The Quiet Violence of Empire

The Quiet Violence of Empire

How USAID Waged Counterinsurgency in Afghanistan

Wesley Attewell

University of Minnesota Press
Minneapolis
London

The University of Minnesota Press gratefully acknowledges the financial assistance provided for the publication of this book by the Department of Geography at the University of Hong Kong.

Portions of chapters 3 and 5 are adapted from "'The Planet That Rules Our Destiny': Alternative Development and Environmental Power in Occupied Afghanistan," *Environment and Planning D, Society & Space* 35, no. 2 (2017): 339–59; copyright Wesley Attewell 2016. https://doi.org/10.1177/0263775816664100.

Published by the University of Minnesota Press
111 Third Avenue South, Suite 290
Minneapolis, MN 55401-2520
http://www.upress.umn.edu

ISBN 978-1-5179-0789-1 (hc)
ISBN 978-1-5179-0790-7 (pb)

A Cataloging-in-Publication record for this book is available from the Library of Congress.

The University of Minnesota is an equal-opportunity educator and employer.

To Juno

From the American people.

Motto of the United States Agency
for International Development

Contents

Abbreviations

ADP/E	Alternative Development Program/East
ADT	Agricultural Development Training
ALP/S	Alternative Livelihoods Program/Southern Region
ANSF	Afghan National Security Forces
ASSP	Agricultural Sector Support Project
AVIPA	Afghanistan Vouchers for Increased Production in Agriculture
BINL	Bureau for International Narcotics and Law Enforcement
CBHAP	Cross Border Humanitarians Assistance Program
CCC	Checchi and Company Consulting
CENTCOM	U.S. Central Command
CIA	Central Intelligence Agency
CJIATF	Combined Joint Interagency Task Force
DAI	Development Alternatives Inc.
DEA	Drug Enforcement Agency
DEC	Development Experience Clearinghouse
FOA	Foreign Operations Administration
HFZ	Helmand Food Zone
HVA	Helmand Valley Authority
HVP	Helmand Valley Project
ICA	International Cooperation Administration
IDEA-NEW	Ideas Driving Economic Alternatives–North, East, West
IDEA-SOUTH	Ideas Driving Economic Alternatives–South
ISAF	International Security Assistance Force
JPEL	Joint Prioritized Effects List
NACP	Narcotics Awareness and Control Project
NARA	U.S. National Archives and Record Administration
NGO	nongovernmental organization

O/AID/REP	Office of the AID Representative for Afghanistan Affairs
OPS	Office of Public Safety
PDPA	People's Democratic Party of Afghanistan
PRT	provincial reconstruction team
RC-EAST	Regional Command–East
SIGAR	special inspector general for Afghanistan reconstruction
SLDP	Shamalan Land Development Project
TCA	Technical Cooperation Administration
TIMER	Technology Innovation and Market-Led Economic Rehabilitation
UNODC	United Nations Office on Drugs and Crime
UNTAM	United Nations Technical Assistance Mission
USAID	United States Agency for International Development
USDA	United States Department of Agriculture
USOM	United States Operations Mission
VITA	Volunteers in Technical Assistance

Introduction

Development, Infrastructure, Race Wars

Decolonization is truly the creation of new men.

Frantz Fanon, The Wretched of the Earth

Here, then, is the fundamental question of our day: how
far can nations who are at present most advanced in
intelligence . . . and technique keep their wealth without
using the land and labor of the majority of mankind
mainly for the benefit of the European world, and not for
the benefit of most men, who happen to be colored?

W. E. B. Du Bois, "The Wealth of the West vs.
a Chance for Exploited Mankind," National Guardian,
November 28, 1955

ON AUGUST 21, 2017, U.S. president Donald Trump outlined a "new"
strategy for resolving the ongoing conflict in Afghanistan. At the time,
America's "longest war" was entering its sixteenth year. Trump was
keen to distinguish his new strategy from that of his predecessor, Barack
Obama. What Trump proposed can be summarized by the following
quip: "We are not nation building again. We are killing terrorists."[1]
As it turns out, however, Trump's "new path" forward had recently
been endorsed by Obama himself. In August 2015, Obama reportedly
opened a meeting of his National Security Council by announcing that
the U.S. mission to Afghanistan would no longer be in "nation building
mode." Instead, U.S. forces would ramp up counterterrorism efforts so
that Afghanistan would not become a "seedbed for extremists again."[2]

Obama's tenure as the commander-in-chief of the U.S. armed forces is
commonly represented as the nation-building phase of the "good war"
in Afghanistan. His "surge" of troops to Afghanistan in 2009 is remembered as signaling a turn toward counterinsurgency in the countryside.

But as Rajiv Chandrasekaran and others have shown, Obama did not assume the presidency as a champion of nation building.[3] Under his watch, military operations slowly but steadily escalated in frequency and intensity. By the time that Trump outlined his "new path" forward in Afghanistan, Obama's "good war" had claimed tens of thousands of civilian lives. In 2016 alone, 3,498 Afghan civilians were killed and a further 7,290 were injured, making it one of the deadliest years for noncombatants on record.[4]

These basic statistics expose how nation building in post-9/11 Afghanistan went hand-in-hand with the killing of insurgents and civilians. More generally, they reveal nation building and killing as the Janus faces of the same imperial coin. And yet, what the debates and presidential jostling described above clarify is the extent to which mainstream publics have implicitly come to accept various forms of nation building—including development and humanitarianism—as a kinder, gentler, and more liberal form of U.S. intervention in the world. From 1945 onward, the United States has appeared exceptional in its ability to wield such forms of "soft power" to secure its broader geopolitical and geoeconomic interests. U.S. soft power, we are commonly told, has historically played a central role in bringing the fruits of capitalism, democracy, and security to a rapidly decolonizing world.[5] In contrast with older, more martial forms of imperial intervention, U.S. soft power was never geared toward defeating enemy armies or rearranging the existing territorial borders of nation-states. Instead, it remains fundamentally concerned with producing what Henry Stimson, the very last U.S. secretary of war, named in a 1947 *Foreign Affairs* article as a "new interrelation of American life with the life of the world." Writing in the immediate wake of World War II, Stimson thought that the United States was uniquely positioned to offer the decolonizing world "leadership towards . . . life."[6] In so doing, Stimson provided other like-minded defense apparatchiks, policy intellectuals, and career diplomats an ideological justification for rescaling foreign struggles over the contours of a global "humanity"—to borrow from the historian Monica Kim—into an "intimate domestic concern."[7] Guided by this expansive geostrategic vision, the United States waged a Cold War against the forces of global communism. From the insurgent Pacific to decolonizing Latin America, the United States subjected local populations to various forms of (para)military violence, while simultaneously enrolling them in imperial infrastructures for fashioning modern, liberal, and capitalist human subjects. These infrastructures tethered subject-making practices at the scale of the individual to a more expansive project of integrating decolonizing nation-states into transplanetary circuits of capitalist production, resource extraction, commodity circulation, and labor racialization.[8] I group these infrastructures under the broader sign of *development*.

Unlike other theaters of U.S. Cold War intervention—including Korea and Vietnam—Afghanistan has never been formally colonized by a Western power. Even so, it has been thoroughly shaped and transformed by U.S. development infrastructures. From the mid-twentieth century onward, successive generations of U.S. technocrats travelled to Afghanistan, where they championed development and the management of rural life as particularly potent vehicles for achieving necessary geopolitical and geoeconomic transformations. These imperial agents relied on Afghanistan as a key laboratory for devising, stress-testing, and refining new combinations of development, soft power, and empire. As I argue in this book, however, they also became adept at concealing violently Orientalist forms of counterinsurgency and race war through the seemingly benevolent infrastructures of technical assistance, marketization, and self-help.

In *Race and America's Long War*, Nikhil Pal Singh insists that American empire has historically been defined by a key contradiction, namely, that the post-1945 "Golden Age" of domestic peace and (military) Keynesian economic prosperity was also the same "epoch in which the United States engaged in continuous and accretive wars all over the world—some named, almost all formally undeclared—whose toll of violence has been excluded from the balance sheet of moral, political, and material costs and benefits."[9] Both at home and abroad, U.S. imperialists developed "infrastructures of violence" and produced various carceral and militarized spaces—suburbs, ghettoes, cantonments, green zones, internment camps, camptowns, and so on—to manage and pacify populations that have long been marginalized along multiple axes of social and racial difference. In practice, then, and despite all official claims to the contrary, the vernacular practices of U.S. Cold War intervention in the post-1945 moment carried forward the "more primal terms of American race war" and, by extension, longer-standing fantasies of achieving "national social and economic regeneration through

(frontier) violence."[10] Building on Singh, *The Quiet Violence of Empire*
asks: What might it mean to center questions of race and violence in
the story of international development and soft power in Afghanistan?
And what might this tell us about how entanglements of racism, war,
and liberalism have historically facilitated the extension and reproduction of capitalist relations across the decolonizing world?

The Quiet Violence of Empire answers these questions by tracing
how imperial infrastructures for developing and pacifying Afghanistan
have evolved over time and space. It pays special attention to the United
States Agency for International Development (USAID) and its transnational "complex" of private sector contractors, military partners,
and local counterparts.[11] Ever since the end of World War II, USAID
and its predecessor institutions have been carrying out the will of
the U.S. empire-state in the Afghan countryside. As part of this intergenerational development mission, the USAID complex built dams and
irrigation canals, established agricultural demonstration programs, led
community development activities, managed cross-border humanitarian relief efforts, supported commercial supply chains, legitimized
counterinsurgency operations, and designed enabling environments
for markets. In this book, I show how USAID assembled these diverse
development activities and interventions into vernacular sociospatial
infrastructures for nurturing particular forms of Afghan life. This
analysis is grounded in three case studies of development in action:
USAID's thirty-year effort to reclaim the deserts of the Helmand Valley
for agricultural resettlement (1946–1978); the transnational development and humanitarian operations that USAID launched during the
Soviet–Afghan conflict to supply war-devastated communities with
the means of rehabilitation and insurgency (1980–1992); and finally,
USAID's ongoing "alternative livelihood" effort to stop Afghan farmers from cultivating poppies (1991–present). I move through these case
studies in chronological order to identify continuities and discontinui-
ties in how USAID has wielded developmental power over Afghans.
Taken together, they reveal that the everyday work of development
has always unfolded through a succession of embodied encounters between rural farming households and USAID agents. USAID's transnational infrastructures of development intervention and expertise seek
to manage these encounters so as to privilege certain outcomes and not
others. In so doing, they structure how ordinary Afghans encounter,

grapple with, and grate against longer historical geographies of political, economic, and imperial power.

What changes when we locate USAID's development mission to Afghanistan in relation to a longer-standing imperial project of racial management? In what follows, I argue that development and the USAID complex played a central role in enabling the U.S. empire-state's post-1945 transition away from an explicitly racist project of globalizing white supremacy toward a more inclusive and liberal one that "suture[d] an 'official' antiracism to U.S. nationalism, itself bearing the agency for transnational capitalism."[12] USAID's development mission to Afghanistan was very much a product of this post-1945 moment: a period defined by the U.S. empire-state's global struggles with the intensifying forces of decolonization. Confronting a decolonizing world devastated by the slow and spectacular violences of total war, the U.S. empire-state found itself seeking to perfect a form of power capable of engaging these emerging "darker nations," to borrow the (racist) terminology of commentators such as Gunnar Myrdal.[13] Development, as we shall see, fit the bill.

USAID and Empire

Political geographers and international relations scholars have long theorized the securitization of development as a direct response to post–Cold War shifts in the drivers of armed conflict and (para)military violence. In contrast with previous conflicts, which were ostensibly fought over "traditional" geopolitical concerns such as territory and sovereignty, the "new" or "globalization-induced" wars stemmed from conditions of chronic poverty and state failure.[14] It was in this context that development was recast as a novel pathway to the security of both states and humans.

This literature has much to tell us about how development's relationship with geopolitics, warfare, and counterinsurgency has shifted over the last thirty years. It is less useful at helping us understand the historical entanglements of development, imperialism, and colonialism. Imperial powers—ranging from the British in India to the French in Indochina—have long used development as a mechanism for pre-empting the threats of decolonial revolt and communist insurgency. Infrastructure building, police training, agricultural transformation, economic development, and scientific modernization have long been hallmarks of colonial and imperial rule.[15] This was especially true of U.S. empire building throughout the twentieth century. The U.S. colonial occupations of the Philippines, Hawai'i, and Guahan were all interconnected spaces of nation building, development, and decolonization.[16] Although World War II ostensibly marked a rupture in the Euro-American colonial project—particularly in the Pacific—the entanglements between empire building and development only intensified in the post-1945 moment, when an ascendant U.S. empire-state took on the responsibility of rebuilding Europe and Japan into regional "engines" of an emerging (racial) capitalist world order.[17] This was part of a concerted effort by the U.S. empire-state to consolidate its growing military might and economic influence across the decolonizing world. What the U.S. empire-state assembled over the Cold War was a transnational infrastructure for steering decolonizing nations away from the gravitational orbit of global communism toward an ostensibly brighter future of capitalist integration and liberal democracy.

The United States laid the first building blocks for this infrastructure during World War II, which scholars have identified as an important moment of imperial transition and transformation.[18] As Takashi Fujitani shows in *Race for Empire*, both the U.S. and Japanese governments experimented with "new postcolonial models of imperialism" that were designed to help manage and mobilize racialized populations "within the larger demands of conducting total war."[19] Over the course of the war, both empires came to realize that it was not in their strategic interest to let the racist logics of white or Japanese supremacy narrowly restrict their ability to procure civilian and military labor power. At the level of day-to-day imperial praxis, Fujitani argues, this realization manifested as a gradual but substantive transition from exclusionary or vulgar forms of racism to inclusionary or polite ones. Under these new total war regimes of polite racism, "newly constituted national subjects such as Japanese Americans and Korean Japanese" were welcomed "into the nation with promises and practices of health, education, sustenance, security, and even greater access to political rights."[20] Such an inclusionary biopolitics of total war, in other words, demanded that abjected and racialized populations be regarded as "worthy of life," even as they were asked to sacrifice their lives for the empire as soldiers, coerced laborers, and sexual slaves.[21]

The gradual mainstreaming of polite and inclusionary forms of racism was one of the key legacies of the war years, offering U.S. imperialists a practical blueprint for carrying out subsequent geopolitical and geoeconomic interventions abroad. Michael Omi and Howard Winant famously theorize World War II as a key inflection point that launched a clear break—or "epochal sea change," in Jodi Melamed's words—in the racial projects of empire. From the end of World War II through the 1960s, an overt U.S. commitment to entrenching and reproducing white supremacist forms of rule, both at home and abroad, was increasingly seen as fundamentally incompatible with—and perhaps even actively detrimental to—its ambitions to assume leadership of the so-called free world. As Nikhil Singh explains, U.S. global power needed a way to "cleanse [imperial] sovereignty of its colonial-racial taint," for it could not "claim to be fighting 'Communist slavery'" while "continuing state-sanctioned discrimination against the descendants of US slaves." It therefore made geostrategic sense for the U.S. empire-state to incorporate an "inclusive, modestly ameliorative form of racial liberalism" as part of its day-to-day workings.[22] This is not to suggest that the U.S. empire-state no longer trafficked in vulgar racism or lethal forms of white supremacist violence. Rather, it is simply to emphasize that such overt forms of race war gradually came to coexist uneasily with an operational framework of foreign intervention that "conceived of racism as prejudice and promised to release liberal freedoms from racial restrictions by extending equal opportunity, possessive individualism, and cultural citizenship" to historically marginalized populations. The U.S. Cold War leadership first perfected such forms of "racial liberalism"—as exemplified by the civil rights movement—at home, where they showed great promise at managing domestic race relations. Over time, however, frameworks of racial liberalism came to "structure the [U.S.] fields of global intervention."[23]

The Quiet Violence of Empire builds on this work by situating USAID's ongoing development mission to Afghanistan within this much longer genealogy of imperial statecraft: one that exposes and emphasizes how America's "outer" race wars on communism, decolonization, and terrorism have historically been animated by its "inner" race wars on poverty, crime, and drugs. In the face of intensifying insurgencies for decolonization and self-determination, development—and by extension, capitalist integration—became a way for the U.S. empire-state to prove its commitment to global antiracisms. What crystallized out of such Cold War desires was a particularly American form of development theory and practice that I theorize as an *infrastructural technology* of racial liberalism.

These transnational infrastructures of development intervention did not emerge fully formed in the post-1945 moment. Rather, as Mona Domosh has shown, the origins of U.S. Cold War development can be traced back to the Jim Crow South in the early decades of the twentieth century. Concerned that Southern plantation economies were on the brink of a significant labor crisis, the U.S. Department of Agriculture (USDA) became obsessed with correcting the biological and moral flaws that supposedly defined rural African American households, and seemingly explained their tendencies toward impoverishment and ill health. To this end, the USDA dispatched technicians to the Jim Crow South, tasked with enrolling African American communities into projects of rural improvement, extension, and uplift. This team included local leaders such as Thomas Campbell, the African American field agent in charge of extension projects in the seven lower Southern states. Campbell set up demonstration farms and conducted home visits, offering technical assistance in the areas of health, sanitation, and home improvement. According to Domosh, Campbell was a "firm believer" in the promise of technical assistance to "create a healthier and more 'modern' agricultural workforce" and, by extension, to "uplift" African Americans "out of poverty into positions of leadership."[24]

Domosh argues that this racialized biopolitics of technical assistance, demonstration, and rural uplift went on to shape the everyday work of international development throughout the Cold War. The Jim Crow South, in other words, was an important site in the imperial genealogy of U.S. development theory and practice. Attending to these transnational connections, in turn, exposes the "often unexamined racialized underpinnings" of the liberal modernization schemes that became popular among USAID technocrats working in Afghanistan and elsewhere, whose populations effectively experienced Jim Crow and the slow violence of racial segregation as an inheritance of U.S. empire. Domosh singles out President Truman's Point Four program as exemplary in this regard. Truman unveiled Point Four as part of his second inaugural address in January 1949, during which he outlined a "bold new program for making the benefits of our scientific advances and industrial progress available for the improvement and growth of underdeveloped areas," where more than half of humanity was living in "conditions approaching misery." Plagued by inadequate access to food, ravaged by disease, and constrained by primitive modes of living, the poverty of these masses was a "threat both to them and to more prosperous areas."[25]

For many commentators, Point Four's obvious point of reference is the Economic Cooperation Act—commonly known as the Marshall Plan—that the Truman administration passed in 1948 as an "emergency tool of assistance" for restoring the economic health and stability of war-devastated Europe.[26] The United States used the Marshall Plan to supply key European allies with the money and other forms of assistance they required to stave off the looming threat of communist subversion. But a comparative reading of the Marshall Plan and Point Four reveals that the U.S. empire-state distributed assistance unevenly across the globe. The Marshall Plan set in motion enormous flows of development capital to Europe, thereby limiting the material resources available to Point Four. Point Four closed this resource deficit by mobilizing the apparently "imponderable" stores of U.S. technical expertise, which were "constantly growing" and seemingly "inexhaustible." Instead of transferring development capital directly into the hands of the "free peoples of the world," Point Four promised to provide them with the technical knowledge they needed to produce, through their own efforts, "more food, more clothing, more materials for housing, and more mechanical power to lighten their burdens." Truman contrasted Point Four with older forms of imperialism on the grounds that it offered "cooperation" and "democratic fair-dealing" as alternative mechanisms for helping decolonizing subjects to "realize their aspirations for a better life."[27] But following Domosh, Point Four actually carried forward the racialized logics of the USDA's extension work in the Jim Crow South, effectively repurposing them into a *technical* solution to the thorny problem of global underdevelopment. In the minds of U.S. imperial planners, the racialized inhabitants of the Jim Crow South and the rest of the decolonizing world were interchangeable. As " 'foreign' peoples of different 'races' who were potential threats to American geopolitical rule," they were in need of uplift and racial improvement.[28] The net effect of the Marshall Plan and Point Four, then, was to map an unevenly racialized terrain of global development intervention: one that ironically reproduced the imaginative geographies that defined past imperialisms, colonialisms, and racial capitalisms, even as it worked overtime to disavow such inheritances.

Initially, the story of Point Four was the story of the Technical Cooperation Administration (TCA). Formally established within the Department of State in October 1950, the TCA dispatched American technocrats to participant nations, where they collaborated with nongovernmental organizations (NGOs) and local counterparts to implement a diversity of projects.[29] Afghanistan became a recipient of Point Four assistance on February 7, 1951, when it agreed to cooperate with the TCA in the "interchange" of technical expertise and skills. The resulting mission was "designed to contribute to the balanced and integrated development of the economic resources and productive capacities of Afghanistan."[30] As we shall see over the course of this book, this seemingly technical relationship was also a thoroughly imperial one, laying the groundwork for future frictional encounters with an emerging Cold War infrastructure of pacification, counterinsurgency, and race war.

Truman clearly never intended racial liberalism to fully supplant (para)military violence as the primary expression of U.S. imperial power. He made this clear on May 24, 1951, when he called on Congress to establish a "Mutual Security Program." In his pitch, he stressed the necessity of "help[ing] other free countries to build the military and economic power needed to make impossible the communist dreams of world conquest."[31] His address was undoubtedly haunted by the ongoing U.S.-led "police action" on the Korean peninsula, which served as a potent reminder of how unresolved class conflicts and economic grievances could fester and erupt into communist, anticolonial insurgencies.[32] Concerned that this "hot" moment of decolonization was a harbinger of things to come, the Truman administration established the Mutual Security Agency on October 31, 1951. Its mission was to coordinate U.S. military assistance with the economic development projects unfolding under the umbrella of Point Four.[33] In theory, the Mutual Security Agency provided the U.S. empire-state a way of flexibly responding to communist military power on the one hand, and communism's allies of "starvation and sickness" on the other. The end-state goal was an imperial framework for coordinating previously disconnected military and development interventions into a planet-spanning infrastructure of anticommunist containment and control. The Mutual Security Agency and the Technical Cooperation Administration were each conceived as distinct action arms of the U.S. empire-state. On August 1, 1953, however, they were both transferred into an autonomous Foreign Operations Administration, which operated for only twenty-three months before it was incorporated into the State Department's new International Cooperation Administration (ICA). Although the ICA was first founded in 1955 with a "vast and far-reaching" mandate to administer aid for "economic, political, and social development purposes," its location in the State Department meant that it had no control over the distribution of military and food aid.[34] These constraints made it difficult for the ICA to operate in an environment where economic and technical assistance were increasingly being recast as tools of military and political security.[35] From the mid- to late 1950s, the ICA was dogged by a number of critical accounts of its overseas activities. The form of these criticisms ranged the gamut from commissioned congressional reports to quasi-fictional novels, the most famous being Eugene Burdick and William Lederer's *The Ugly American*.[36] Their common refrain was that American military and development assistance was poorly planned and executed.[37] The Kennedy administration responded to these narratives of failure by pledging to overhaul America's foreign aid programs.

The cornerstone of this reorganization effort was the Foreign Assistance Act.[38] Unveiled in March 1961, the act was meant to consolidate a fragmented foreign aid landscape into one overarching agency, organized around "country-based strategies" and longer-term development timelines.[39] Kennedy justified the act on geopolitical grounds, warning House Representatives that "widespread poverty and chaos" would "lead to a collapse of existing political and social structures which would inevitably invite the advance of totalitarianism into every weak and unstable area." A comprehensive program of development assistance was required to neutralize this looming threat to American security and prosperity. Kennedy's geopolitical arguments for closing an ostensibly expanding "aid gap" between the United States and the Soviet Union proved persuasive, and in August 1961, both the House and the Senate ratified the act. As a result, the Kennedy administration was given the green light to establish USAID, which began operations in November 1961.

What we can glean from this crude history of USAID, I think, is a revealing sense of how a nascent U.S. development-industrial complex expanded a domestic project of racial retrenchment into an international project of imperial retrenchment. What began as a biopolitical infrastructure for managing African American communities in the U.S. South was, in the post-1945 period, gradually upscaled into a supposedly antiracist project for capturing the forces unleashed by global decolonization movements and redirecting them toward liberal, modern, and racial capitalist futures. Under such conditions, Melamed argues, "liberal antiracism . . . entered US governmentality . . . specifically as a geopolitical racial project that associated Americanism with the benefits of capitalism."[40] The consequence of this shift was to "unevenly detach" imperial racialization from older conceptions of the color line, and to also universalize U.S.-style capitalism—that is, racial capitalism—as a fundamentally antiracist force for good across the decolonizing world.[41]

From the outset, USAID administrators were under no illusion regarding the role that the agency was expected to play in upholding and reproducing this global racial project. As David Bell, the agency's administrator from 1962 to 1966, put it, "fundamentally, AID's purpose is national security." Here, Bell was advancing a multiscalar understanding of national security. Within decolonizing nations, Bell argued, "we're not aiming for standards of living," but rather, for "internal dynamics of self-sustaining growth." Bell's hope was that such efforts would lead into a "world of independent nations capable of making economic and social progress through free institutions."[42] Market participation and capitalist integration, Bell strongly implied, were essential to realizing such a utopian vision. It was imperative that USAID help decolonizing nations achieve independence, but only "so that they may be 'interconnected' in terms that feed capital."[43] Building on the work of Cedric Robinson and Ruth Wilson Gilmore, Jodi Melamed identifies the above dialectic of partition and integration as the "base algorithm" for a particularly racialized form of capitalism. As the wielder of a state-sanctioned form of power that is meant to mitigate and eliminate—yet invariably produces and exploits—"group-differentiated vulnerabilities to premature death," USAID has historically contributed to the entrenchment and reproduction of racial capitalist relations across the

decolonizing world.⁴⁴ As Melamed puts it, "official antiracism now explicitly required the victory and extension of US empire, the motor
force of capitalism's next unequal development."⁴⁵

To be sure, Afghanistan has always been a space of Western empire building. But if—as Melamed, Singh, and others insist—there is
something qualitatively distinct about how the U.S. empire-state leveraged antiracism and racial liberalism to secure its geopolitical and
geoeconomic interests during the Cold War, this book also emphasizes
how such a project of global rule was undoubtedly felt across the decolonizing world as a more intimate geography of racial encounter and
subject making. In her pathbreaking history of U.S. detention and interrogation practices during the Korean "police action," the historian
Monica Kim argues that "stories of war hold allegorical power because
at their most fundamental, they are stories about intimate encounter."
"It is the small," she emphasizes, "rather than the epic, that moves the
story of war forward." Like Melamed, Singh, and Fujitani, Kim also
identifies the post-1945 period as a key inflection point in the story of
U.S. empire. As both the U.S. empire and revolutions "claimed the central project of decolonization," the "geography of war was not limited
to a traditional sense of sovereignty in the state-territorial sense," but
rather, expanded "into the most intimate corner of humanity—the individual human subject."⁴⁶ While Kim narrates this shift through the
Korean War, a similar story can—and has—been told about the subsequent counterinsurgencies that came to define the post-1945 period.
In Korea, Vietnam, Guatemala, Thailand, Indonesia, and Afghanistan,
military counterinsurgents, covert operatives, and communist revo-
lutionaries fought to determine "who would fashion the new human
subject for the world after 1945."⁴⁷ This was, as Kim acknowledges, a
"vast, impossible question." Yet its stakes were such that the struggle to
definitively answer it invariably spilled off the battlefield to encompass
the most ordinary spaces of everyday civilian life. As an institution that
was ostensibly designed to straddle battle and civilian spaces, USAID
was ideally positioned to inherit this colonial project of subject making.
Over the course of the Cold War, USAID came to value Afghanistan as
a "uniquely valuable" node in a transnational infrastructure of development experimentation, the purpose of which was to draft a portable
blueprint for producing legitimate human subjects: ones who were, in
Kim's evocative turn of phrase, "worthy of life."⁴⁸

How did all of this unfold in Afghanistan? One of the key claims of this book is that USAID—and the U.S. empire-state more broadly—relied heavily on Afghanistan as a key field site for experimenting with development as a transcalar tool for bridging these multiple scales of imperial activity.[49] This is to say, *The Quiet Violence of Empire* offers a more "infrastructural" account of U.S. empire building in Afghanistan. In particular, it emphasizes how Afghanistan has historically doubled as a field site where overlapping civilian and military best practices for managing and ordering Afghan life brushed up against each other, clashed, and combined to produce new hybridized, sociospatial configurations of imperial rule and control. These processes of hybridization were neither smooth nor coherent. Instead, they were jagged and uneven, generating frictions along and connections across entrenched axes of imperial sedimentation. For this reason, the ongoing USAID mission to Afghanistan remains an ideal case study for contemplating the infrastructural character of development and counterinsurgency, and by extension, for building a more geographically nuanced theory of U.S. empire.

Development as Infrastructure

What does it mean to bring an infrastructural edge to the study of development, counterinsurgency, and empire? Much critical work in human geography and other cognate fields—including international relations, security studies, and anthropology—has drawn on the writings of Michel Foucault to theorize development as a biopolitical technology for managing the "population" as a "multiplicity of men" that is "affected by overall processes characteristic of birth, death, production, illness, and so on."[50] By intervening in these processes, development seeks to reorient them toward particular ends.

Despite sharing a broader commitment to Foucauldian frameworks, however, this literature has advanced different understandings of vernacular development practices and their ultimate consequences for marginalized populations. Postdevelopment scholars such as Mark Duffield and Arturo Escobar have historically treated development as a hopelessly corrupted biopolitical mechanism of carceral control.[51] Development's sole purpose, they argue, is to maintain—not reduce—the destabilizing "life chance divide" that continues to bifurcate and inoculate the "developed" world from its "underdeveloped" other. More ethnographically minded geographers and anthropologists, in contrast, caution against such a "facile negation" of development, offering instead more grounded accounts that recognize the "impossibility of not trying (or desiring) to develop."[52] They have therefore turned to Foucault's concept of governmentality for a "far more precise diagnosis" of the "rationalities of development, the forms of knowledge and expertise they construct, and the specific and contingent assemblages of practices, materials, agents, and techniques through which these rationalities operate to produce governable subjects."[53] Driven by a technical "will to improve," development-as-governmentality works as a desiring machine, bringing together a diversity of "parts"—farmers, technicians, government officials, institutions, technologies, and non-human organisms—that were once held separate. The net effect of development here is to unleash a "multiplicity of forces to reassemble matter in space and summon particular sorts of 'conducts' from human and nonhuman actors."[54]

What does this look like in practice? As I have noted previously, international development emerged during the Cold War as a response to the threat posed by popular insurgencies in the decolonizing world. Development promised a *technical* solution to the global problems of poverty and hunger and, by extension, a pathway for reorienting the "hearts and minds" of decolonizing peoples toward liberal and capitalist ideologies. Afghanistan was one of the first places where development turned the Cold War technical. In 1955, the Soviet Union launched its first "economic offensive" in Afghanistan, thereby providing U.S. empire builders with an opportunity to showcase how their supposedly unparalleled technical prowess might be converted into geopolitical influence.[55] The first half of this book tracks these geographies of "competitive coexistence," emphasizing how Cold War Afghanistan became a testing ground where various forms of technical assistance were tailored to accommodate an imperial governmentality of uplift and improvement, one that saw rural farmers as a docile and malleable mass that was in dire need of technocratic guidance.[56]

The Quiet Violence of Empire follows scholars such as Tania Li and Vinay Gidwani in acknowledging the multiple ways in which development can transform the prospect of a better life from a "fleeting abstraction" into a "visible possibility."[57] But it also insists that under conditions of empire and race war, development also functions as a technology of *antirelationality*, in the sense that it assists, to paraphrase Jodi Melamed, in the "production of social separateness—the disjoining or deactivating of relations between human beings (and humans and nature)—needed for capitalist expropriation to work."[58] From this perspective, then, even an expansive governmentality framework is less well equipped to capture the uneven, violent, and contradictory "power geometries" that have always organized how different "handlings" of development brush up and grate against one another in imperial theaters of empire building, race war, and counterinsurgency. If development is best understood as a technology of racial liberalism that offered the U.S. empire-state a technical way of recasting the "more primal terms of American race war" for a new and supposedly antiracist age, the key question then becomes, what new geographies of "(frontier) violence" did development help unleash across the decolonizing world?[59]

The Quiet Violence of Empire adopts an infrastructural framework as a way of better attending to the violent proximities between development, counterinsurgency, and empire building. This is to say, I theorize USAID's development work in Afghanistan as fundamentally *infrastructural* in nature. Here, I follow Deborah Cowen and Michelle Murphy in using the term *infrastructure* expansively to encompass both physical structures, as well as the "spatially and temporally extensive ways" in which the everyday violences of imperialism, settler colonialism, and racial capitalism are "sedimented into and structure the world." Such a "capacious sense of infrastructure," Murphy argues, must necessarily include "social sedimentations such as colonial legacies, the repetition of gendered norms in material culture, or the persistence of racialization."[60] Placing Murphy in conversation with Ara Wilson, infrastructures, as the "material manifestation[s]" of imperial ideologies, can help us track, over space and through time, the various throughlines connecting the exclusive racial formations that defined U.S. empire building in the early twentieth century to the inclusive ones that came to predominate from 1945 onward.[61] Engineered to order social and natural worlds, infrastructures have always played an essential role in building and sustaining life. Given infrastructure's centrality to the waging of race war on the one hand, and the uplift of racialized and marginalized populations on the other, it has historically been the object of political struggle. There is an important subset of critical development studies that showcases how traditional infrastructure projects have undergirded postcolonial state-building efforts.[62] USAID's development mission to Afghanistan has undoubtedly been infrastructural in this sense. From the outset, it was centrally concerned with building the concrete components of a modern nation-state—dams, irrigation systems, highways, pipelines. But as *The Quiet Violence of Empire* shows, rural development interventions were also grounded in less obvious infrastructures of community building, commodity circulation, knowledge production, technical assistance, market participation, gender integration, labor recruitment, and racialized counterinsurgency. What all of this shows is that USAID has long attempted to develop Afghanistan by unleashing various forms of "infrastructural power" throughout the countryside. Laleh Khalili advances the concept of "infrastructural power" as a framework for understanding the broader geopolitical and geoeconomic consequences of the U.S. military's peacetime construction activities. Khalili defines infrastructural power as the authority to "forge and maintain the assemblage of practices, discourses, physical fixtures, laws, and procedures necessary for the government of subjects and citizens, including their economies."[63] She shows how the U.S. Army Corps of Engineers wielded this form of power across the decolonizing world by laying down the physical and virtual infrastructures necessary for the spread, consolidation, and enforcement of capitalist relations.

The Quiet Violence of Empire shows that there is nothing about infrastructural power that makes it the exclusive purview of military actors. Placing Khalili in conversation with Cowen, Murphy, and Wilson, in fact, foregrounds infrastructural power as a useful heuristic for reckoning with how a civilian institution like USAID has championed development and the intimate management of everyday rural life as potent mechanisms for achieving broader geopolitical and geoeconomic objectives in Afghanistan. In the early days of the Cold War, USAID wielded infrastructural power to bring Afghan households into ongoing relations with national projects for building spaces of agricultural transformation, economic modernization, and community uplift in the countryside. USAID's use of infrastructural power took on an increasingly transnational character from the late 1980s onward, when nurturing spaces of market development and capitalist circulation became the sine qua non of rural development in the countryside. Interventions like the Commodity Export Program (chapter 2) and, eventually, Ideas Driving Economic Alternatives (chapter 4) familiarized ordinary Afghans with the new "grammar[s] of the capitalist geoeconomic order," creating an "environment conducive to incorporation into capitalist networks and relations."[64] Through infrastructural power, USAID connected the localized spaces of everyday Afghan life to the globalized spaces of capitalist production, accumulation, and circulation.

As the Cold War transitioned into the long war on terror, Afghanistan increasingly became the target of both civilian and military modes of infrastructural power. But military and civilian actors have not always seen eye to eye on how to go about wielding infrastructural power across the countryside. This is exemplified in the post-9/11 period, when USAID was expected to collaborate with the U.S. military to produce interagency infrastructures for pacifying and ordering insurgent populations. On paper, USAID and the U.S. military seemed like natural partners, especially given how they often found themselves "working in the same spaces."[65] The Bush administration's 2002 National Security Strategy elevated development into one of the core pillars of the global war on terror.[66] By the end of the same year, U.S. soldiers were already collaborating with representatives from USAID and other civilian institutions in carrying out the everyday work of occupation in Afghanistan. Over time, it became increasingly apparent to U.S. forces in Iraq and Afghanistan that high-technology forms of conventional warfare—which were first introduced during the 1991 Gulf War and subsequently honed during the so-called Revolution in Military Affairs—were inadequate to the urgent task of pacifying rural and urban insurgencies.[67] When considered together, all of these developments signal the extent to which the U.S. military began to take development seriously as a pathway to stabilization.

Jodi Melamed foregrounds the 2002 National Security Strategy as an example of how Cold War discourses of racial liberalism gradually evolved into a new civil-military commitment to extend the benefits of what she calls "neoliberal multiculturalism" to the rest of the world. If racial liberalism remained, for most of the Cold War, "sutured to US governmentality," proponents of neoliberal multiculturalism sought to sever these chains on the grounds that "the market is better than the state at distributing resources and managing human life."[68] From their perspective, the United States, as the world's preeminent multicultural democracy, had a moral obligation to "include all the world's poor in the expanding circle of development" by opening their societies to capitalist markets as well as global flows of foreign investment and commodities. Capitalist integration, in other words, was a "multicultural imperative." Melamed is undoubtedly correct to suggest that the entanglements between racial capitalism, empire, and the U.S. national security state only deepened as the twentieth century transitioned into the twenty-first. But what Melamed overstates, I think, is the actual operational coherence of the civilian and military arms of the U.S. national security state. The U.S. military's turn toward development was not formally codified until November 28, 2005, when it published Directive 3000.05, requiring that "stability operations" be "given priority comparable to combat operations" across all Department of Defense activities.[69] But even then, as Jennifer Morrison Taw observes, the directive only offered a very vague definition of stability operations as any civilian or military interventions undertaken during times of peace or conflict to help establish and maintain the particular forms of order that are essential to advancing U.S. interests across the globe.[70] This meant that stability operations, at least as conceptualized in doctrine, were expansive in scope. Indeed, the directive itself championed stability operations as a way for combat soldiers to participate in—and perhaps even contribute substantively to—the essential work of "develop[ing] indigenous capacity for security essential services, a viable market economy, rule of law, democratic institutions, and a robust civil society."[71] But in practice, the net effect of Directive 3000.05 was twofold. First, it reintroduced a particular civil-military division of development labor. The military's expertise in stabilizing so-called nonpermissive environments meant that it could create the security bubbles necessary for civilian actors and institutions to implement more comprehensive and long-term forms of development programming. Second, Directive 3000.05 was constrained by the idea that functioning states—as opposed to failed or rogue ones—were the only legitimate source of security in the post-9/11 world. Guided by such a framework, the U.S. military came to prize state normalization as one of the "fundamental measures of success in conflict transformation."[72]

Directive 3000.05 did not introduce the concept of stability operations to U.S. military doctrine. As the historical record shows, they have long been a defining feature of U.S. settler colonialism and imperialism. The United States waged a number of domestic and foreign conflicts through stability operations, including the Indian Wars, the colonization of the Philippines, the Korean War, and the Vietnam War, to name only a few examples.[73] This trend continued in the aftermath of the Cold War when the U.S. military found itself engaging in more stability operations than ever before. But even if stability operations remained a "contemporary manifestation of race war" well into the twenty-first century, the intensifying challenges confronting the U.S. military occupations of both Afghanistan and Iraq made it clear that a top-down, state-centric approach to stabilization was inadequate to the task of "winning the hearts and minds" of insurgent populations.[74] The U.S. military responded with a "rush to the intimate" that culminated in the publication of a revised counterinsurgency field manual (FM 3-24) in December 2006. From this point forward, the "operative dogma" of the global war on terror gradually shifted from conventional forms of counterterrorism to an "inclusive doctrine" of population-centric counterinsurgency, one that key military leaders hoped might help rescale the occupations of Iraq and Afghanistan into "full-spectrum operations" that could substantively intervene on the "forms of liberal 'underdevelopment' seen as a threat to the 'Western way of life.'"[75]

It is not a stretch to imagine population-centric counterinsurgency—with its emphasis on cultural sensitivity, "hearts and minds," and imperial mimesis—as an especially lethal mode of military multiculturalism.[76] But while FM 3-24 undoubtedly elevates free markets and frontier entrepreneurship into indicators of what Melamed calls "multicultural inclusiveness," what is less clear is the extent to which the U.S. military actually prioritized such neoliberal deliverables in its day-to-day operations.[77] By 2006, the U.S. military was already using Afghanistan as a formative site for stress-testing new infrastructures of full-spectrum warfare, such as Provincial Reconstruction Teams and Village Stability Platforms. Contrary to initial expectations, they proved to be key sites of tension, negotiation, and struggle. The U.S.

military wielded infrastructural power to bring about stabilization, while USAID's long-term objective remained the establishment of an enabling environment for self-help and internal dynamics of market-based, self-sustaining growth. A more comparative analysis, in other words, shows how the U.S. military and USAID developed variegated and incoherent infrastructures for managing Afghan life. *The Quiet Violence of Empire* therefore pays special attention to the frictions, anxieties, and tensions that have sparked at the points of contact between civilian and military infrastructures for developing Afghanistan.

It would also be a mistake to assume that infrastructural power has only ever been wielded in Afghanistan by empires. Development interventions, whether civilian or military in nature, have always been shaped by their encounters with alternative and localized infrastructures for provisioning rural life. These have ranged the gamut from nomadic forms of pastoralism to traditional practices of social reproduction and household management, to the complex and modern agricultural systems that continue to support Afghanistan's booming narco-economy. *The Quiet Violence of Empire* maps how Afghanistan has long served as a space of friction between imperial infrastructures of development, stabilization, and improvement, and the vernacular materialities and social relations that continue to shape and organize communal life in rural Afghanistan. These frictional encounters have served as grist for the mill of development innovations and experimentation, elaborating new, hybridized infrastructures for "guiding population and economy together."[78]

Such an infrastructural perspective is important because it emphasizes the fundamental spatiality of development. Critical development studies has emphasized how particular spaces—the hotel, the car, the embassy, the bunker, the aid compound—shape the everyday practices of development.[79] Key contributors have also demonstrated how development spatializes and materializes state power in the lifeworlds of beneficiary populations.[80] *The Quiet Violence of Empire* builds on this work by emphasizing how development does not just occur in or over particular spaces, but rather, through space. Each of the book's case studies considers how USAID technocrats sought to achieve their development goals in Afghanistan by intervening on the spatial milieu of life and work. As part of this broader effort, they established community development centers, demonstration farms, and model villages where rural Afghans could learn how to help themselves. They also enacted measures such as land consolidation, market development, and crop eradication that were meant to reorganize the spatial configurations of everyday Afghan life. USAID hoped that these spatial interventions would eventually transform rural Afghanistan into an environment conducive to perpetual self-improvement. Theorizing USAID's development activities as vehicles of infrastructural power offers a productive way of knitting together the multiple scales, geographies, and histories that animated my three case studies of imperial intervention in Afghanistan. An infrastructure framework, however, also makes it possible for scholars of empire to think relationally across the "stretched out and sequential connections" that have linked the various overseas "fields of development caused by US counterinsurgency and modernization campaigns."[81] To tell the story of USAID's development mission in Afghanistan is necessarily to situate it within a broader geography of imperial forces, relations, and struggles that encompasses other sites in South Asia, the decolonizing Pacific, Latin America, and ultimately, the "covert capital" of Washington, D.C., itself. What, then, are the intellectual and political stakes of this relational method?

Great Games . . .

Afghanistan has long been a terrain of imperial struggle. British colonial officials infamously spoke of Afghanistan as the prize of a "Great Game." The term is attributed to Captain Arthur Conolly, an officer of the British East India Company, itself a colonial nexus of war, finance, and development.[82] Between 1823 and 1842, Conolly conducted a number of expeditions into Afghanistan. In a letter dated July 1840 and addressed to Major Henry Rawlinson, a newly appointed British imperial agent based out of Kandahar province, Conolly proclaims: "You've a great game, a noble game before you." To play this game, the British colonial office would have to juggle a number of strategic geopolitical relationships with key regional stakeholders—Russia, Persia, the Oosberg states, the Bokhara Amir—so that they might be "just to us." This was necessary to ensure that Britain could "play the part that the first Christian nation of the world ought to fill."[83]

Conolly was writing to Rawlinson at a time when Britain's victory in the First Anglo-Afghan War seemed all but assured. Ghazni, Kandahar, and Kabul were all nominally under British control. The defeated Afghan leader, Dost Mohammed Barakzai, had surrendered to the British occupying force, which was in the process of evicting him to India. These conditions were the backdrop for Conolly's optimistic assessment that judicious geopolitical maneuvering would allow Britain to consolidate its military victories and open up a space for colonial officers like Rawlinson to begin the "noble" and "humanitarian" work of civilizing the Afghan people. Such a vision never came to pass. The British occupiers were first surprised—and eventually routed—by an armed insurgency led by Dost Mohammed's son, Wazir Akbar Khan. Khan and his "horde of 'pagan savages'" forced the British out of Kabul on January 6, 1842, who then spent the next seven days retreating through hostile territory to Jalalabad. What began as a column of sixteen thousand men was almost completely decimated by an unrelenting stream of guerilla ambushes. As the story is commonly told, only one British soldier—an assistant surgeon, Dr. William Brydon—made it back safely. Regardless of whether this detail is historically accurate, it is nonetheless the case that the First Anglo-Afghan War was a "patent triumph for the Afghans," who morally and physically crushed the British East-India Company Army.[84]

Contemporary commentators often cite this spectacular defeat as evidence for how Afghanistan has always been a "graveyard of empires." Imperial interventions always fail, we are told, because the Afghan people are stubbornly tribal, wildly ungovernable, and inherently barbaric. These are, as Nivi Manchanda emphasizes, geographically deterministic, ahistorical, and racialized renditions of the Afghan people. But these virulent Orientalisms left a lasting impression on British imperial policy in the region, justifying a strategic and military negligence of Afghanistan that was occasionally punctuated by moments of intensified engagement.[85] All of this is confirmed by how successive generations of British colonial officials rescripted Conolly's Great Game from a "humanitarian" justification for a noble civilizing mission into a narrow metaphor for macroscale geopolitical relations and conflicts.[86] Even Lord Curzon, the viceroy of India himself, came to frame Afghanistan as a "[piece] on a chessboard upon which is being played out a game for the domination of the world." While this was, as Derek Gregory observes, an "extraordinarily instrumental view of a land and its peoples," it nonetheless provides an "accurate summary" of how the late nineteenth- and early twentieth-century "geopolitical maneuverings" of imperial Britain and Russia "shaped the formation of the modern state of Afghanistan—a 'purely accidental' territory, Curzon called it—out of the shards of rival tribal fiefdoms and ethnic loyalties."[87]

The British colonial office played its first chess piece in 1878, when it launched a second war against the Emirate of Afghanistan. Britain won this rematch and extracted a series of concessions from the defeated Afghan emir. Under the terms of the treaty that formally ended the war, Britain seized control over Afghanistan's foreign relations as well as key frontier territories bordering India.[88] Britain's geopolitical objective was to fortify Afghanistan into a buffer state that would protect India from Russian territorial expansion.[89] As a way of staving off potential Russian interference, Britain supplied its new proxy regime with the cash and weapons it required to quell any internal and external threats to its rule. This status quo held until 1919, when Britain and Afghanistan engaged in a third war. While Britain was not able to secure a decisive victory over the Afghan Emirate, it was nonetheless able to preserve the territorial integrity of India's western borders. What Afghanistan regained from Britain was its sovereign right to conduct foreign relations.[90]

The fact that Afghanistan was never fully colonized, Manchanda argues, is more a function of British indecisiveness and negligence than any indication that the Afghans were a particularly unconquerable people.[91] Nor did Afghanistan's quasi-colonial status give way to full decolonization in the post-1945 moment. Instead, Afghanistan precariously navigated a tense period of imperial succession, whereby a longstanding British regional presence gradually gave way to more direct forms of U.S. intervention.[92] What the U.S. imperial administrators inherited from their British predecessors was the goal of keeping Afghanistan free of Russian—now Soviet—influence. Throughout the Cold War, Afghanistan continued to serve as a playing field upon which broader geopolitical struggles for power unfolded. This revamped Great Game began innocuously enough as a kind of "competitive coexistence" between the United States and the Soviet Union, which manifested in development interventions and not military operations (see chapter 1). Eventually, however, the Great Game escalated into a full-blown proxy war (see chapter 2). During both of these phases, Afghanistan became adept at leveraging its broader geostrategic importance to extract increasing levels of aid from both superpowers. Afghanistan, in Barnett Rubin's estimation, "became a sort of rentier or 'allocation' state, deriving over 40 percent of its revenue in every year since 1957 from 'revenue accruing directly from abroad.'"[93] These external revenue streams enabled the state to expand and consolidate its power in ways that lessened the need for democratic accountability.

As the Cold War wound down, Afghanistan gradually lost its geopolitical importance as a buffer state. After the Berlin Wall fell in November 1989, the United States and the Soviet Union attempted to peacefully resolve a number of outstanding conflicts, including the proxy war in Afghanistan. This turn of events did not bring the Great Game to a close, but rather fundamentally transformed it. Despite a joint U.S.–Soviet commitment to assist the United Nations in transitioning Afghanistan toward peace, the insurgency against the communist regime escalated into a civil war. As Afghanistan descended into violence and anarchy, it began to take on characteristics typically associated with "failed" states.[94] Such states are seen as incapable of meeting the basic needs of their citizens. For this reason, they are feared as sources of regional insecurity and as threats to the international order. When the Taliban eventually seized power in 1996, it was widely hoped that they would exert a stabilizing influence on Afghanistan. Unfortunately, while the Taliban reinforced the security and commercial components of the state apparatus, it nonetheless remained an "internally ruthless, totalitarian political entity, linked to a transnational shadow economy," as well as "opposition and terrorist groups on a region-wide basis, including al-Qaeda."[95] While Afghanistan could no longer be described as a "failed" state, it had, in the eyes of the international community, become a "rogue" threat to be managed, contained, and pacified through a combination of geopolitical and geoeconomic interventions. The events of 9/11 only confirmed these perceptions, unleashing the military engagements that foreshadowed the ongoing occupation of Afghanistan.

Barnett Rubin and Ahmed Rashid take all of this as evidence of how, despite a century of geopolitical machinations, the Great Game continues to unfold across the region: except now, "the number of players has exploded, those living on the chessboard have become involved, and the intensity of the violence and the threats it produces affect the entire globe."[96] Grand narratives of this sort, where one Great Game dissolves cleanly into another, are powerfully seductive. But as Manchanda and Gregory remind us, the imperial tendency to shroud Afghanistan in a "world of misleading metaphors" obscures as much as it reveals. The main consequence of these imaginative geographies is to render Afghanistan legible "as a pawn in a game of imperial stratagems, deliberately divested of agency and deprived of a narrative in which the history of Afghanistan is the history of Afghans."[97] The protagonists of Great Game narratives are invariably states (and state actors) who operate at the "macroscales of policy and strategy, security and design." What often falls out of such state-centric frameworks are the "micromovements of peoples who are subject and scarred, beholden to and invested in these empires on the ground."[98] This is to say, they tell us remarkably little about how broader "imperial predicaments" have historically "exerted an insistent presence" on the "intimate social ecologies" of the Afghan people.[99]

This is not, as Ann Stoler and David Bond usefully clarify, a "matter of advocating the micro over the macro or vice versa."[100] Rather, it is merely to suggest that if development in Afghanistan has always been felt in the space of the everyday as an embodied, intimate, and uneven geography of encounter between imperial agents, local counterparts, and beneficiary households, the resulting relationships were never, following Sara Ahmed, "simply in the present." Instead, each embodied encounter between a development professional and beneficiary subjects necessarily "reopens other encounters" that "always hesitate between the domain of the particular—the face to face of this encounter—and the general—the framing of the encounter by broader relationships of power and violence."[101] Given USAID's overarching commitment to blending a high-modernist biopolitics of technoscience with a liberal ethos of self-help and a (racial) capitalist vision of continuous market expansion, highly localized development encounters in Afghanistan frequently resonated with other, seemingly unrelated interventions across the decolonizing world.

This became especially true when the Cold War in Afghanistan finally turned hot in 1979. Indeed, the Soviet invasion and occupation of Afghanistan was haunted in so many ways by the specter of the Vietnam War. Once a mujahideen victory seemed likely in the late 1980s, venerable mastheads such as the *Washington Post* were quick to identify Afghanistan as "the Soviet's Vietnam."[102] But the Vietnam

War was important in other ways. As I argue elsewhere, USAID used war-torn South Vietnam as a crucible for forging a more explicitly violent approach to postcolonial improvement.[103] For this reason, USAID's leadership of the "other" war for South Vietnamese "hearts and minds" remains exemplary of the ways in which violence and destruction often enable the work of development. Over the course of the war, USAID, through its many police training and public safety activities, became increasingly implicated in the assassination, administrative detention, and torture of suspected National Liberation Front insurgents. In carrying out these activities, USAID aptly demonstrated its expertise in what George Orwell named the "dirty work of Empire."[104] As I show in chapter 2, USAID applied what it learned in Soviet-occupied Afghanistan, where it effectively reverse engineered development into a form of insurgency.

The Vietnam War remained an important historical touchstone for the long wars on terror in the post-9/11 era. It was during the invasion and occupation of Iraq that the U.S. military first rediscovered Vietnam-era counterinsurgency as a way of reversing a rapidly deteriorating situation on the ground. Defense intellectuals such as Anthony Cordesman never tired of drawing connections and comparisons between the Vietnam and Afghan wars. "We are fighting a war a half century later," Cordesman famously quipped to *Voice of America,* "that we lost for similar reasons a half century earlier." Vietnam veterans like Retired Army Lieutenant Larry Wilkerson—then the chief of staff to Secretary of State Colin Powell—were also struck by the "frightening" similarities between the two counterinsurgencies. This was made especially clear in the "various and sundry ways that we're trying to win people's hearts that aren't working."[105] But some of the other afterlives of Vietnam in post-9/11 Afghanistan are less obviously connected to the challenges of conducting "armed social work" under intensifying conditions of rural insurgency. If Lisa Bhungalia is correct to assert that counterinsurgency entails a "restrategization of war through the civil realm," then it is important to remember that policing, like development, has historically doubled as a civilian technology of race war, pacification, and order-making, both at home and abroad. As Nikhil Singh, Stuart Schrader, and Micol Seigel all show so forcefully, one of the most damaging legacies of USAID's development work in Vietnam has been the entrenchment and reproduction of transnational infrastructures for training police and other violence workers in the art of using force to quell disturbances and manage social conflict and unrest.[106] At the height of the Vietnam War, major U.S. cities, ranging from Detroit to Los Angeles to New York, became key hotspots in a broader struggle for social justice, racial equality, and civil rights. In response to these eruptions of black urban unrest, U.S. police forces were mobilized to first quell the riots, and then to wage an inner race war on the supposed scourges of poverty, drugs, and crime. Drawing inspiration from the ongoing counterinsurgency in Vietnam, U.S. police forces deliberately sought to transform America's streets into what one police commissioner revealingly called "foreign territory."[107]

What began as an inner war, however, soon boomeranged back outward as the so-called War on Drugs. Under the guise of global narcotics control, the U.S. national-security state supplied key allies in drug-producing countries with police training and other forms of assistance, including infusions of development capital and military hardware. USAID's mission to Afghanistan from the Soviet occupation onward must be understood through its connections to this global war on drugs. Over the course of the Soviet–Afghan conflict, U.S. covert operatives tacitly encouraged their mujahideen counterparts to fund their insurgency through poppy cultivation and opium production.[108] By the "end" of the occupation, Afghanistan was well on its way to surpassing Myanmar to become the world's leading exporter of opium resin. USAID, which had spent the duration of the conflict turning a blind eye to such activities, suddenly found itself under intensifying pressure to develop a comprehensive counternarcotics response. USAID's subsequent efforts in this field were undeniably haunted by its prior and current experiences carrying out police training, eradication, interdiction, and alternative development work in other drug-producing hotspots, such as Myanmar, Thailand, Peru, Bolivia, and Colombia.[109] In this way, Afghanistan became thoroughly entangled with the transnational geographies of (para)military violence, racialized policing, and development intervention that have, since 9/11, combined the War on Drugs and the War on Terror into what Emma Shaw Crane describes as a "new mode and stage of liberal empire": one that, as we shall see in chapters 3 and 4, subjected ordinary Afghans to new triangulations of rehabilitation, racialized dispossession, and political terror.[110]

I am not the first scholar to situate Afghanistan within a broader geohistorical context of warfare, development, and counterinsurgency. Derek Gregory's *The Colonial Present* is pathbreaking in this regard for how it maps the contrapuntal geographies that suture the U.S. empire-state's post-9/11 invasion and occupation of Afghanistan to its subsequent military interventions in Iraq, as well as to Israel's ongoing project of settler-colonial genocide in Palestine. These connective sinews, he cautions, are never transparent, nor can they be made so "by narratives in which moments clip together like magnets, or by maps in which our unruly world is fixed within a conventional Cartesian grid." What we need, in Gregory's estimation, are "other ways of mapping the turbulent times and spaces in which and through which we live."[111] In this vein, the contrapuntal geographies that I have mapped thus far suggest that we might also take seriously Afghanistan's geographical location in Central Asia. So much of modern Afghanistan's history has been shaped by its tumultuous relationship with British colonial India and, after the violence of Partition in 1947, Pakistan. But as I have also shown, Afghanistan is a generative site for contemplating the transnational afterlives of the U.S. wars against decolonization in Asia. By locating Afghanistan more explicitly in the "shadows of the long war," we can arrive at a more complex and nuanced understanding of how the everyday workings of the various U.S. counterinsurgency and counternarcotics campaigns in the decolonizing Pacific got reproduced as an inheritance for ordinary Afghans living at the very edges of that unwieldy geographical formation we call "Asia."[112] What allows for "inter-referencing" between the Golden Triangle and the Golden Crescent, in other words, are the transnational afterlives of U.S. empire.[113]

It is well beyond the scope of this book to fully consider the scholarly and political implications of approaching the long and bloody histories of U.S. empire building in Afghanistan from an explicitly inter-Asian perspective. But it is important to locate Afghanistan at the intersection of the "Middle East" and "Asia" as a way of moving beyond the methodological nationalism that seems to organize so much of the scholarly literature on U.S. interventionism abroad, which, according to Andrew Friedman, has tended to remain narrowly focused on singular moments of imperial warfare, violence, and occupation. What links many of the seemingly unrelated "fields" of development and counterinsurgency identified above is the quiet yet nonetheless insistent presence of USAID and the varied assortment of technicians, managers, and contractors that always follow in its wake. These development workers lead fundamentally transnational lives, shuttling back and forth between the field and the so-called Beltway metropolitan region that has come to serve as the nerve center of U.S. empire-building activities overseas. *The Quiet Violence of Empire* maps these transnational geographies from the everyday landscapes of the Beltway itself, taking special care to showcase how international development produces spaces and transforms spatial relations, both at home and abroad.

. . . and the USAID Complex

If development is a form of infrastructural power, then who wields it? One of the protagonists of *The Quiet Violence of Empire* is the USAID complex. This is the name that Susan Roberts gives to the constellation of institutions, contractors, and counterparts that carries out the everyday work of development in the field. Although this complex is almost as old as USAID itself, it became an especially powerful "distribution channel" for development capital in the post–Cold War period. As of 2019, USAID was handling more than $19 billion worth of projects annually.[114]

The sheer size, scale, and complexity of the USAID complex makes it a bit of a black hole to study. These difficulties have not stopped geographers like Roberts from combing through audits, contracts, and budgets to track how this complex "feeds and is nourished by spatializations" that invoke "far-flung spaces of need and intervention," as well as agglomeration economies and material circulations that are much closer to home.[115] Although this is important and difficult work, it nonetheless provides us with no sense of what the main players of this development-industrial complex actually do on a day-to-day basis.

From where might one begin the hard work of grounding the USAID complex in the everyday development geographies of the field? I originally thought my own research for this book would take me to Afghanistan. But the mounting ethical, logistical, and financial challenges inherent to conducting field research in a rapidly expanding war zone made it necessary for me to pivot away from a conventional "ethnography of locations" to a more wide-angle "ethnography of circulations."[116] I would go on to conduct the majority of the research for this book in the geographical heart of the USAID complex: the Beltway metropolitan region. Encompassing the city of Washington, D.C., as well as other suburban municipalities in Maryland and Virginia—hence its other colloquial moniker, the DMV—the Beltway is an ideal home base from which to better understand how the USAID complex has wielded infrastructural power across the decolonizing world. Home to USAID, the State Department, the Pentagon, the World Bank, and many of the major NGOs and private contractors that carry out the vernacular work of development, the Beltway is what Ananya Roy calls a "circulatory matrix": a key center of development calculation where whole "worlds are put into motion." Conducting research in a circulatory matrix like the Beltway, Roy acknowledges, invariably entails a "loss of the subaltern" on some level.[117] For this reason, *The Quiet Violence of Empire* cannot fully recover the thoughts and motives of the ordinary Afghans who benefited from, were the targets of, and, on more than one occasion, disrupted USAID's development activities in Afghanistan. But my fieldwork did bring me face-to-face with the civilian and military professionals who, at one point in their career, worked for or with the USAID complex in Afghanistan. These figures do not occupy elite positions of power within the U.S. empire-state. Rather, they generally work as middling and highly mobile technocrats who implement and refine their "practices of expertise" while circulating throughout a "vast web of empire" that stretches from Washington, D.C., and its suburbs—Bethesda, Fairfax, Arlington, Alexandria—all the way to the foreign guesthouses and field sites that dot the countryside of rural Afghanistan. Following Roy's injunction to render the familiar strange, I critically engage these figures, appreciating both the breadth and the depth of their mundane forms of expert knowledge as well as the sincerity of their desire to make Afghanistan better than it is, all the while refusing to take what they say at face value. In so doing, I illuminate the forms of power and knowledge through which they are constituted, as well as the ways they navigate a "complex terrain of complicity and resistance" to produce the multiscalar spaces of development work.[118]

I conducted fifteen interviews with these actors in a variety of settings: the cafeteria of the Ronald Reagan Building, suburban office complexes, local cafes, and participants' homes. These interviews do not—and were never meant to—provide a comprehensive account of USAID's development mission to post-9/11 Afghanistan. Instead, they shine a spotlight on the ways in which particular members of the USAID complex attempted to secure Afghanistan through development in specific times and places. They also surprised me as an invaluable source of industry gossip and rumor, offering new insights into the various institutional communities that populated the domestic landscapes of the USAID complex, and the everyday ways in which they related to each other. Working in a world as high-stakes and as cutthroat as the Beltway, my interviewees came to embrace and traffic in gossip, rumor, and speculation as a kind of survival strategy, as well as a way of constituting and reproducing certain kinds of community. From this perspective, gossip and rumor were just as important to the everyday work of development in the Beltway as policies, budgets, and contracts.[119]

Ultimately, these interviews were generative in their particularity and partiality, opening up a series of fraught questions that I took up in the archives of U.S. imperialism. *The Quiet Violence of Empire* wrestles with the immense paper bureaucracy that the USAID complex has accumulated over its long history of intervention in Afghanistan. These documents range the gamut from policy memoranda and meeting minutes to audits, project reports, and archived dissertations. I sourced the majority of this material from the U.S. National Archives and Records Administration (NARA) at College Park, where I focused on the records of the Agency for International Development (Record Group 286) and its predecessor agencies (Record Group 469). I also collected documents from the National Security Archives at George Washington University. For more contemporary projects, I trawled through the depths of USAID's Development Experience Clearinghouse (DEC), employing all of the search tricks in the book to unearth relevant documents and reports. Monica Kim argues that to "create a certain kind of paper archive [is] to claim a certain kind of legitimacy in international politics."[120] It is through paper—or, in today's increasingly digital world, PDFs—that Afghanistan is brought back and rendered legible to the Beltway, thereby setting the stage for further rounds of development programming in the field.

But even as the USAID complex was busy remaking Afghanistan into a "space of constructed visibility," the Beltway itself remained a "landscape of denial." The U.S. empire-state, Friedman observes, has a vested interest in "strategically, collectively, and cognitively [evading] the ethical implications of its violent actions" across the decolonizing world. Friedman argues that it accomplishes this ethical buffering through its "design and use of the most intimate spaces, relationships, and everyday spatial pathways of its own suburban life."[121] Hidden away in suburban Maryland, NARA is physically disconnected from the Dulles National—Reagan National Corridor that Friedman identifies as the geographical backbone of the covert capital. Nonetheless, College Park remains one of the main epistemological hinges structuring how critical scholars have understood the longer geohistories of U.S. imperial intervention abroad.

Ann Stoler has written extensively on how colonial and imperial archives like NARA double as "shadowed places" where state agents can convert certain social facts into qualified knowledge, and render others—whether through loss, miscategorization, or deliberate redacting—unusable and irrelevant.[122] But it is also important to remember that digital portals like the DEC are plagued by the same thorny problems. The DEC was first established in 1975 as a paper archive at the USAID library in Rosslyn. But it is curiously difficult to find any information at all about this analog iteration of the DEC. Some of the only tangible evidence of the library's offline existence is buried in the bibliography of books like Jim Glassman's *Thailand at the Margins*. From Jim, I've heard stories that certain paper documents were never scanned into the DEC.[123] Like NARA, then, the DEC is also one of the shadowed places of the covert capital, where imperial sovereignty continues to "reside in the power to designate arbitrary social facts of the world as matters of security and concerns of the state."[124] Its purpose is to tell a very particular story about how USAID has evolved as an institution. Here, a close reading of the DEC's own web page chronicling "USAID's History" is instructive. In the 1970s, USAID pivoted away from "technical and capital assistance" toward basic needs programming. In the 1980s, USAID discovered the market and the private sector. In the 1990s, USAID's mandate expanded to encompass sustainability and democracy. And in the 2000s, USAID was increasingly consumed by war and rebuilding. Nowadays, USAID's new buzzwords are self-reliance and resilience.[125]

What is striking about this timeline is the way it aligns with Foucauldian critiques of the development–security nexus that have become popular in international relations and political geography in

recent years. How, then, might we use these archives to undermine—
and not reinscribe—the authority of the U.S. empire-state? The standard approach is to read colonial archives "against their grain": to
locate "'structure' with the colonizers and the colonial state, and
'human agency' with subalterns, in small gestures of refusal and si-
lence amongst the colonized."[126] Although this is where I began *The
Quiet Violence of Empire,* I eventually arrived at Stoler's "less assured
and perhaps more humble" commitment to instead read along the archival grain.[127] My aim here is "not to follow a frictionless course" but
rather to "[draw] our sensibilities to the archive's granular rather than
seamless texture, to the rough surfaces that mottle its hue and shape
its form."[128] This entails a twofold commitment: first to take NARA and
USAID's DEC seriously as archives of how the everyday work of U.S.
empire building has been both biopoliticized and neoliberalized, and
second to sit with those moments in the archival record where USAID's
investments in a neoliberal biopolitics of development come undone,
exposing its long-standing entanglements with the ugly violences of
race war and counterinsurgency.

These moments of "countermand" take on a diversity of forms. Some
of these "discrepant accounts"—like Dick Scott's personal collection of
documents and testimonies pertaining to the Helmand Valley Project—
quietly "hover in the archive's long shadows."[129] But other dissenting
voices are louder and more insistent. WikiLeaks' databases of leaked
diplomatic cables and war diaries are exemplary in this regard, offering concerned publics a partial glimpse of the banal, everyday violence
that came to define counterinsurgency in Afghanistan. More generally, journalists and independent researchers are an invaluable source
of reporting on an empirical context as volatile as occupied Afghanistan. To be sure, newspaper articles, blog posts, and research reports
do not offer unfiltered access to the real world.[130] Nor can it be assumed
that the *New York Times, Washington Post,* Afghanistan Research and
Evaluation Unit, and Afghan Analysts Network do not bear the marks
of imperial rule. But journalists and independent researchers have
doggedly exposed the negative consequences of USAID's development
activities in post-9/11 Afghanistan. For this reason, they have an important role to play in the radical critique of the colonial present.

All of this is suggestive of how conducting research in the Beltway is
"to enter a field of force and a will to power."[131] On occasion, my program

of research butted up against and clashed with this will to power. In the summer of 2013, one key informant abruptly cancelled a scheduled interview on the grounds that they were afraid of discussing potentially controversial subjects on record. This was a time when USAID and its development contractors were facing increased levels of public scrutiny for potentially wasting taxpayer dollars in Afghanistan. But I am also reminded of the ways in which academics—even critical ones—are interpellated by the U.S. empire-state. One informant took time out of their busy schedule to sit down for an interview, partially because they remembered how hard it had been for them to do similar work in graduate school. And in hindsight, the ease with which I had been able to strike up conversations and make research plans with development contractors in Jalalabad or provincial reconstruction teams in Helmand speaks to the ways in which the presence of academics on the battlefield has been normalized, even valorized. Counterinsurgency, after all, is supposed to be the graduate level of warfare, weaponizing disciplines such as English, anthropology, and geography to carry out close readings of enemy populations and environments.[132] These very real proximities between academia and empire make it all the more difficult to "understand how unintelligibilities are sustained" and why "empires remain so uneasily invested in them."[133] The story that follows is not meant to be a comprehensive engagement with such imperial unintelligibilities. What *The Quiet Violence of Empire* offers instead is a first rough attempt at thinking through some of their methodological and political implications for the study of U.S. empire in the colonial present.

Chapter Outlines

The Quiet Violence of Empire is divided into four chronological chapters, each one tracking the gradual evolution in USAID's methods for wielding development as an *infrastructural technology of racial liberalism* across the Afghan countryside. The first two empirical chapters cover the Cold War period of this history. Chapter 1, "The Unfinished Symphony," focuses on the Helmand Valley Project. First conceived in 1946 as a showcase for the spectacular transformative potential of U.S. hydraulic engineering expertise, the Helmand Valley Project was an ambitious attempt at laying down the irrigation infrastructures necessary to reclaim large, arid swaths of southern Afghanistan for agricultural resettlement. What resulted instead was the widespread salinization of prime agricultural land. To address these problems, USAID began testing a different approach to rural development in the Helmand Valley. USAID came to believe that rural Afghans were not being held back by their technical inability to capture, store, and unleash the productive energies of regional hydrological systems. Rather, the true constraint to the development of Afghanistan was rural Afghans themselves. USAID would have to install within the Afghan inhabitants of the Helmand Valley the will and the ambition to work for higher standards of living. For this reason, USAID began to experiment with other, less spectacular infrastructures of development, a politics of improvement that prioritized technical assistance, extension services, and community uplift as the keys to building new and modern forms of rural Afghan life. While these various infrastructures of "community development" promised more inclusionary modes of development encounter, they were actually undergirded by techniques and strategies that were first developed to uplift African American households in the Jim Crow South. The net effect of these transnational connections was therefore to reproduce longer-standing historical geographies of race war and racial management as a transnational inheritance of U.S. empire. Unsurprisingly, these experiments were not always well received by their intended beneficiaries. On at least one occasion, Afghan farmers actively resisted—and eventually derailed—USAID's attempts at reorganizing already existing infrastructures for building and sustaining communal life. What emerged out of such failures was a new, more "people-centric" blueprint for rural development in Afghanistan: one that would go on to serve as a core pillar of USAID interventions through the Soviet–Afghan conflict and into the global war on terror.

Chapter 2, "From Factory to Field," explores how USAID practiced development as a form of insurgency in Soviet-occupied Afghanistan. Barred by international law from operating within Afghanistan, USAID eventually chose to support the mujahideen resistance from offices located across the border in Pakistan. USAID coordinated the Cross Border Humanitarian Assistance Program, which is notable for reconceptualizing rural development as the logistical problem of procuring and distributing commodities across a transnational borderland: or, what I name elsewhere as a problem of *just-in-time imperialism*. This is to say, USAID intervened in the Soviet–Afghan conflict by offering mujahideen insurgents, Afghan farmers, and local entrepreneurs the logistical support they needed to carry out the infrastructural work of securing rural Afghanistan for a postracial future of liberal peace and capitalist prosperity. Initially, USAID's Cross Border Humanitarian Assistance Program sought to stem the flow of refugees from Afghanistan to Pakistan by supplying rural households with the food, medicine, and other vital commodities they required to remain in their war-devastated communities and, by extension, serve the mujahideen "fish" as a "sea" to "swim" in. Buoyed by USAID's success at repurposing development into a kind of insurgent logistics, mujahideen forces eventually liberated the vast majority of the countryside from communist control, thereby opening the door for more substantive forms of cross-border rehabilitation and reconstruction work. Convinced of the urgent need to preempt a looming food crisis by rehabilitating levels of agricultural production to prewar levels, USAID worked with a private-sector implementing partner to transform the Afghanistan–Pakistan borderlands into an environment conducive to the market-driven circulation of agricultural inputs. These cross-border development efforts, however, soon brushed up against alternative infrastructures for provisioning rural life, as USAID began to suspect that certain unruly mujahideen commanders were covertly diverting agricultural assistance to illicit poppy cultivators. USAID tried to break these alternative infrastructures of rural rehabilitation by introducing the dialectic of law enforcement "anger" and development "mercy" that would go on to become the hallmark of counternarcotics operations in post-9/11 Afghanistan.

The final two chapters connect USAID's Cold War interventions in Afghanistan to its ongoing alternative development efforts to wean Afghan farmers off of poppy cultivation. Over the course of these chapters, I compare and contrast a number of different alternative development programs that were implemented by the USAID complex in Afghanistan's southern and northeastern regions. Chapter 3, "Fast Development, Slow Violence," tracks how the U.S. race wars on drugs and terror combined to produce new forms of empire building and counterinsurgency capitalism in post-9/11 Afghanistan. In the early days of the occupation, the U.S. empire-state leveraged its civilian and military components to transform and reorganize the rural landscapes of southern Afghanistan through a new dialectic of anger and mercy: one that paired broken-windows-style police training with crop substitution interventions that had first been put to work in other theaters of the global race war on drugs. In particular, I focus my attention on the different forms of alternative development programming that emerged in the southern provinces of Helmand and Kandahar between 2005 and 2013. Tapped to play a leading role in the broader counternarcotics campaign, USAID drew from its prior experiences working with drug cultivators—both in Afghanistan and elsewhere—to develop a more market-based approach to alternative development programming. From 2005 to 2009, USAID set about reorienting Afghan farmers in Helmand and Kandahar away from traditional subsistence livelihood strategies toward more modern forms of commercial agricultural production. USAID hoped that these infrastructures of alternative development assistance would help cushion the shocks that poppy-cultivating households were experiencing due to more traditional forms of counternarcotics activities, namely, crop eradication. Beginning in 2009, however, USAID's ability to set Afghan households on the path toward racial liberal, market-based futures became increasingly constrained by a rapidly worsening insurgency. Because of this deteriorating security situation, USAID found itself becoming increasingly reliant upon military support to carry out activities in the field. What resulted from this convergence of civilian and military operations was a so-called stabilization model of alternative development, grounded in quick-impact crop substitution programs that sought to provide poppy cultivators with heavily subsidized access to improved wheat seeds and fertilizers. While the USAID complex likes to critique such hybridized forms of alternative development for unsustainably distorting local economies and for negatively compromising the operational space of civilian actors, it nonetheless glosses over the real problem with stabilization programs, which is that they led to the dispossession and displacement of land-poor households across southern Afghanistan. These displaced households survived under such dire conditions by migrating to the more remote and unhospitable desert regions of Helmand province, where they once again turned to poppy cultivation as a strategy for accessing land and subsistence. For these farmers, poppy cultivation functioned as a bulwark against successive waves of U.S.

infrastructural power, or, to put it in more theoretical terms, as a form of infrastructural resistance.

Chapter 4, "Alternative Developments?," interrogates the "rural development" model of alternative livelihoods programming that came to the fore in northeastern Afghanistan. In contrast with the alternative development programs analyzed in chapter 3, the "rural development" model championed more long-term interventions that sought to establish an "enabling environment" for licit, market-based forms of agricultural production and exchange. But while these comprehensive attempts at marketizing all facets of rural Afghan life made certain farming households live, they also let others die: specifically, those who were already disadvantaged by virtue of their gender and their geographical location. To make matters worse, these gendered infrastructures of rural improvement were also secured by geographical techniques of population management that were fundamentally destructive of life, including crop eradication, nexus targeting, and even assassination. USAID's vision of a seemingly frictionless "environment" of market governance was therefore fully embedded in and undergirded by imperial infrastructures of abandonment, violence, and death. From this perspective, alternative development in eastern Afghanistan appears more precisely as a violent hybridization of lethal and nonlethal forms of infrastructural power that severed or eliminated certain undesirable patterns of rural life while simultaneously nurturing other connections and circulations that might better serve the geopolitical economic interests of U.S. empire.

The conclusion, "Development in a Time of Abolition," considers the political stakes of *The Quiet Violence of Empire* in this ongoing moment of crisis, emergency, and possibility. It does so by reading some of the recently leaked exit interviews that the special inspector general for Afghan reconstruction conducted with development professionals and counterinsurgents in the immediate aftermath of the war. It then places these interviews in conversation with Frantz Fanon's reflections on decolonization and development in *The Wretched of the Earth*. For the most part, the lessons offered by the interviewees are largely reformist in nature. And yet, some seized the opportunity to articulate a more "structural" critique of their involvement in the war. The USAID complex repeats the same mistakes over and over, they argue, because it is structurally organized to channel the lion's share of development capital into the pockets of American contractors and not Afghan households. Development, in other words, is first and foremost a metropolitan project of racial capitalist accumulation. And yet, despite having diagnosed the problem as such, their investments in and commitments to the USAID complex effectively preclude them from proposing the most obvious solution, one that was anticipated by Frantz Fanon some fifty-seven years ago: abolish the USAID complex and, in its place, build alternative infrastructures for channeling development capital directly to marginalized communities. Here, my use of abolitionist language is deliberate, drawing inspiration from the struggles for black life against white supremacy, police brutality, mass incarceration, and immigrant detention that continue to rage across cities in the present moment. But it also recalls the successful histories of leftist and anti-imperialist organizing against USAID's long and bloody history of providing overseas police training assistance as a form of development. Putting these histories and geographies of abolitionist struggle in conversation, I think, opens a window for outlining an explicitly transnational and multiscalar concept of abolition: one that might serve as a building block for an intercommunalist politics of presence, aimed at ensuring that the "last shall be first."

This book does not offer a blueprint—or even a series of recommendations—for moving forward into abolitionist, anti-imperial, and intercommunalist futures. But what it does emphasize is the importance of attending to the everyday acts of refusal that make life possible, and perhaps even livable, under the enduring conditions of counterinsurgency and racial capitalism. Rural development in Afghanistan and elsewhere has always been a frictional terrain of imperial encounter, shaped by broader relations of power and violence, yet never fully subsumed by them. Afghan farmers have historically demonstrated their capacity to refuse the promises of imperial development, choosing instead to align themselves with alternative infrastructures for provisioning and supporting life. In this fraught time of what Shaw Crane and others call "afterwar," such small, particular, and localized practices of refusal and making do must, I think, be understood as essential to the abolitionist and anti-imperialist work of building and sustaining Afghan lifeworlds that can, to paraphrase Ruth Wilson Gilmore, "flourish, and be voluptuous, and quite beautiful."[134]

1

The Unfinished Symphony

Infrastructural Power in the Helmand Valley

[Afghans] are exploding out into the open. . . . The spirit of a
new era is driving them at a furious pace.

> *Glenn Foster, Morrison-Knudsen engineer, 1952,*
> *in Monica Whitlock, "Helmand's Golden Age,"* BBC News

ON JULY 5, 1962, the United States Agency for International Development (USAID) invited the "combined American community" of
Kandahar to "come out and enjoy [themselves]" at a "Fourth of July Celebration" in Mansil Bagh Park. The following program (Figure 1) shows
that from 8:00 in the morning until 6:00 in the evening, American and
Afghan revelers partook in a variety of activities, including a pie-eating
contest, a dizzy relay, and tonga cart rides. According to Marvin Green,
the acting assistant area executive officer for USAID/Kandahar, this
celebration was a "long overdue" opportunity to bring the community
"together in mind and purpose." He predicted that it would "do won-
ders in cementing relations" with local Afghans.[1]

This program captures a slice of what life was like for Americans living and working in the southern Afghan province of Helmand during the
Cold War. Long-time BBC World Service correspondent Monica Whitlock frames this history as "all but forgotten." In a long-form mixed media
essay published by *BBC News,* she recovers this period as Helmand's
"Golden Age." During this "hopeful moment" in Helmand's history,
Whitlock argues, ordinary Afghans "faced the future with confidence."[2]

Whitlock's nostalgic retelling of Helmand's glory days draws heavily from a collection of recently rediscovered silent films that were shot
and produced by a young American engineer, Glenn Foster. Employed
by the legendary American construction and heavy engineering firm
Morrison-Knudsen, Foster lived and worked in southern Afghanistan
for seven years. During his time in Afghanistan, Foster used a 16mm

PROGRAM

08:30	Ball Game	(Mr. Jose Tayani)
10:00 – 11:15	Swimming	
11:15	Flag Raising & National Anthem	(Mr. Curtis)
	Ambassador Stevens addresses this group if he wishes to do so.	
11:30 – 13:00	Lunch	
13:00	Sack races	(Mr. John Givman)
	First group – age 5 years – 8 years	
	Second group – age 9 years – 12 years	
	Third group – Men	
	Fourth group – Women	
14:00	Water Show	(Mrs. Hillbolt)
14:30	Greased Pole Contest	(Mr. Jim Aispaugh)
15:00	Dizzy Relay	(Mr. Ed Wholan)
15:30	Three-legged race	(Mrs. Reilly)
	Age group – 5 thru 8 years	
	– 9 thru 12 years	
	– Adults	
16:00	Pie Eating Contest	(Mr. Ed Wholan)
	Age group – 12 years and under	
	– Adults	
16:30	Potato Push	
17:00	Races	
	50 Yards dash – 5 thru 8 years	
	50 Yards dash – 9 thru 14 years	
	50 Yards dash – Women	
	1000 Yards dash – Men	
17:15	Sponge Relay	(Mrs. McMillan)
17:30	Nuts and Bolt Contest	(Mr. Pacifico)
	Nail Pounding Contest	
17:45 – 18:00	Group Singing	

Bingo games will be held through the afternoon. Cards will cost 10 afghanis for each game. Winner takes all.

Tonga cart will be available for rides all afternoon.

We will try to show Movies in the Palace during the afternoon.

FIGURE 1. *Program, Marvin Green, "Fourth of July Celebration— Kandahar," June 11, 1962, P 58, Box 1, Record Group 286: Records of the United States Agency for International Development (hereafter cited as RG 286), National Archives and Records Administration, College Park, Md. (hereafter cited as NARA). Re-created by the author.*

camera to film scenes of "Afghan life and landscapes, of engineering projects, of Christmas parties in the American community."[3] Many of Foster's films were shot in and around Mansil Bagh. Formerly a royal palace, the Afghan king Zahir Shah had bequeathed Mansil Bagh to Morrison-Knudsen for use as both an administrative center and as a residential compound. What Foster captured on film was not some exotic Oriental landscape, but rather one dotted by "modern American-built houses, with lawns, low fences, and front gardens." The viewer, Whitlock enthuses, is taken right inside this faithful reproduction of American suburbia and immersed in its "lively details": large drinks, endless cigarettes, Christmas dinners, swimming parties, and beauty pageants.

These spaces were not exclusively inhabited by American expatriates. Over the course of the Cold War, approximately one million Afghans were lured to the Helmand Valley by the prospect of good jobs, schools, and land.[4] These migrants gravitated to the nascent "Little Americas" of southern Afghanistan, such as Mansil Bagh or Lashkar Gah, the newly established capital of Helmand province.[5] They shared these spaces with the American imperialists, with whom they forged comfortable working and living relationships rooted in mutual amusement and curiosity. As Saeeda Mahmood, the daughter of an Afghan civil servant who also ran the local cinema in Lashkar Gah, reminisces, these were the happiest of times:

> We grew up all together. No-one said, you are this, and we are that. Some of our neighbours were Americans. We used to invite them at Eid, they'd invite us for their parties. I remember Santa Claus would come, on a donkey, bringing us all presents.[6]

Young Afghans like Saeeda flicker in and out of Foster's footage. Educated, ambitious, and progressive, they dressed not in burqas and *shalwar kamezes* but in flower-print dresses, high heels, and letterman jackets. According to Foster, they were even known to enjoy a competitive game of baseball and tug-of-war, both of which were American imports to southern Afghanistan.

Published during the early days of the U.S. military's "drawdown" from Afghanistan, Whitlock's essay is no doubt meant to remind the BBC's readership that the history of Western intervention in the region has not always been synonymous with insurgency and (para)military violence. But its other effect is to counter imperial amnesia with imperial nostalgia. U.S. imperialists, we are reminded, once knew how to coexist with and inspire their Afghan counterparts. These imperial encounters may have been uneven and asymmetrical, but they nonetheless offered a potential pathway for nurturing more modern, liberal, and capitalist forms of Afghan life. The Afghans who settled in the Helmand Valley under American guidance gradually became "aware that there is a better way of life beyond their borders and they [began to want] some of these things."[7] U.S. imperialists, therefore, brought something else with them to Afghanistan: the promise of development.

In *The Colonial Present*, Derek Gregory argues that "postcolonial critique must not only counter amnesiac histories of colonialism, but also stage 'a return of the repressed' to resist the seductions of nostalgic histories of colonialism."[8] Whitlock's yearning for the "Little Americas" of Helmand's "Golden Age" speaks to the enduring liberal nostalgia for development and its empty promise of a kinder and gentler form of imperialism abroad. The "Little Americas" filmed by Foster were not idiosyncratic to Afghanistan. Rather, they were a reoccurring trope of U.S. imperialism abroad. The United States, as Andrew Friedman reminds us, "did not just have an empire, but imperialists."[9] The Cold War rollout of U.S. imperial power abroad went hand-in-hand with the establishment of new systems for building and maintaining imperial life. What resulted was a transnational infrastructure of imperial suburbanisms that included not only Lashkar Gah and Mansil Bagh, but also the Aramco oil camps of Saudi Arabia, the colonial villas of Vietnam-War-era Saigon, and the secluded cul-de-sacs and tree-lined vistas of the Dulles Corridor, to name only a few examples.[10] These "(extra)ordinary entanglements of US-corporate colonial domesticity," in turn, were underpinned in so many ways by the violence work of U.S. empire.[11] In contrast with some of the other "Little Americas" mentioned above, Lashkar Gah and Mansil Bagh were not as obviously undergirded by the spectacular forms of extractive and kinetic violence that had come to define U.S. empire building elsewhere. But they still served as key nodes in a subtler, yet no less damaging sociospatial infrastructure of imperial power, pacification, and control. This was the U.S. empire-state's thirty-year mission to improve Cold War Afghanistan through successive phases of integrated rural development programming.

In this chapter, I consider how the U.S. empire-state used Cold War

Afghanistan as a "uniquely valuable" laboratory for applying a geo-political-economic edge to rural development theory and practice.[12] Between 1955 and 1979, Afghanistan became one of the largest per capita beneficiaries of American foreign aid. A significant percentage of these funds was channeled into the Helmand Valley Project (HVP). This was an ambitious state-building scheme to harness the watersheds of the Helmand Valley—mapped in Figure 2—as part of a broader project of resettling the deserts of southern Afghanistan. Over the course of the Helmand Valley Project, American imperialists worked alongside local elites and farmers to lay down the infrastructural prerequisites for modernizing Afghanistan. These infrastructures of Cold War development were animated by an interplay between capital- and people-centric methods for managing rural Afghan life.

When considered from the vantage point of the colonial present, however, the overall arc of the HVP is immensely suggestive of how an ideology of racial liberalism, as Jodi Melamed puts it, "came to structure

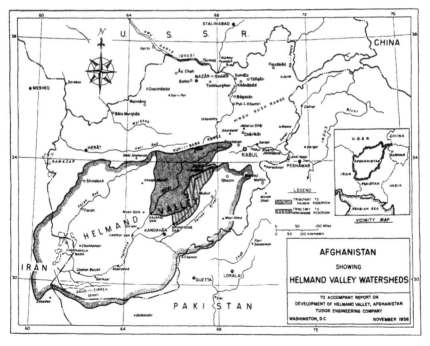

FIGURE 2. *Map of the Helmand Valley Watersheds. Harold Schwartz, "Helmand Valley Development," November 8, 1960. P 58, Box 14. RG 286, NARA.*

the [U.S. empire-state's] fields of global intervention."¹³ From the outset
of the Cold War, the U.S. empire-state hoped to leverage its considerable technical prowess—whether in the field of heavy engineering, or
in the everyday forms of extension and community development that
came to define the later stages of the Helmand Valley Project—to realize its "vision of a global, American-centered, racially inclusive world,
one organized around formally equal and independent nation-states."¹⁴
Interventions like the Helmand Valley Project were supposed to showcase the benefits of this vision for decolonizing populations and, ideally, orient them toward liberal and anticommunist futures. But U.S.
modernizers, even in supposedly neutral Afghanistan, could never
quite cleanse development of what Nikhil Pal Singh calls its "colonial-
racial taint."¹⁵ Rural development in Cold War Afghanistan, in other
words, was as much a *racial* project as it was a technopolitical or even
geopolitical one. At the level of everyday practice, it drew heavy inspiration from longer genealogies of race war, topologically connecting
the Helmand Valley to other domestic and foreign theaters of imperial
racial management, including the Jim Crow South, the American inner
city, and insurgent South Vietnam, to name only a few examples.¹⁶ But
the HVP's commitment to foregrounding the American suburban form
as an ideal organizing framework for rural Afghan society is significant
for what it tells us about the unspoken racialized and gendered underpinnings of the development mission more generally. It is by now well
known that the American suburb has historically served as a stage for
racial cleansing, domestic violence, settler dispossession, and transnational militarism.¹⁷ How did rural communities scattered across the
Helmand Valley feel these histories and geographies in their everyday
lives as an inheritance of empire?

    I broach this question by triangulating recent critical scholarship on
Cold War hydropolitics, self-help approaches in development, and the
transnational infrastructures of colonialism, race war, and empire. My
aim here is to construct a new framework for understanding rural development interventions like the HVP as a conduit for a particularly racialized mode of infrastructural power. In so doing, I expose the HVP as
a contradictory patchwork of capital- and people-centric infrastructures
for developing southern Afghanistan and, by extension, integrating the
region into transnational circuits of imperial pacification and racial
management.

I then analyze archival documents to track the HVP's evolving conception of underdevelopment in southern Afghanistan as a problem of infrastructure. In its initial phases, the HVP was focused on modernizing hydraulic infrastructures across southern Afghanistan. These heavy engineering schemes, however, resulted in the widespread salinization of reclaimed land. In order to address these problems, the HVP began to experiment with other infrastructural practices for improving the conditions of everyday life. After rescripting salinization as the natural consequence of Afghan backwardness, USAID established a network of spaces—including agricultural training centers and demonstration farms—where farmers were introduced to modern agricultural practices. In so doing, USAID realized that it was not enough to simply "extend" agricultural assistance to Afghan farmers. Rather, change in the Helmand Valley had to be "total," comprising "all aspects of life at the same time."[18] This total approach to rural development was exemplified by the Shamalan Land Development Project (SLDP). Implemented from 1967 to 1973, the SLDP indexed a complete reengineering of the biophysical landscape to a comprehensive community building effort. The SLDP, however, failed to consider the needs and desires of the "mass of the people," spurring them to resist and ultimately derail the project.[19]

All of this occurred at a moment when USAID more generally was refining its development best practices to prioritize the basic needs of beneficiary populations across the decolonizing world. True to form, Afghanistan soon became a laboratory for stress testing these "New Directions" in integrated rural development programming.[20] But while USAID paid lip service to the idea of putting Afghans first, local needs and desires continued to take a back seat to the technical expertise of U.S. imperialists, who remained the final arbiters of possibility in the field. On the eve of the Soviet occupation, then, USAID found itself caught between two ways of wielding infrastructural power across Afghanistan—and the decolonizing world more broadly.

Infrastructures of Development

Throughout the twentieth century, Timothy Mitchell observes, "the politics of national development and economic growth was a politics of techno-science, which claimed to bring the expertise of modern engineering, technology, and social science to improve the defects of nature, to transform peasant agriculture, to repair the ills of society, and to fix the economy."[21] Such a technopolitics of modernization is clearly exemplified by the ways in which colonial, settler-colonial, and postcolonial elites have historically depended upon infrastructures to wield power over space, across scale, and through time. Gyan Prakash shows how the constitution of British India went "hand in hand with the establishment of a grid of modern infrastructures and economic linkages that drew the unified territory into the global capitalist economy."[22] More recent work also emphasizes the similar role that transportation infrastructures played in settler-colonial contexts such as the United States and Canada. Transcontinental railroads, in particular, are notable for how they triangulated nationalist space-making projects with the genocide of Indigenous populations and the entrenchment of a virulent racial capitalism.[23]

While colonial and imperial elites were seduced by the nation-building potential of transcontinental railroads, they also championed hydrological infrastructures as another crucial prerequisite for "[engineering] a stable, prosperous, and loyal political and social order."[24] This was particularly true during the Cold War, which saw the rapid proliferation of river basin development projects throughout the decolonizing world.[25] Such projects were appealing to Cold Warriors and postcolonial elites alike. U.S. Cold Warriors sought out stages for flaunting the prodigious transformative capacities of Western technoscience. Instantly recognizable as spectacular feats of modern heavy engineering, river-basin development projects resonated with the geopolitical imaginations of the U.S. empire-state, which played a central role in "identifying regions and resources suitable for programs of technological intervention."[26] This geopolitical context made it easy for river basin development projects to be enrolled in the global effort to contain the expanding influence of the Soviet Union in the decolonizing world.

From the perspective of postcolonial elites, however, river basin development projects were valuable scale-jumping technologies that could help them leverage the broader "geopolitical economy of the Cold War" to support home-grown visions of state formation and nation building.[27] Majed Akhter argues that the Cold War effort to develop the Indus River Basin "increased the strength and spatial extent of the Pakistani state" by improving its ability to control the watershed over a wider swath of territory.[28] The construction of hydraulic infrastructures, in other words, went hand-in-hand with the production of state space. River basin development projects were therefore able to serve as a crucial weapon of the broader Cold War precisely because they articulated with the intertwined geopolitical, geoeconomic, and sociocultural processes that were driving decolonization across the Third World.

For the most part, this literature on the "hydropolitical" dimensions of the Cold War remains largely focused on state infrastructures.[29] The HVP was certainly concerned with the task of building the concrete sinews of a modern nation-state. Nick Cullather's work on the HVP serves as an important starting point in this regard. Cullather argues that American advisors detailed to the Helmand Valley subordinated "complex social and political problems within the more manageable engineering problem of overcoming the water constraint."[30] Development in Afghanistan was initially framed as a problem of water scarcity. In the eyes of U.S. modernizers, rural Afghans were primarily held back by their inability to capture and unleash the productive energies of regional hydrological systems. "Resolution," as Cullather writes, "became a matter of apportioning cubic yards of water and kilowatt-hours of energy."[31] Timothy Nunan concurs, emphasizing how the HVP framed water as a resource that had to be "mastered" through infrastructural development "if Afghanistan was to become a territorial state with a national economy."[32]

But if large-scale hydropolitical projects like the HVP symbolically, and perhaps unfairly, carried the hopes and dreams of Afghan nation builders—King Mohammed Zahir Shah was a particularly vocal champion of damming and reclamation work—their impact on everyday forms of rural life making was nonetheless equally complex and fraught. Over time, one of the consequences of the HVP was to subject rural households to evolving and ever more intimate forms of governmentality. As dam- and irrigation-building schemes ran their course across southern Afghanistan, often to disastrous effect, they opened up new and more intimate terrains of development intervention, such as the community and the household. This second phase of the HVP, in turn, was anchored by "less obvious" infrastructures of technical assistance, agricultural development, and community building, all of which played an increasingly central role in "[ordering] social and natural worlds."[33]

Instead of targeting and transforming whole ecosystems, these infra-structures operated at the scale of everyday life, intervening on the be-haviors and practices that sustained and reproduced vernacular social relations.

(Post)colonial nation builders, of course, have always valued large-scale infrastructural projects for their everyday governmental effects. At the turn of the twentieth century, for example, British East India Company officers and their local proxies leveraged a racialized and highly unequal politics of infrastructural improvement to develop major urban centers, such as Bombay and Bangalore. Colonial *dewans* in particular took a personal interest in building "circulatory infra-structures and residential extensions that sought to inculcate new norms of propriety in natives and raise the value of landed property."[34] Similarly, Cullather hints that American modernizers often conceived of Afghans as deficient subjects requiring a "revolution in mental con-cepts."[35] Cullather, however, does not expand on how this insight in-formed development practice. Building on Cullather, I argue that the HVP attempted to launch such a revolution through infrastructural interventions that were meant to help rural Afghans develop the will and capacity to participate in their own self-improvement. This imper-ative to "create a spirit of self-help" was one of the leitmotifs that ran through the different phases of the HVP.

Recently, there has been a groundswell of geographical work on the concept of self-help.[36] David Nally and Stephen Taylor usefully explore how self-help was enrolled in Cold War agricultural development pro-gramming as a way of steering the conduct and aspirations of rural households. The aim of a self-help approach was to "make subsistence-level existence seem alien and commercial farming appear both de-sirable and imminently attainable."[37] Farmers, in other words, would demonstrate their capacity for self-help by conducting themselves as rational economic subjects. At first blush, the relevance of Nally and Taylor's work to the context of Cold War Afghanistan seems obvious. The goal of the HVP, however, was not to universalize the figure of the market subject, but rather, to establish an internally coherent and self-sustaining agricultural economy in southern Afghanistan.[38] This is to say, it was animated by a different vision of self-help, animated by a desire to "shore up small-scale solidarities to encourage demo-cratic liberation and civic action on a local level, and to embed politics and economics within the life of the community," or what Daniel Immerwahr summarizes as a "quest for community."[39] From the 1930s through the 1960s, the United States bankrolled many community development schemes across the Global South, including in Afghanistan. As Immerwahr points out, this global "quest for community" was never at cross-purposes with the "urge to modernize." Instead, they often "shared space" as "rival impulses" that were "felt sometimes by the same people simultaneously, coiled tightly around each other."[40]

This was the case with the HVP. Over time, U.S. modernizers came to believe that southern Afghanistan could only be developed by laying down the infrastructures necessary for rural Afghans to participate in new forms of communal life. To this end, self-help activities needed what Stuart Schrader calls a "definite spatial locus," carefully delineated to maximize the chances that the "target population" might naturally feel compelled to "invest in its members' own security and controlled uplift."[41] Elsewhere across the decolonizing world, this spatial locus was "the community." Given that the formerly nomadic communities now settling the Helmand Valley were generally not "extant and cohesive formation[s]," however, the USAID complex had to tease them into existence through participation.[42] One of the most common ways in which communities were asked to participate in development interventions was by articulating their needs and desires. Armed with this knowledge, development professionals could then prioritize certain activities over others. As these projects were ostensibly an expression of community needs, members would presumably be invested in bringing them to fruition. This whole exercise, of course, assumed that "village councils were the proper vehicles through which those desires could be expressed."[43] Like similar interventions in India, however, community development programs in the Helmand Valley conflated "'what the people want' with 'what the village wants,' assuming the village to be a corporate body capable of articulating and acting on the general will."[44] What the HVP unleashed, then, was not the individualizing model of self-help identified by Nally and Taylor, but rather one that was designed to massify rural Afghans into populations. As part of this process, the felt needs of individual Afghans were aggregated and fixed in space.

For all of these reasons, the HVP is productively understood as a form of what Laleh Khalili names as *infrastructural power*.[45] Placing Khalili in conversation with Stuart Schrader and Mona Domosh, however, it was also an infrastructural power that was fundamentally grounded in a transnational biopolitics of race war and race making. This takes us beyond Immerwahr's theorizations of community development, which, as Domosh makes clear, "never make explicit the racialized context for those interventions." Domosh herself points to the Jim Crow South as another site and time that played a central role in the emergence and evolution of community development practices, "thus making explicit the racialized biopolitical concerns that form an important pillar of liberal [empire]."[46] Schrader has also reworked and extended Immerwahr's ideas by tracking how Lyndon Johnson's so-called War on Poverty picked up the idea of "participation as pacification" from overseas theaters of decolonization and development—primarily, occupied South Vietnam—and put it to work in the equally racialized and insurgent landscapes of the American inner city. First outlined in a commencement speech that Johnson delivered at the University of Michigan on May 22, 1964, his vision of building a domestic "Great Society" free of economic hardship and racial injustice rested on new methods of poverty alleviation that championed "individual improvement, within a framework of community relationships."[47] This is exemplified by the piece of legislation that inaugurated Johnson's Great Society, the 1964 Economic Opportunities Act, which required its (often racialized) beneficiaries to participate in the management of their own aid. Given that the act came into force during a "long, hot summer" of widespread urban unrest and race war, stretching from Rochester to Harlem to Jersey City to Philadelphia to Chicago, participation in Johnson's Great Society invariably became entangled with pacification: a point that the *New York Times* hammered home when it described the Act as an "anti-riot bill."[48]

These homologies between participation, race war, and counterinsurgency, furthermore, take on a fundamentally transnational character when we consider that very similar community development programs were simultaneously being honed and stress tested in occupied South Vietnam. From 1963 onward, U.S. counterinsurgents were turning to concepts such as community development, self-help, and popular participation as a way of combining development and security in the South Vietnamese countryside. The significance of these transnational connections was not lost on contemporary commentators like

Samuel Huntington, who worried that Vietnamese family and community structures were in the process of being fractured by many years of ground warfare and aerial bombardment, potentially reproducing a situation "not altogether dissimilar from that which the [1965] Moynihan report found to exist among Negro families in American urban slums."[49] Community development, U.S. counterinsurgents hoped, could play a role in preempting some of these concerns. As self-help cadres traveled the countryside, consulting with hamlet governance structures, proposing various construction projects, and helping communities transform their visions into reality, they sought to build infrastructures that could orient rural households toward anticommunist futures of order, security, and prosperity.[50]

By 1967, Johnson's dream of building a Great Society at home was already beginning to crumble. The act and its participatory mandate had not prevented urban unrest from worsening and spreading to cities such as Detroit. For six sweltering days in July 1968, Detroit became the stage for one of the most destructive race riots in U.S. history, which was only quelled once the state's Republican governor, George Romney, dispatched the Michigan Army National Guard to the city.[51] The stage was therefore set for Johnson's War on Poverty to be subsumed into Nixon's War on Crime and, by extension, for security to supplant development as the guiding logic of the U.S. inner race war on historically marginalized communities.[52] Despite these domestic setbacks, popular participation and self-help remained important to the U.S. empire-state's outer race wars on communism, even in the face of some spectacular failures. The U.S. military responded to the National Liberation Front's devastating Tet Offensive in 1968 by doubling down on its commitment to community development: a curious and somewhat counterintuitive decision, given the general lack of evidence that this strategy had actually paid out any counterinsurgency dividends.[53] But as we shall see later on, this was also around the time that previously disparate community development interventions scattered across Afghanistan coalesced into their most comprehensive form in the Helmand Valley. All of this, in turn, is immensely suggestive of how the theory and praxis of community development came to function as a transnational infrastructure of U.S. race war and pacification, tethering a seemingly neutral field of Cold War "competitive coexistence" like Afghanistan to the scorching "hot" counterinsurgencies simultaneously engulfing key occupied territories, such as South Vietnam and the American inner city.

Over the course of this chapter, then, I track how rural Afghans experienced the infrastructural power of the HVP as an inheritance of empire and race war. In so doing, I offer a more nuanced understanding of the HVP as an anxious hybridization of variegated infrastructures for managing and sustaining Afghan life. I pay particular attention to the development frictions that sparked when these combinations of heavy engineering and community development came into contact with the vernacular materialities and social relations that had long organized rural Afghanistan.[54] In the next section, I explore how early river basin development efforts in the Helmand Valley resulted in the waterlogging and salinization of prime agricultural lands. American modernizers responded to these challenges by assembling an infrastructure of spaces for extending technical assistance to Afghan farmers. Initially, this technopolitical effort to instill a spirit of self-help within Afghan farmers was confined to demonstration farms and agricultural training centers. Gradually, however, USAID realized that the situation in the Helmand Valley called for a more total approach to rural development.

Technopolitics in the Helmand Valley

Although Lloyd Baron notes "evidence of a long history of agricultural production" in the Helmand Valley, he nonetheless traces its transformation into an object of modern development back to the dawn of the twentieth century.[55] Between 1910 and 1914, Kandahar's governor, Osman, resurrected the traditional canal—or *kareze*—system that had once supplied copious amounts of irrigation water to this former "bread basket" region of Central Asia.[56] These efforts were supplemented throughout the 1930s by German and Japanese engineers, who were hired to repair and improve the original hand-dug canals.[57]

This work was interrupted in 1942, when the Afghan government, led by King Zahir Shah, succumbed to heavy Allied pressure and evicted all Axis engineers from the southern provinces. World War II, however, proved to be a blessing in disguise, furnishing Afghanistan with profitable export markets for certain key commodities. Afghan farmers were mobilized to provision the Allied armies in India, while shepherds benefited from a wartime explosion in the demand for karakul pelts.

The Afghan government tapped these lucrative circuits of wartime exchange to accumulate a substantial reserve of foreign currency.[58]

Concerned that Afghanistan would soon "die as a nation," Shah's prime minister, Mohammad Daoud, argued that these reserves were best spent tackling the pressing problem of underdevelopment.[59] To this end, the Afghan government devised a plan to bring modern irrigation infrastructures to the Girishk, Nad-i-Ali, and Marja districts of the Helmand Valley. Convinced that local engineers possessed neither the expertise nor the equipment necessary to implement this plan, the Afghan government instead looked abroad for a capable implementing partner. In 1946, the Afghan government hired the largest American heavy engineering firm, Morrison-Knudsen, to oversee the reclamation of the Helmand Valley.

Prior to the outbreak of World War II, Morrison-Knudsen had largely operated within the territorial confines of the continental United States. It was perhaps most well known for being a member of the Six Companies consortium that built the Hoover Dam.[60] When America finally entered the conflict in December 1941, the logics of total war meant that strategic firms like Morrison-Knudsen were called upon to serve U.S. military interests overseas. Morrison-Knudsen, in particular, was enrolled into Contractors, Pacific Naval Air Bases, a conglomerate that was hired by the U.S. military to build critical infrastructure in key hotspots across the Pacific theater. These wartime projects established path dependencies that kept the contractor tethered to the U.S. empire-state throughout the Cold War. While the HVP was the first Cold War project that Morrison-Knudsen was hired to execute in the decolonizing world, it would certainly not be the last. The Cold War would eventually take Morrison-Knudsen to Sri Lanka, Iran, the Congo, and South Vietnam, to name only a few examples.[61]

From the outset, Morrison-Knudsen's engineers—or the Emkayans, as they were known colloquially—framed the task of developing the Helmand Valley in narrowly technical terms, judging "water scarcity" to be the "critical constraint to agricultural surplus generation."[62] Irrigation, accordingly, became the "sine qua non of agricultural development" and, by extension, the "logical priority for the allocation of scarce" reserves of foreign aid capital.[63] Such conclusions were not idiosyncratic, but rather, were very much in line with development thinking at the time, which "favored capital formation, *primarily for infrastructure,* as the best means for moving the stagnant economies and traditional societies of Third World countries towards sustainable economic growth."[64] Decolonizing nations were also drawn to capital-intensive infrastructure projects, precisely because they promised to bring about modernization without requiring fundamental changes to the "deeply entrenched" social, political, and cultural geographies that shaped and organized everyday lifeworlds.[65]

Most accounts of the HVP stress that Morrison-Knudsen wanted to vet its plans with detailed soil, groundwater, and drainage surveys. The historical consensus is that the Afghan government talked Morrison-Knudsen out of doing this preparatory work.[66] Consequently, Morrison-Knudsen produced flawed engineering designs that were inappropriate for the unfavorable topography and soil composition of the Helmand Valley.[67] Unsurprisingly, early rounds of infrastructure development triggered widespread waterlogging and salinization. The construction of a dam at the mouth of the Boghra canal "raised the water table to within a few inches of the ground," resulting in a "snowy crust of salt [that] could be seen in areas around the reservoir."[68] As farmers living in nearby Nad-i-Ali discovered—many of whom had been settled "before the character of the soil and conditions affecting irrigation were understood"—the primary consequences of salinization was a catastrophic decline in agricultural productivity.[69]

In the heat of the moment, the significance of these trends was apparently minimized by all of the parties involved.[70] Although Morrison-Knudsen seized upon the crisis as evidence of the urgent need to conduct a thorough survey of the Helmand Valley, its interim plan of constructing subsurface drains in all of the affected areas showed that its faith in the transformative power of capital-centric infrastructure development remained largely unshaken.[71] Unsurprisingly, the Afghan government once again refused to sanction what it believed would be costly and time-consuming surveys, arguing that "even a 20 percent margin of error in estimating the acreage of water supply could not detract from the project's intrinsic value."[72] Contemporary commentators roundly criticized this controversial decision for being "guided by political expediency, rather than technical merit."[73]

Even without the surveys, however, Morrison-Knudsen faced other, more pressing obstacles in translating its new plans into reality. By 1946, the Afghan government had blown the HVP's budget, which, in turn, jeopardized Morrison-Knudsen's ability to respond to the intensifying salinization crisis. Afghanistan's agricultural export economy had been devastated by two years of drought, and the global demand for karakul lambskins was also declining.[74] The Afghan government was forced to balance the resulting trade deficit by dipping into its once significant reserve of foreign exchange. In order to retain Morrison-Knudsen as the primary contractor for the HVP, the Afghan government had to secure an external source of funding. The Shah regime signaled its intentions of taking on this task in the fall of 1948, when it dispatched an economic mission to Washington, D.C. In so doing, the Afghan government set in motion a series of processes that would substantively shape future rounds of development in the Helmand Valley. By explicitly targeting the United States as a potential source of funding, the Afghan government opened the door for the HVP to become further enrolled in the machinations of American Cold War empire building. From this point forward, Afghanistan would become an increasingly key node in the U.S. empire-state's multifront struggle to secure its geopolitical and geoeconomic interests across the decolonizing world.

Competitive Coexistence

Once in D.C., the Afghan economic mission wasted no time in soliciting the American Export-Import Bank for a loan. The Roosevelt administration had created the bank on February 2, 1934. The bank's founding mandate was to stimulate economic revitalization across Depression-era America by using a variety of financial instruments to facilitate the circulation of commodities between domestic markets and the rest of the world.[75] Many of the bank's domestic functions, however, were in danger of being made redundant by the U.S. empire-state's deepening involvement in World War II, which was playing an increasingly dominant role in reigniting industrial production at home. The bank therefore shifted focus and began to take a much greater interest in catalyzing economic development abroad.[76] As part of this effort, the bank offered to fund sound international development projects through long-term loans at "reasonable" interest rates. The bank marketed these ostensibly benevolent loans as the fundamentally "non-imperial" type of foreign aid "which private investors could scarcely be expected to make."[77] This framing proved persuasive, and throughout the 1940s, the bank played an increasingly central role in funding development projects overseas. By the time that the Afghan Economic Mission arrived in Washington, D.C., the bank's international lending capacity had reached a staggering $4 billion.[78] Swept up by this new climate of largesse, the mission set for itself the comparatively modest objective of securing a $55 million loan from the bank.

This proved more difficult than anticipated. In October 1948, Afghanistan's position on the "checkerboard" of the nascent Cold War remained unclear.[79] Lacking an obvious geopolitical justification for the HVP, the Afghan Economic Mission instead tried to sell it as well planned and economically sound. The bank, however, remained skeptical of the mission's claims. In addition to challenging the mission's estimates of the HVP's potential income stream, the bank also worried that the Afghan government lacked the financial and administrative capacity to serve as a reliable counterpart. The mission responded to these criticisms by representing the HVP as a "necessity beyond price." The value of the HVP was likened to that of an "operation to a person suffering from acute appendicitis," or "food to a starving man." Framed thusly as a stark matter of life and death, the mission argued that the HVP was "therefore properly not to be considered as a subject of economic study."[80]

Unconvinced, the bank flatly rejected the Afghan Economic Mission's original proposal. In November 1949, however, it reversed course and agreed to provide Morrison-Knudsen with a significantly reduced loan of $21 million, which was more than sufficient to cover the costs of completing the existing Kajaki Dam and Boghra Canal projects.[81] If all went according to plan, Morrison-Knudsen could then use the remaining resources to extend the HVP into Kandahar's Arghandab Valley. Although the bank still considered the mission's economic justifications for the HVP "exaggerated," it nonetheless agreed that "the potentialities of the [agricultural] projects appear so great that even if the claimed benefits are discounted substantially, the resulting benefits could still be of a magnitude which would justify the undertaking of these important projects."[82] The bank also concurred that there was a general paucity of reliable data on the Helmand Valley, but it nonetheless refused to fund the surveys that Morrison-Knudsen had reinserted into the mission's original proposal. As one commentator argued, this "later proved to be [a] fatal weakness of the project."[83]

According to contemporary commentators, the bank's decision to reward the Afghan Economic Mission with a reduced loan was motivated by a convergence of geopolitical and geoeconomic concerns.[84] Throughout 1949, the bank found itself under mounting pressure to fund the HVP so that it could then anchor Afghanistan's eventual incorporation into Truman's anticommunist Point Four program. This came to pass on February 7, 1951, when the United States and Afghanistan agreed to cooperate "in the interchange of technical knowledge and skills and in related activities designed to contribute to the balanced and integrated development of [its] economic resources and productive capacities."[85] Afghanistan's new relationship with the U.S. empire-state was soon made concrete through the launching of the United States Operations Mission (USOM) in Afghanistan in early 1951.[86]

As the first Technical Cooperation Administration (TCA) technicians arrived in Lashkar Gah to set up USOM/Afghanistan, bank personnel were busy conducting their own evaluation of the HVP, which singled out the division of development labor as a major area of concern. In the early days of the HVP, Morrison-Knudsen focused on building irrigation infrastructures, leaving the task of preparing and resettling the newly reclaimed land to the Afghan government. By early 1951, however, the Afghan government had become overwhelmed, and it tried to offload its resettlement responsibilities onto Morrison-Knudsen.[87] The bank was unhappy with this solution, and in 1952 it called on the Afghan government to establish an autonomous Helmand Valley Authority (HVA) to oversee the whole resettlement process.[88] Although the HVA was initially successful at accelerating the pace of resettlement, it soon became clear that many of the new arrivals were former nomads who possessed no knowledge of proper farming techniques and practices. Within three short years, the salinization crisis had quickly followed the expanding irrigation infrastructure network into Darweshan, Seraj, Tarnak, Garmser, Shakhansur, and the Arghandab Valley. By 1956, "more than 35 percent of the irrigable lands in the Helmand Valley [were] seriously affected by salinity and alkali conditions."[89] As salt "[whitened] the land," many of the new settlers simply decided to abandon their farms.[90] Those who remained were "barely able to subsist, as each year, the problems multiplied."[91]

Although Morrison-Knudsen was a private sector contractor, its continued failure to solve these problems reflected poorly on the U.S.

empire-state. This was because many of the new settlers in the Helmand Valley did not "distinguish between the TCA or [International Cooperation Administration] adviser who was supposed to 'recommend' but not 'do,' and the Emkayan engineer who was supposed to 'do' but not 'recommend.'"[92] Afghan settlers, in other words, were (correctly) diagnosing both the HVP and USOM/Afghanistan as entangled components of an emerging transnational nexus of development, capitalist, and imperial power, or what Susan Roberts would later call a "development-industrial complex."[93] For this reason, USOM technicians became increasingly concerned with managing the positive or negative effects that localized development practices in the Helmand Valley could potentially have upon the U.S. empire-state's "prestige" across the rest of the decolonizing world. Indeed, this obsession with "prestige" would go on to become the "touchstone" responsible for driving and sustaining "higher levels of official US funding for the Helmand Valley Project over the next two decades."[94] The implication here is that USOM/Afghanistan had great geopolitical and geoeconomic incentives to paint an unrealistically optimistic portrait of development progress in the Helmand Valley.

These imperial concerns acquired additional urgency in 1955, when the Soviet Union ushered in a new era of "competitive coexistence" in Afghanistan by distributing over $100 million in foreign aid to the governing regime.[95] This "economic offensive" financed infrastructure construction in some of the other key regions of Afghanistan. Embroiled in a "'strange kind of cold war,' fought with money and technicians instead of spies and bombs,'" Afghanistan became "a new kind of buffer, a neutral arena for a tournament of modernization."[96] These new conditions of "competitive coexistence" meant that the TCA— now known as the International Cooperation Administration (ICA)— had no choice but to get further "sucked into a haphazard effort with no prospect of final success." Failure to do otherwise would "result in 'chaos and dire' consequences for American political interests in that part of the world."[97] As the director of USOM/Afghanistan emphasized in a cablegram dated January 10, 1956, "any spectacular canal failure (such as December 14 Seraj, see above) particularly dangerous to US in that it would strengthen hand; (A) those in USA who desire to drop HVA project before successful results shown (which disastrous US prestige) or (B) those who discouraged possibility carrying through financing HVA from GOA/US sources and strongly tempted turn USSR take over."⁹⁸

So far, I have traced some of the mechanisms through which the HVP was enrolled into a transnational infrastructure of anticommunist empire building. The TCA and the Export-Import Bank valued the HVP as a hinge that could thread multiple scales of imperial activity. As I argue in what follows, however, the HVP's rescaling from a regional development project to a Cold War weapon in the struggle against global communism occurred alongside an important shift in how U.S. imperialists went about wielding development as a form of infrastructural power in the Helmand Valley. Subsequent phases of the HVP were marked by a gradual, partial, and contested transition away from capital-centric approaches to modernization toward more people-centric forms of development theory and practice. As part of this process, U.S. imperialists began to experiment with less obvious infrastructures for managing and ordering Afghan lifeworlds.

"A New Potent Force"

By the mid-1950s, Morrison-Knudsen was facing mounting criticism over its capital-centric approach to reclamation. In 1956, the Tudor Engineering Company prepared a survey on behalf of the ICA that described the "cultural techniques" of the new settlers as antiquated and inefficient.⁹⁹ The survey identified three problems that required immediate attention. First, many farmers over-irrigated their fields to preempt future water shortages. Second, farmers were "strongly influenced by precedent and not easily induced to alter methods of cultivation which have been practiced for centuries, if not millennia," and consequently, were "able to do little more than feed and clothe [themselves] and [their family]."¹⁰⁰ Finally, farmers were "seriously handicapped" by a lack of modern farming equipment. In other words, the problem was not so much the HVP, but rather, the farmers themselves.

Accordingly, Tudor recommended that the ICA develop and implement a "realistic and practical" program of "capacity building" meant to "extend" improved agricultural practices to Afghan farmers.¹⁰¹ This was not a new idea. On January 13, 1954, the Export-Import Bank had asked Morrison-Knudsen to consider the potential benefits of carrying out "technical assistance" activities in the field. When Morrison-Knudsen declined on the grounds that it lacked the expertise to carry out such a task, the bank then invited the Foreign Operations Administration (FOA)—the institution that preceded the ICA—to develop a new technical assistance program for the HVP.[102]

The FOA was well positioned to take on this task, having already launched extension activities in the Helmand Valley. On October 4, 1953, it opened an Extension Training Center, responsible for producing a cadre of village-level workers. Trainees took classes in agricultural extension and went on tours of field sites. Once trained, they were dispatched to local communities, where they demonstrated modern agricultural techniques to their fellow Afghans. The purpose of this exercise was not only to help rural communities help themselves, but also to identify other candidates for extension training.[103]

The FOA furthered these extension efforts by establishing a Helmand Valley Advisory Service.[104] From its inception, the advisory service worked with the HVA to chart new directions in land reclamation, resettlement and extension.[105] On any given day, advisory service technicians might have distributed new seed varietals; demonstrated proper fertilization, pest control, and castration techniques; and helped plan crop rotations.[106] Nally and Taylor treat the kind of extension work pictured in Figure 3 as an important catalyst of self-help. They emphasize how extension agents did not merely function as neutral conduits of agricultural knowledge, but rather, had to become "an 'encouraging companion' to farmers, urging them to question '*why they do the things they do, and are the way they are,*' and making them '*aware of the alternatives.*'" Afghan elites, however, remained unconvinced that the "path to successful development work lay in the *conditioning of conditioners* via grassroots extension work."[107] Key officials, in fact, deemed farmers incapable of self-help. In one memorandum dated March 23, 1955, Dr. Abdul Wakil, the HVA's vice president in charge of agriculture, proclaimed that he had "been associated with FOA technicians for the past two years and had come to the conclusion that the U.S. assistance program had not been geared to the unique type of problems faced in the Helmand Valley Project."[108] According to Dr. Wakil, the FOA was too accustomed to working with farmers who possessed a baseline knowledge of traditional agricultural practices. Settlers in the Helmand Valley, in contrast, knew next to nothing about farming.[109]

To compound matters, certain Cold Warriors found it difficult to

FIGURE 3. *Robert Snyder discusses plowing methods in the Logar Valley. International Cooperation Administration, "Afghanistan 108," May 10, 1957. Box 1, Prints and Negatives: Photographs of Foreign Assistance Activities, 1947–1967, NARA. Courtesy National Archives, RG 286-C: Photographs of Assistance Programs in Foreign Countries, ca. 1961–ca. 2002.*

imagine how extension work might help contain Soviet influence in the decolonizing world. These geopolitical-economic concerns acquired additional urgency in 1955, when the Soviet Union ushered in a new era of "competitive coexistence" in Afghanistan by launching an "aggressive campaign of economic penetration" in key northern provinces, including Nangarhar.[110] As Ambassador Angus Ward quipped, "the Soviets have trained their heavy economic artillery on Afghanistan and the United States has in effect replied with technical advice on how to construct a popgun."[111] Ward felt that while technical assistance was "no doubt very worthwhile per se," it unfortunately lacked both "dramatic value and economic impact," making it "compare unfavorably, in Afghan minds, with the eye-catching projects undertaken by the Soviets." As one Afghan official lamented, "We have American advisers running out of our ears, but what do we have to show the people for all this American activity?"[112]

Despite these criticisms, the spectacular heavy engineering projects prized by Cold Warriors like Ward increasingly shared space with technical interventions aimed at nurturing a culture of self-help throughout the Helmand Valley. The changing tenor of the HVP was signaled in three ways. First, self-help became a mantra of the Afghan government's Five-Year Plan for Rural Development. Drafted in 1957, the plan argued that installing an "ambition" to work for higher standards of living in the Afghan people would "provide a foundation" for "self-perpetuating" economic, social, and mental progress.[113]

Second, by July 1959, Afghan officials were lambasting Morrison-Knudsen for failing to make the HVP "beneficial for Afghanistan."[114] Unfortunately for Morrison-Knudsen, its contract with the Afghan government was slated to expire in the fall of 1959. Given the Afghan government's obvious dissatisfaction with Morrison-Knudsen's performance, it is unsurprising that the new ICA—which had succeeded the FOA in 1955—decided to replace the firm with the U.S. Bureau of Reclamation.

Third, the ICA responded to critics such as Ambassador Ward by doubling down on the FOA's commitment to developing the Helmand Valley through a program of technical assistance. For E. D. White, director of the ICA's Office of Food and Agriculture, technical assistance was becoming "part of a new potent force on a new type of quiet battleground" where "more kinds of food and improved living together with what men think is far more important than lead and gunpowder." Unlike Ambassador Ward, White embraced technical assistance—and particularly extension—as a "typically" American form of development that "neither the Soviets nor any other nation can claim."[115]

White's intention here is undoubtedly to reposition technical assistance as an inclusive and ameliorative technology of racial liberalism. Pitched by White as a "quiet" pathway to improved life chances, technical assistance promised to be more effective at reconfiguring the thoughts and attitudes of decolonizing subjects than violence and coercion. What White implies here is that technical assistance approaches could complement—and perhaps even supplant—the spectacular heavy engineering and construction projects that had, up until this point, been the most visible expression of "competitive coexistence" in neutral Cold War arenas such as Afghanistan. Moving forward, then, technical assistance interventions were poised to become the building blocks for a new kind of imperial infrastructure: one that might serve, to para-phrase Ara Wilson, as the "unexamined background" for new and brighter futures of transnational empire building across the decoloniz-ing world. While this is all undoubtedly significant, I am nonetheless also struck by what seems to fade into the "unexamined background" of White's own vision: the incredible racialized violence of technical assistance itself. Ara Wilson argues that "when infrastructure works as it should, we often stop seeing it."[116] When scholars notice infrastruc-ture, they have tended to grapple with it as a technopolitical project of geopolitical economy, as opposed to one of racial management and rule. White's use of the adverb "typically," I think, invites precisely this kind of response. The obvious reading here is that it invokes President Truman's Point Four address, especially when he champions Ameri-ca's "imponderable resources in technical knowledge."[117] But I argue that technical assistance was also "typically American" in other, much more vulgar and exclusionary ways. As Domosh reminds us, the suite of rural development practices that would eventually be bundled under the umbrella term of technical assistance and then exported overseas in the Cold War period to places like Afghanistan were first put to work in the heavily racialized and segregated agricultural landscapes of the Jim Crow South.[118] When development professionals established demonstration farms, extension sites, or community uplift centers in the Helmand Valley, then, they were effectively building on and extend-ing longer-standing theories and practices of racial management that had first emerged in what Nikhil Pal Singh and others have identified as the quintessential spatial loci of U.S. race war: the plantation and the reservation.[119]

The upshot here is that by seeking out ways of actualizing the la-tent geopolitical-economic potential of technical assistance, the ICA was also repurposing the Helmand Valley into a laboratory of racial management, albeit one where racialization had become "unevenly de-tached" from taken-for-granted color lines.[120] As part of this process, the administration folded existing extension activities into a broader intervention on rural life as a totality. This new "total" approach sought to create an infrastructure for compelling rural Afghans to partici-pate in the improvement of their communities. In advancing such a massifying—and not an individualizing—mode of self-help, the ICA was gambling that rural communities could be transformed into "collectively constructed systems" for "building and sustaining" modern forms of liberal life.[121] Technical assistance, in other words, was expected to complement heavy engineering interventions as vehicles of infrastructural power.

Total Development

The emergence of this "total" approach was foreshadowed by the United Nations Technical Assistance Mission's (UNTAM) Shewaki-Charasia Demonstration and Training Unit in the province of Kabul. Established in 1954, this unit sought to "change" Shewaki and Charasia from traditional to modern villages. This change was to be a "total one, comprising all aspects of life at the same time." Through their interactions with UNTAM, villagers would "develop an incentive . . . to change and continue to change."[122]

In the ICA's eyes, UNTAM's interventions had failed to realize their "total" potential. Instead, they were better understood as a "series of service operations in which most everything is given to the individual villagers with little apparent village contribution."[123] The ICA argued that UNTAM had two "basic weaknesses." First, by servicing individuals rather than communities, UNTAM failed to mobilize rural populations for self-action. Second, UNTAM made no effort to meet the needs of the people. In order for UNTAM's total approach to succeed in Afghanistan, it would have to be rescaled into a biopolitical intervention that focused on rural populations, rather than individual Afghans.

The Galloway report also argued that the Helmand Valley Advisory Service shared many of these weaknesses. Despite a "relatively successful" extension phase, a "total community development process" was "not taking place at the village level" in the Helmand Valley. Consequently, the "basic needs in self-improvement" of the "mass of the people" were not being met.[124] In response, the ICA worked with the Afghan government to establish a number of community development centers in various parts of the country. These centers were meant "to help people to help themselves," "to increase the income of the farmers through economic activities," "to improve their health and living conditions," and "to expand educational opportunities for the rural people."[125] These centers also sought to catalyze changes in the "mental outlook of the people," instilling within them a will to uplift their communities, as well as their nation.

Although this new "total" development effort was represented as a "cooperative enterprise," the Afghan government limited its involvement to supporting activities that concerned rural communities as a whole. This meant that a "substantial part of the development" necessarily fell "on the shoulders of the villagers themselves."[126] Spontaneous participation in these programs would only occur if they were guided by the "immediate needs of the people." Ideally, priority would be given to those needs which were expressed by the people themselves during a process of "discussion and close contact." Development professionals recognized, however, that the majority of the rural population might prove incapable of articulating a coherent set of demands. In such a situation, experts would be called upon to speak on their behalf.

What "total" development championed, therefore, was not necessarily the "individualistic expectation of market participation" that is foregrounded by Nally and Taylor but rather a community-based model for popular participation that sought to provide "impoverished people a direct say in what constituted poverty, how it could be managed, and what its mitigation might encompass on an everyday level."[127] Under this new rubric, individual Afghans were asked to articulate their needs and desires in aggregate terms. These communal expressions, in turn, would serve as the basis for further rural development interventions.

In principle, participation in rural development was meant to precipitate a democratization of planning processes. Plans for interventions would originate at a grassroots level, and then flow upward through the infrastructures of the broader development mission. Such a "frontal assault on the top-down planning model," however, never fully materialized in the Helmand Valley.[128] It proved difficult for American modernizers to abandon the notion that centralized planning was necessary to establish infrastructures for popular participation. This became a source of tension between Americans and Afghans. One memorandum dated May 15, 1958, complained that Afghans would "take precipitous action" regardless of whether "definite plans" had been made.[129] By the time that the ICA was succeeded by USAID in 1962, tensions over the HVA's supposed "lack of appreciation of the necessity of planning" had reached new heights. Alarmed by the HVA's willingness to do things "too fast, without adequate resources," USAID insisted that the only way to "attack" the economy of the Helmand Valley as a "whole" was with a "comprehensive" plan.[130]

The HVA resisted these efforts. When USAID "tried to discuss the need for economic analysis," its "arguments were peremptorily brushed aside" by Dr. Wakil, who said "such studies are not really required."[131] The HVA had come to see planning as synonymous with delays and cancellations, rather than development.[132] Guided by the assumption that the HVA could "afford to make a few mistakes," Dr. Wakil argued that the project should instead be "developed as rapidly as possible."[133] By the early 1960s, the HVA and USAID had reached a "complete psychological impasse."[134] In hopes of breaking this stalemate, USAID attempted to circumvent the HVA by opening direct lines of communication with rural populations. One notable strategy adopted by USAID was to reposition local Islamic authority figures as potential conduits of secular agricultural expertise. Whereas USAID might have previously framed Islam—and all of its gendered traditions, including the veiling and segregation of women—as antithetical to modernization and liberalism, technicians in the field began to emphasize the value in mobilizing religion as a potential infrastructure of total development. Although the "Moslem religion" has "much to say about agricultural matters," one technician argued, many "farm people" remained "poorly informed about what the Koran, the Traditions say about agriculture; and about what they mean in light of the new problems and technology in Afghanistan's agriculture today." "As important and respected leaders," judges and mullahs in particular had a

> big responsibility and opportunity to inform and guide the villagers. The Judges can give leadership with the Mullahs, as well as interpret wisely the Koranic Law on land inheritance, water rights, and related matters. The Mullahs talk with the villagers before and after prayers; they teach the children; they have a major influence on their thinking. Moreover, through history, the more effective Mullahs have constantly looked for things to improve their communities: better seed, new plants, improved livestock. With the world-wide, far-reaching move to produce more and better agricultural products to furnish a better living, and to feed and clothe the growing population, the Mullahs have a greater task than ever before.[135]

USAID hoped that by bringing Islamic agricultural teachings to the attention of rural communities, religious authority figures could help spur popular participation in and engagement with emerging infrastructures for disseminating agricultural expertise. "In this day," writes Reynolds, "when all countries have men who are specializing to find the best methods of successful farmers, and the secrets of nature, to improve agriculture; and when countries are helping each other, we find that: . . . Mohamed said that any professional man is a friend of God; which gives encouragement to the modern specialists with their tools, fertilizer, better crops, and livestock to teach farmers to produce more; and which means greater happiness to all."[136]

U.S. imperialists like Reynolds, in other words, envisioned Islam and total development coming together as two mutually reinforcing biopolitical infrastructures for ordering and managing Afghan lifeworlds. Like development, Islam was traversed by a will to improve.[137] This was, however, a selective will to improve, one that specifically empowered Afghan *men*. Rajiv Chandrasekaran argues that HVP was as much about progressive social engineering as it was about development.[138] American and Afghan modernizers alike saw mixed schooling and the abolishment of the veil—and the practice of purdah more generally—as eminently desirable. These shared aspirations for a more egalitarian future, however, effectively concealed the ways in which the logics of total development helped reproduce longer-standing patterns of gendered, uneven development. U.S. imperialists such as Reynolds could wholeheartedly endorse Islam as a vehicle for agricultural modernization because their work in the field was, in some very crucial ways, uncritically reproducing traditional forms of household management. In Reynolds's writings, the protagonist of agricultural development is always male. "The Farmer and *His* Work," as Reynolds was keen to emphasize, "Are Important."

USAID's attempt to work through Islamic authority figures is nonetheless important, for it betrayed a growing obsession with making the "traditional attitudes of subsistence peasants" yield to a "revolution in mental concepts."[139] In this sense, the "total" approach to rural development was conceived as a way of fine-tuning how American modernizers went about wielding infrastructural power across the Helmand Valley. As the above discussion reveals, the "total" approach supplied American and Afghan modernizers with an infrastructure for managing the everyday needs and desires of rural populations. This emerging regime of infrastructural power aimed to uplift rural populations in ways that reinforced the established order of things. In order to better understand this interplay between improvement and ordering, I turn my attention to the Shamalan Land Development Project (SLDP). Implemented from 1967 to 1973, the SLDP combined engineering and communitarian interventions to completely remake a rural district from the ground up. The resulting hybridization of conventional and "less obvious" infrastructures, however, failed to enact a more egalitarian (re)distribution of life necessities and instead, reinforced existing geographies of uneven development. Unsurprisingly, the rollout of the SLDP was resisted by the rural masses, catalyzing further shifts in development theory and practice.

Bulldozers and Rifles

In 1969, Mildred Caudill published a hagiography of the HVP that painted an optimistic picture of Afghanistan's "Agricultural Awakening." Whereas farming had once "been a simple operation in the Valley, with methods and equipment virtually unchanged from one generation to another," the future of agriculture in Afghanistan looked bright. According to Caudill, this was because the "Green Revolution that is sweeping Asia has reached the Helmand-Arghandab Valley."[140]

The "Green Revolution" was launched in the early 1960s by Norman Borlaug, who developed a revolutionary new type of high-yield wheat. Impressed by its test results, USAID imported 170 tons of this experimental wheat into southern Afghanistan.[141] Existing patterns of settlement, however, initially confounded USAID's efforts to "add intelligence" to the HVP. In order to grow Borlaug's wheat efficiently, the small and uneven parcels of land that were common in the Helmand Valley would have to be "turned back into vast open spaces."[142] A "typical village distribution system" is depicted in Figure 4. Note how the various fields are not only of irregular size and shape, but also appear to be organized by crop type—corn, wheat, and vegetables—rather than property ownership. If an individual farming household was tending to more than one crop, their landholdings would likely be scattered throughout the village.

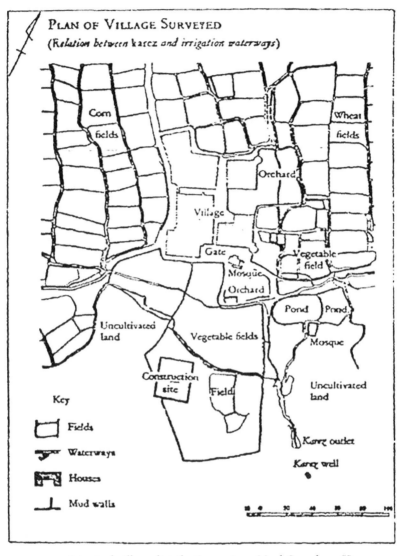

FIGURE 4. *A typical village distribution system. Mark Svendsen, "Some Aspects of Irrigation Technology in Afghanistan," USAID DEC, 1977, http://pdf.usaid.gov/pdf_docs/PNAAD121.pdf.*

Billed by USAID as the "total package of canal construction and land development," the SLDP transformed a 200-acre section of the Shamalan district into a test case for the Green Revolution.[143] The plan was to level the demonstration site with bulldozers, removing all existing structures—houses, fields, orchards, and so on—in the process. Each farmer's fragmented land holdings would be consolidated into a single rectangular plot of equal size. These reorganized agricultural households would then be integrated into a new grid of modern irrigation and extension infrastructures.[144] Figure 5 documents some of the infrastructural improvements that might have been typical of this process. As part of the SLDP, the land of a local farmer—Muhammadin— was upgraded through the construction of a diversion structure, a ditch, and a lateral. In order for Muhammadin to make the most of these infrastructural improvements, he was also introduced to improved farming practices, inputs, and agricultural machinery.[145]

USAID expected that Muhammadin's experiences would eventu-

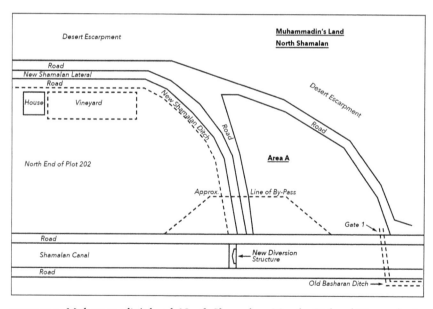

FIGURE 5. *Muhammadin's land, North Shamalan. Map by Richard Nisa, adapted from Richard Scott, "New/Old Approaches to the People in the Shamalan," Helmand Valley Archive, January 13, 1973, http://scottshelmandvalleyarchives .org/docs/sld-73–20.pdf.*

ally serve as the blueprint for Green Revolution technologies across the Helmand Valley.[146] Traditional agricultural formations would be swept away by bulldozers and replaced by an ordered and modern landscape. This reorganized environment was meant to do two things. First, it would cultivate communal forms of sociality by forcing farmers to live and work in two different places. Second, the move to centralize and regularize land holdings anticipated an eventual transition from subsistence to commercial agriculture. According to Udall, Dominy, and Whitaker, irregular land holdings of inadequate size perpetuated subsistence agriculture in the Helmand Valley by "denying the farmer the base and business volume upon which to build a commercial unit."[147] Under the aegis of the SLDP, technopolitics would articulate with biopolitics to infrastructurally reengineer an entire community from the ground up. In practice, the diverse infrastructural components of the SLDP worked at cross-purposes. Launched as a "demonstration," one of the SLDP's core objectives was to secure community support for a comprehensive program of infrastructural transformation. To this end, SLDP technicians established an "epistemic" infrastructure of surveys, questionnaires, and field researchers that targeted two separate groups of local elites.[148] According to Husick and Uyehara, the traditional leaders—or "khans"—were to be "given reasons to support [the project]" because they were the "key decision makers in the Helmand area." Husick and Uyehara also argued that a major effort should be undertaken to win over "progressive farmers" who were "more aware of the need for change" than the "mass of the people." Husick and Uyehara, however, remained unconvinced of the need to secure the active support of the "mass of the people." As they write:

> The decision to support or not support the project will not be made by the mass of the people. . . . This does not mean, however, that these people can be ignored. They must understand the project and what it will mean to them if we expect to receive the active cooperation we will need for the success of the project. They can also influence their leaders if they understand and support the project.[149]

This particular passage is revealing of how the SLDP was riven by an internal tension. On the one hand, SLDP officials firmly believed that local elites were perfectly "capable of articulating and acting on the general will."[150] On the other hand, they also recognized that the SLDP was more likely to succeed if the "mass of the people" could be encouraged to participate in some capacity. SLDP representatives therefore found themselves confronting the challenging task of designing a public relations campaign that was not meant "to gain an active commitment from the people," but to "create within them a favorable impression of the project."[151]

To this end, USAID hired a social anthropologist, Richard Scott, to engage local farmers and identify their felt needs and desires. USAID tasked Scott with answering the following questions: "Are preparations for the on-farm land reshaping O.K. as far as the people problems are concerned?"; "Is there going to be significant, preventable discontent?"; "Are the tenants going to be odd-men out?"; "Who makes farm management decisions on the affected land?"; "Who do they listen to for farm management advice?"; "Who should be chosen for agricultural development committees to move farm practice forward after leveling? How?"; "What should be the basis of such committees?"; and finally, "Do the extension men in the Shamalan need special training because of the new problems arising from land leveling, etc.?"[152] These questions suggest that Scott was hired to build the epistemic infrastructures required to support a biopolitics of population management.

Significantly, Scott was unable to find villagers who had been subjected to a "long-term contact explanation" of the project. Most locals had no "clear, consistent picture of the details of how the project is to function."[153] Contact was made with local elites, but contrary to expectations, most of them were opposed to the project on the grounds that it would lead to losses in the size and the productivity of their landholdings. Scott's fieldwork therefore challenged the wisdom of focusing outreach on elites whose own self-interests predisposed them to oppose development activities.

Scott also discovered that Afghan survey crews were instructed not to discuss their activities with local villagers. In addition to believing that "villagers' opinions are unimportant because they are too ignorant to understand what is good for them in the first place," Afghan technocrats also assumed that "as long as no one knows anything and no one begins the actually socially disruptive process of land consolidation and leveling, peace can be maintained."[154] In Scott's estimation, this reluctance to engage with the "mass of the people" was problematic. In order to succeed, implementers needed "as much detailed information about the socio-cultural-economic context of the areas as [they] have about soil, subsoils, and topography." Armed with this information, USAID would have a better "indication of potential problems and from what quarters they are likely to come."[155]

According to Scott, surveys would have shown that the Shamalan was being farmed relatively successfully through irrigation schemes that were technically imperfect yet nonetheless adequate for local purposes.[156] As development would bring little new land into cultivation, most farmers did not understand its potential benefits. Instead, they chose to "see the work as reducing the size of their landholdings via the new canals, ditches, and drains."[157] Villagers were particularly concerned about what would happen to their vineyards, orchards, and trees. While the HVA was supposed to reimburse farmers for any losses stemming from reclamation work, these payments were generally delayed and sometimes nonexistent. For these reasons, farmers began to "sharpen [their] arms." These tensions came to a head over the issue of land leveling. Although land leveling was the most technically efficient solution to the Shamalan's drainage problems, farmers faced "tremendous uncertainty as to what land they would get back, where it would be located, and if it would be as much as they had before."[158] Consequently, they refused to leave their land.

Scott's investigations also revealed that agricultural production in the Shamalan was not being constrained by a lack of water, but rather by an unevenly distributed infrastructure for allocating vital resources.[159] Irrigation infrastructures were overseen by *mirabs* who were traditionally appointed by local elites. Given that one khan would often act as the *mirab* for another, this practice safeguarded elite interests. This meant that questions of water distribution were entangled with local patronage infrastructures. Sharecroppers and small farmers were expected to offer their political support to their local khan in exchange for water access. Each khan possessed the power to ensure that any one of these farmers could be left water short, should they step out of line. Unsurprisingly, a number of farmers in the Shamalan indicated that they supported the project because "it meant they would then get enough water."[160] They also correctly surmised that most khans would oppose the project precisely because it promised to disrupt their control over the allocation of scarce water resources.

Unable to function independently of the material relations in which they were embedded, *mirabs*—and by extension, the hydraulic infrastructures that they managed—both emerged from and reflected an uneven geography of power. Frustrated by the SLDP's unwillingness to confront this unequal distribution of infrastructure, farmers began to meet bulldozers with rifles. Although these localized incidents of resistance never coalesced into a coherent antidevelopment movement, their combined effect was to jam the everyday workings of the SLDP. As one SLDP manager, J. Shankland, noted, it became apparent that the "necessary clearing of land titles and farmer's acceptance of the [SLDP]" was not obtainable in "any reasonable length of time."[161] Given these insurmountable "socio-economic problems," it was not "feasible or prudent" for all parties involved to "carry out the coordinated work plans for development of the Shamalan."[162]

By painting a more complex picture of life in the Shamalan, Scott's reports help us understand the SLDP as a fraught moment of imperial encounter that momentarily opened a breach in the Cold War order of things. Scott, however, should not be misread as a critic of rural development. Scott's objective was not necessarily to empower rural populations, but rather to outline a more effective way of securing their willing participation in their own pacification. What Scott shared with USAID, in other words, was an imperial commitment to perfecting Western developmental expertise as a tool of infrastructural power.

USAID's ability to act on Scott's recommendations was constrained. In late 1973, the Afghan monarchy was overthrown in a coup led by the former prime minister, Daoud. Already beleaguered by an ongoing drought and a looming lack of funding, USAID seized upon the coup as a pretext for disengaging from Afghanistan.[163] Unfortunately for USAID, the gravitational pull of Afghanistan proved difficult to escape. At this point in time, Afghanistan remained an important node in the broader geopolitical-economic infrastructures that buttressed the U.S. Cold War regime. Thus, when Daoud described the HVP to then secretary of state Henry Kissinger as an "unfinished symphony" that required further assistance, the new president of Afghanistan was quickly reassured that the United States would "live up to its responsibilities."[164]

USAID technicians were subsequently dispatched back to the Helmand Valley, armed with new "people-centered" understandings of how best to practice development in the field. When USAID suspended its Afghan mission in 1973, it did so in the midst of a major overhaul to the American Foreign Assistance Act. Under the terms of this New Directions mandate, USAID was obligated to prioritize the "basic needs" of the world's "poorest majority."[165] USAID's return to Afghanistan served as an early test case for these sea changes in development theory and practice.

USAID supported the HVA in developing a project to address the drainage problems that continued to cripple agricultural production across the Helmand Valley. This Central Helmand Drainage Project would ostensibly benefit the "poorest majority" of households who were "barely eking out an existence" on waterlogged land that otherwise had the potential to produce a "respectable living by Afghan standards." While USAID acknowledged that "deeply ingrained" water use practices were exacerbating the salinization of land in the Helmand Valley, innovations in this area would have to account for "complex interactions among technical, bureaucratic, and cultural systems."[166] A new drainage system, in contrast, would be cheap and "virtually self-managed."[167]

By focusing narrowly on the "technical details," rather than on the "total scene," USAID demonstrated that it had not yet fully absorbed the lessons of the SLDP.[168] This disconnect was flagged by none other than Richard Scott, who was again hired to serve as USAID's eyes and ears in the field.[169] Scott criticized USAID for ignoring "some of the most basic issues that have been recognized as having hampered the Valley development for the past 20 years." "A project," Scott writes, "does not help farmers by simply constructing a system of ditches." Rather, USAID needed to find some way of encouraging farmers to self-identify with the drainage project. Scott proposed a "detailed information scheme" that would allow all parties involved to "clearly register their desires relative to what is planned." A successful development intervention would have to be "guided to some degree by these desires."[170]

Like the SLDP before it, the Central Helmand Drainage Project served as an important moment in USAID's longer history of wielding infrastructural power across Afghanistan. When read together, both projects emphasize how USAID was increasingly caught between two distinct ways of practicing development in the Afghan countryside. On the one hand, both the SLDP and the drainage project carried forward USAID's persistent "urge to modernize" the Helmand Valley through capital-centric infrastructure schemes that rendered complex problems technical. On the other hand, they both signaled the emergence of a new approach to rural development in Afghanistan: one guided less by a schematic view of Afghans as "productive units, 'abstract citizens' whose motives conformed to the goals of the planner," and more by a growing imperative to manage their felt needs and desires by inscribing them within "less obvious" yet equally infrastructural regimes of technical assistance, community building, participatory development, and knowledge production.[171] In combination, both projects emphasize the importance of mapping the infrastructural underpinnings of USAID's long-standing development mission to Cold War Afghanistan.

The blockading of the SLDP is represented in the archival record as a singular and isolated incident: an unfortunate moment of miscommunication that nonetheless offered USAID a blueprint for improving future rounds of development in the Afghan countryside. The lessons of the SLDP were clear. Instead of assuming that the benefits of development were self-evident, USAID technicians needed to do a better job of explaining how specific projects could help rural communities fulfill their goals and aspirations. Only then could they be induced to participate in the unending "struggle" against poverty, illiteracy, and underdevelopment.[172] But what such a framing obscures are the contradictory logics of race war and racial liberalism that have always lurked just underneath the surface of the U.S. empire-state's development mission to Afghanistan. After all, the SLDP was not the first time that U.S.–Afghan relations in the Helmand Valley were brought to the brink of insurgency. On December 21, 1959, the city of Kandahar was the site of widespread rioting. In a letter sent to the commissioner of reclamation eight days after the incident, P. R. Nadler reported that an Afghan mob had "set fire to the theater, busted up the girl's school, and then headed for the ICA area," where they beat up Americans—some of whom had taken their wives into town for a little bit of pre-Christmas shopping—damaged a number of automobiles, threw rocks at windows, cut screens, and engaged in other acts of petty vandalism. A few U.S. technicians were "pretty badly beaten up." One suffered broken ribs, cuts, a broken hand, and many bruises, and was robbed of some valuables. The "pretty daughter" of one Afghan engineer was also "reportedly hurt." It is therefore unsurprising that "retaliation by the army" was swift, eventually resulting in government forces parking a "couple of tanks" in the street near the ICA's headquarters. Eventually, the military commandant in Kandahar "permitted the Americans, stranded there, to return to Lashkar Gah with military escort—via Girishk." From that point forward, according to Nadler, tensions "eased up" and improved dramatically.[173]

In Nadler's postmortem of the riot, he draws on the combined wisdom of other "elder heads" in southern Afghanistan to speculate that the "basic cause" of the riot "is resistance to change and particularly the removal of the chaderi." However, Nadler's report also invokes one of his Afghan counterparts, Dr. Kayeum, to downplay the significance of the riots, specifically by underscoring their exceptional nature. Dr. Kayeum, Nadler emphasizes, "knows his mullahs, and he is sure that while it is unfortunate that this has occurred while the BuRec is contemplating entering the picture, he feels that it may be a blessing after all, because the RGA [Royal Government of Afghanistan] will take firm steps to make sure it will not happen again." While Nadler was quick to hedge that only "time will tell," as it is "very difficult to evaluate [the impact of the riots] from this distance," we can now confidently and unfortunately say, with the blessing of sixty-three years of hindsight, that Dr. Kayeum's predictions were wildly off base.[174] It is unclear whether USAID technicians in 1968 would have thought to connect the blockading of the SLDP with the Kandahar riots that had punctuated the final weeks of the previous decade. If they did, such speculations were left out of the reports, memoranda, and telegrams that I eventually found in the archive. But when read together, these seemingly distinct moments of rural unrest expose the everyday violence work that went into maintaining the "Little Americas" of the Helmand Valley, and by extension, the U.S. empire-state's vision of bringing racial liberalism to southern Afghanistan. Contra U.S. imperialists like Nadler, what the Afghan rioters in Kandahar shared with their armed counterparts in the Shamalan is perhaps not so much a racialized "resistance to change" as a general and well-founded suspicion that U.S. empire building in Afghanistan was never really going to transform their lives for the better. No amount of Fourth of July celebrations, Christmas parties, baseball games, or suburban bungalows could truly conceal the counterinsurgent violence and uneven development that lay at the heart of U.S. empire building in Afghanistan. Faced with such a transformative onslaught of slow violence work, resistance and unrest might have seemed like the only way of making do under the seemingly bloodless and racial liberal conditions of "competitive coexistence" that gradually became the public face of the Cold War in Afghanistan.

In this chapter, I analyzed archival documents to establish that the Helmand Valley has long served USAID as a laboratory of development theory and practice. Over the course of the Cold War, the inhabitants of the Helmand Valley were subjected to a number of different development experiments, which ran the gamut from capital-centric infrastructure projects, technocentric extension programs, and racial biopolitical community building schemes. These experiments in postcolonial racial management, in turn, served as grist for the mill of developmental innovation. What emerged from the HVP was a more refined and inclusionary—or, in the language of Jodi Melamed, "racial liberal"—method for wielding infrastructural power across Afghanistan and, by extension, the rest of the decolonizing world more broadly.

Rural development infrastructures in Cold War Afghanistan may have served as conduits for a new, racial liberal mode of imperial power, but they also doubled as terrains of resistance. Instead of playing the role of passive beneficiaries, Afghan farmers confounded American efforts at every turn. Afghan farmers clung stubbornly to traditional agronomic practices. They refused to see the value in plans and surveys. They rioted in the streets. They resisted rural development efforts, meeting USAID's bulldozers with rifles. They asserted themselves as political subjects with real needs and desires. Successive development failures gradually attuned USAID to the importance of taking these needs and desires seriously. Development in the Helmand Valley, in this sense, was fundamentally shaped by its interactions with alternative infrastructures for provisioning rural life.

The effects of these iterative encounters were felt unevenly by the inhabitants of the Helmand Valley. Salinization and desertification were common—and devastating—consequences of poorly planned rural development interventions. Gender relations within the Little Americas of southern Afghanistan may have been liberalized, but outside of these more progressive enclaves, traditionally patriarchal forms of household management were largely left undisturbed. But in some localized pockets of the Helmand Valley, certain rural development interventions did materially improve the life chances of local communities. From the mid-1970s onward, for example, there were some indications that the Central Helmand Drainage Project was actually beginning to show some positive results. As Chandrasekaran observes, "on the first farms to receive new drains, yields increased to 75 percent of optimum production within a year," leading some excited Americans and Afghans to believe that they "finally had a solution to the problem that had hounded them for thirty years."[175] This optimism was reinforced in 1975 with the publication of a Farm Economic Survey, which ostensibly provided "conclusive evidence" that USAID assistance was finally having a real impact on the per capita farm owner income in the Helmand Valley.[176] USAID, unfortunately, never got the chance to assess the sustainability of these gains. Its plans to expand the drainage project across the Helmand Valley were put on hold in 1978, when the Afghan Communist Party staged a political coup. Washington responded by ordering all government personnel stationed in southern Afghanistan to pack their bags and return home.

The communist coup did not end USAID's Cold War mission to Afghanistan, but instead, radically transformed it. Immediately after seizing power, the nascent communist regime found itself confronting an intensifying rural insurgency. This struggle rapidly escalated into a full-blown proxy war between Soviet military forces and American counterintelligence operatives. USAID faced enormous bipartisan pressure to intervene in the conflict. By the early 1980s, the agency had caved and launched a new phase of development and humanitarian programming from offices located across the border in Pakistan. The logistical challenges inherent in operating on a transnational war footing forced USAID to innovate new ways of wielding infrastructural power across rural Afghanistan. Under such conditions, USAID reimagined rural development as a way of laying down the infrastructural prerequisites necessary to help rural Afghans survive both the Soviet occupation and its eventual aftermath. To this end, USAID implemented a diversity of projects that were meant to introduce the market as the only effective system for sustaining and nurturing rural lifeworlds. As the first in a longer series of attempts at schooling rural Afghan households in the global grammar of modern capitalist relations, these interventions entrenched infrastructural power as the guiding logic of liberal empire in Afghanistan.

2

From Factory to Field

The Insurgent Logistics of Development

> You said, once, there are other ways to fight the Soviets.
> Maybe I'd be more useful here. . . . You can't underestimate
> the importance of the supply line from Karachi.
>
> *Kamila Shamsie,* Burnt Shadows

ON DECEMBER 24, 1979, Soviet forces invaded Afghanistan to prop up the floundering communist regime. Led by the People's Democratic Party of Afghanistan (PDPA), the communist regime had seized power only twenty months prior through a military coup. This so-called Saur Revolution resulted in the formation of a coalition government between the two main factions of the PDPA: Parcham and Khalq. This power-sharing arrangement did not last long. In July 1978, Khalq launched a sustained campaign of violence and repression against Parcham, which eventually culminated in the former asserting its dominance over both party and government. From this position of power, Khalq embarked on a radical program of socialist transformation, aimed at eliminating entrenched infrastructures of rural class oppression. One of Khalq's primary objectives was to indoctrinate rural Afghans in the "principles of scientific socialism." As part of this effort, cadres went to the countryside to make its inhabitants aware of the "economic and social conditions that consigned [them] to lives of brutal poverty."[1] As part of this campaign, Khalq tried to regulate traditional marriage practices and inaugurate comprehensive land reform. Unfortunately, what followed was not an era of revolutionary promise, but instead, one of violence and chaos.

Although Khalq's "revolution from above" is often represented as an attempt to "redistribute wealth and power from the rural rich to the rural poor," Barnett Rubin argues that these reforms were also meant to help the state wrest control of the countryside away from traditional elites.[2] Convinced that these reforms were not in their best interest, rural Afghans began to engage in isolated acts of resistance. Although the grievances that inspired rural populations to take up arms against the Khalqi regime varied from region to region, the most commonly cited included a disrespect for Islam, government corruption, interference in domestic affairs, and the dispossession of private property.[3] Spurred by the communist regime's unwillingness to compromise its reform agenda, these local uprisings gradually coalesced into a nationwide jihad, or holy war. Weakened by internal strife, the communist regime lacked the military capacity necessary to pacify this intensifying insurgency and consequently, teetered on the brink of total collapse. The Soviet Union dispatched troops across the Amu-Darya to prevent such a geopolitical embarrassment from coming to pass.[4]

The Soviet intervention was meant to be short lived. Its objectives were simple: stabilize the communist regime by crushing the jihadist forces, known as mujahideen.[5] The insurgents, however, proved more resilient than expected, and what began as a short-term ground invasion rapidly morphed into a protracted occupation. Much has already been written on the role that the U.S. government played in both kick-starting and fanning the conflict. In December 1979, the Carter administration asked the Central Intelligence Agency (CIA) to work with Pakistan's Inter-Services Intelligence agency in establishing an "arms pipeline" to the mujahideen. While the Carter administration did not believe that the Soviet forces could be defeated, it hoped that a campaign of "harassment" would make the occupation prohibitively costly. Initially, CIA logisticians routed bolt-action rifles and rocket-propelled grenade launchers to mujahideen forces. In the hands of the mujahideen, these outdated weapons proved effective, and by late 1981, rebel forces were operating in nearly every Afghan province. Emboldened, the CIA began to pump advanced weaponry, including AK-47s and portable air-defense systems, into Afghanistan.[6]

Less well documented is the role that USAID played in supporting these "ghost wars." In the early 1980s, USAID found itself under intensifying pressure to support the mujahideen insurgency. Although USAID was initially reluctant to intervene in the conflict, it was eventually persuaded to establish the Office of the AID Representative for Afghanistan Affairs—hereafter, O/AID/REP—across the border in Pakistan. This office coordinated a Cross Border Humanitarian Assistance Program (CBHAP), which channeled emergency relief to rural populations living in Soviet-occupied Afghanistan. In this chapter, I theorize the CBHAP, much like the Helmand Valley Project that preceded it, as a vehicle of infrastructural power. Under the sign of the Helmand Valley Project, U.S. imperialists unleashed inward-looking forms of infrastructural power that were concerned with nurturing self-improvement and communal uplift throughout southern Afghanistan. The CBHAP, in contrast, sought to supply rural Afghans with the means of surviving both the myriad violences of war and insurgency and the dislocations and upheavals that would likely accompany an expected peacetime transition toward a future of market participation and transnational commodity exchange. Under the umbrella of the CBHAP, USAID enabled both geopolitical intervention and geoeconomic integration by wielding infrastructural power over rural households. In so doing, O/AID/REP introduced free Afghan farmers to what Laleh Khalili calls a "capitalising *dispositif*."[7]

I begin by considering how the Soviet occupation effectively transnationalized USAID's long-standing development mission to Afghanistan. As an arm of the U.S. empire-state, USAID was legally prohibited from overtly operating in occupied Afghanistan. USAID had to adapt its existing repertoire of development best practices to these unique operational constraints. This is to say, it had to figure out how to develop Afghanistan from a distance. USAID's strategy was to reconceptualize development as a problem of procuring and distributing commodities across a transnational borderland, in other words, *logistics.* More specifically, USAID saw its role as offering the various protagonists of the conflict—mujahideen insurgents, Afghan farmers, local entrepreneurs, and so on—with the logistical support necessary to carry out the infrastructural work of pacifying rural Afghanistan, whether through military or capitalist means.

Initially, O/AID/REP designed the CBHAP to strengthen the mujahideen insurgency by shoring up its base of popular support. In hopes of escaping the conflict decimating the countryside, many rural households were fleeing their communities for the refugee camps located just across the border in Pakistan. The CBHAP sought to stanch—or even reverse—these refugee flows so that the mujahideen "fish" would have a "sea" to "swim in." To this end, it supplied rural Afghans with the vital commodities, including food and medicine, they required to remain in their war-devastated communities. The CBHAP, in this sense, functioned as a form of war by other means.

Buoyed by this support, the mujahideen liberated vast swath of the countryside from Soviet forces. O/AID/REP adapted by transitioning its humanitarian programming into longer-term development projects designed to improve the health, educational, and agricultural prospects of rural populations. I focus my attention on the Agricultural Sector Support Project (ASSP), which was established in 1987 to rehabilitate Afghanistan's devastated agricultural economy to prewar levels. The need for rehabilitation was urgent. At the time, agricultural production levels were insufficient to satisfy the food requirements of rural populations, to say nothing of the millions who had already fled to the refugee camps in Pakistan. Over the course of the ASSP, O/AID/REP advanced two distinct approaches to meeting these agricultural needs. The first, as implemented by the Afghan nongovernmental organization (NGO) Volunteers in Technical Assistance (VITA), adapted the Helmand Valley Project's "total" approach to rural development into an effort to lay down an infrastructure of quasi-governmental spaces across the Afghan countryside. The second was the brainchild of the private sector contractor Development Alternatives Inc., which unleashed a series of measures aimed at transforming the Afghanistan-Pakistan borderlands into an environment conducive to the market-driven circulation of agricultural inputs. It was the latter approach that came to dominate the cross-border development effort, thereby setting the stage for a profound reorganization of how USAID would go about wielding infrastructural power in Afghanistan.

As with the Helmand Valley Project, however, O/AID/REP's cross-border development efforts soon brushed up against alternative infrastructures for provisioning rural life. O/AID/REP began to suspect that certain unruly mujahideen commanders were covertly diverting agricultural assistance to illicit poppy cultivators. USAID attempted to smooth this developmental friction by launching a Narcotics Awareness Control Project. Although this project was a spectacular failure, it was nonetheless important for introducing the dialectic of "anger" and "mercy" that would go on to become the hallmark of counternarcotics operations in post-9/11 Afghanistan.

Development as Logistics

Thus far, I have emphasized the infrastructural aspects of the U.S. empire-state's Cold War development mission to Afghanistan. Over the course of the Helmand Valley Project, the U.S. development-industrial complex built a plethora of new infrastructures for ordering and managing rural Afghan life. These infrastructural interventions took on a diversity of forms, ranging from the traditional (extending networks of dams, irrigation canals, and drains) to the less obvious (establishing extension, community development, self-help, and intelligence programs).

The communist coup, however, threw USAID's development mission into a state of crisis that was only further exacerbated by the Soviet invasion and occupation. Prior to the coup, the United States Operations Mission in Afghanistan had enjoyed a relative degree of proximity to the rural populations that it was in the process of managing. The communist takeover, however, made it impossible for U.S. imperialists to carry out the everyday work of development in the countryside through intimate, face-to-face encounters. Having decamped from Afghanistan in 1978, the USAID complex could not return without officially becoming party to the conflict, according to the international laws of war. USAID eventually came up with an imperfect, yet workable solution to this thorny geographical problem: relocating its base of operations to Pakistan. Over the course of the subsequent conflict, USAID designed and built transnational infrastructures for managing and improving rural Afghan life. These cross-border conduits of infrastructural power, in turn, recalibrated the very geographies of development in Afghanistan, which quickly stretched to encompass the transnational borderlands straddling both sides of the infamous Durand Line.

How did USAID/Afghanistan carry out the everyday work of development across transnational space? Once USAID entered the Soviet–Afghan conflict on the side of the mujahideen insurgents, development almost immediately became a transnational problem of logistics. Instead of assembling and dispatching teams of technicians to work among rural populations, USAID chose to focus its considerable development expertise on the urgent task of distributing emergency relief commodities to communities in need. What began as an urgent effort to transform the Afghanistan/Pakistan borderlands into a smooth space of humanitarian circulations, however, was gradually supplanted by market logics. Having maintained and supported free Afghan life under conditions of extreme duress and crisis, the USAID complex saw and seized an opportunity to (re)orient rural households and communities toward more global and market-based futures.

In recent years, the topic of logistics has enjoyed a renaissance among critical scholars. Against mainstream understandings of logistics as a "mundane science of cargo movement," this nascent literature argues that "it is better understood as a calculative rationality and a suite of spatial practices aimed at facilitating circulation—including, in its mainstream incarnations, the circulatory imperatives of capital and war." In the introduction to a recent special issue on "Turbulent Circulations," Charmaine Chua, Martin Danyluk, Deborah Cowen, and Laleh Khalili emphasize how logistics thinking was mainstreamed in the decades following World War II, triggering a "paradigmatic shift" in the operations of both capital and empire.[8] Danyluk's own contribution to the issue draws on Harvey and Lefebvre, showing how this "logistics revolution" offered a spatial fix for capitalism's tendency toward crises of surplus and overaccumulation. "By remaking the geographies of circulation as well as production, consumption, and dispossession," Danyluk writes, "this 'logistical fix' has played a vital role in promoting the accumulation of capital—and the reproduction of capitalist social relations—into the twenty-first century." In so doing, it has reorganized the spatial architectures of global capitalism by accelerating the outsourcing of industrial production to nations across the decolonizing world.[9]

As I argue elsewhere, however, the Cold War logistics revolution also ushered in new, more "just-in-time" forms of imperial intervention, or what I call "just-in-time imperialism."[10] Beginning with the Korean "police action" and continuing into the Vietnam War, the U.S. military-industrial-development complex recombined existing infrastructures of accumulation, exchange, and circulation to produce new geographies of logistical power that promised ever more flexible and all-encompassing futures of just-in-time management and control. By the time that the Soviets invaded Afghanistan in the early 1980s, modern logistics management technologies and practices—such as computers, containers, and database management software—had thoroughly transformed the everyday work of U.S. empire building. The Vietnam War, in particular, was a key inflection point in this imperial turn toward logistics management. Over the course of the war, the U.S.

military gained invaluable experience in managing the transnational supply chains required to sustain a prolonged military occupation. In the war's early days, the logistical challenges facing the U.S. military were enormous. As General Earle Wheeler, then the chairman of the Joint Chiefs of Staff put it in 1967, "it was as if one were to move a major American city some 10,000 miles, place it in a radically new environment, and expect that every aspect of its existence—public and private—would be provided for without delay or confusion."[11] Woefully understaffed, the U.S. military responded to these challenges by outsourcing the everyday work of transpacific logistics. It hired a consortium of U.S. and foreign contractors to build a nationwide grid of intermodal transportation infrastructures, and recruited a multinational labor force, largely composed of East and Southeast Asian migrants, to run them. But as General Kenneth B. Hobson also notes, "The war in Southeast Asia provided the *first live test* of the effectiveness of our modern logistics systems and *brought out the defects* that had to be corrected."[12] In this vein, the U.S. military used occupied South Vietnam as a crucible for designing and stress-testing new movement control systems and labor management techniques. Its aim was to "provide the combat troops with just the right amount of supplies required at time which he needs to use or consume it." What the U.S. military tried to do, in other words, was to keep "inventory in motion" along transpacific supply chains.[13]

While the U.S. military's entry into the Vietnam War was undoubtedly a major catalyst for technological innovation in the realms of wartime transportation and distribution, it is also important to recognize that U.S. imperialism in Southeast Asia has always been animated by a logistical vision of building and securing transpacific supply chains for commercial commodities and raw materials. In 1953, President Eisenhower infamously invoked logistics as one of the reasons why his administration was "really" concerned with the struggles for decolonization that were unfolding in some "far off corner in Southeast Asia." "If Indochina goes," he argued, the "tin and tungsten that we so greatly value from that area would cease coming." A $400 million support mission was therefore the "cheapest way that we can prevent the occurrence of something that would be of the most terrible significance for . . . our security, our power, and ability to get certain things we need from the Indonesian territory, and from Southeast Asia."[14] What Eisenhower was offering here, then, was a logistical justification for continued intervention across the region, one explicitly concerned with ensuring the circulation of vital commodities across transpacific space.

But if the U.S. empire-state valued Southeast Asia as a crucial source of raw materials, it also had the potential to serve as a destination for commercial exports. In 1954, for example, the State Department established the Commercial Import Program to help market actors in Vietnam meet the import needs of the regional economy.[15] USAID eventually assumed responsibility for the program, which had gradually evolved into a complex transpacific system for financing wartime commodity imports. Although USAID was not directly involved in the day-to-day buying and selling of commodities, it nonetheless helped produce smooth spaces of transpacific circulation and exchange by serving as a financial middleman between South Vietnamese and U.S. entrepreneurs. By the end of fiscal year 1966, the State Department and USAID had distributed $1.99 billion in commodities through the program, accounting for approximately 64 percent of all U.S. foreign assistance obligations to South Vietnam during this time frame.[16] In concrete material terms, what the program unleashed was a massive transpacific flow of consumer commodities—including motorcycles, refrigerators, and radios—from the United States to South Vietnam.

Whether these commodities arrived in the hands of South Vietnamese consumers is another question entirely, as the program itself was plagued by problems in the realm of last-mile distribution.[17] But what all of this emphasizes is that USAID began to see logistics as a key pathway to modernization and national development. As one anonymous USAID official told a group of South Vietnamese trainees during their visit to the U.S. Army Logistical Center at Camp Tokorozawa in May 1965:

> The work in which you are engaged is, in my opinion, of the utmost importance. If you succeed in establishing an efficient supply and maintenance system for your Government, *you will have made the most important step it is possible to make in the social and economic development of your country.* Agriculture, public health, public safety, law and order, highway department, and education are all important to development. Not one of these can be administered without a good supply and maintenance system.[18]

By tying logistics to national development in this manner, USAID was merely rearticulating a longer-standing consensus shared by empire builders of all stripes, that transnational logistics infrastructures are the "material manifestations" of an enduring racial capitalist ideology that has always prized connectivity, circulation, and exchange as one of the clearest expressions of imperial power—and, by extension, drivers of imperial competition—across the colonial and decolonizing worlds.[19] If racial capitalism, as Jodi Melamed and Ruth Wilson Gilmore both emphasize, is best understood as a technology of *antirelationality*—that is to say, a "technology for reducing collective life to the relations that sustain neoliberal democratic capitalism"—it is therefore logistics that makes it possible for differentially subjugated and racialized forms of humanity to be partitioned and reconnected "in terms that feed capital."[20]

This is exemplified by how the U.S. empire-state turned to logistics as a way of intervening in the Soviet–Afghan conflict. Effectively separated from Afghan communities by the communist coup, USAID launched a cross-border effort to reintegrate rural Afghans into transnational infrastructures of humanitarian assistance and commodity circulation. By taking on the task of covertly supplying Afghan communities with the everyday means of survival and insurgency, USAID opened the door for logistics to become, following Deborah Cowen, the "calculative practice that defines [development]."[21] Indeed, a close engagement with the archival record reveals that this logisticization of development only intensified as the war ran its course. Once it became clear that a Soviet withdrawal from Afghanistan was imminent, USAID's concerns transitioned from fomenting war and insurgency to jumpstarting recovery and rehabilitation. When the Soviet occupation collapsed, the result was not a cessation of hostilities between the mujahideen and the communist regime, but rather an intensification of them. For this reason, the Afghanistan–Pakistan border remained a barrier for USAID advisors, who were still legally prohibited from crossing it and rebuilding working relationships with rural communities.

USAID tried to adapt the communal forms of self-help that became popular during the Helmand Valley Project to these constraints, resulting in an uneven infrastructure for providing "quasigovernmental services" to liberated Afghans. Concerned that these community-oriented measures were incapable of improving agricultural productivity in time to stave off the potential threat of mass starvation, USAID abruptly phased them out in favor of more market-oriented interventions. Unlike development professionals, market actors were not constrained by international restrictions on cross-border mobility, allowing them to play an essential role in facilitating trade and circulation in both Afghanistan and Pakistan. In collaboration with these market actors, USAID introduced Afghan households to advanced agricultural inputs—such as improved seeds, chemical fertilizers, and modern machinery—that could only be procured through an emerging infrastructure of bazaars and trade centers. USAID hoped that these trade facilitation activities would encourage Afghan households to understand agricultural modernization as synonymous with market integration and, by extension, to see the market as a more effective distributor of essential resources than the state.

It is tempting to parse USAID's intervention in the Soviet–Afghan conflict into distinct phases. Over the span of a few years, USAID went from supporting insurgent forces to nurturing market relations. Reading these humanitarian and development activities together, however, exposes the extent to which USAID understood its role in war-torn Afghanistan as one of ensuring that communist pacification went hand-in-hand with capitalist integration and incorporation. What USAID found in logistics management was a way of consolidating these military and civilian projects into a coherent expression of infrastructural power. In USAID's hands, logistics became both the enabler and the objective of development.

USAID's attempts to wield infrastructural power across the Afghanistan–Pakistan borderlands, however, were invariably plagued by the "frictional problems of waging [counterinsurgency] from a distance."[22] USAID's enduring inability to devise an effective method for monitoring cross-border flows of assistance left its supply chains vulnerable to predation. While pilferage and racketeering were common problems, USAID was especially concerned by how shipments of agricultural commodities seemed to be ending up in the hands of poppy cultivators. As a response to the rural devastation wrought by almost a decade of war and occupation, poppy cultivation directly competed with licit agricultural production as a pathway to rural recovery and rehabilitation. Horrified that development capital was being used to fuel an alternative—and competing—infrastructure for provisioning rural life, USAID launched a suite of counternarcotics programs that explicitly tied the provision of further agricultural assistance to the immediate eradication of poppy fields. All of this is immensely suggestive of how agricultural uplift and market development remained deeply implicated in the dirty work of race war and empire. Licit supply chains had to be secured from disruption, while alternative—i.e., noncapitalist and/or illegal—infrastructures for provisioning rural life had to be stamped out through force, coercion, and violence. The net effect of these counternarcotics activities was to unevenly impose huge body burdens on the very rural communities that USAID was supposed to be assisting in the first place.[23]

In what follows, I track how USAID's methods for wielding infrastructural power evolved through the different phases of the CBHAP. I begin by showing how the program's first iteration mobilized humanitarian logistics to maintain Afghan households at a minimum threshold of subsistence. This infrastructure of humanitarian management was meant to help mujahideen forces consolidate their control over the means of violence. In O/AID/REP's hands, logistics functioned simultaneously as a pipeline of relief supplies and as a form of war by other means.

Keeping the "Sea" Full

Derek Gregory argues that war in the post-9/11 world is being shaped by the "slippery spaces within which and through which it is conducted." The U.S. military and its allies, he emphasizes, are increasingly conducting their military operations in key borderlands across the globe. These borderlands have consequently become crucibles for developing, refining, and hardening a "distinctly if not uniquely American way of war."[24] This should come as no surprise, given the historical role of borderlands as key zones of imperial contact and encounter. The feminist Chicanx theorist Gloria Anzaldúa famously describes borderlands as vague, undetermined, and transitional spatial formations, "created by the emotional residue of an unnatural boundary." At such boundaries, "the Third World grates against the first and bleeds," producing a creolized "border culture" defined by its multiple contradictions. Anzaldúa argues that for marginalized subjects, borderlands are as much spaces of joy, desire, resistance, and exhilaration as they are spaces of hatred, anger, exploitation, unrest, and death.[25] As Mark Duffield observes, however, imperial actors have long associated the border-lands of the decolonizing world with the characteristics of "brutality, excess, and breakdown."[26] Such an imperial imaginative geography re-duces borderlands to uncivilized enabling environments for sectarian and extremist violence, as well as the forms of sociocultural decay, de-development, widespread civilian death, and humanitarian abuse that invariably follow. For this reason, borderlands are in urgent need of liberal governance, economic management, and military or develop-mental pacification.

Gregory identifies the so-called Af-Pak borderlands as one of the primary geographical anchors of the contemporary "everywhere" war on terror. But these borderlands, as Gregory acknowledges, emerge out of longer regional histories of imperial intervention and pacification. They straddle the infamous Durand Line, which was first surveyed from 1894 to 1896 to demarcate the edge of British India. This act of colonial bordering effectively "bisected the cultural region of Pash-tunistan, dividing villages and extended families with strong culture and kinship connections between them."[27] Ever since 1947, when the partition of India led to the formation of Pakistan, the Afghan govern-ment has insisted that the Durand Line should no longer be enforced. Although Afghanistan's position has consistently been rejected by in-ternational law, the question of the Durand Line to this day remains unresolved. As a result, these "syncretic" borders have remained an ambiguous and slippery space of intermingling. Against the "endlessly destructive efforts" taken by both colonial and postcolonial govern-ments to "partition people into boxes defined by language, religion, and ethnicity"—a suite of practices and policies that, by 1947, had become a "standard part of Britain's decolonization toolkit"—the inhabitants of the Af-Pak borderlands have found ways of surviving and making do under conditions of war and its aftermath, many routinely crossing from Afghanistan into Pakistan and back without observing any bor-der formalities.[28]

Mujahideen insurgents used this to their advantage during the Soviet–Afghan conflict, establishing most of their bases, training grounds, and supply chains in the borderlands. Concerned by the pos-sibility of causing an international furor, Soviet commanders forbade their soldiers from engaging mujahideen insurgents anywhere within five kilometers of the border. As Lester Grau and Ali Ahmad Jalali show, however, ground soldiers in the heat of battle routinely disobeyed this order, and often found themselves in dangerous and legally untenable situations.[29] Soviet air forces also entered Pakistani air space to pursue fleeing enemies, flatten their sanctuaries, and disrupt their lines of communication. In so doing, Soviet forces extended Afghanistan's eastern borders into Pakistan's frontier provinces on a whim, transforming the border from a "colonial draftsmen's line" into a "violence curtain."[30]

The borderlands, however, were not only traversed by local mujahideen, foreign jihadists, religious fundamentalists, spies, drug traffickers and gun runners, but also by an expanding network of private contractors, USAID direct hires, NGOs, expatriate Afghans, and embassy officials. These civilian noncombatants were working behind the scenes to distribute much-needed humanitarian and development assistance among Afghan communities devastated by years of conflict and occupation. There has been some writing on these other cross-border flows and circulations. Magnus Marsden shows how the Soviet–Afghan conflict was intimately entangled with complex "trading worlds" that straddled both sides of the border. According to Marsden, many merchants "came to embark on a life of trade when they or their fathers ceased to be employed by the Afghan state as the struggle with the mujahideen intensified."[31] These commercial circuits were supplemented by humanitarian ones. Helga Baitenmann observes that the Soviet–Afghan conflict erupted at a time when NGOs were playing an increasing role in alleviating the "pain that accompanies war and displacement." Baitenmann identifies three different kinds of NGOs that began to operate in and around the Afghan theater. The first group provided humanitarian assistance to Afghan refugees in Pakistan. The second publicized the mujahideen cause to Western audiences.[32] I focus, however, on the third group, which mounted cross-border relief operations into Afghanistan.

In the early days of the conflict, only a few well-established NGOs, such as Médecins Sans Frontières, were willing to jeopardize their claims to neutrality by conducting cross-border operations that violated international norms. These "humanitarian guerillas" blazed a trail that many smaller NGOs soon followed.[33] The intended beneficiaries of their humanitarian activities were the civilians and combatants who continued to live and wage war in Afghanistan. Initially, the scope of these efforts was limited. The deteriorating security situation meant that NGOs could supply rural populations with only basic survival assistance. NGO efforts were also hampered by a dearth of centralized infrastructure for distributing humanitarian assistance within Afghanistan. NGOs were limited to working in areas where local authorities had managed to maintain functioning administrative infrastructures. While it is never easy for NGOs to work in conflict zones, these cross-border operations were particularly fraught. Cross-border operations were illegal in both Pakistan and Afghanistan, which meant that NGOs had to bribe police and government officials to work unmolested.[34]

The nature of these cross-border operations began to change in 1985, when USAID finally succumbed to mounting political pressure and intervened in the conflict. In the years following the Soviet invasion, Congress made several million dollars available to USAID so that it could support the mujahideen with humanitarian assistance. A concrete mechanism for disbursing this aid, however, was not established until 1985, when a bipartisan coalition of frustrated pro-mujahideen lawmakers passed legislation that tasked USAID with launching the CBHAP. USAID established O/AID/REP to fulfill this responsibility.[35]

The existence of the CBHAP is often acknowledged, yet its contours have only been sketched out in broad brush strokes.[36] While the stated objective of the program was to alleviate the "suffering of the people in 'free' areas of Afghanistan," it was also designed to counter what Congress described as the Soviet "depopulation campaign."[37] Soviet aerial operations were driving a growing number of Afghans into both the communist-controlled urban areas and the refugee camps located in Pakistan and Iran. During my conversation with Elaine Kingsley— one of O/AID/REP's first employees—she argued that the CBHAP was meant to discourage Afghans from fleeing their homes:

> If you wanted the mujahideen to be successful in Afghanistan, they needed a base of operations. . . . You needed to keep a civilian population center through the villages in Afghanistan both to serve as . . . resources for R and R, for food, for intelligence. So it made sense to have assistance in Afghanistan, both from a purely humanitarian perspective, but also . . . so that the mujahideen could blend in normally and naturally within the community . . . as they were fighting.[38]

If, as one U.S. advisor put it, the "Soviets [were] trying to kill the fish by draining the sea," O/AID/REP was "trying to keep the sea full."³⁹ The implication here is that the United States saw fomenting insurgency in Soviet-occupied Afghanistan as a problem of humanitarian logistics. This is to say, USAID increasingly came to value logistics as a flexible tool of population management that could provision deserving Afghans with the means of life, while simultaneously supplying the mujahideen with both the commodities and the conditions necessary to sustain their insurgency.

The CBHAP was designed to capitalize upon logistics' potential to efficiently modulate between a politics of life and death under conditions of conflict and emergency. Its purpose was to establish a life-sustaining infrastructure of humanitarian care in the Afghanistan-Pakistan borderlands that would nourish the spectacular life-eliminating violence of population-centric insurgency. From the outset, the program faced "unique operational circumstances." At the time, the U.S. empire-state was preventing its agents from entering Soviet-occupied Afghanistan, forcing O/AID/REP to operate out of offices based in Islamabad, Peshawar, and Quetta.⁴⁰ As Kingsley explains, USAID and its American partners could not go cross-border "because it was an act of war and we had no embassy presence that could provide us any support or guarantees."⁴¹ Additionally, O/AID/REP was torn between its geostrategic mandate to achieve short-term, war-related objectives, and its institutional desire to address long-term development concerns. Despite USAID's bloody history of participating in Cold War counterinsurgencies, the securitized nature of the CBHAP "generated confusion and suspicion" among employees who still believed that technical concerns were the only legitimate basis for development activities.⁴² Many also worried that the secrecy surrounding the program would lead the domestic public to believe that it was not justifiable on either development or humanitarian grounds. In contrast with the CIA, USAID could not afford to be "misperceived" as an "agency engaged in clandestine activities."⁴³

O/AID/REP worked around these constraints by tapping into existing NGO networks, further implicating them in the unfolding insurgency.⁴⁴ Initially, the force of the U.S. travel ban meant that European NGOs "were the only channels available to AID for reaching Afghans living in Afghanistan."⁴⁵ Many European NGOs, however, tried to maintain a façade of neutrality by refusing to accept direct U.S. funding, making it difficult for O/AID/REP to monitor their activities. Accordingly, O/AID/REP began to favor U.S.-based NGOs, especially those that had established working relationships with the few mujahideen commanders who possessed a measure of institutional capacity.[46]

What gelled over time was a geographically uneven infrastructure for circulating vital commodities along a number of key cross-border corridors. The most important of these corridors are charted in Figure 6, which was drawn up in 1989 on the basis of interviews conducted in the regions marked "Survey Areas" on the map. It is highly unlikely

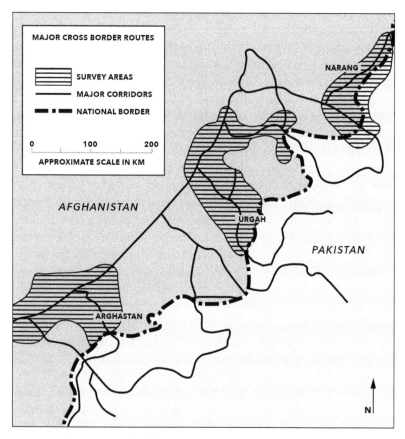

FIGURE 6. *Major cross-border routes. Map by Richard Nisa, adapted from Nathan Berger, "Profile of Private Sector Cross-Border Trade Routes between Afghanistan and Pakistan," 1989, AF02305, RA, NSA.*

that these routes remained exactly the same from one year to the next. Nonetheless, Figure 6 reveals a very particular geography of humanitarian distribution that unevenly benefited some areas of Afghanistan over others. This uneven geography of distribution was a function of the decentralized mujahideen command structure. As Mike Martin reminds us, the mujahideen insurgency was not a unitary front, but rather was primarily animated by local power dynamics.[47] Its basic building block was a "band of men led by a commander."[48] Commanders accessed supplies, cash, and legitimacy by affiliating with one of the Peshawar-based mujahideen parties, or *tanzeems.* Generally, the ties linking commanders to their *tanzeems* were instrumental, not ideological. For this reason, individual *tanzeems* exercised minimal authority over the day-to-day operations of insurgents.

The mujahideen command structure became more centralized in May 1985, when the seven main *tanzeems* were encouraged by their U.S., Pakistani, and Saudi benefactors to form the Islamic Union of Mujahideen of Afghanistan (henceforth, the Alliance).[49] O/AID/REP represented its relationship with the Alliance as mutually beneficial. The Alliance supplied the O/AID/REP with the local connections it needed to broaden the geographical scope of its cross-border programming. In return, O/AID/REP not only provided the Alliance with access to Western expertise but also helped it establish technical committees that were meant to execute development programming in the fields of education, health, and agriculture.[50] These committees were expected to improve the Alliance's "institutional capability" to perform the "civil functions of government" and, in so doing, position it as a credible alternative to the communist regime.[51]

To accelerate this process, O/AID/REP worked with the Alliance to distribute humanitarian relief—which included food, medical supplies, temporary shelters, vehicles, and pack animals—under the banner of a new Commodity Export Program. O/AID/REP conceived the program in 1986 to reinforce mujahideen supply lines against Soviet disruption. Soviet military operations were also displacing rural populations, further compromising their ability to access the necessities of life.[52] Confronted by these urgent procurement needs, O/AID/REP turned to many of the "modern logistics techniques" and "sound supply management practices" that had become increasingly central to both capitalist accumulation strategies and imperialist interventions from the

1960s onwards.[53] O/AID/REP believed that the recent "revolutions" in capitalist, military, and imperial logistics management had laid down the foundation for a centralized supply system capable of distributing large quantities of commodities on a just-in-time basis to "free" Afghan households across the war zone.

O/AID/REP subcontracted these responsibilities to a Texas-based logistics specialist, the American Manufacturer's Export Group. The Export Group was not directly involved in moving commodities from factory to field. Instead, it coordinated a diverse set of land, sea, and air transportation services.[54] Generally, relief commodities were transported to Pakistan on commercial carriers, and then transferred to Export Group or Pakistani government warehouses by local truckers. Each *tanzeem* was permitted to request warehoused commodities on a specific day of the week. *Tanzeem* representatives presented program agents with letters signed by senior Alliance functionaries that indicated the commodities being requested, as well as their destination inside Afghanistan. Upon issuance, the commodities were transferred to *tanzeem* warehouses, where they awaited last-mile delivery.[55]

The Export Group also managed the field activities of the Pentagon's Humanitarian Relief Program, whose effect was to insert Afghanistan into transnational infrastructures of militarized procurement, transportation, and distribution. This was a multistep process. First, military logisticians forwarded excess nonlethal materiel—primarily clothing, tents, and rations—from domestic defense reutilization and marketing offices to Andrews Air Force Base in Maryland. Once a month, these commodities were loaded onto cargo planes and transported to Islamabad. Along the way, these planes stopped at Rheine-Main Air Base in Germany to pick up the excess nonlethal materiel that had been collected from European defense reutilization and marketing offices. Upon arrival in Islamabad, the cargo was primarily unloaded by Pakistani officials. The Export Group's role was limited to monitoring the discharge process and cross-checking warehouse inventories against manifests provided by the Air Force.[56]

In its role as the coordinator of civilian and military relief pipelines, the Export Group worked to supply Afghan populations with the means to live and reproduce themselves in an environment ravaged by war. Driven by the biopolitical imperative to "make live," the Export Group also found itself responsible for managing the circulation of bodies. As part of the Humanitarian Relief Program, U.S. Air Force planes also doubled as ambulances of last resort, evacuating injured Afghans in need of advanced medical care to U.S. and European hospitals. The Export Group brought on an NGO, International Medical Corps, to streamline the screening process. Each month, the Alliance selected approximately 150 Afghans for screening at International Medical Corps's facilities. Of these, only a handful were selected to receive the "enormous gift of free medical care."[57] These patients were then flown out of Pakistan to Rheine-Main Air Base, where they were transferred to their final destination. What resulted was a complex choreography of wounded bodies, convalescing patients, and relief commodities that linked and blurred the boundaries between far-flung spaces of caring and violence.

In this way, the Export Group set in motion a transnational space of humanitarian flows in the Afghanistan–Pakistan borderlands, plugging local populations into broader philanthropic infrastructures of capital and commodities. To keep the mujahideen "sea" full, USAID worked with partners in the public and private sectors, as well as the military, to link a network of docks, warehouses, hospitals, and supply depots together through various land, sea, and air lines of communication. USAID's intervention in the Soviet–Afghan conflict therefore targeted the in-between spaces that are often forgotten by critical scholars of the development-humanitarianism-security nexus. These humanitarian supply chains coexisted uneasily with the parallel infrastructures of (c)overt violence that had been strung across the Afghanistan–Pakistan borderlands by the CIA. The implications of blurring the humanitarian and arms pipelines were not lost on USAID and its implementing partners, who struggled to distinguish themselves from their CIA colleagues.[58] While humanitarian actors recognized that "the entire population . . . which supports the resistance consider themselves involved in a *Jihad* . . . and thus *Mujahideen*," they also argued that the war was "no respecter of person," as civilians and combatants alike could become injured, hungry, and cold.[59] Given that the need for medical care, food, and clothing seemingly transcended the narrow legal categories of civilian and combatant, humanitarians claimed that "the only distinction of importance" for the Commodity Export Program was "between lethal and non-lethal support."[60] This distinction, however, does not hold under scrutiny. As I have shown, the ostensibly nonlethal support provided by the Export Group functioned as a form of war by other means. Through humanitarian logistics, the Export Group nurtured and sustained certain forms of "free" Afghan life so that the mujahideen, in turn, could more effectively wage war among the population.

USAID launched its humanitarian logistics effort just as the military situation on the ground was beginning to shift. The Soviet Union, in particular, was beginning to grow weary of occupying Afghanistan. At the Twenty-Seventh Communist Party Congress held in March 1986, General Secretary Gorbachev called for a swift resolution to the Afghanistan problem, which he likened to a "bleeding wound."[61] Recent developments in the conflict were no doubt weighing heavily on Gorbachev's mind. The United States was intensifying the pressure on Soviet forces by providing mujahideen insurgents with portable air defense systems and a steady supply of Stinger surface-to-air missiles. The mujahideen used these Stinger missiles to wreak havoc on enemy helicopters and transport aircraft, "sowing fear" among Soviet forces. But while it is clear that the U.S. introduction of the Stingers had an immediate military impact on the Soviet–Afghan conflict, archival evidence suggests that the missile's "potency" was only one of the many factors driving Gorbachev's desire for disengagement in the months leading up to the Twenty-Seventh Congress.[62] It did not take long for Gorbachev to win over the Politburo. On November 13, 1986, it officially announced its intention to withdraw all Soviet troops from Afghanistan by the end of the following year.[63]

As the Soviet will to occupy Afghanistan crumbled, USAID started the process of transitioning O/AID/REP away from a war footing. In anticipation of peacetime conditions, O/AID/REP preemptively launched three subprojects that targeted the pressing problems plaguing Afghanistan's health, education, and agriculture sectors. These were the Health Sector Support Project, the Education Sector Support Project, and the Agricultural Sector Support Project (ASSP). Whereas the Commodity Export Program had been focused on helping war-affected Afghans meet their subsistence needs, the three Sector Support Projects instead prioritized longer-term questions of reconstruction and rehabilitation.

Unfortunately for O/AID/REP, the "unique operational circumstances" that shaped the Cross-Border Humanitarian Program persisted into the post-Soviet period. Even though the tide of the Soviet–Afghan conflict was rapidly turning in favor of the mujahideen, the U.S. government insisted on keeping its restrictions on cross-border travel in place. These enduring constraints on the mobility of U.S. civilian imperialists prevented O/AID/REP and its implementing partners from simply reintroducing many of the same rural development infrastructures that had previously been refined over the course of the Helmand Valley Project. O/AID/REP was therefore forced to modify established rural development approaches to account for the difficulties inherent in operating across an international border. What resulted was a partial blueprint for constructing new and improved rural development infrastructures, capable of managing and ordering rural life over transnational space.

In what follows, I track this evolution in how USAID wielded rural development as a form of infrastructural power in Afghanistan. I do so through a close reading of the ASSP. First established in 1987 by O/AID/REP and its implementing partner, VITA, the ASSP began its life as an attempt to reestablish quasi-governmental infrastructures of community development throughout the Afghan countryside. O/AID/REP hoped that these efforts would produce viable alternatives to the communist regime. These local proxies would manage rural populations on O/AID/REP's behalf. Over time, however, O/AID/REP became increasingly disenchanted with community-based infrastructures for rehabilitating agricultural production. This is signaled by how O/AID/REP forced VITA to split the ASSP contract with another implementing partner, Development Alternatives, which championed market integration as the only possible pathway to development. According to Development Alternatives, the Saur Revolution had inhibited the functioning of "free market" forces. Its plan was to restore Afghanistan to a precommunist "open market situation."

This marketization of rural Afghanistan, however, was partial, tentative, and contested. I argue that this was symptomatic of the difficulties that O/AID/REP and its two implementing partners faced in cleanly delineating where wartime humanitarian interventions and peacetime development activities began and ended under conditions of conflict and emergency. Although the establishment of the ASSP was meant to signal a turn away from emergency response toward development and improvement, a closer look at its day-to-day operations reveals that it remained guided by humanitarian concerns. As we shall see, the ongoing nature of the humanitarian crisis both enabled and constrained the extension of market infrastructures into Afghanistan.

A Matter of Life and Death

The origins of the ASSP can be traced back to a noncompetitive grant that USAID awarded to the US-based VITA NGO in September 1986. The grant called on VITA to "design a project for assisting the agricultural sector of Afghanistan."[64] VITA was one of the first NGOs to establish a comprehensive rural works program inside of Soviet-occupied Afghanistan.[65] Many VITA personnel had first cut their teeth on rural development projects during the period of "competitive coexistence." One member of VITA's senior staff team, Dr. Abdul Wakil, had served as the vice president of the Helmand Valley Authority. VITA's familiarity with and embeddedness in the field, in turn, helped it forge and maintain a "good network of relations" with the mujahideen *tanzeems* and their commanders. For this reason, O/AID/REP saw VITA as "overqualified" to lead the effort in restoring agricultural production to prewar levels. O/AID/REP formalized this working relationship on June 14, 1987, when it offered VITA a three-year, $6 million contract for the ASSP project.[66]

As the lead implementor for the ASSP, VITA worked with the Alliance to expand agricultural production across liberated Afghanistan. VITA's first "Activity Approval Memorandum" proposed a two-track strategy.[67] The Alliance's in-house Agricultural Council would take the lead in implementing Track I, which involved carrying out a so-called Afghan Agricultural Project in targeted rural areas. VITA, in contrast, envisioned itself playing a more supporting role in the broader project. As part of this Track II, VITA would work alongside O/AID/REP and Pakistani government officials to establish an "Informal Steering Committee" focused on channeling financial and technical assistance to the Council, as well as any other private sector actors working in liberated Afghanistan.[68]

From the outset, however, this neat division of development labor proved untenable. This was largely due to the Council's lack of experience in actually executing rural development projects. By September 1987, VITA was already lamenting that the Council's "principal accomplishment to date" is the "fact that they continue to meet on a weekly basis, to talk about what they might do." While this was, VITA acknowledged, "an important step forward for the Alliance," it was "not enough." VITA was particularly concerned by how the Alliance remained divided along geographical, linguistic, sectarian, and personal lines. In VITA's eyes, these "serious and far reaching" divisions effectively precluded the Council from quickly making the practical decisions necessary to "provide meaningful policy direction for the Afghan Agricultural Project."[69] VITA, in other words, was concerned by how the Council was serving as a key source of developmental friction.

Nor was it possible for VITA to wait for the Council and the *tanzeem* to "agree to a unified course of action which accommodates the myriad ideological issues which currently divide them." The persistence of emergency conditions, VITA argued, meant that "the provision of agricultural equipment, supplies, and related infrastructure" had become "*literally a matter of life and death* for people in some of the rural areas of Afghanistan."[70] Instead of supporting the Council, VITA began circumventing it. This process culminated in VITA cobbling together an alternative infrastructure for meeting the "virtually unlimited" agricultural needs of rural Afghans. Known as the "Rural Works Division," this third Track is best understood as a scaled back version of the Helmand Valley Project that had been adapted to the "unique operational circumstances" that continued to constrain U.S. imperial activities in the field.[71]

Mindful of how "rural development activities in a context as heterogeneous as rural Afghanistan can become an all-inclusive labour," VITA deliberately limited the mandate of the Rural Works Division to a "realistic package of activities which can be undertaken by a small group of engineers and technicians working under war time conditions."[72] A significant proportion of this Rural Works effort involved rehabilitating key transportation and irrigation infrastructures that had been damaged by the war. VITA's objective here was to reestablish the infrastructural grid necessary to jumpstart agricultural development across liberated Afghanistan. These infrastructure building activities were also designed to be labor intensive so that they could "generate extensive employment." According to one cable, an average road rehabilitation activity could employ upward of three hundred daily laborers for almost six months. It is therefore unsurprising that the ASSP's infrastructure building components eventually came to represent the "largest single donor employment generation activity which far exceed[ed] all activities combined of PVOs [private voluntary organizations], NGOs, and all other donors."[73] Here, we can begin to see how rural development activities in occupied Afghanistan were increasingly grounded in racialized and gendered laboring systems. Under the guise of rehabilitating rural economies, O/AID/REP and its implementing partners exploited populations of young and unemployed Afghan men as a source of precarious unskilled labor for local infrastructure building projects. What the Rural Works Division laid down, in other words, was the foundation of an infrastructure for producing "native" workforces across the countryside. These wartime initiatives, in turn, foreshadowed the eventual emergence of a particular mode of developmental power that explicitly relied on exploitative processes of labor proletarianization as a way of pacifying potentially insurgent populations.[74]

VITA, in turn, used this Rural Works program to anchor an extended network of "area development schemes" (ADS) across the countryside. The first area development scheme was piloted in the summer of 1987, and it was followed by others in June of the following year. Area development schemes, as their name implies, were a highly spatialized bundle of rural rehabilitation activities. VITA channeled development assistance into key "areas of opportunity" that met certain predetermined characteristics.[75] These included an urgent need for agricultural rehabilitation, as well as a stable security bubble—often maintained by local mujahideen commanders or political leaders—within which to work.[76] Given VITA's insistence on grounding area development schemes in local security infrastructures, it should come as no surprise that they were, as Figure 7 reveals, unevenly concentrated in Afghanistan's eastern border provinces. The geographies of rural development, in this sense, mapped neatly on to the geographies of the rural insurgency.

One document offers a detailed description of how this process might have unfolded in the field. First, a team composed of an engineer and two technicians would "undertake a survey of four possible area development schemes and begin limited activities on the two which appear to be most feasible." In this hypothetical scenario, the team eventually located the scheme "in a quiet corner of Nooristan," where they began focusing their attention on assisting a cluster of approximately fifteen villages with a combined prewar population of approximately 20,000 residents.[77] According to the authors of the report, this proposed site was ideal because:

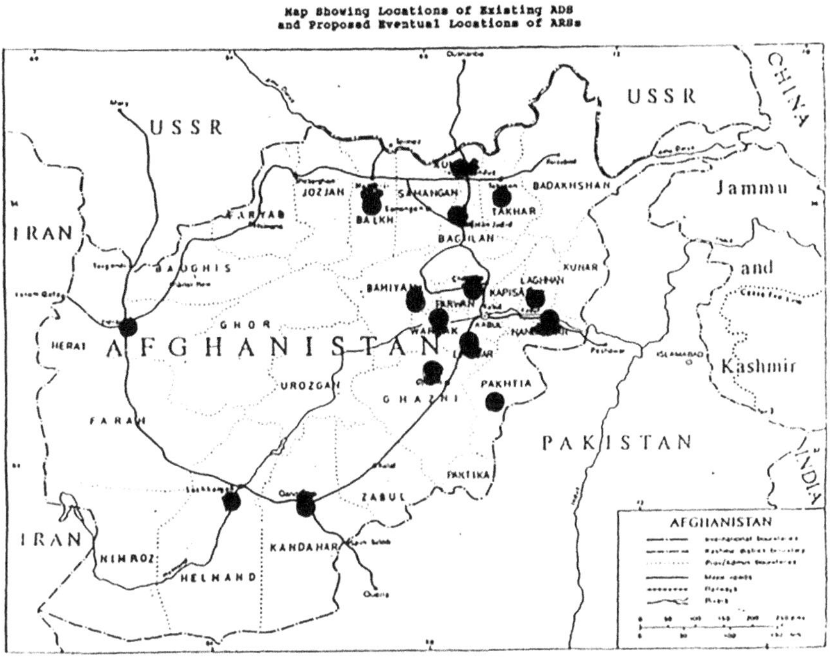

Map Showing Locations of Existing ADS
and Proposed Eventual Locations of ARUs

FIGURE 7. *Map showing the location of existing and future ADS. The ADS are indicated on the map as the large black dots. RONCO Consulting Corporation, "Assessment of the Agriculture Sector Support Project," USAID DEC, 1989, http://pdf.usaid.gov/pdf_docs/PDABB828.pdf, 41.*

access is relatively good; transportation costs are not astronomical; the people want to stay in the area, or return to it; the area is now defendable; the social structure is relatively homogenous and the people are relatively easy to work with; the villagers of the impact area are relatively close together and *form an integrated unit*; there are two principal irrigation canals which sustain agriculture and *tie the proposed villages together socially and economically*; the kinds of inputs required to assist the area are reasonable and within the scope of the project.[78]

Having settled on a site, the team could then go about allocating agricultural assistance in "ways which reflect Afghan rural village sociology," as well as the "prevailing economic conditions."[79] As demonstrated by the above quote, the ultimate aim was to strengthen, stabilize, and integrate war-damaged communities into cohesive regional formations, or "areas."[80] As part of the hypothetical case study sketched out above, the area development team proposed cash-for-work initiatives as a way of mobilizing local populations to reactivate two major irrigation canals, which would go on to provide an infrastructural scaffolding for further development activities.

By laying down an extensive infrastructure of area development schemes, VITA hoped to furnish liberated communities with what it named as "quasi-governmental services." This is to say, VITA pitched area development schemes as offering "an institutional mechanism for delivering goods and services to facilitate agricultural rehabilitation, and in that sense, could help fill the 'institutional' void left by the defunct [Agricultural Council]." In this sense, VITA was "totally unlike a contractor providing technical assistance to a government." Instead, it had taken on "operating functions normally associated with those of a government agency."[81] VITA's expanded responsibilities were signaled by how it worked hard to ensure that liberated communities were serviced by some form of local authority. VITA considered *shuras,* in particular, a necessary pathway to more participatory forms of development. If a *shura* did not exist, VITA's agricultural development officers often "[went] to the mosque and [asked] people to set one up." "While not a formally elected body," as one evaluation of VITA's performance observes, "its members do *appear to represent the collective will of an area.*" VITA fixated on *shuras* as "grassroots organizations" that had an important role to play in catalyzing a "critical change in Afghan politics." Rural Afghans who participated in *shuras,* VITA hoped, would come to believe that they "have the right to select local representatives themselves and hold them responsible for their actions." Such a shift also had important implications for development practitioners, who would have to "learn to deal with rural villagers as development *clients* rather than its *objects.*"[82]

As part of this process, VITA's agricultural development technicians increasingly put *shuras* to work in devising projects for addressing the basic needs of local constituencies. VITA, in other words, sought to reposition *shuras* as the anchor nodes of an expanding infrastructure of self-help. Area development schemes that worked with *shuras* to plan and execute projects, one report boasted, produced "far more than completed karezes and roads." Apparently, they also mobilized "communities to work on their own behalf, [helped] organize a rural population divided by war, and sometimes catalyzed rebuilding efforts in devastated areas that might [have] otherwise [appeared] hopeless to refugees considering returning to their prewar homes."[83] In reality, however, agricultural development officers carefully managed their assigned *shura*, adjudicating each proposed subproject on the grounds of feasibility, desirability, and sustainability. This is to say, *shuras* only *participated* in the work of agricultural development. They did not *lead* it.

In this sense, the area development scheme concept is productively understood as an extension of the *total* approach to rural improvement that first came to prominence in Afghanistan under the aegis of the Helmand Valley Project. Both the total approach and the area development scheme envisioned rural communities as both the loci and the protagonists of agricultural improvement. But whereas USAID had only ever operationalized the total approach at the level of individual communities—as exemplified by the Shamalan Land Development Project—VITA upscaled it, producing a regional infrastructure of rural improvement that, by 1989, stretched across 15 different Afghan provinces. Even under conditions of transnational war and emergency, participation and self-help remained key technologies for ordering, managing, and pacifying rural life.

As VITA's contract approached termination, however, these continuities were increasingly reframed as a liability. Influenced by early evaluations of the ASSP, O/AID/REP entered into contract renegotiations with VITA, convinced of the need for substantive changes. The two parties reached a new cooperative agreement in March 1990 that preserved some aspects of VITA's prior mandate, while also subtly shifting the tenor of rural development in other crucial ways. The geographies of the Soviet–Afghan conflict had shifted dramatically in the months leading up to the negotiations. By February 15, 1989, the Soviet Union had withdrawn all of its troops from Afghanistan.[84] While the Soviets continued to supply the Kabul proxy regime with aid and weapons, the troop withdrawal crippled the communist counterinsurgency against mujahideen forces. The mujahideen responded by accelerating their liberation of communist-controlled provinces, which, in turn, made it safe for VITA to "work in more areas with greater selectivity regarding subprojects to be implemented."[85] VITA's renegotiated mandate ambitiously reflected these new geo-strategic realities by further upscaling the area development scheme concept from a regional to a provincial intervention. What began as a more localized attempt to exert a "positive influence on the establishment of government-like institutions" in rural communities transitioned over time into a multiscalar "Agricultural and Rural Rehabilitation" infrastructure for implicating ordinary Afghan households in the pacification of entire provinces.[86]

O/AID/REP also used the pretext of contract renegotiations to shift the direction of the ASSP in other, more substantive ways. One critical evaluation published in December 1988 argued that while VITA had been mostly unsuccessful at "developing a specific agricultural assistance program," the one promising exception was a small, but highly "experimental activity in distributing agricultural equipment through private commercial channels." As part of this experiment, VITA offered local entrepreneurs a number of subsidies, incentives, and rebates that were explicitly crafted to help them launch competitive cross-border trading operations.[87] Keen to narrate the story of these exploratory initiatives as one of "success," O/AID/REP began to champion "the reestablishment of this private sector agribusiness system" as "the most effective and therefore sustainable method of supplying the immediate and long-term support required for the rehabilitation of Afghan refugees and the farming community."[88] Swayed by consultants who had previously panned VITA for lacking the developmental experience necessary to carry out such a task, O/AID/REP formally signaled its commitment to nurturing cross-border trade and circulation in 1989. This was when O/AID/REP hired a new implementing partner—Development Alternatives—to add a formal "Private Sector Agribusiness" (PSA) component to the revamped ASSP.

With these reconfigurations of the ASSP, O/AID/REP effectively threw its weight behind two distinct—yet supposedly complementary—transnational infrastructures for managing and ordering Afghan lives. Whereas VITA sought to upscale preexisting community institutions of self-help and self-improvement, Development Alternatives sought instead to (re)introduce market spaces and relations across liberated Afghanistan. These two vehicles of infrastructural power, in turn, were shaped and constrained by their frictional encounters with the materialities and social relations that organized rural Afghan life under conditions of war and emergency. As mujahideen forces liberated increasing swath of Afghanistan, they made it possible for O/AID/REP to engage in longer-term rural development activities. But mujahideen victories also set the stage for refugees who had previously fled to Pakistan and Iran—a diaspora that, according to some estimates, accounted for approximately one-third of Afghanistan's total population—to repatriate en masse. This was a problem for two reasons. First, the general consensus among U.S. imperialists was that by 1987, agricultural production in Afghanistan had fallen to about 53 percent of prewar levels, and as such, was "insufficient to support the existing in-country population, let alone [the] large number of refugees that will be returning as the political situation stabilizes further."[89] In a column penned for the ASSP's monthly newsletter, Fayaz Khan prophesized that a massive "influx of returning refugees without a corresponding increase in agricultural production will certainly lead to the disruption of what is already a fragile socio-economic and political fabric."[90] Second, U.S. imperialists such as Robert McCorkle and Clyde Hostetter lamented how many young mujahideen had "missed learning how to farm through a traditional father-to-son relationship."[91] If these young men were not trained, Afghanistan, in the words of one local technician, would "lose a generation of farmers."[92]

As an implementing partner for the ASSP, DAI's interventions were guided by these two overarching concerns. In another, less volatile context, DAI might have been able to actualize its framing vision of the ASSP as a vehicle for transitioning Afghan farmers toward more commercial forms of agriculture. DAI's day-to-day activities in the field, however, remained constrained by the ever-looming threat of humanitarian catastrophe. Under such circumstances, DAI was only able to familiarize rural households with the potential of market infrastructures to meet urgent subsistence needs. What DAI introduced, in other words, was a more market-based method for wielding infrastructural power over rural Afghans.

Natural Neoliberals?

In order to sell O/AID/REP on the idea that market-based approaches were better suited to the task of developing Afghanistan from a distance, private sector contractors such as DAI and RONCO Consulting

Corporation, went to great lengths to show that rural Afghans were naturally predisposed to behaving as entrepreneurial subjects. In an assessment of the ASSP, RONCO stressed that Afghan farmers have historically "resisted government interventions and are skeptical of outsiders telling them how to farm."[93] Similarly, DAI emphasizes how rural Afghans have historically been traders as much as they have been subsistence farmers. Prior to the outbreak of the war, Afghans reportedly "enjoyed a vibrant private sector market economy consistent with their independent nature," trading a wide range of commodities with their Russian, Pakistani, Iranian, Chinese, and Indian neighbors.[94] One can read the archival record to map a transnational infrastructure of trade and goods movement that connected major urban centers in Afghanistan with more well-developed markets in Pakistan. Over time, two distinct circuits of trade came to organize the economic geographies of Afghanistan. The larger of the two linked Kabul with Peshawar, while the smaller threaded the southern borderlands dividing Quetta and Kandahar. These routes were maintained and reproduced by a diverse and intergenerational group of Afghan and Pakistani merchants, wholesalers, shippers, smugglers, truckers, middlemen, and money dealers, who plied their trade across the borderlands.[95]

    DAI argues that Communist aggression inhibited these "free market forces." By 1989, the previous "open market situation" had deteriorated to the point where farmers in liberated Afghanistan had no cost-effective way of procuring agricultural inputs and other essential commodities.[96] But even if the conflict had crippled Afghanistan's national economy, market and trading infrastructures remained functional in certain localized areas. For this reason, DAI understood market actors as constituting the "most efficient way of distributing commodities even if there is no effective central government."[97] DAI's a priori commitments to liberalizing market relations in Afghanistan meant that it unsurprisingly envisioned local entrepreneurs playing an outsized role in revitalizing Afghanistan's ailing agricultural sector. DAI, in particular, hoped to collaborate with market actors in reorganizing liberated Afghanistan into a frictionless space conducive to the smooth circulations of commodities and capital. If Afghanistan, as DAI worried, could not receive a substantial influx of refugees without becoming "deficient in food for about nine million people," then the most pressing task confronting development professionals moving forward was to figure out some way of "[making] the country self-sufficient in the fastest possible time."[98] Because DAI had neither the time nor the capital required to bring more rural land under sustained cultivation, it instead had to narrow its focus on helping farmers improve their wheat yields.[99] To this end, DAI worked to mainstream modern agricultural inputs among rural communities.

This was not a new idea. USAID had previously distributed improved Mexipak wheat seeds to Afghan farmers as part of the Helmand Valley Project. By the late 1980s, however, these older varieties had lost their high-yield potential and developed a vulnerability to rust diseases. DAI's plan for the new PSA component was therefore twofold. First, to introduce Afghan farmers to newer seeds—such as Pak 81, Pirsabak 85, and Bezostaya—which would be used in combination with chemical fertilizers and agricultural machinery to squeeze even more productivity out of the land.[100] And second, to "promote and encourage the increased flow of critically needed production inputs to Afghan farmers using Afghanistan and Pakistani private sector agribusiness channels."[101] DAI ostensibly designed these market-based interventions to complement VITA's upscaled "Agricultural and Rural Rehabilitation" activities. One report evocatively described the two subcomponents as the "left" and "right" hands of the ASSP.[102] Although DAI paid lip-service to the notion that both hands were equally important, in reality, it believed that VITA's approach was fundamentally misguided. DAI was keen to reorient rural development "away from a [NGO] perspective of short-term relief and high-visibility to a more mercantile and commercial perspective."[103] As DAI elaborated in its technical proposal for the ASSP, the NGO strategy of donating commodities and providing free services was unsustainable, and risked distorting the economics of agricultural production in Afghanistan. "Rather than being encouraged to produce useful outputs," DAI wrote, "the Afghan farmers may be devoting their energy to entering the queue that receives free handouts."[104]

DAI vowed to avoid these mistakes by instead establishing commercial linkages between market actors and "paying agricultural 'customers'" across liberated Afghanistan. DAI's first order of business was to create a base of "paying agricultural 'customers'" through "Agricultural Development Training" (ADT). Echoing prior rounds of extension and demonstration work in the Helmand Valley, farmers who participated in DAI's training program learned how to use modern agricultural inputs, such as improved seeds, chemical fertilizers, and farm machinery. What distinguished DAI's efforts, however, was the extent to which it was integrated with emerging market infrastructures. DAI represented ADT as the hinge that would bridge VITA's "limited quasi-public sector" activities with the "commercial agribusiness activities of the [Private Sector Agribusiness] component."[105] DAI carried out the majority of this extension work at so-called ADT sites. The likelihood that DAI might designate a particular community as an ADT site largely depended on its popularity as a refugee destination, its agricultural potential, its proximity to other nodes of development, its investment in community infrastructures, and its commitment to remaining poppy free.[106] By 1992, DAI had established active ADT sites in Helmand, Kandahar, Logar, Paktika, Wardak, Ghazni, Nangarhar, Baghlan, Takhar, Parwan, and Bamyan. Each site was staffed by anywhere between three to thirteen extension agents, who were often wealthier land-owning farmers recruited from the very communities they were supposed to serve. DAI targeted these so-called progressive thinking or "contact" farmers because they were better equipped to absorb the risks associated with agricultural experimentation.[107] For this reason, they were crucially regarded by their peers as "early adopters" who were "able and worthy of imitation."[108]

DAI trained these farmers in Pakistan, dispatched them back to their home communities, and tasked them with establishing a variety of demonstration plots. Local farmers then visited these plots, where they evaluated for themselves the potential benefits of adopting modern inputs and best practices. Extension workers such as Pir Mohammad often parsed these "nonprogressive" farmers into one of two categories: the "undecided" majority who expected their progressive counterparts to "do all the work for them"; and the "tradition-bound" minority who were "indifferent or hostile to any innovative techniques or practise." Mohammad nonetheless remained confident that given enough time and resources, even the latter group of farmers could be "reached and educated."[109]

Having encouraged rural Afghans to desire modern agricultural inputs, DAI then set about (re)assembling transnational market infrastructures for satisfying such demands. To this end, DAI mobilized a number of "Commercial Agricultural Sales" teams to supply "10 key provinces with a significant range of commodities . . . essential to get agricultural production moving" at "affordable prices."[110] Almost immediately, the teams found themselves navigating a series of "obvious tensions" between their broader ideological commitment to laissez-faire approaches and their more practical attempts to accommodate the realities of the field.[111] Tariq Husain, one of DAI's trade and marketing advisors, squared this potential contradiction by arguing that interventions in market activity were justified so long as they created opportunities for trade and arbitrage. Once these conditions were set, "traders in hot pursuit of profits" would "move goods from one place to another."[112] Here, Husain understands a certain degree of manipulation as necessary to bring about a "more sustainable" future in which market forces, not rural development programs, play a leading role in introducing the latest agricultural inputs to farmers. DAI shared these views, prioritizing the complex task of encouraging "additionalities" in "agricultural exports and on-farm availabilities" while simultaneously minimizing the creation of "long-term market distortions."[113]

In this vein, DAI indirectly supported private sector distributors with "trade facilitation" and "market development" incentives, which were meant to reduce the costs and risks of circulating commodities under conditions of war and emergency.[114] DAI's incentives identified and targeted three different logistical frictions. First, transportation costs continued to remain high, even in the post-Soviet period. Agricultural supply chains were particularly "vulnerable to fraud, theft, and abuse," reportedly suffering more losses than any other project in O/AID/REP's Afghanistan portfolio.[115] Seeds, fertilizers, machinery, and vehicles were in great demand across liberated Afghanistan and easily fungible, making them attractive targets for would-be thieves and hijackers. This problem became particularly acute when DAI began to extend its supply chains over greater distances, especially into northern Afghanistan. In order to convince market actors to ply some of these riskier routes, DAI offered to subsidize all security-related transportation costs.[116]

Second, DAI blasted the complex regulatory infrastructures governing cross-border trade between Pakistan and Afghanistan for dampening market activity. Under the terms of the 1965 Afghanistan-Pakistan Transit Trade Agreement, only representatives of the Afghan government were permitted to import commodities tariff-free. By implication, mujahideen commanders were barred from accessing these preferential trading rates. Initially, DAI tried to circumvent these regulatory regimes by strategically naming the U.S. government as the final importer of agricultural commodities into liberated Afghanistan. Given that DAI's long-term objective was to eventually extricate itself—and, by extension, the U.S. government—from the business of managing these transnational supply chains, it had to find some way of helping local distributors avoid Pakistani duties and taxes. Otherwise, the business of exporting agricultural inputs into Afghanistan would remain "time consuming, prohibitively expensive, or even impossible."[117]

DAI's strategy was to reposition market actors as providers of humanitarian assistance. In September 1990, O/AID/REP assured DAI that the Pakistani government's Afghan Affairs Advisors would accept a "definition of humanitarian assistance to include subsidies to the agricultural business sector."[118] One agribusiness advisor, Cary Raditz, subsequently called on DAI to secure an official agreement from the Pakistani government to "extend blanket coverage of 'humanitarian aid' provisions to cover private sector trade of fertilizer and other restricted ag-inputs to Afghanistan." To support this position, DAI argued that rural households were using inputs such as chemical fertilizers for purely humanitarian purposes and offered to retain a neutral inspection service to prove it.[119] All of this underscores how DAI saw commercial channels and humanitarian supply chains not as distinct from each other, but rather, as part and parcel of the same transnational infrastructure for managing rural life in liberated Afghanistan.

Third, market actors were concerned that Afghan households were an unsustainable customer base. DAI sought to assuage these fears by engaging in so-called market development activities. These involved identifying products with a high potential to generate future profits, and then incurring losses to create a market for them.[120] Specific market development activities included: subsidizing procurement and promotion costs; offering goods on consignment; and agreeing to repurchase unsold commodities from local merchants at a predetermined price. Through these efforts, DAI hoped to "demonstrate that the private sector can disseminate certain new technologies as effectively as agricultural extension services, and with more sustainability, since innovations will be marketed based on farm level profitability, rather than solely agronomic rationales."[121]

DAI carried out most of this market development work in liberated Afghanistan, establishing a number of bazaars and trade centers in rural communities that had become important as hubs of rural development activity. DAI staffed each one of these market spaces with three to four agribusiness agents who worked at maintaining an environment conducive to the continuous circulation of commodities and capital. Figure 8 is a sketch of a typical bazaar, located at Now Zad in Helmand province. What is particularly interesting about Figure 8 is that every stall depicted either sells "grain" or "fert[ilizer]."[122] The extent to which improved wheat seeds and chemical fertilizers dominated these highly localized trading networks speaks to the ongoing importance of subsistence agricultural production to the livelihood strategies of households served by the bazaar.

Bazaars and trade centers, however, were not free spaces of exchange. DAI used them as laboratories where various techniques for unleashing market forces could be put to the test. DAI representatives, for example, often held title to particular commodities until they were delivered to bazaars. Through such "forward placement" practices, DAI reduced the risk assumed by merchants in pioneering new products.[123] DAI also went to great lengths to ensure that fertilizers and improved wheat seeds were equally distributed to all bazaars, irrespective of local supply and demand conditions. Instead of ignoring underperforming bazaars, DAI instead decided that the market could not always be trusted to develop liberated Afghanistan in an equitable manner.

In many ways, DAI's market development work is symptomatic of its broader approach to agricultural rehabilitation across liberated Afghanistan. DAI travelled in the wake of the insurgency, laying down physical and virtual infrastructures for integrating newly pacified regions into transnational circuits of market-driven circulation and exchange. Following Laleh Khalili, DAI wielded rural development as a transnational form of infrastructural power across liberated Afghanistan. These new market-based infrastructures for managing and ordering rural life did not emerge in a vacuum. As James Ferguson reminds us, all development interventions have unintended consequences.[124] The Soviet–Afghan conflict is especially noteworthy for launching, nurturing, and entrenching opium production as an alternative infrastructure for provisioning rural life. O/AID/REP and DAI had long suspected that some proportion of agricultural assistance was being

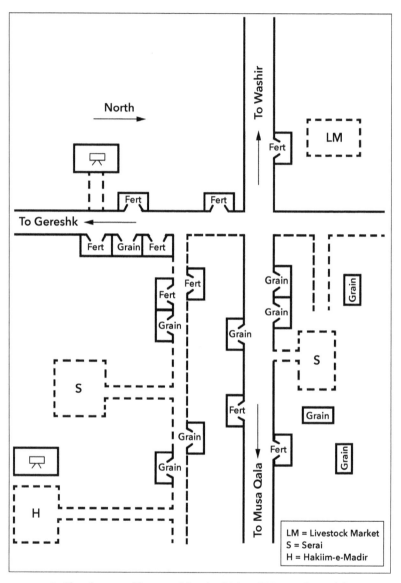

FIGURE 8. *Sketch map of bazaar. Map by Richard Nisa, adapted from DAI, "Report of Findings of Bazaar Survey IV," USAID DEC, 1990, https:// pdf.usaid.gov/pdf_docs/PNABS692.pdf.*

illegally diverted toward poppy cultivators. Prior to the withdrawal of Soviet troops, O/AID/REP was able to downplay these suspicions. From the late 1980s onwards, however, O/AID/REP found itself under increasing domestic pressure to tackle the problem of poppy cultivation. Accordingly, O/AID/REP implemented a series of projects that were meant to dissuade Afghan farmers from cultivating poppy and, by extension, eliminate a potentially threatening source of infrastructural friction. These counternarcotics interventions subjected poppy cultivators to an interplay of "anger" and "mercy." While the frictional problems of waging counternarcotics from a distance rapidly derailed these projects, they nonetheless foreshadowed the shape of things to come.

Anger and Mercy

It is by now well-established that CIA covert operations helped transform the Afghanistan-Pakistan borderlands into the world's largest heroin producing region. Alfred McCoy exposes how the CIA was aware that many mujahideen commanders were directly involved in the production and distribution of high-grade heroin. Because ruthless narco-lords "made effective anti-communist allies and opium amplified their power," the CIA chose to "tolerate" their drug dealing, and "when necessary, blocked investigations." This is to say, the CIA regarded Soviet-occupied Afghanistan as an "enforcement free zone where all US foreign policy priorities"—in this particular case, the U.S. "War on Drugs"—"were [subordinated] to the agency's mission." While the Drug Enforcement Administration made some "weak" and "distant" attempts at drug interdiction, the force of these interventions was ultimately blunted by the CIA's "direct alliances" with Afghan drug lords.[125] Unlike in the domestic context, where the race war on drugs, crime, and subversion was only beginning to ratchet up, the U.S. empire-state curiously placed counternarcotics on the back burner in Afghanistan. Crime, as it turned out, could be used to fight communist subversion overseas.[126]

Initially, O/AID/REP was reluctant to challenge this culture of impunity. Elaine Kingsley recalls that poppy cultivation was generally considered an "acceptable income generation activity" for "certain muj in the east and southeast on the part of their managers and handlers."[127] Kingsley insists that O/AID/REP never directly collaborated with the CIA. Yet she also acknowledges that O/AID/REP likely distributed agricultural assistance to rural households living in known poppy producing regions and, by implication, indirectly aided and abetted the emergence of the regional narco-economy. As O/AID/REP chief Larry Crandall reportedly quipped: "until we were sure that the Soviets would go . . . we basically put drugs on the back burner."[128] By 1988, however, the security situation had improved sufficiently for Crandall to greenlight O/AID/REP's first counternarcotics program for Afghanistan. "Since it now looked like we were going to win this thing," Crandall argued, "we couldn't countenance a situation where we were supporting a group of people who were freedom fighters but also drug traders."[129] The situation had become urgent, as Afghan farmers were turning to poppy cultivation in droves. Years of war had decimated homes, farm-to-market roads, irrigation systems, and draft animal stocks. Afghan farmers adopted poppy cultivation as a strategy for surviving in this devastated environment. In comparison with wheat, poppies were easier to grow, produced greater yields, and fetched better farm-gate prices.[130] Afghan opium, as it turns out, was in high demand across Pakistan's Northwest Frontier Provinces. These borderlands had once been a significant poppy cultivating region. With the help of the U.S. State Department's Bureau of International Narcotics and Law Enforcement, the Pakistani government launched an aggressive eradication campaign that succeeded in displacing poppy cultivation from the region.[131] This counternarcotics victory, however, was only partial, as local poppy cultivation infrastructures were eventually replaced by a booming heroin manufacturing industry. The growth of this heroin complex was fueled largely by a steady supply of raw materials from Afghanistan. Poppy cultivation in Afghanistan, in other words, was rapidly being integrated into transnational infrastructures of production, distribution, and consumption.

As poppy cultivation spread across liberated Afghanistan, it eventually became a problem that O/AID/REP could no longer ignore. Figure 9 shows that by 1989, poppy was being grown at varying intensities in at least 22 provinces. Alarmed, O/AID/REP began to question its policy of funding "activities in areas where poppy is known to be cultivated."[132] From this point forward, development assistance would be tied to counternarcotics concessions. O/AID/REP's first opportunity to pilot this new strategy came in November 1988, when it received

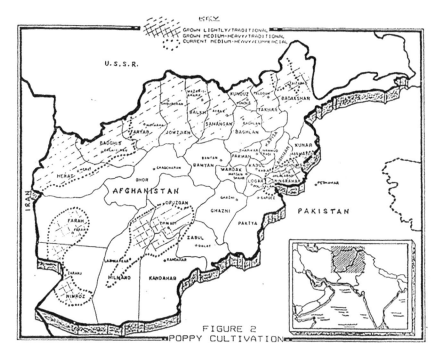

FIGURE 9. *Poppy cultivation areas in Afghanistan. USAID, "Activity Approval Memorandum: Afghanistan—Narcotics Awareness and Control Project."*

a direct request for counternarcotics assistance from a mujahideen commander based in Nangarhar province. The commander offered to curtail poppy cultivation in exchange for a steady supply of food and agricultural inputs.[133] Dubbed Project Alpha, O/AID/REP conducted this pilot program under the umbrella of broader commodity export initiatives. From November 1988 through June 1989, O/AID/REP provided the commander with agricultural tools, 600 metric tons of wheat, 46,788 kilograms of sugar, and 104,000 kilograms of ghee. O/AID/REP transported the commodities from Peshawar to the commander's warehouse in a tribal agency located just adjacent to Nangarhar. The commander then assumed responsibility for bringing the commodities into Afghanistan, as well as for last-mile distribution at the district level.[134] Over the course of Project Alpha, the commander was careful not to directly link the distribution of agricultural assistance with the eradication of poppy fields. This was because the commander did not want to get sucked into the "business of paying [farmers] not to grow poppy every year."[135] Instead, the commander represented poppy cultivation as haram and forbade farmers from engaging in it. The commander then permitted farmers who "[behaved] correctly" to access Project Alpha assistance. As the commander put it, "what works best is a combination of 'mercy and anger': he supplies the anger, and [O/AID/REP] supplies the mercy."[136]

By spring 1989, both the commander and independent monitors confirmed that Project Alpha had successfully eliminated poppy cultivation in the pilot areas. Eager to reproduce these results across the rest of liberated Afghanistan, O/AID/REP wasted no time in tapping DAI to expand Project Alpha into a broader Narcotics Awareness and Control Project (NACP). The NACP's initial goal was to reduce—and eventually, eliminate—poppy cultivation by stimulating rural development opportunities throughout liberated Afghanistan. O/AID/REP, however, rapidly discovered that it was "nearly impossible for any development program to replicate the income available from the cultivation of narcotics corps." Drug traffickers were making so much money that they could easily crush emerging markets for licit alternatives by simply raising the farm-gate prices for opium resin. For this reason, O/AID/REP dismissed "strictly voluntary" approaches as "doomed to failure."[137] Instead, O/AID/REP drew from the historical "experiences" of other narcotics producing countries—especially Pakistan, Thailand, and Myanmar—to emphasize the "importance of linking crop/income substitution initiatives with adequate enforcement."[138]

Afghanistan, however, lacked a centralized government institution capable of carrying out these law enforcement responsibilities. The Kabul regime's grip on the countryside was increasingly tenuous, and the fragmented Alliance possessed neither the authority nor the expertise to carry out police actions.[139] O/AID/REP instead followed the blueprint established by Project Alpha and negotiated a series of "poppy elimination agreements" with relevant local commanders or *shuras*.[140] O/AID/REP reasoned that cultivation bans, whether total or partial, would be more likely to succeed if farmers perceived them as Afghan initiatives. Afghanizing poppy eradication in this manner, however, also enabled O/AID/REP to strategically insulate itself from any of the negative repercussions that would likely result.[141]

To secure Afghan consent for eradication, DAI did two things. First, it sought to "establish a psychological environment which will actively discourage . . . poppy cultivation."[142] As a way of inducing attitudinal changes among Afghan farmers, DAI encouraged local authority figures to participate in "community awareness programs," largely on the assumption that they were "more culturally attuned" to the sensibilities of rural Afghans.[143] DAI worked with these community leaders to produce pamphlets, posters, banners, dramas, radio programs, educational films, sports programs, and even popular songs. Through this "social marketing" work, community leaders "[took] a highly visible, public stance against narcotics cultivation, trafficking, and abuse."[144] In so doing, they ostensibly helped anti-narcotics messages reach a much wider audience.

Gerald Owens, the NACP's Chief of Party, observed that while these community awareness programs may have "seemed reasonable from a Western cultural standpoint," they made no sense from an "Afghan point of view." Instead, farmers justified poppy cultivation on the grounds that they were only "[producing] the stuff for corrupt westerners."[145] For this reason, counternarcotics interventions needed to "attack" poppy cultivation from "all fronts" by combining eradication and education campaigns with "effective area" or "human capital" development.[146] "Even Afghan hospitality wears thin," wrote one official, "if the only reciprocation is words."[147]

To this end, DAI proposed the idea of forming "Poppy Reduction and Elimination Units," which would provide rural development assistance to underserviced opium producing communities.[148] Once a site had been identified, poppy cultivators would receive rural development assistance on a staggered basis. In the first year of project operations, farmers would not be provided with any inputs that might facilitate poppy cultivation. Once farmers had proved their commitment to poppy elimination, they would then become eligible to receive greater amounts of rural development support. Eventually, these "committed" farmers would help their communities return to a "pre-war agricultural status" by cultivating higher value crops, such as cumin, caraway, licorice, fruit trees, grapes, and vegetables.[149]

DAI believed that if Poppy Reduction and Elimination Units were correctly managed, they could have a "major" counternarcotics impact in "non-traditional growing areas."[150] Unfortunately, the establishment of Poppy Reduction and Elimination Units was plagued by a series of problems. From the outset, DAI found it difficult to grasp the complex and nuanced dynamics of poppy cultivation in rural Afghanistan. DAI established an Information and Research Office, which carried out a number of studies, surveys, and small-scale extension projects in hopes of determining the precise combination of development activities most likely to precipitate a general reduction in poppy cultivation. Unfortunately, a number of different social, political, economic, cultural, and environmental variables ensured that crop substitution remained an "agricultural planning task that [was] clearly location specific." Although DAI agents were able to identify a number of licit alternatives to the opium poppy that offered competitive returns on investment when planted in easily accessible and irrigated land, these crops were "not likely to be identical from one valley to another."[151] To compound matters further, it proved impossible to find a crop that matched the income generated by poppy cultivation in more remote, rain fed locations.

Second, it was never clear as to whether Afghan poppy cultivators actually understood themselves as the "beneficiaries" of a project that essentially asked them to act against their own economic interests. By making the provision of development assistance contingent upon poppy eradication, DAI effectively gave itself no margin for error. If alternative crops proved less than satisfactory to beneficiary populations, nothing was really preventing them from simply resuming poppy cultivation, leaving DAI with no choice but to cut off rural development assistance to particularly recalcitrant areas.

The most significant problem, however, was legal in nature. While Congress approved NACP operations in August 1990, it delayed the full implementation of the Poppy Reduction and Elimination Unit concept.[152] Congress was particularly suspicious of O/AID/REP's working relationships with opium producing commanders such as Nasim Akhundzada and Shakeel Durrani, both of whom had "a mixed reputation for honesty."[153] In one letter, Congressmen Stephen Solarz and Lawrence Smith called on AID Administrator Ronald Roskens to explain why Nasim Akhundzada would have "voluntarily cut opium production in the Helmand Valley," as this "would be the first time a producer had voluntarily reduced production without replacement income in hand."[154] Congress justified its cautious approach by arguing that Sections 2291 (b) and (f) of the Foreign Assistance Act effectively prohibited O/AID/REP from "reimbursing" former poppy cultivators.[155] NACP operatives such as Steven Weerts, however, protested these restrictions, arguing that Section 2291 should not have created problems for DAI "unless it was interpreted in a very twisted way."[156] Weerts argued that it was irresponsible to deny Afghan farmers rural development assistance on the supposed basis of their "connection" to drug trafficking. This was because all "anti-drug programs . . . [have to] be conducted in drug-growing or drug-using communities or there would be no point to [them]."[157]

DAI tried to assuage Congress by adopting what were widely considered to be the "most stringent policies regarding assistance programs to poppy growing areas."[158] In-house and external monitors would conduct unannounced visits to field sites, producing audits, evaluations, and reports that would be cross-checked with analyses of satellite imagery.[159] Congress remained unconvinced, forcing O/AID/REP to drop the NACP's poppy elimination and income substitution components. In October 1991, DAI tried to resubmit a revised NACP with augmented research and awareness elements, but this, too, failed to receive Congressional approval.[160] These bureaucratic troubles ultimately proved insurmountable, and on December 4, 1991, O/AID/REP officially terminated the NACP.

By all accounts, the NACP was an abject failure, making no impact on levels of poppy cultivation. It nonetheless remains an important moment in the history of counternarcotics in rural Afghanistan. The NACP mainstreamed the notion that successful counternarcotics operations in Afghanistan would have to entail a dialectical interplay of "anger" (eradication) and "mercy" (development). In so doing, it exposed the violence at the core of the imperial development mission to Afghanistan. Certain infrastructures for provisioning, managing, and ordering rural life would be supported and nurtured. Other illegal alternatives would be eliminated by violence, force, and coercion. Development in this instance appears as the dirty work of empire, pacifying rural communities, and preparing them for a peacetime future of market integration and commercial agricultural production.

Abandoning Afghanistan

USAID's legal troubles were not the only source of developmental friction to plague the ASSP throughout the early 1990s. Instead of improving as expected, the security situation in post-Soviet Afghanistan continued to worsen, leaving O/AID/REP's supply chains increasingly vulnerable to attack. This problem peaked into a full-blown crisis from between July 17 to December 29, 1991, when O/AID/REP suspended all cross-border flows of assistance, largely in response to a string of mujahideen attacks on development operations in Afghanistan. In the weeks leading up to the ban, renegade mujahideen hijacked a convoy of eleven vehicles, blew up a truck, and kidnapped three O/AID/REP employees. The intent of O/AID/REP's ban was to pressure Pakistani and Afghan actors into improving the security climate in the field. The force of the ban, however, was blunted by the fact that it only affected flows of nonlethal assistance. Many mujahideen commanders continued to receive shipments of arms and munitions from the Gulf War and elsewhere. The upshot was that Afghan populations were punished even while the CIA continued to arm individual commanders.[161]

Although the ban only delayed the delivery of agricultural inputs, its consequences were severe. The ban was imposed at the beginning of the fall planting season, when the potential impact of modern agricultural inputs is the highest. Farmers were forced to plant improved seeds without the chemical fertilizers necessary to unlock their high yield potential. DAI calculated that the "amount of wheat not produced because of the ban would have been enough to provide wheat to 205,000 people for one year."[162] Many households experienced a decline in living standards, as they met their subsistence needs only by consuming some of the seed stocks that they were saving for the next planting season. Although the ban was lifted in December, the fall crop had already been planted, wasting an entire year's worth of inputs. This imposed further body burdens on marginalized populations already living under conditions of slow violence and death.[163]

The ASSP never fully recovered from the disruptions that the ban imposed on both field activities and Afghan lifeworlds. This was most clearly signaled on November 16, 1992, when DAI's FY 93 budget for the ASSP was dramatically reduced from $50 million to $20 million.[164] No longer capable of running rural development activities at full capacity, both DAI and VITA began the process of phasing them out. USAID briefly considered transferring VITA's responsibilities to an independent NGO, but this never came to pass. Afraid of losing directional control over rural development activities, USAID eventually instructed VITA to terminate all operations on December 31, 1993.[165]

Throughout each phase of the Soviet–Afghan conflict, O/AID/REP's cross-border development mission functioned as a vehicle of infrastructural power. O/AID/REP supported the mujahideen insurgency by laying down the physical (logistics) and virtual (trade facilitation, regulatory frameworks, etc.) infrastructures necessary to unleash transnational circulations of goods, capital, and people. What began as a humanitarian intervention eventually transitioned into a more market-based approach to provisioning, managing, and ordering rural life. O/AID/REP envisioned these transnational development interventions preparing rural communities in liberated Afghanistan for an eventual peacetime future of capitalist agricultural production.

But as one DAI employee named Gerry Owens acknowledges in his end-of-contract report, very little went according to plan. O/AID/REP designed the ASSP with conditions of stability and certainty in mind, yet the "assumption that an Afghanistan free from Soviet invaders would be free to get on with the business of rebuilding never quite worked out."[166] Instead, political concerns constantly complicated the ostensibly technical task of developing Afghanistan from a distance. Through their day-to-day struggle to overcome the many challenges inherent in wielding infrastructural power across a transnational borderland, O/AID/REP employees were made acutely aware of their embeddedness within multiscalar configurations of geopolitical and geoeconomic power. Perhaps this is why O/AID/REP and its implementing partners worked so hard to extricate themselves from the business of providing rural Afghans with technical assistance. The market, they hoped, might serve as an antidote to the creeping politicization of rural development programming.

But as Owens usefully reminds us, DAI's—and by extension, O/AID/REP's—vision of a (not too distant) future where neutral market actors have assumed a leadership role in rural development efforts around the globe was not hegemonic. Owens specifically draws attention to the controversy that erupted "over the role that USAID should play in supporting the private sector as part of a solution to rebuilding Afghanistan."[167] Jamey Essex asserts that by the late 1980s, neoliberalism had taken a "firm hold" within American development theory and practice.[168] Evaluations of DAI's trade facilitation activities, however, highlight just how uneven USAID's neoliberal turn actually was. Although evaluators praised DAI for successfully channeling a "considerable volume of materials" to Afghan farmers, they nonetheless felt that market development had fallen short of "meeting initial expectations."[169] The evaluators explained this failure by suggesting that DAI had received "less than full support" from USAID, whose "characteristics" have historically been directly oppositional to "those most associated with the private sector operations in developing countries."[170] To solve this problem moving forward, USAID would have to do more than become "fully conversant" with market forces: it would have to learn how to operate "as if [it] were a private sector company."[171]

USAID's post-9/11 mission to Afghanistan has internalized these criticisms, championing the entrenchment and reproduction of capitalist market relations as the most effective pathway to rural improvement and pacification. The rural geographies of 21st-century Afghanistan, however, have also been indelibly shaped by another transnational configuration of infrastructural power. In the intervening years since USAID cancelled the NACP, Afghan farmers have increasingly relied on poppy cultivation to provide subsistence for their families. What resulted was a series of frictional encounters between these two competing infrastructures—one legal, the other illegal—for provisioning, managing, and ordering rural life. As we have seen, the U.S. development-industrial complex has always turned to violence as a way of smoothing over developmental frictions. These tendencies were exacerbated once the U.S. military occupation of Afghanistan rescripted poppy cultivation as a problem of counterinsurgency. As an increasingly integral supporter of U.S. military stabilization operations in Helmand and Kandahar provinces, USAID found itself becoming implicated in a "dirty" war on poppy cultivation, grounded in eradication, interdiction, and dispossession. In so doing, USAID played a central role in consigning the most marginalized farming households to conditions of life approximating slow violence and death.

[3]

Fast Development, Slow Violence

Development as Race War

Back then, a few clumps of poppy were enough to provide for
a household's needs, leaving a little over, to be sold: no one was
inclined to plan more because of all the work it took to grow
poppies—fifteen ploughings of the land and every remaining
clod to be broken by hand, with a dantoli; fences and bunds
to be built; purchases of manure and constant watering; and
after all that, the frenzy of the harvest, each bulb having to be
individually nicked, drained, and scraped. Such punishment
was bearable when you had a patch or two of poppies—but
what sane person would want to multiply these labours when
there were better, more useful crops to grow, like wheat, dal,
and vegetables?

Amitav Ghosh, Sea of Poppies

Afghanistan needs a homespun version of the broken windows
theory.

Sandeep Gopalan, "Pulling the Afghan Bus
From the Ditch—'Broken Windows' Strategy to
Fix Government Can Inspire Hope," Washington Times

IN THE EARLY 2010S, at the height of the U.S. occupation of Afghanistan, commentators writing for a diversity of publications—including
The Economist, Small Wars Journal, and the *Washington Times*—began
calling on the U.S. military to draw counterinsurgency inspiration
from longer genealogies of policing work in the domestic context. In
particular, they offered New York City as a model of how a "broken
windows" approach to order management might help U.S. occupying
forces combat the intensifying insurgency in Afghanistan. If New York

City was the first successful test-case of broken windows theory, then rural Afghanistan would be its next and somewhat unlikely frontier.

First introduced by James Wilson and George Kelling in a 1982 issue of the *Atlantic Monthly,* broken windows is a theory of policing that fixates on "controlling low-level disorder" as a way of "preven[ting] more serious crime."[1] According to Bench Ansfield, "Wilson and Kelling's signal intervention revolved around their understanding of how signs of disorder, such as subway graffiti or public drunkenness, ostensibly push 'law abiding' residents toward vandalism and crime by reducing 'community controls' against incivility."[2] Confronted by these everyday signs of disorder, the afflicted community begins to fear the specter of "more injurious crime," leading to the further deterioration of neighborhoods and communities. From Kelling and Wilson's perspective, then, the task of the police is not to fight crime, but rather to cultivate a broader sense of community safety by "eradicating the visual cues of disorder": this is to say, by fixing broken windows, removing abandoned cars, or painting over graffiti.[3]

In the intervening forty years since *Atlantic Monthly* published Kelling and Wilson's article, their theory of broken windows has been debunked for its racist underpinnings, its lack of evidentiary basis, and its practical ineffectiveness. And yet, the broken windows theory has thoroughly transformed policing practices in the United States and elsewhere, granting beat cops an enormous amount of discretionary power to subject marginalized communities to lethal levels of violence and coercion. More recent engagements with the broken windows theory have emphasized the thoroughly transnational nature of its reach.[4] Counterinsurgent technologies and techniques such as the checkpoint or the night raid, for example, all have domestic corollaries, such as stop-and-frisk and no-knock warrants. But even if broken windows *is* a travelling theory of counterinsurgency, any attempt to apply it in Afghanistan should give us pause: what could a theory of policing first developed and put to work in New York City possibly offer to counterinsurgents trying to quell a raging insurgency in the sparsely populated agricultural landscapes of rural Afghanistan?

As it turns out, there was little consensus among this group of boosters as to what broken windows might look like in the Afghan context. In their hands, broken windows was rescaled from a theory of policing to a theory of governmentality. Writing for the *Small Wars Journal,*

Lieutenant Colonel Andy Bell—then the operations branch chief for the Operations, Plans, and Policy Division of the Army Capabilities Integration Center at Army Training and Doctrine Command—proposes a very literal translation of the broken windows metaphor into concrete counterinsurgency practice. When Bell arrived in Afghanistan, he was "taken aback by the trash and destruction left by years of fighting." "Could keeping our areas clean and orderly," Bell wondered, "positively affect Counter Insurgency efforts?" Although Bell transitioned into a military career with twenty years of law-enforcement-related experience under his belt, it was the question of cleanliness that captured his attention, and that offered a pathway to winning community "hearts and minds." By working with local communities to keep areas "clean" and "orderly," he argued, U.S. counterinsurgents could "make things difficult for the enemy to operate without fear of discovery as being suspicious, or out of place."[5]

If Bell's vision of broken windows counterinsurgency undoubtedly appears to some less sympathetic readers as nothing less than a call to beautify the imperial landscapes of war making—what one of my colleagues memorably described as "military KonMari"—it is important to note that other commentators presented more polished versions of the same idea.[6] *The Economist* invoked the broken windows theory to explain why coalition forces needed to quickly rebuild Kabul's Faroshga market, which had been leveled by two Taliban suicide bombers on January 18, 2010. "The best way to discourage that kind of attack," writes the anonymous author, "is to snuff it out, clean it up, and pretend it never happened."[7] Other commentators, such as Sandeep Gopalan, applied broken windows to broader problems of nation building and governance. What Afghanistan needed, Gopalan declared, was a "homespun version of the 'broken windows' theory, in which small problems are addressed quickly to foster confidence in management's competency." While Gopalan identifies the fight against corruption as one arena where broken windows thinking might pay dividends—"New York," he quipped, "offers a telling lesson in this regard"—it was not the only possible "battleground." As Gopalan writes:

> Afghanistan cannot be secured without offering alternatives to poppy cultivation for its farmers. Conventional counternarcotics strategies are unlikely to work and often push the farmers into

criminal hands. Unless a green revolution at the grass-roots level makes a sustainable agricultural income feasible, the Taliban will continue to be well-funded. Regional models—from India, for example—can be adopted to make legitimate agriculture profitable. While subsidies and intensive government support at the village level will be needed in the immediate term, as farmers are weaned from the poppy trade, results will become evident.

Here, Gopalan's implication is clear: poppy cultivation, like corruption, is a problem that needs to be addressed at the scale of the everyday through community-centered agricultural interventions, so that rural households can develop an investment in the Afghan government. To paraphrase Gopalan: "Unless the common man sees that [agricultural development] is being tackled in his local community, it will be business as usual."[8]

At first glance, Gopalan's move from broken windows to crop substitution does not seem like an obvious one, especially given how they are often understood to be two contradictory—and perhaps even opposed—methods for managing potentially insurgent populations. But what makes Gopalan's uneasy slippage between the two forms of pacification possible, I think, is broken windows' longer-standing connections to the thorny and evolving problem of "national security." When Kelling and Wilson first proposed a broken windows approach to policing the South Bronx in the early 1980s, they did so in a context of a "nationwide urban crisis" that showed no signs of either slowing down or ameliorating.[9] Beginning with the urban uprisings in the late 1960s and continuing through the new period of intensifying austerity, deindustrialization, and social state retrenchment that came to define most of the 1970s, the specter of racialized insurgency and unrest loomed large over the American inner city.[10] As Ansfield notes, Kelling and Wilson's vision of broken windows "broadcast a real-time ruination that conjured long-established fears of racial degeneration and newly developing anxieties of national economic and political decline."[11] At its core, then, broken windows was a form of counterinsurgency that sought to quell these nationwide fears by making the mundane, the small, and the everyday the central concern of beat policing. By targeting and intervening on low-level forms of disorder, broken windows theoretically secured the American inner city for capital, thereby setting the stage for new rounds of urban renewal, redevelopment, and reinvestment.

It was precisely broken windows' proximity to race war on the home front that allowed it to travel—however imperfectly—abroad, eventually arriving in the insurgent landscapes of post-9/11 Afghanistan. If broken windows could secure the American inner city at home, resolving a festering urban crisis in terms that were amenable to the racial capitalist state, then surely, as some commentators came to believe, it could also be upscaled to achieve similar results in hotspots of decolonization and insurgency across the globe. In recent years, the most vocal proponent of this thesis has been the conservative commentator Bret Stephens, who most recently argued that the United States' spectacular defeat in Afghanistan signals how we have fully "turned the corner" into a "broken windows world" of "unlit streets, more hospitable to predators than it is to prey." After multiple decades of neglecting the "small things," Stephens warns, the world is about to "learn just how high the costs can go when the policeman walks off the job."[12]

Although both Gopalan and Stephens invoke broken windows thinking as the solution to the problem of Afghanistan, it is nonetheless important to note that they are not asking for the same thing. As Stephens's many critics are quick to remind us, his various writings on the subject can be summarized as a barely concealed reactionary call for a "much larger military" that acts like an "expeditionary force."[13] Gopalan, in contrast, perhaps hews much closer to Kelling and Wilson's original formulation in his emphasis on enforcing the rule of law at the grassroots or the village level. Where Gopalan departs from Kelling and Wilson—and certainly from Stephens—is in his recognition of the need to build up rural communities, and to promote agricultural development in ways that reach as many farming households as possible. There is, in other words, a reparative element to Gopalan's version of broken windows that seemingly departs from the revanchist origins of the concept. In Gopalan's hands, then, broken windows becomes an elastic framework that can be stretched to encompass rural development, community uplift, and law enforcement interventions, all at the same time. Broken windows can speak to each of these seemingly distinct fields of intervention because Gopalan rescripts it into a technical theory of improved management.

What Gopalan obscures in this framing is of course broken windows' ties to longer-standing forms of racialized order maintenance and management. Critics of broken windows thinking have long emphasized the role that it has played in upholding entrenched infrastructures for policing and managing surplus populations of racialized and marginalized subjects, or, what W. E. B. Du Bois famously named as "the basic majority of workers who are yellow, brown, and black."[14] By the advent of broken windows in the early 1980s, these communities had already been rocked for decades by various interlocking "practices of place annihilation."[15] These ranged the gamut from the Johnson administration's Great Society initiative that created an enabling environment for the rise of the carceral state, to the predatory forms of inclusion that preserved the racist underpinnings of U.S. housing markets in the post-1945 period, to the outright forms of police violence and brutality that came to define the domestic counterinsurgencies in the "occupied territories" of Watts and Harlem, all of which were so powerfully documented by contemporary Black radicals such as James Baldwin.[16] Broken windows' innovation was to take these "practices of place annihilation" and filter them through an ever more banal and routinized politics of everyday encounter, which in turn cleared the ground for increasingly comprehensive forms of urban reinvestment and renewal. As we shall see later on in this chapter, it is precisely this dialectic of place annihilation and renewal that also came to define the everyday work of counterinsurgency in southern Afghanistan in the post-9/11 period. Gopalan's invocation of broken windows thinking is therefore significant, opening intellectual and political spaces for considering how the United States' inner race wars on poverty, crime, and drugs have always been entangled with the United States' outer race wars on decolonization, disorder, and insurgency.

For the specific purposes of this chapter, it is broken windows' bloody entanglements with the United States' race wars on drugs and poverty—both at home and abroad—that are perhaps most relevant. By the time that Gopalan penned his op-ed for the *Washington Times* in 2010, poppy cultivation in Afghanistan had proven itself to be an intractable problem. Although poppy cultivation first took root in Afghanistan during the Soviet–Afghan conflict, the local narco-economy grew rapidly under the enabling conditions of war and insurgency. By 1991, Afghanistan had surpassed Myanmar to become the world's largest producer of opium resin.[17] In the years leading up to this inflection point, USAID's Pakistan-based Office of the Aid Representative for Afghanistan Affairs had taken some preliminary steps toward confronting poppy cultivation. This cross-border counternarcotics campaign, however, was crippled by a restrictive regulatory regime and never fully got off the ground. All the while, poppy cultivation continued to spread across the countryside.

Undeterred, USAID drew up ambitious plans to consolidate these nascent efforts into a "full-scale alternative development project."[18] Confident that mujahideen forces would replace the communist regime with a stable interim government, USAID scheduled the launch of its new project to follow a peaceful transfer of power.[19] What USAID did not anticipate was that certain mujahideen commanders might see the impending communist defeat as an ideal opportunity to seize power for themselves.[20] Ahmad Shah Massoud and Abdul Rashid Dostum—the leaders of Jamiat-i-Islami and Jombesh-i-Milli, respectively—forged an uneasy "Northern Alliance" in hopes of wresting control of Kabul away from the reeling communist regime.[21] Concerned Pashtun commanders, who disliked Dostum and the other Tajik and Uzbek power brokers in the Northern Alliance, responded by throwing their weight behind Gulbuddin Hikmatyar's Hizb-i-Islami and helped his fighters infiltrate Kabul.[22] The stage was therefore set for a multifront battle to capture Kabul and, by extension, dictate the terms of regime change.

The Northern Alliance struck first, entering Kabul on April 25, 1992. Hikmatyar soon followed, and the combined offensive "liberated" Kabul in five days. Instead of marking the end of the conflict, however, the fall of Kabul freed the rival factions to go "at one another's throats." They laid down roadblocks and checkpoints, reorganizing Kabul into a matrix of conflicting enclaves. From these bases, mujahideen commanders launched explosive campaigns of looting, rape, and murder.[23] Pitched street battles killed and injured thousands of Kabulis and displaced countless others from their homes. In the words of Amnesty International, Kabul had become a "human rights catastrophe."[24]

When reflecting on this "time of 'anarchy,'" Elaine Kingsley acknowledges that USAID had been "naïve" and "blind" to let Afghanistan "[fall] off the map."[25] Although the U.S. empire-state was concerned by the worsening situation in Afghanistan, it ultimately decided against intervening in what was shaping up to be a bloody civil war. Kingsley explains

USAID's inaction as an understandable response to Gorbachev's resignation as the president of the Soviet Union on December 26, 1991. The resulting dissolution of the communist bloc meant that the U.S. empire-state no longer saw Afghanistan as a national security priority. To quote Kingsley: "We'd won the [Cold War], who cares, we left."[26]

But even if USAID never fully disengaged from Afghanistan, the conditions necessary to launch its "full-scale alternative development project" never materialized. Local stakeholders who might otherwise have benefited from continued USAID largesse instead became increasingly reliant on informal sources of funding—including poppy cultivation—to run their (para)military operations. This remained true even in 1996, when Taliban fundamentalists supplanted Northern Alliance warlords as the dominant politico-military force in Afghanistan.[27] Formed in the madrasas that sprang up to service Afghan refugee camps in Pakistan, the Taliban "sought to restore law, order, and stability . . . through the removal of the warlords and the imposition of a radically purified Islam."[28] Despite the Taliban's hardline ideology, it protected and taxed poppy cultivation, which flourished under such enabling conditions.[29] In July 2000, however, the Taliban shifted gears and imposed a total ban on poppy cultivation. Many observers speculated that the Taliban was hoping to leverage the ban for increased levels of international recognition and foreign assistance.[30] The United States responded accordingly on May 17, 2001, when Secretary of State Colin Powell announced $43 million in emergency agricultural aid for Afghan farmers who were enduring a severe drought.[31]

Although Powell promised that further deliveries of aid would be forthcoming if the Taliban could sustain the ban, 9/11 and the subsequent invasion of Afghanistan made this all but impossible. The U.S. War on Terror officially arrived in Afghanistan on October 7, 2001. Code named Operation Enduring Freedom, the invasion was spearheaded by Northern Alliance proxies, who worked with CIA advisors to mount a combined air and ground offensive against the Taliban regime. The eventual collapse of the Taliban made it safe for farmers to resume cultivating poppies, prompting commentators to frame Operation Enduring Freedom as an opportunity to synchronize America's longer-standing War on Drugs with its new War on Terror. As Tim Golden put it, Afghanistan's opium problem was once again "America's to solve."[32]

What coalesced in the Afghan countryside over time was a hybridized War on Drugs *and* Terror, or, perhaps more accurately, a multiplicity of hybridized wars, waged concurrently by different organs of the U.S. empire-state. What linked these hybrid wars was an overarching belief that the Afghan counterinsurgency could only be won through a comprehensive counternarcotics offensive. USAID contributed to this interagency effort by trying to bring about the kind of "green revolution at the grassroots level" that Gopalan would eventually call for in his op-ed.[33] To this end, USAID drew from its prior experiences working with drug cultivators, both in Afghanistan and elsewhere, to design and carry out "alternative development" programming across the countryside. Whenever possible, USAID championed markets as the best mechanism for providing Afghan farmers with sustainable and economically viable alternatives to opium poppies. By reorienting farming households away from subsistence livelihood strategies toward commercial forms of agricultural production, USAID's alternative development programming would set them on the path toward more liberal, market-based futures.

When understood in this way, alternative development seems to offer something other than a broken windows approach to the problem of poppy cultivation in Afghanistan. It is rural uplift, not racialized order management, that lies at the heart of USAID's alternative development mission. But I want to linger on Gopalan's invocation of alternative development as another potential "battleground" for broken windows, because I think it reveals something about the violent racial logic that undergirds the everyday work of counternarcotics in Afghanistan. Paying closer attention to the transnational afterlives of broken windows thinking, I argue, can help us better understand how the United States' inner race wars on drugs and crime came to be felt as an inheritance by rural Afghan households, whether they were entangled with local narco-economies or not. USAID may not have been directly involved in counternarcotics law enforcement, but its alternative development programming took root in landscapes that were being transformed by the everyday work of poppy eradication. USAID seized every possible opportunity to reframe alternative development as the antidote to such interventions. But the State Department's involvement in training Afghan police forces recalls USAID's own bloody history of carrying out "public safety" work in key Cold War hotspots of counterinsurgency. What I want to do in this chapter, then, is to refuse the story that USAID wants to tell us about alternative development programming in Afghanistan, to take seriously Gopalan's attempts to apply broken windows thinking to alternative development, and to show how the various forms of rural uplift promulgated in its name were undergirded by longer-standing racialized logics of imperial and domestic order management.

In what follows, I track how the United States' outer race war on terror collided with its inner race war on drugs and crime in southern Afghanistan. The former site of the Helmand Valley Project, southern Afghanistan became infamous in the post-9/11 period as the heartland of the neo-Taliban insurgency. Given southern Afghanistan's centrality to the broader Afghan counterinsurgency, it is unsurprising that provinces like Helmand and Kandahar became the testing grounds for different alternative development experiments. These ranged the gamut from the explicitly civilian—USAID's own "Alternative Livelihoods Program/South" or the State Department's police training efforts—to hybridized civil–military interventions, such as the Helmand Food Zone initiative or International Relief and Development's "Afghanistan Vouchers for Increased Production in Agriculture." What hardened over time was a distinction between two competing models of alternative development: first, the stabilization model, which relied on quick-impact crop substitution programs to provide poppy cultivators with heavily subsidized access to improved wheat seeds and fertilizers; and second, the rural development approach, which prioritized more long-term commitments to market building and capitalist integration. USAID went to great lengths to uphold this distinction. This often manifested as a critique of how stabilization-style projects—even the ones USAID was involved in—unsustainably distort local economies and negatively affect the operational space of civilian actors. But what USAID's critique ignores are the ways in which alternative development is often experienced as what Micol Seigel calls "violence work."[34] Violence work is often visible and spectacular. But it can also be slow, its effects accumulating over time. This slower kind of violence work is exemplified by alternative development interventions such as the Helmand Food Zone, which resulted in the dispossession and displacement of land-poor households across southern Afghanistan. These displaced households migrated to the more remote desert regions of Helmand and Kandahar provinces, where they once again relied on poppy cultivation to survive. When considered from this perspective, poppy cultivation functioned as a bulwark against successive waves of U.S. infrastructural power. Poppy fields, then, might perhaps be better understood not as broken windows, but rather as visual reminders of how an everyday politics of survival and making do can be forms of political resistance.[35]

War Economies and Counterinsurgency Capitalisms

Scholars have long understood that war making invariably produces new economic geographies.[36] Post-Soviet Afghanistan is often held up as a case study of how a national economy can be thoroughly "adjusted" by extended periods of conflict. According to Jonathan Goodhand, Afghanistan's "war economy" is made up of three distinct yet related components. These are the *combat, shadow,* and *coping* economies. Although these subeconomies are interconnected, each one involves "different types of actors, incentives, commodities, and relationships."[37] Afghanistan's combat economy supplies the resources that belligerents need to wage war. The shadow economy, in contrast, largely exists outside of state-regulated frameworks. While its protagonists benefit economically from war, they may "have an interest in peace, if peace can enable the maintenance or increase of profits."[38] Finally, the coping economy encompasses the livelihood strategies that the poorest households rely on to meet their daily subsistence needs. These households participate in Afghanistan's war economy not to accumulate assets or to predate on resources, but rather to survive.

The widespread consensus is that poppy cultivation weaves these combat, shadow, and coping economies together. For rural households struggling to make ends meet, poppy cultivation is simultaneously a livelihood strategy, a means of accessing land and credit, and a consistent store of value.[39] The poppy and its derivatives also help economic entrepreneurs—such as landowners or opium traders—participate in the circuits of "shadow globalization."[40] Finally, poppy cultivation fuels combat economies, as belligerents finance their paramilitary operations by extracting rents from farmers and traders. In rural Afghanistan, then, the opium poppy functions simultaneously as a conflict good, an illicit commodity, and as a means of survival.

Writing at the turn of the twenty-first century, Barnett Rubin worried that "ending war in Afghanistan might transform the criminalized war economy into an even faster-expanding criminalized peace economy."[41] Goodhand echoed Rubin's concerns, arguing that a strong centralized state was required to readjust Afghanistan's war economy for peacetime conditions. But what is obscured by these concerns is any sense of how Afghanistan's war economy is the by-product of U.S. empire building across the region and, for this reason, always already entangled with longer genealogies of racial capitalism. Over the course of the Soviet–Afghan conflict, CIA covert operatives deliberately encouraged mujahideen commanders to cultivate poppies, which subsequently became a central element in the logistics of anticommunist jihad. But the U.S. empire-state's post-9/11 war on poppy cultivation in Afghanistan also had the effect of linking the battle space to other transnational configurations of race war, counterinsurgency, and geopolitical economy. From this perspective, Afghanistan's narco-economy shares much in common with the globalized military-industrial complex that has long fueled U.S. imperial interventions overseas. The United States, as Nikhil Pal Singh reminds us, has always been a war economy.[42] Forged in the crucible of what Sven Beckert calls "war capitalism"—or, a globalized system of world making grounded in "slavery, the expropriation of Indigenous peoples, imperial expansion, and the assertion of sovereignty over people and land by entrepreneurs"—the United States would eventually go on to become its foremost practitioner across the globe. Beckert uses the concept of war capitalism to explain how the "violent expropriation of land and labor in Africa and the Americas" enabled "Europe's extraordinary economic development by the nineteenth century and beyond."[43] But what distinguishes the American brand of war capitalism from the European iterations, Singh emphasizes, is how it has developed and perfected "infrastructures of violence" to "manage a population sharply divided along multiple racial lines."[44] This is even true of the period that is described as the "golden age" of U.S. capitalism, which began in the late 1930s, when the Roosevelt administration first put the national economy on a wartime footing. As Ruth Wilson Gilmore reminds us, the United States "has since committed enormous expenditure for the first *perma-*

nent warfare apparatus in the country's pugnacious history," effectively laying the infrastructural groundwork necessary to wage its outer race wars on communism, insurgency, and terrorism at the same time as its inner race wars on poverty, crime, and subversion.[45]

If descriptions of Afghanistan as a nation caught between criminalized war and peace economies disavow the central role that U.S. war capitalism has played in entrenching and exacerbating poppy cultivation across the rural landscape, they also racialize Afghan households in very particular ways. Here, the net effect is to reinforce imperial representations of Afghan livelihood strategies as not only backward or traditional—and hence, in perennial need of modernization through development—but also as always potentially implicated in criminal and insurgent activity. In this way, rural lifeworlds became available to a widened suite of interventions that encompasses development, policing, and other forms of violence work. By conflating poppy cultivation, crime, and insurgency, such discourses necessarily evoke domestic historical geographies of racialized order management. As Stuart Schrader argues in *Badges Without Borders,* decolonization movements abroad and civil rights struggles at home both emerged as a response to new and complex arrangements of formal equality and de facto inequality. In both the domestic and the foreign spheres, such "emergent forms of social and political protest" were "labeled crime and subversion": terms that offered a "political vocabulary and governing grammar" through which entrenched "[matrices] of racial difference" could be reproduced and mapped on to new configurations of insurgency and unrest. This is not to suggest that "the specific US experience of racism and policing" can be used to explain how counterinsurgency works in the Afghan context.[46] But it is to emphasize that the post-9/11 war on Afghan poppy cultivation was haunted by the transnational afterlives of the United States' inner race wars on poverty, crime, and drugs. In her reflection on the infrastructural underpinnings of intimacy, Ara Wilson argues that our consciousness of infrastructure—which otherwise "aims to be invisible"—is heightened under certain conditions: during times of crisis, for example, or when infrastructures are being "installed" or "displayed as the 'colonial sublime.'"[47] In a rapidly destabilizing southern Afghanistan, U.S. counterinsurgents had to install new transnational infrastructures of pacification and order management in real time. Under such conditions, it is unsurprising that they turned to strategies, techniques, and technologies that had already been honed elsewhere.

If alternative development was a central and highly visible element of the U.S. empire-state's counternarcotics playbook in Afghanistan, another suite of interventions, which were seemingly more banal in character, centered on police training and force professionalization. Scholars such as Schrader and Seigel have emphasized how the everyday work of policing blurs the foreign and domestic spheres, and a similar story can be told of counternarcotics interventions in post-9/11 Afghanistan. Carried out by the private security contractor DynCorp at the behest of the State Department's Bureau for International Narcotics and Law Enforcement (BINL), police training in Afghanistan recalled USAID's own Cold War effort to tie law enforcement assistance to economic development across the decolonizing world. Spearheaded by the Office of Public Safety (OPS), USAID's police training program provided various forms of technical and material assistance to at least fifty-two countries with the goal of preventing communist revolution and crime. In the eyes of OPS advisors, a professional police force was a necessary prerequisite to modernization and development. From Indonesia to Vietnam to Turkey to Brazil, OPS advisors extolled the developmental virtues of police professionalization, championing its ability to clear the ground for further interventions designed to reformat existing social orders, thereby facilitating their integration into global infrastructures of war capitalism.[48]

In theory, OPS advisors worked hard to reform policing in aid-recipient countries through a judicious application of "big-city" techniques and technologies. In practice, OPS assistance "often landed in furrows already plowed by colonial powers, strengthened by authoritarian militaries, and bolstered by caudillos, tycoons, and compradors."[49] For this reason, OPS advisors found themselves directly implicated in what George Orwell once named the dirty work of empire.[50] In the context of the Vietnam War, OPS advisors helped unleash new geographies of targeted killing, prison building, administrative detention, and enhanced interrogation. The incendiary story of Dan Mitrione, an OPS advisor who infamously trained Uruguayan police officers in torture techniques, also did significant damage to the OPS's reputation. As scandal after scandal rocked the OPS, leftist organizers ramped up their political campaign to halt the global provision of police training under the umbrella of development assistance. Their efforts bore fruit in 1974, when Congress passed a law that effectively abolished the OPS, ostensibly ending USAID's implication in the everyday violence work of empire.

Police training, unfortunately, continued under other institutional guises. Former OPS advisors continued to provide police assistance under private auspices, establishing security contractors such as Vinnell. But as Schrader notes, the OPS's now illegal mission to train and modernize overseas police forces was given new life by President Nixon's War on Drugs. The OPS, to be sure, had long served as a conduit of counternarcotics assistance. As early as 1951, OPS advisors working in drug hot spots such as Turkey were "[incorporating] antinarcotics routines and training into [their] repertoires." But this entanglement of counternarcotics and public safety work deepened after Nixon inaugurated the War on Drugs in June 1971. According to Schrader, OPS organized some of the first interagency meetings on narcotics control in October 1971, and went on to play a substantive role in newly formed "coordinating bodies," such as the East Asia Working Group on Narcotics. By the early 1970s, then, the OPS was already exploring how it might leverage narcotics control to ramp up police assistance overseas, even as it was confronting an intensifying crisis of political legitimacy back home on Capitol Hill. The OPS's turn toward narcotics control would prove prescient, given how its responsibilities were eventually transferred to successor agencies, such as the new Drug Enforcement Administration (DEA) and the BINL. These imperial continuities are most clearly exemplified by the five OPS agents that "remained overseas in official capacities after the phase out of police assistance, now as 'narcotics advisors.'"[51]

When USAID describes its alternative development programming in Afghanistan, it sets up an opposition between its own market-based interventions and other approaches to counternarcotics that instead prioritize law enforcement or stabilization objectives. While development and police training might both be "construed as fungible activit[ies] intended to achieve security" in the Afghan countryside, only the latter intervenes on rural communities with "intertwin[ed] discourses and practices of criminalization and racialization," heightening their vulnerability to violence work.[52] Under such conditions, alternative development becomes not only the antithesis of more conventional forms of counternarcotics work, but also the antidote to some of its worst consequences. This is, however, a convenient fiction. Alternative development, I argue, cannot be understood in isolation from the longer history of racialized order management, police modernization, and public safety work that I traced above. Not only was USAID formerly implicated in the overseas work of police training, but it also made the calculated decision to latch on to narcotics assistance as a way of maintaining its grip over the global public safety advisory effort. The institutional continuities between the OPS, the DEA, and the BINL, in turn, emphasize the need for a more expansive conception of alternative development as a form of *slow violence work.*

In Seigel's book on state power and the limits of police, she defines violence work as "work that relies upon violence or the threat thereof." It is through violence work, Seigel emphasizes, that "police realize . . . the core power of the state." In the concluding chapter, however, Seigel posits the need for a broader critique that also exposes the "lethal capacity of state-*market* violence inflicted at home and abroad."[53] Building on Seigel, I argue that USAID development professionals are also violence workers, in the sense that they help realize the core power of the state–market nexus. Contrary to USAID's lofty claims, alternative development in Afghanistan was not geared toward alleviating the geographies of inequality, slow violence, and organized abandonment produced by global capitalism, but rather toward reproducing them.

If the alternative development, law enforcement, and stabilization approaches to counternarcotics share an investment in reshaping rural Afghanistan through slow and spectacular forms of violence work, then it is also unsurprising that, given the transnational circulation of imperial order management techniques and technologies, they might also traffic in broken windows thinking. What these supposedly distinct elements of the Afghan counternarcotics campaign take for granted is the idea that poppy cultivation is a visible manifestation of disorder that can stand in for more serious problems, such as rural poverty, transnational crime, or insurgency. Because broken windows is an elastic concept that can be made to mean different things, how it translated into operational practice varied between projects. Some forms of counternarcotics, chiefly eradication, targeted the visible sign of disorder itself—the poppy field—prioritizing its excision from the rural landscape. Others, such as alternative development, intervened on rural ecosystems, championing a politics of community uplift that aimed to dissuade beneficiary households from breaking windows—or growing poppies—in the first place.

On the surface, the latter approach seems less violent than the former. But they reconverge when they reframe Afghan poppy cultivators as the true broken windows plaguing rural communities. Whether poppy cultivators are criminal actors who have chosen to engage in deviant behavior or rational economic subjects who just need developmental guidance, they become a "threat to the already existing normative order."[54] If USAID believed that it could neutralize this threat by transforming poppy cultivators into farmer entrepreneurs, the regional opium complex instead offered them access to another, proven infrastructure for building, sustaining, and managing rural life.[55] Given the illegal nature of poppy cultivation, the complex has historically depended upon smaller-scale farmers to supply opium resin. From a security perspective, larger monocropping operations are more likely to be targeted by counternarcotics operations. But, perhaps more importantly, poppy cultivation is not easily mechanized, making economies of scale elusive. The task of scoring poppy capsules so that opium resin can be harvested, for example, is still largely carried out by hand. It is for this reason that Afghan narco-entrepreneurs are perennially concerned with securing steady access to both land and unskilled labor.[56]

Over time, then, southern Afghanistan became a contact zone between two competing projects of rural life making. In a conversation with the historian Robin Kelley that was held in the wake of the 2014 police murders of Eric Garner and Michael Brown, Fred Moten argued that "to fix a broken window is to fix another way of imagining the world, to literally fix it, to destroy it, to regulate it, to exclude it, to incarcerate it . . . but also, at the same time, to incorporate it, to capitalize upon it, to exploit it, to accumulate it."[57] If the USAID complex, through alternative development, sought to "fix" rural Afghans by incorporating them into broader racial capitalist systems of exploitation and accumulation, we might also argue, following Moten, that poppy cultivation offered rural Afghans an alternative way of relating to local, regional, and global economies. As Operation Enduring Freedom ran its course, these two modes of infrastructural power worked at cross-purposes. Rural Afghanistan became a space of infrastructural friction, where fantasies of marketization and circulation grated against the lived materialities and social relations that leave poppy cultivation as the only practical choice for marginalized farmers struggling to make ends meet. Under such asymmetrical conditions of imperial encounter, poppy cultivation can be read as a vernacular practice of resistance: one rooted in the "ordinary work" of living on, making do, and survival.[58] This was especially true for the smaller-scale and land-poor farmers who, from 2009 onward, were gradually displaced from southern Afghanistan's traditional agricultural regions by an intensified civil–military war on poppy cultivation. These farmers settled in remote deserts, where they relied on poppy cultivation as a precarious strategy for eking out a subsistence living. But even if poppy cultivation allowed for the reproduction of marginalized Afghan life under conditions of extreme duress, this is, to paraphrase Lauren Berlant, "not identical to making it or oneself better, or a response to the structural conditions of a collective failure to thrive, but to making a less bad experience." Survival, in such a context, is articulated as *slow death*, which Berlant defines as a form of historical existence defined by conditions of physical and mental deterioration, crisis ordinariness, and truncated life. Berlant here is more pessimistic than other scholars who have also reflected on the political potential in everyday acts of survival or making do. But the question nonetheless remains: when racialized and marginalized subjects are "increasingly devoted to the work of merely reproducing their lives," in Neferti Tadiar's words, what forms of resistance remain within the horizon of the possible?[59]

As a way of answering this question, I track the evolution of these geographies of infrastructural power, friction, and resistance through the different phases of the U.S. empire-state's post-9/11 counterinsurgency in southern Afghanistan. More specifically, I show how the effort to wean Afghan farmers off of poppy cultivation went from being a largely civilian problem of either "rural development" or "law enforcement" to a fundamentally civil–military one of "stabilization." The civilian "rural development" approach was exemplified by USAID's Alternative Livelihoods Program for the Southern Region of Afghanistan, or ALP/S. First launched by Chemonics International in 2005, ALP/S championed "value chains" and "agribusiness clusters" as the solution to southern Afghanistan's poppy problem. Chemonics believed that establishing an enabling environment for agribusiness activity would generate sufficient "trickle-down benefits" to discourage farmers from cultivating poppies.[60] Instead of being coerced into fixing the countryside's broken windows problem through violence work, Afghan communities could be induced through the right combination of incentives into shouldering such responsibilities themselves. What resulted, however, was a thoroughly uneven geography of rural development, one that counterintuitively intensified poppy cultivation in southern Afghanistan.

"The Real Deal"

On December 22, 2001, Hamid Karzai exercised his newfound powers as the leader of the recently established Afghan Transitional Administration to pass an edict criminalizing poppy cultivation.[61] Karzai's decision was predictably unpopular among rural households, who were celebrating the military defeat of the Taliban regime by recultivating poppies.[62] At this early stage of the occupation, the Karzai regime lacked the ability to enforce its ban. International stakeholders therefore began clamoring for the U.S. empire-state to take charge of the nascent counternarcotics campaign.[63] Antonio Maria Costa—then the executive director of the United Nations Office on Drugs and Crime (UNODC)—was typical in this regard, arguing that the U.S. could not hope to defeat terrorism without "going against drug trafficking."[64] Costa described Afghanistan as being "at a crossroads": "either (i) energetic interdiction measures are taken now, and supported by the international community, or (ii) the drug cancer in Afghanistan will keep spreading and metastasize into corruption, violence, and terrorism—within and beyond the country's borders."[65] While Costa here does not explicitly invoke the language of broken windows, his racialized conflation of crime and subversion, as well as his commitment to an oncological metaphor, would undoubtedly be familiar to the first boosters of order-maintenance policing, who similarly described the South Bronx of the 1970s as an "urban cancer" that "unless checked," would infect the rest of the city, and perhaps even, the very fabric of the nation-state itself.[66]

Karzai legitimized the transnational circulation of these discourses when he endorsed the UNODC's framing of Afghanistan's poppy problem as a "cancer" requiring intense "chemotherapy." Karzai upped the stakes by warning that poppy cultivation was more dangerous to the project of developing Afghanistan than the Soviet occupation, the bloody civil war that followed, or even contemporary terrorism. "Just as our people fought a holy war against the Soviets," Karzai proclaimed, "so we will wage jihad against poppies."[67] The effect of Karzai's rhetoric here is not merely to criminalize poppy cultivation, but also to pathologize it as a malignant disease that must be eliminated irrespective of the short-term damage that this would inflict on households participating in local narco-economies to make ends meet. Given the urgency of Karzai's call for chemotherapy, it was likely triggered by a conjunction of factors. While the Taliban's 2001 ban had confined poppy cultivation to the Northern Alliance strongholds of Samangan and Badakshan, by 2004 it had expanded to all thirty-two of Afghanistan's provinces (see Figures 10 and 11). It became particularly entrenched in Helmand, Kandahar, Uruzgan, Nangarhar, Laghman, and Kunar, key borderland provinces that were showing clear signs of infiltration by the Taliban's successors, or the neo-Taliban.[68]

Extrapolating from these trends, commentators speculated that the neo-Taliban had reactivated their longer-standing linkages to the opium trade. These fears were soon confirmed by reports that neo-Taliban forces were once again offering protection and logistics services

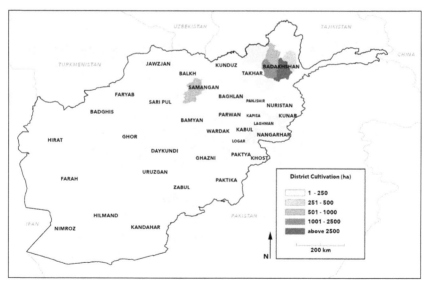

FIGURE 10. *Afghanistan poppy cultivation in 2001. Map by Richard Nisa, adapted from UNODC, Afghanistan Opium Survey 2004 (New York: United Nations, 2004).*

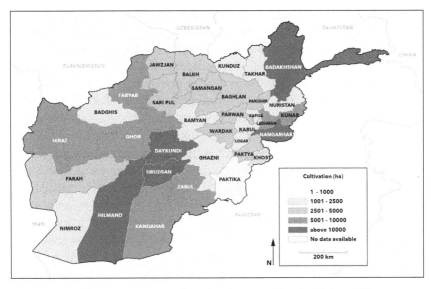

FIGURE 11. *Afghanistan poppy cultivation in 2004. Map by Richard Nisa, adapted from UNODC, Afghanistan Opium Survey 2004 (New York: United Nations, 2004).*

to narco-entrepreneurs.[69] Afghan policy makers nonetheless remained hesitant to endorse a militarization of counternarcotics. Karzai's minister of finance, Ashraf Ghani, instead emphasized that a "winning" counternarcotics strategy would have "four key elements." These were a "long-term" plan for training Afghanistan's police forces; a commitment to stimulating economic growth by "rebuilding the country physically"; an agricultural strategy for marketizing rural Afghanistan through land reform, microcredit, agroindustrialization, and trade; and a mechanism for reestablishing government control across the countryside.[70] Ghani's vision here is noteworthy for reframing poppy cultivation as a problem best solved by assembling the right mix of infrastructural incentives and disincentives necessary to transition farming households toward alternative livelihoods. Counternarcotics, in its ideal form, would double as a conduit for infrastructural power.

At this stage of the occupation, the U.S. military had no interest in articulating a competing vision for counternarcotics, which it framed as a form of "mission creep" that would siphon valuable resources away from the intensifying war on the neo-Taliban.[71] For this reason, the U.S.

empire-state's contributions to the Afghan counternarcotics campaign were initially provided by three civilian agencies. Each one assumed lead responsibility for supporting a different counternarcotics "pillar." The DEA backstopped interdiction operations across Afghanistan, working with local police forces to seize precursor chemicals, destroy clandestine laboratories, and arrest drug traffickers.[72] But if drug warlords have always been familiar to domestic publics as acceptable targets of violence work, the widespread popularity of poppy cultivation as a rural livelihood strategy emphasized the need for a more comprehensive counternarcotics response. By criminalizing poppy cultivation and making eradication the second pillar of the Afghan counternarcotics campaign, the U.S. empire-state set ordinary Afghan households on a direct collision course with emerging law enforcement infrastructures. The U.S. State Department's BINL contributed to this eradication effort in two ways. First, the BINL hired a private security firm, DynCorp International, to train a centralized police force capable of carrying out eradication in insecure environments.[73] Second, the BINL provided financial and technical assistance to provincial governors who had launched their own eradication efforts. One BINL initiative rewarded provincial governors with $135 every time they eradicated a hectare of poppy.[74] Another tasked DynCorp with dispatching "Poppy Elimination" teams to seven of the top opium-producing provinces—Helmand, Kandahar, Farah, Uruzgan, Nangarhar, Badakshan, and Balkh—where they supported governor-led eradication efforts with a mix of community outreach, development liaison, and information gathering.[75]

This multiscalar combination of centralized and governor-led eradication was seemingly vindicated by some early success stories. The most widely cited example is Nangarhar, which by 2004 had more or less become poppy free. Eradication statistics, however, tell a more complex story, exposing how interventions at both the national and provincial scales were consistently falling short of predetermined targets.[76] Such difficulties are potentially explained by the fact that eradication was doing little to slow down the trade in illicit drugs, while also generating widespread resentment among rural farming communities.[77] As early as 2005, the UNODC was warning that "eradicated fields leave families in economic distress, trigger humanitarian disaster, and increase the temptation to join the insurgency."[78] This alienation regularly manifested itself through violent forms of protest. At the height of the 2005 growing season, the Afghan government dispatched eradication units to the Maiwand district of Kandahar, where they encountered armed farmers blocking access to local poppy fields. The two sides exchanged gunfire that killed at least one Afghan farmer and wounded several others. Over the next eight days, the resistance spread to the Panjwayi district, forcing local officials to solicit help from the Karzai administration, which proved less than forthcoming.[79] In Nagarhar, too, the ban on poppy cultivation similarly "imposed a toll on the economic well being of the population" that "changed its level of support for the government." Between 2004 and 2006, farmers in Nangarhar reluctantly complied with the provincial government's ban on poppy cultivation. In the spring of 2007, however, farmers began to meet eradication units with resistance. On April 2, more than 1,000 residents of Bati Kot protested the ban by blocking the Torkham–Jalalabad highway for an extended period of time. In the ensuing clash with government security forces, twelve villagers were injured, while a further twenty residents were arrested.[80]

What lies at the heart of DynCorp's work in Afghanistan, then, is the conceit that a professionalized police force could surgically eradicate the poppy fields spreading across rural Afghanistan, paving the way for the USAID complex to usher in a future of development and modernization. But instead of preventing insurgency, police interventions sparked riots and blockades, which had to be pacified through further rounds of violence work. The conditions were therefore ripe for USAID to claim a central role in diffusing these tensions. Drawing from prior experiences of carrying out counternarcotics activities in Afghanistan, USAID argued that it could complement the "anger" of eradication with the "mercy" of alternative development. The United Nations General Assembly formally defines alternative development as a "process to prevent and eliminate the illicit cultivation of plants containing narcotics and psychotropic substances through specifically designed rural development measures" that recognize "the particular socio-economic characteristics of the target communities and groups."[81] According to David Mansfield, this definition is vague and confusing, offering an "unsatisfactory" shorthand for any form of rural development taking place in a "drugs environment."[82] USAID's first opportunity to clarify its vision for alternative development in southern Afghanistan came in 2005. This was when USAID solicited bids for three different Alternative Livelihood Programs, each one targeting a different region of Afghanistan. The objective of these programs was, in the words of one prospective implementing partner, to "improve the licit income opportunities and well-being of thousands of rural families" in key poppy cultivating provinces by integrating them into a "rapidly growing" horticultural economy.[83] This implementing partner was Chemonics International, whose obvious obsession with market integration undoubtedly helped it secure the four-year, $119 million USAID contract to implement the Alternative Livelihoods Program for southern Afghanistan. Although Chemonics was first formed in 1975 to implement a fertilizer program in Afghanistan, it had recently become famous for accomplishing alternative development "miracles" in Latin America.[84] USAID's expectation was that Chemonics would achieve similar results in Helmand and Kandahar.

Unfortunately for Chemonics, the usual challenges inherent to carrying out alternative development activities in a "drugs environment" were exacerbated by conditions of intensifying insurgency and (para)military violence. By the time Chemonics launched the ALP/S in 2005, the neo-Taliban resurgence in southern Afghanistan was well under way. As early as 2004, the neo-Taliban was dispatching infiltration teams to Helmand and Kandahar. In addition to skirmishing with Afghan National Army patrols, assassinating local officials, distributing "night letters," and establishing shadow institutions, these teams also stirred up unrest by manipulating intertribal rivalries as well as longer-standing resentments over ongoing forms of warlord predation. These efforts bore fruit, and by June 2006 key districts had fallen under neo-Taliban control.[85]

It is impossible to understand ALP/S's trajectory in isolation from this context of intensifying violence. Given the extent to which eradication was fanning the flames of insurgency in contested districts, and cognizant of the central role that poppy cultivation has always played in helping rural households cope with crushing poverty, Chemonics focused the ALP/S on transitioning farmers in southern Afghanistan away from subsistence production toward "value-adding, agro-processing endeavors."[86] Here, Chemonics' goal was to help local farmers interface with global value chains in mutually beneficial ways. The origins of the value chain concept can be traced back to the foundational work of Terence Hopkins and Immanuel Wallerstein, who posited the existence of transnational "commodity chains"—networks of "labour and production processes whose end result is a finished commodity"—that serve as the backbone of a globalized economy.[87] This pathbreaking work proved influential among political economists, who gradually shifted the focus from commodity to value chains. Gary Gereffi, in particular, uses the value chain heuristic to describe how developing countries often access global markets by positioning themselves as suppliers—of raw materials, of intermediary commodities, of unskilled labor—to multinational enterprises. By virtue of their status as "gatekeepers," these "lead firms" invariably dictate how developing "suppliers" participate in global value chains. Understanding these processes can help economic actors "upgrade" their ability to capture greater shares of the "value" that is added to commodities over the life of the production process.[88] As Marion Werner and her coauthors note, this kind of thinking has found a receptive audience among development professionals, who have demonstrated a voracious appetite for "new ways of explaining how globalized trade and investment flows can be harnessed to promote outcomes such as international competitiveness, growth, and employment." This was particularly the case among an expanding cadre of USAID employees and contractors whose various experiences had convinced them to seek out a more active role in "making markets work." For these actors, value chain frameworks offered a way of moving beyond problematic laissez-faire approaches to capitalist integration while still foregrounding markets as the "means and ends of development."[89]

This was precisely how USAID and Chemonics deployed the value chain concept in southern Afghanistan. The starting point of Chemonics' analysis was the transnational infrastructure for transforming poppy resin into heroin, which it admired as a "lucrative, model value chain" that excelled at supplying Afghan cultivators with credit, water, labor, land, and inputs. Chemonics' goal was to reorganize the agricultural "environment" of southern Afghanistan by re-creating similar value chain infrastructures for other alternative crops. To overcome this "enormous challenge," Chemonics mobilized a combination of private- and public-sector resources to establish "agro-industrialized zones" across the project area.[90] Here, Chemonics was likely drawing inspiration from the "clusters" framework that came to prominence in the 1980s when a group of scholars began extolling the virtues of agglomerating smaller-scale enterprises for the purposes of helping developing countries realize greater economic efficiencies and market competitiveness.[91] While the cluster model was useful for mapping localized geographical configurations of economic activity, it was less suited to grasping the increasingly globalized nature of capitalist accumulation in the late twentieth and early twenty-first centuries. In hopes of finding some way of jumping scales, development professionals began to explore the potential of synergizing the cluster and value chain frameworks.[92] Their aim was to identify connections "between the upgrading prospects of clustered firms and the governance dynamics of the global value chains in which these firms participate."[93]

Chemonics drew on these frameworks to upscale alternative development activities in southern Afghanistan. By and large, Chemonics targeted broader regions with "area-based development [strategies]" in which "discrete economic interventions became linked and supported each other in integrated clusters."[94] Anchored by key urban nodes for infrastructure and service development, these agricultural clusters were supposed to generate "trickle-down" benefits for individual farmers.[95] Chemonics identified seven different livelihood strategies as having a strong potential for clustering and upgrading: horticulture, dairy, wheat flour, livestock feed, fish farms, drip irrigation, and oilseed.[96] Chemonics eventually selected livestock, horticulture, and seed production for further agribusiness development. Chemonics devoted the majority of its resources to developing the regional "livestock complex" into a "major driver of licit economic development in southern Afghanistan."[97] Chemonics collaborated with local producers, subcontractors, and agricultural associations to demonstrate the commercial viability of livestock-based agribusinesses, including a commercial feed mill, veterinary networks, dairy production, fattened lamb breeding, a price information system, and rural financial services. Chemonics complemented these efforts by developing a secondary horticultural cluster focused on demonstration and market trial activities, as well as a stand-alone wheat seed distribution program that would provide farmers with a stop-gap alternative to poppy.[98]

The above analysis clarifies that Chemonics conceptualizes the small-scale agribusiness as the ideal building block of a reinvigorated agricultural economy. This vision assumed the existence of a critical mass of farmers eager to transform themselves into "farmers-as-businessmen."[99] Chemonics tried to accelerate this process by making various business development services available to rural households. In addition to improving access to credit and price information systems, supporting local business associations, and launching mass media campaigns, Chemonics even drew up plans to construct an industrial park, which it pitched as a "concentrated version of the more dispersed clusters" that would provide "developed sites for business persons investing in agroprocessing."[100] In combination, these various alternative development interventions show how Chemonics used the ALP/S to establish the physical and virtual infrastructures necessary for agribusiness cluster and value chain development across southern Afghanistan. The intended effect of the ALP/S was to replace one of the most visible symbols of the Afghan insurgency—poppy fields—with other, equally visible symbols of capitalist modernization: state-of-the-art factories, gleaming industrial parks, and bustling market communities. What the ALP/S promised Afghan beneficiaries was a frictionless geography of market efficiency that would evenly distribute economic benefits generated in very particular spaces across the countryside.

Chemonics' ability to wield infrastructural power over farmers, however, was gradually constrained by the intensifying violence of the insurgency. In the spring of 2006, neo-Taliban forces launched an unprecedented offensive that took both the U.S.-led coalition and the North Atlantic Treaty Organization's newly established International Security Assistance Force (ISAF) by surprise. The neo-Taliban ratcheted up the frequency of suicide bombing attacks sixfold, which, in turn, contributed to a 45 percent increase in the number of U.S. and ISAF casualties.[101] ISAF countered by dispatching thousands of British and Canadian soldiers to Helmand and Kandahar provinces, respectively. ISAF, however, severely underestimated the strength and morale of its adversary. Its counteroffensive was too small to reverse the neo-Taliban advance, yet "just large enough to antagonize the local population and drive them further into the arms of the insurgency."[102] British forces, in particular, defended key districts in Helmand—including Now Zad, Sangin, Musa Qala, and Garmser—through the indiscriminate use of violence, killing civilians, and destroying homes in the process. ISAF's inability to defeat the insurgency had implications for the ALP/S. According to USAID's Office of Inspector General, British forces determined the areas in which Chemonics would be allowed to operate. Owing to an upswing in convoy hijackings, suicide bombings, and improvised explosive device attacks, the British forced Chemonics to abandon prime poppy-cultivating districts—such as Nad-i-Ali and Marja—in favor of safer field sites, specifically the villages surrounding Lashkar Gah.[103]

Chemonics adapted by replacing its initial alternative development strategy with one that promised to "win the confidence of the population." No longer concerned with developing regional agribusiness clusters, Chemonics reconceptualized ALP/S as an "attitudinal and behavioural change program" that would "create a critical mass of leaders and supporters from the grassroots upwards to the provincial level in favour of the possibility of socio-economic change."[104] Worried that "market-driven development" was fast becoming an empty slogan among target communities, Chemonics rebranded itself as a "deal maker" that could plug local farmers into global value chains.[105] Chemonics, for example, began to promote local agricultural fairs as a way for "producers, traders, buyers, investors, and input suppliers to make deals and contacts, show off Helmand agriculture, and learn new technologies and opportunities."[106] One particular fair hosted more than 1,700 people, who apparently conducted "$5,404 in actual sales on the day of the event, and $70,874 of agriculture and related products after the fair."[107] Chemonics encouraged farmers to participate in these fairs in the hope that they would enter into longer lasting agribusiness arrangements, such as contract farming.

When read together, the reports that Chemonics produced to keep USAID informed on ALP/S's progress tell a very particular story about how alternative development programming unfolded in southern Afghanistan during the early days of the neo-Taliban insurgency. What began as an attempt to impose a top-down vision of market integration on a fragmented rural landscape flexibly transitioned into a more grassroots effort to provide local communities with the "attitudinal and behavioural change" assistance they needed to bring about market-driven futures of socioeconomic transformation. Especially when compared to the forms of order-maintenance policing that were subjecting rural communities to various forms of economic hardship and slow violence, the ALP/S seems like a relatively beneficial program with the potential to serve as a model for further alternative development interventions across Afghanistan.

This is a narrative that obscures more than it reveals. One way of critically unpacking it might be to close read formal audits of the ALP/S.[108] Auditors such as Checchi and Company Consulting (CCC) were skeptical of Chemonics' commitment to sustainable development, arguing that the ALP/S's agribusiness components generally produced quick impacts rather than long-term effects. Chemonics may have constructed feed mills, trained paravets, cultivated orchards, and established micronurseries, but there was no indication that these interventions could be sustained when funding ran out.[109] CCC argues that nothing changed when Chemonics switched the ALP/S's focus to Afghan attitudes and behaviors, as the contractor only provided training in the "strict sense of the word."[110] When Chemonics did conduct training activities, their effect was to reproduce traditional gendered divisions of agricultural labor. Checchi specifically slammed the ALP/S's impact on women for being "very weak or nil."[111] Early on in the life of the project, Chemonics pledged to hire a "Senior Gender and Economic Safety Specialist" who would find "appropriate" ways of integrating women and other marginalized groups into local agricultural economies.[112] Chemonics' own gender participation metrics suggest that this objective remained unfulfilled. The ALP/S trained only 30 women in agricultural practices, compared to 43,030 men. Similarly, only 202 women received seeds and fertilizers, as opposed to 110,478 men. Checchi notes that Chemonics targeted women for training in business skills, but "even this was very low."[113] Given these skewed gender dynamics, it is also likely that Chemonics' attempts at nurturing a regional "livestock complex" had the unintended consequence of masculinizing one of the only livelihood strategies that women could participate in to help boost household incomes.[114]

Checchi's most damning criticism of the ALP/S, however, was that it may have encouraged farmers in southern Afghanistan to cultivate poppy. Checchi argues that UNODC maps show a simultaneous intensification and concentration of poppy cultivation in key agricultural districts straddling the Helmand River. These were the districts that Chemonics targeted with the ALP/S. Checchi hypothesizes that the ALP/S made cash, land, and labor available for agricultural production in Helmand and Kandahar at the moment when counterinsurgent forces were ramping up their war on poppy cultivation elsewhere in Afghanistan.[115] As a result, southern Afghanistan effectively pulled all of the poppy cultivation that was being pushed out of other provinces.

Like the Helmand Valley Authority before it, Chemonics exacerbated the very problem that it had been tasked with solving.

Even after accounting for all of these problems, Checchi still described the ALP/S as "mostly successful."[116] But "mostly successful" for whom? From the outset of the ALP/S, Chemonics channeled resources to communities where conditions for economic development were already favorable. Chemonics planned on eventually expanding the ALP/S into some of the more remote regions of Helmand and Kandahar. Farmers in these regions, however, spent the life of the project "[waiting] their turn."[117] Given that these farmers were generally more prone to cultivating poppy, their eventual abandonment was highly problematic. Nor was this uneven geography of alternative development assistance unique to ALP/S. As Mansfield and Pain observe, market-based forms of alternative development that prioritize horticulture and livestock invariably favor the most well-resourced and integrated farmers, while simultaneously ignoring the "interests and needs of the poor."[118] The Afghan government tried to tackle this problem by revising its National Agricultural Development Framework in 2008 to foreground the "middle-scale farmer"—defined as anyone who owns between one to fifty hectares of irrigated land—as a key "backbone for sustainable growth."[119] While this change was meant to bring about a more egalitarian distribution of resources, it nonetheless reinforced widespread understandings of male landowners as the rightful protagonists of rural development.[120]

The untold story of the ALP/S, then, is that it exacerbated existing geographies of uneven development, channeling capital and resources to relatively privileged groups of rural households while subjecting others to various forms of slow violence and organized abandonment, or what Ruth Wilson Gilmore names in her famous definition of racism as "group-differentiated vulnerability to premature death."[121] As an infrastructural technology of racial liberalism, ALP/S exemplifies how the USAID complex has continued to "[innovate] racial procedures beyond color lines," crafting "new terms of racialized stigma" (farmers-as-businessmen) out of complex articulations of gendered, geographical, colonial, class, and other social differences.[122] Chemonics' refusal to acknowledge the growing levels of polarization along class and gender lines was not unique to ALP/S, but rather a defining characteristic of alternative development work writ large. In the context of southern Afghanistan, U.S. counterinsurgents were quick to repurpose the ALP/S into an alternative development program that was clearly shaped by the evolving geographies of the military occupation. As security conditions deteriorated in the south, the USAID complex found it increasingly difficult to operate independently of military forces, who were starting to rediscover counternarcotics as a central element of their war on the neo-Taliban. What emerged was a new kind of militarized alternative development, one closely synchronized with stability operations and full-spectrum counterinsurgency.

This gradual turn toward a stabilization model of alternative development was not smooth but rather highly contentious. While certain members of the USAID complex championed the new stabilization approach, others offered staunchly market-based critiques of flagship projects, including International Relief and Development's Afghanistan Vouchers for Increased Production in Agriculture (AVIPA). These critics dismissed the stabilization approach as a stopgap that only generated quick impacts among local populations. From this perspective, stabilization appears as fundamentally antithetical to development, which is supposedly defined by its longer-term commitment to addressing the root causes of poverty and marginalization through market integration. Such a framing is undergirded by a problematic disavowal of how development in Afghanistan has historically been yoked to a politics of race war, counterinsurgency, and violence work. The real problem with the stabilization model is not that it refused to conform with an idealized conception of how development should be carried out in the field. Rather, it is that stabilization-style projects—including AVIPA as well as the Helmand Food Zone Initiative—carried forward ALP/S's tendency to gloss over thorny questions of land tenure. In so doing, they dispossessed land-poor households of their access to the means of subsistence, heightening their "group-differentiated vulnerability" to various forms of slow violence, organized abandonment, and premature death.

Stabilizing Southern Afghanistan

Beginning in 2007, the U.S. military's assessment of counternarcotics as mission creep slowly shifted. Military leaders were undoubtedly concerned by the latest geographical reorganization of poppy cultivation in

Afghanistan. The UNODC's 2007 poppy cultivation report maps these shifts, showing how Afghanistan's insurgency and drug trade were flourishing in the "same lawless terrain," often in "mutually reinforcing ways."[123] Within a year, concerted eradication efforts had increased the number of poppy-free provinces from six to thirteen. Yet levels of poppy cultivation remained at an all-time high. Figure 12 explains this contradiction by highlighting a concentration of poppy cultivation in Helmand and Kandahar.[124]

The UNODC seized upon this geographical trend as clear-cut evidence for treating poppies as a military problem. Helmand and Kandahar were not only two of the "richest" provinces in Afghanistan, they were also neo-Taliban strongholds. If poppy cultivation was once a symptom of poverty, it was now inextricably linked with insurgency. Neo-Taliban insurgents, the UNODC argued, were funding their operations by extracting rents from local narco-economies. For this reason, the U.S. military needed to become more directly involved in the counternarcotics effort. Otherwise, Afghanistan would collapse under the combined "blows of drugs and insurgency."[125]

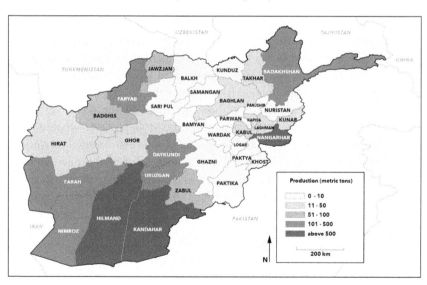

FIGURE 12. *Opium production in Afghanistan by province, 2007. Map by Richard Nisa, adapted from UNODC, Afghanistan Opium Survey 2007 (New York: United Nations, 2007)*

Many commentators have debunked the UNODC's claims as "misguided." Drawing on the UNODC's own data, Mansfield and Pain show that "rich" households in Helmand earned an average daily income of $1 per person, which was only $0.30 more than their "poor" counterparts in Balkh.[126] And yet, farmers in both provinces still fell under the threshold of "extreme poverty" set by the UN Millennium Development Goals.[127] Furthermore, while the neo-Taliban was taxing the drug trade—an income stream that the UNODC conservatively values at approximately $125 million per year—to pay for wages, guns, and supplies, these "protection services" were not their only source of funding.[128] Nonetheless, the UNODC's metaphorization of "drug money" as the "oxygen in the air that allows [insurgents] to operate" was gradually mainstreamed among U.S. war managers. These arguments were used to depoliticize and delegitimize both the neo-Taliban and poppy cultivators.[129] In September 2009, Antonio Maria Costa suggested that "drug money . . . is starting to trump ideology," in the sense that it has "gone from being a funding source for [the neo-Taliban] to becoming an end itself."[130] The neo-Taliban, Costa implied, should be understood not as an insurgent movement fighting to address political grievances, but rather as a profit-hungry narco-cartel. Similarly, many U.S. counternarcotics experts were representing Afghan farmers as nothing more than greedy opportunists who were undeserving of alternative development assistance.[131]

By October 2008, ISAF was publicly framing the narcotics–insurgency nexus as a "force protection issue" that had to be dealt with in a "military way."[132] Within a month, the Pentagon gave U.S. forces the green light to support counternarcotics activities across rural Afghanistan. This decision proved controversial among some U.S. military and civilian allies.[133] And yet, the U.S. military's newfound commitment to counternarcotics was consistent with its doctrinal turn toward stability operations and population-centric counterinsurgency. Relevant army field manuals envision U.S. soldiers playing a "significant role" in helping local populations generate economic opportunities, establish trading linkages, reconstruct destroyed infrastructures, and develop free markets.[134] In largely rural Afghanistan, where agriculture remains a "cornerstone" of the national economy, this meant working with farmers to carry out everyday farming tasks—such as rebuilding irrigation systems or assessing livestock herds—alongside conventional kinetic operations.[135]

In theory, this endorsement of market-based agricultural development was supposed to open up spaces for collaboration with USAID. In practice, the military's conception of infrastructural power rarely synergized with USAID's. The U.S. military did find an eager collaborator in Richard Holbrooke, who, from January 2009 until his death in December 2010, served as the U.S. special envoy for Afghanistan and Pakistan. Holbrooke was responsible for managing the civilian component of Obama's "new strategy for Afghanistan and Pakistan."[136] Unveiled on March 27, 2009, it called for a "surge" in troops and civilian support to hotspots of insurgency across Afghanistan. The massive civil–military buildup was supposed to provide the manpower necessary to wage a comprehensive counterinsurgency campaign among the Afghan people. The Obama administration was particularly keen on making counternarcotics a central pillar of the surge. In the years leading up to the surge, Holbrooke had been a vocal critic of the Afghan eradication effort, describing it as the "single most ineffective program in the history of American foreign policy."[137] Consequently, when Obama asked his new special representative to help the Afghan government "develop an economy that isn't dominated by illicit drugs," Holbrooke wasted no time in "phasing out" eradication.[138] As Holbrooke quipped, "We are going to stop making the farmers the victims."[139]

Holbrooke, however, was equally critical of USAID's market-based approach to alternative development in Afghanistan, arguing that it had been "tried elsewhere with almost no success."[140] The interviews I conducted reveal that Holbrooke tried to shake up USAID's Afghan mission by "[coming] in hard," highlighting how "everything is broken," and putting a "block" on procurements.[141] Many alternative development programs were caught in this "limbo period," including Chemonics' follow-up to ALP/S, Ideas Driving Economic Alternatives—South (IDEA-South). Chemonics first proposed IDEA-South to Holbrooke in April 2009 as a plan to "support market-based value chains that could independently compete with poppy and provide a longer-term incentive for farmers." Convinced that Chemonics had failed to learn the lessons of the ALP/S, Holbrooke wanted to redesign IDEA-South into a "New Deal" for Afghan farmers, based on a "soup-to-nuts" system of subsidies.[142] Chemonics and Holbrooke could not compromise, forcing USAID to cancel IDEA-South on June 14, 2009.

What emerged in its place? Guided by the belief that alternative development should serve as a "counterinsurgency-stability tool," Holbrooke replaced IDEA-South with "rapid and targeted assistance deliveries" in "areas that have been cleared and secured by coalition and Afghan forces."[143] These "quick response" programs exemplified what the special inspector general for Afghan reconstruction would later describe as the stabilization model of alternative development.[144] By this phase of the occupation, USAID was no stranger to stability operations. USAID personnel had acquired substantial stabilization experience through their contributions to provincial reconstruction teams and village stability platforms. The Pentagon first conceived the former in the early 2000s as "super-sized" stabilization teams that partnered soldiers with civilian counterinsurgents to interface with local populations and facilitate reconstruction efforts in "non-permissive environments."[145] In so doing, provincial reconstruction teams took over some of the stability operations responsibilities traditionally associated with U.S. special forces, who were now free to apply their expertise in Afghanistan's most remote and insecure districts, setting up village stability platforms, which were temporary bases for conducting patrols, assembling militias, and nurturing local entrepreneurs.[146] From 2006 onward, U.S. Special Operations Command began recruiting USAID development advisors to support these platforms. According to one advisor, this relationship was mutually beneficial. Special Forces soldiers became more adept at "shaping" the local human terrain, while USAID advisors gained access to military resources as well as the ability to operate in areas that would otherwise be considered off-limits.[147]

USAID's enrollment in stability operations has always been controversial. One USAID director enthusiastically described their experience working with the U.S. military as a "love fest."[148] Although they were initially "totally allergic to the US military," by 2013, they had a change of heart. As they summarized to me, "I love them, and they love us, and we really have a deep respect and appreciation for each other now." Others were more practical, offering examples of how "integrating civilian agencies down to the tactical level" can incentivize communities to support counterinsurgency objectives.[149] Critics such as Elaine Kingsley, however, were loath to name these activities development:

The military doesn't do development. They do hearts and minds—
also known as quick impact—projects. They build, they repair,
they hand out. They do things with a short-term goal in mind
and . . . much of it does not address a root cause. It does not fix
the problem. It's a palliative. . . . It is like a band-aid. . . . It's a
piece of the development equation, but it isn't development, because as we have always said, development takes a long time. It's
not about throwing lots of money. It's a process, it's about local
ownership . . . and when you are fighting a war and [you] tell a
general, "Oh, it's going to take us five years to really show a long-
term impact," he doesn't want to fight for five years, he wants it
over and done with.[150]

The thrust of Kingsley's criticisms here is to position stabilization as the
inverse of development. Whereas development plans for the future, stabilization is mired in the here and now, undermining security instead
of shoring it up. As Kingsley makes clear, the problem was not so much
the goal of civil–military cooperation, which was a "good" concept.
Rather, it was that civil–military interventions were poorly executed
and more likely to negatively impact rural populations, who would then
view USAID as "tainted" by its ties to the U.S. military occupation.[151]

Proponents of civil–military integration might claim that these negative consequences are never the intended outcome of stabilization operations. Critics like Kingsley would disagree. But I also want to push back
against Kingsley's reading of actually existing stabilization as somehow
corrupting or undermining development. Instead, I want to suggest that
what the development, stabilization, and policing approaches to counternarcotics in Afghanistan all share is an imperial connection to longer-
standing genealogies of race war, counterinsurgency, and violence work.
In their distinct yet related attempts to eliminate "discrepant forms of
habitus" and replace them with "rational" ways of being and acting in
the world, each project of imperial order making (re)produced "group-
differentiated vulnerabilities" to slow violence, organized abandonment,
and premature death.[152] The brunt of this slow violence work, as always,
was borne by the most marginalized segments of rural communities.
Much like Chemonics' ALP/S, the stabilization-style alternative development projects that came to define the U.S. surge in the south failed to
account for households that access land in highly precarious ways. Here,

I follow Mansfield and Pain's assertion that "the rise of opium poppy cultivation in Afghanistan has in a sense been a stay of execution on an inexorable decline in the land-based economy of poor households with restricted assets and limited access to resources."[153] Land-poor Afghans have historically relied on poppy cultivation as a bulwark against broader processes of dispossession and displacement. Stabilization practitioners did not attend to these nuances, inadvertently carrying out the dirty work of dispossession that the USAID complex disavows yet nonetheless remains a central prerequisite of market-based alternative development work in the field.

Such a conjunction of stabilization, alternative development, and dispossession is by no means unique to southern Afghanistan. Recent work by Kevin Woods and Teo Ballvé identifies similar processes at work in Myanmar and Colombia, where diverse coalitions of state, military, and private-sector actors have used alternative development programs to dispossess drug-producing farmers of their land and then subsequently channel them into lucrative plantation economies.[154] The experiences of poppy cultivators in southern Afghanistan conform to yet also complicate this narrative of dispossession, displacement, and proletarianization. Stabilization-style alternative development initiatives such as AVIPA or the Helmand Food Zone certainly dispossessed and displaced land-poor poppy cultivators. Southern Afghanistan, in contrast, lacked a robust infrastructure capable of capturing and proletarianizing them into a surplus labor force for agribusiness development. As a result, they were able to resettle in some of the remote desert regions of southern Afghanistan, where, in desperation, they once again turned to poppy cultivation as a viable livelihood strategy. Even under such dire circumstances, poppy cultivation offered land-poor households a method for eluding the long grasp of U.S. infrastructural power, effectively reaffirming its crucial importance as a key subaltern strategy of both resistance and survival.

Making the Desert Bloom, Again

In 2008, Helmand's governor, Golub Mangal, launched a civil–military initiative designed to "open an in-road into poppy country." Under Mangal's leadership, USAID came together with the British Department for International Development and the Helmand Provincial

Reconstruction Team to combine "alternative livelihoods with improved security and governance." The result was a 25,000-hectare Helmand Food Zone (HFZ) near Lashkar Gah where farmers were only permitted to grow licit crops such as wheat.[155]

The HFZ exemplifies an "anger and mercy" approach to counternarcotics. Dell offers a succinct chronology of the HFZ's three phases:

> First, a governor-led public information campaign used local *shuras* to enroll farmers in a program to provide seed/fertilizer for wheat and fodder cultivation. Village elders and farmers have signed no-poppy pledges. Breaking the pledge will make their fields, along with any other poppy fields in these areas, liable to eradication. Second, in early October, the governor's officials distributed seed and fertilizer (or vouchers for them), renewing the no-poppy pledges from recipients. Finally, in January through March, farmers who plant poppy will see their fields eradicated by the governor's police and the Poppy Eradication Force.[156]

In 2008 alone, the HFZ program reportedly provided free wheat seed and fertilizers to over 30,000 poppy cultivators. The initial response was positive, with farmers in Nad-i-Ali, Gereshk, and Garmser moving their land back into wheat production.[157] The UNODC eventually confirmed these trends, reporting at the end of the 2008–2009 growing season that poppy cultivation within the HFZ had declined by 37 percent and had mainly been replaced by cereal crops.[158]

In addition to supporting the HFZ, USAID also funded another "relief and stabilization" program, AVIPA.[159] AVIPA was launched in 2008 by International Relief and Development, who worked closely with the Afghan government to provide distressed farmers living in eighteen provinces with heavily subsidized vouchers that could be exchanged for inputs or training in best agricultural practices. In May 2009, USAID rescaled AVIPA to "provide counterinsurgency-stability programming in Helmand and Kandahar provinces within an agricultural framework."[160] In the run-up to the surge, the U.S. military reportedly asked USAID to prepare stabilization activities that could be implemented on a moment's notice.[161] Holbrooke selected AVIPA—now renamed AVIPA Plus—as one such project. While USAID proposed spending $150 million on AVIPA Plus—itself a "staggering amount of money to disburse over just one year in two insecure provinces"— Holbrooke signaled his commitment to the program by doubling its budget.¹⁶² The component of AVIPA Plus that was specifically focused on southern Afghanistan was called AVIPA Plus South. While AVIPA Plus South followed the voucher-based model of its predecessor, it subsidized seeds and fertilizers at much higher rates. This was done to ensure that AVIPA Plus South provided a "substantial economic benefit" to as many farmers as possible, thereby maximizing its counterinsurgency impact.¹⁶³ AVIPA Plus South also introduced farmers to higher-value crops, launched a suite of cash-for-work activities, and provided microfinance services.

Both the HFZ and AVIPA Plus South were widely represented as counternarcotics success stories. Governor Mangal linked declining levels of poppy cultivation in Helmand to the establishment of the HFZ.¹⁶⁴ Embassy officials made similarly upbeat claims, describing the HFZ program as the "decisive factor in reducing poppy cultivation in Helmand this year."¹⁶⁵ According to one official, local authorities were so impressed by the HFZ that they were demanding that similar initiatives be launched in their own backyards. Insurgents also began targeting wheat distribution centers, seemingly testifying to the HFZ's counterinsurgency prowess.¹⁶⁶

AVIPA Plus South also got off to a successful start. In Nad-i-Ali and Arghandab, elders defied Taliban directives by insisting that villagers participate in the project. Insurgents in Nawa reportedly began laying down their arms, choosing the certainty of cash-for-work wages over the dangers of jihad.¹⁶⁷ By "carpet bombing" Nawa with dollars, AVIPA Plus South "jolted" the local economy by a factor of three to four, substantively impacting the environment of insurgent formation. To locals, district officials, the Marines, and USAID agents, AVIPA Plus South "seemed to be a wonder drug."¹⁶⁸

These sentiments were echoed by one of my interviewees, Infantry Officer Andrew Metcalf. Approximately ten months into Metcalf's Afghan deployment, he took over a battalion based in Kandahar. Metcalf credited AVIPA Plus South with helping land-poor farmers extricate themselves from a "permanent poverty trap." He singled out two aspects of AVIPA Plus South for praise. First, the project discounted the costs of agricultural inputs by up to 90 percent, making them accessible to even the poorest farmers. Second, IRD used local Afghans to "sell the seeds" and "provide the coordination," furnishing them with a sense of ownership over the project. The only problem with AVIPA Plus South— and this was "the problem with a lot of the money in Afghanistan"— was that it was "regulated through such a burdensome bureaucracy." Metcalf recalled:

> AVIPA had a one-year contract, we did one seed distribution, highly, highly beneficial. All the people came back and said, "Hey, we want this again," and other people came, like "Hey, we . . . didn't have this in our area, but we'd be willing to come here to get it." You know, just received rave reviews while [AVIPA Plus South's] money ran out because the contract was up. . . . The guy told me it was a six-month review process to see if they'd get any more money. And so, you just lose kind of any sort of momentum.[169]

This is, of course, the familiar critique of civilian development programming that represents USAID as incapable of producing concrete results within a reasonable time frame. But as other, less enthusiastic stakeholders pointed out, both the HFZ and AVIPA Plus South would have benefited from *more* bureaucratic oversight. Some of the IRD's civilian employees bemoaned that AVIPA Plus South was fueling local tensions, raising Afghan expectations to unsustainable levels, promoting waste and fraud, and finally privatizing a lot of agricultural work that had previously been done in common.[170] Some critics accused the HFZ program of distributing inferior strains of wheat seed to local farmers, an "avoidable error" that "needlessly undercut the long-term investment by the UN and Western governments in Helmand's legal agricultural markets."[171]

What these otherwise critical accounts all gloss over, however, is the central role that both the HFZ and AVIPA Plus South played in displacing land-poor households from prime agricultural areas. On some level, this is hardly surprising. For the longest time, the "whole phenomenon of uprooted Afghans" was "barely visible on the aid community's radar screens."[172] This has changed in recent years, with an increasing number of authors investigating the linkages between counternarcotics and rural displacement. David Mansfield, for instance, observes that while poppy "represents an important source of on-farm income for many farmers, its labor intensive nature means that it also provides opportunities for the land-poor to either rent or sharecrop land, as well as offering off-farm employment to laborers during the weeding and harvest seasons."[173] Generally, poppies cannot be easily harvested through the labor of an average-sized household. Accordingly, land-wealthy Afghans often subcontract the task of cultivating poppy to other community members through sharecropping or leasing arrangements. Under the terms of such agreements, the sharecropper or the tenant is allowed to cultivate poppy on the understanding that the landowner will be entitled to a cut of the harvest. The viability of these arrangements is dictated in large part by the health of the local narco-economy. As Mansfield and Pain point out, "were the land-wealthy to cultivate less labor-intensive crops, the land would no longer be available for sharecroppers or for lease, but would instead be farmed using family labour of the landowner or relatively few wage labour inputs."[174]

This is precisely what happened in the HFZ. Fishstein argues that "the forced shift from opium poppy to less labour intensive crops such as wheat set in motion a chain of events which reduced the amount of land available for renting or sharecropping, hurting the landless and the land poor who rely on such arrangements."[175] As the demand for tenants and sharecroppers in the HFZ plummeted, the land-poor found it increasingly difficult to continue living in the area. To compound matters, the USAID complex typically made it difficult for the landless and the land-poor to participate in initiatives such as the HFZ or AVIPA Plus South.[176] In so doing, stabilization forms of alternative development programming effectively dispossessed sharecroppers and tenant farmers of their access to the means of subsistence. Instead of being absorbed into the informal economies of urban centers such as Lashkar Gah or Kandahar City, this displaced population attempted to escape the reach of both government and international forces by migrating to the *dasht*—or desert—areas north of the Boghra Canal. This land was not held in common, but rather, had been enclosed immediately after the fall of the Taliban regime by local commanders who lived adjacent to the canal. Beginning in 2004, the commanders commoditized this land and made it available for purchase or rent at relatively affordable prices. Swayed by the tantalizing prospect of being able to own land, many of the sharecroppers and tenants displaced by the HFZ and AVIPA Plus South decided to buy into the *dasht*. Making the *dasht* bloom, however, proved difficult and costly:

> The desert land needed to be cleared, levelled, and fertilized. Machinery had to be hired and wells drilled into the underground water supply in order to irrigate the land. . . . Generators, pumps, and piping were also needed to draw the water. These were all extra costs that were not associated with farming in the main river valleys. And then of course, there was the diesel required to run the pumps and generators.[177]

To recoup these fixed costs and pay off their debts, farmers had no choice but to monocrop opium poppy. This worked out for the first wave of migrants to the *dasht*, who were able to improve their life chances by cultivating poppies.[178] Later arrivals, unfortunately, found it more difficult to buy land in the *dasht*, forcing them to enter into sharecropping or tenancy arrangements with their more established predecessors. Over time, then, the hierarchical class structures that defined life in the Helmand Food Zone were gradually reproduced in the *dasht*.[179]

This was not enough to dissuade migration during the boom times. For a while, even sharecroppers were able to eat meat and fruit three times a week, purchase medicine, and invest in motorbikes or solar panels.[180] Ever since 2012, however, the situation in the *dasht* has become increasingly grim. Farmers across the class spectrum have endured multiple years of crop failure. Intensive monocropping has exhausted the land, resulting in widespread salinization and alkalinization, and rendered poppy crops increasingly susceptible to yield-crippling diseases.[181] At first, many migrants were willing to suffer through what they perceived to be a temporary inconvenience. Repeated crop failures of increasing severity, however, have demonstrated to them that the situation in the *dasht* is untenable. A once hopeful community has now become angry and bitter, blaming the foreigners and the corrupt Afghan government for their woes. Many believe that their crops were not actually diseased, but rather, had been sprayed by American planes. Regardless of whether residents of the *dasht* are victims of a political conspiracy or ecological circumstances, if such conditions persist, it is highly likely that they will once again find themselves "on the move."[182]

Making Peace with Poppies

When I spoke with Amira Garner, a livelihoods specialist who worked for Development Alternatives Inc., she told me that Holbrooke's tenure as Obama's special representative had been marked by a "series of horrible cooperative agreements." Garner singled out AVIPA Plus South for criticism, arguing that it "really regressed agricultural development." Instead of adopting a more "commercial approach"—which is "how DAI feels things need to be approached at this stage in Afghanistan and that's the only way you really hopefully get sustainability"— Holbrooke and the IRD "just completely distorted the market by flooding it with free inputs." This has "really been at the detriment of good development."[183]

From a certain perspective, Garner's pointed critique undoubtedly rings true, though perhaps not in the way she intended. As I have shown, stabilization-style alternative development projects such as AVIPA Plus South and the HFZ dispossessed land poor Helmandis of their access to the means of subsistence, setting them in motion and forcing them to resettle in inhospitable borderland spaces. Chemonics' ALP/S—the kind of project that Garner might begrudgingly describe as "good development"—never upended rural communities in quite the same way. And yet, it still subjected certain marginalized groups in rural communities—the land-poor, the landless, women, and households located in more remote and insecure districts—to forms of slow violence, organized abandonment, and premature death. All of this clarifies how sharecroppers and tenant farmers have historically fit uneasily within broader alternative development frameworks, exposing the many tensions and contradictions baked into market-based approaches. By displacing poppy-cultivating households from the most fertile areas of southern Afghanistan, AVIPA Plus South and the HFZ might have cleared the ground for the USAID complex, smoothing over a key source of developmental friction that has long confounded its ability to wield infrastructural power over rural communities. In the presurge period, a vibrant narco-economy and a steady supply of underemployed males made it economically rational for well-resourced farmers to reserve a certain percentage of their landholdings for poppy cultivation. Projects like AVIPA Plus South and the HFZ altered this cost-benefit calculus, encouraging middle-scale farmers to free up increasing amounts of land for legitimate agribusiness uses. The implication here is that such interventions have potentially reshaped southern Afghanistan into a more receptive environment for future market-driven agribusiness interventions.

USAID was better able to capitalize upon these reconfigurations when a shifting set of operational circumstances led the U.S. military to distance itself from the stabilization model of alternative development. As the U.S. military's focus in Afghanistan transitioned from counterinsurgency to drawdown, counternarcotics once again became mission creep. In 2013, the U.S. military adopted a whole suite of poppy-related constraints on field operations. American forces and their Afghan proxies were no longer allowed to step foot in, damage, or destroy poppy fields. As David Axe observes, these new rules suggest that the U.S. military has "made peace with poppies, viewing them as a potential good thing for Afghanistan and the Army."[184] No longer forced to work with either the military or Holbrooke, USAID wasted no time in shifting back toward more market-based models of alternative development. This new direction was most clearly signaled when USAID awarded Chemonics a five-year contract to bring a Regional Agricultural Development Program to southern Afghanistan. In so doing, USAID gave Chemonics a second chance to transform the south into an environment conducive to market-oriented agricultural production. Under Chemonics' watch, agricultural sales once again replaced reductions in poppy cultivation as the most important measure of alternative development success.[185]

While implementing the Regional Agricultural Development Program in southern Afghanistan, Chemonics likely drew inspiration from some of Garner's own work at DAI, especially the two projects that have come to embody the "commercial approach" to alternative development. The first was the flagship Alternative Development Program for Afghanistan's eastern region. The second was its successor project, Ideas Driving Economic Alternatives—North, East, and West. Instead of "growing hope" in eastern Afghanistan, both projects produced what the anthropologist Tania Murray Li calls "differentiated subjects of colonial rule," thereby exacerbating already existing geographies of uneven development.[186]

[4]

Alternative Developments?

Economizing Life and Death in Eastern Afghanistan

It was a single poppy seed: prising it out, she rolled it between
her fingers and raised her eyes, past the straining sails, to the
star-filled vault above. . . .

When Kalua asked what she was looking at, she raised her
fingers to his lips and slipped the seed into his mouth.

Here, she said, taste it. It is the star that took us from our
homes and put us on this ship. It is the planet that rules our
destiny.

Amitav Ghosh, Sea of Poppies

ON DECEMBER 21, 2011, USAID uploaded a short two-part YouTube
documentary entitled "Growing Hope in Afghanistan."[1] It was meant
to showcase the achievements of the Alternative Development Program
that Development Alternatives Inc. (DAI) had previously implemented
in eastern Afghanistan. "Growing Hope" foregrounds the testimony of
a farmer named Mohammad Muslim. In Muslim's own words:

We used to grow poppy before. We were desperate. We knew
it was illegal. Now I am very happy and proud that we have
switched to growing vegetables. . . . In the past, we could hardly
cook meat once a week. Now we eat meat every other day. All
these kids you see go to school. Some go on foot to nearby
schools. The others go to farther schools and I pay for their
transportation. I pay for all the school expenses for these kids,
buying them pens, notepads, clothing, backpacks, and other necessary things. Allah has enabled us to do so—through farming.
I hope they become engineers, agriculture experts, and doctors.
It's enough that I have grown up as illiterate. I hope they have

bright futures and that they grow up literate and under the banner of Islamic teachings.[2]

DAI and USAID offer Muslim's story as an example of how Alternative Development Program East (ADP/E) played an instrumental role
in connecting rural households to brighter, more liberal, and capitalist
futures. With DAI's help, Muslim traded a subsistence life of illegality,
desperation, sadness, and shame for one of improved life chances, expanded horizons for individual choice making, and relative consumer
abundance. Once Muslim started growing and selling vegetables,
his ability to procure the "necessary things" of life—meat, clothing,
school supplies, and so on—dramatically improved. But perhaps more
importantly, what Muslim found in horticulture was a clear pathway
for escaping the constraining grip of eastern Afghanistan's land-based
economy. In Muslim's eyes, horticulture promised a life of professionalization and upward class mobility for his children.

At the time of the release of "Growing Hope," ADP/E was the latest
phase in the USAID complex's longer-standing project of developing
a thriving commercial sector in Afghanistan. DAI, in particular, had
long been a champion of what it was calling the "commercial approach"
to rural development. As early as 1992, DAI was asking Dr. Abdul
Wakil—whose successive stints with both the Helmand Valley Authority and the Office of the Aid Representative for Afghanistan Affairs had
earned him a reputation as the "Johnny Appleseed" of Afghanistan—to
articulate a vision of how horticulture might lead Afghan farmers into
a future of prosperity.[3] By this point in time, the broader USAID complex was in the midst of shutting down the cross-border mission to
war-torn Afghanistan. Dr. Wakil therefore never got a chance to put
his vision to work in the Afghan countryside. From this perspective,
ADP/E is important as one of the USAID complex's many belated attempts at translating Wakil's vision for the post-9/11 context. But Muslim's testimony is also suggestive of how alternative development in
eastern Afghanistan became fundamentally concerned with broader
questions of household management. One of the net effects of Muslim's switch from poppy to vegetable cultivation was a substantive reconfiguration of household roles. Muslim's children went from being
agricultural laborers in training to potential bearers of human capital.

Under the aegis of ADP/E, rural household relations were ostensibly oriented away from traditional subsistence economies toward new and emerging market formations.

I trace this evolving trajectory of alternative development encounter through a close reading of two chronological case studies. These are DAI's ADP/E and its successor project, Incentives Driving Economic Alternatives—North, East, and West (IDEA-NEW). While these two alternative development projects intervened on different stages of the agricultural value chain—the former was primarily concerned with improving production, while the latter was keen on facilitating exchange— they nonetheless shared a deep commitment to marketizing all facets of rural Afghan life. For this reason, key players in the USAID complex often hold them up as ideal-type alternative development interventions, especially when compared to the stabilization-style quick-impact initiatives that became popular in the southern region. It is therefore tempting to theorize them as explicitly neoliberal forms of development governmentality, or what Michel Foucault might call "environmental-type interventions."[4]

But as DAI's field experiences reveal, eastern Afghanistan never quite became the seemingly frictionless "environment" of market governance that Foucault preliminarily sketched out in his Collège de France lectures. Both ADP/E and IDEA-NEW were fully embedded in and undergirded by imperial infrastructures of abandonment, violence, and death. Over time, DAI's interventions parsed rural populations along lines of geography and gender, thereby serving as a catalyst of uneven development in eastern Afghanistan. Alternative development activities that were designed to integrate Afghan women into agricultural value chains actually entrenched "traditional" heteropatriarchal models of rural household management that confined them to a carceralized geography of domestic spaces. As in southern Afghanistan, these reconfigured infrastructures of Afghan life were secured by—and provided a legitimating armature for—geographical techniques of population management that were fundamentally destructive of life, including crop eradication, nexus targeting, and assassination. From this perspective, alternative development in eastern Afghanistan appears more precisely as a violent hybridization of lethal and nonlethal forms of infrastructural power that severed or eliminated certain undesirable patterns of rural life while simultaneously nurturing other connections and circulations that better served the geopolitical economic interests of U.S. empire.

The Biopolitics of Alternative Development

The USAID complex often cites ADP/E and IDEA-NEW as examples of what the special inspector general for Afghanistan reconstruction (SIGAR) identifies as the "rural development" model of alternative livelihoods. This model assumes that a well-executed development project will inevitably result in reductions to poppy cultivation. Its approach is therefore to make "rural development the objective, and reductions in poppy cultivation an externality or side effect of that objective."[5] Theoretically, this model promised a form of counternarcotics that would strengthen the relationship between government and farming communities. This is to say, the USAID complex valued projects like ADP/E and IDEA-NEW as conduits for governmental power.

SIGAR's framing is seductive for how it neatly maps on to longer-standing imaginative geographies of Afghanistan as divided between an insurgent south and a governable north and east.[6] In contrast with alternative development programs in Helmand and Kandahar, which were optimized for conditions of violence and conflict, those in Nangarhar could take advantage of a more permissive operating environment. But SIGAR's account is far less useful for understanding how ADP/E and IDEA-NEW were equally—if not primarily—concerned with strengthening the relationships between farming communities and markets. DAI's alternative development vision was for the market, not the state, to serve as the primary source of subsistence, improvement, and accumulation in the Afghan countryside. This is not to suggest that DAI deemed the Afghan government to be irrelevant. For DAI, the role of the government was to establish an enabling environment for commercial agriculture.

One way of unpacking DAI's alternative development work in eastern Afghanistan is by emphasizing its "environmental" characteristics. My use of the term "environmental" is inspired by Foucault's exploration of how biopower is exercised under conditions of market rule. Foucault writes that nineteenth-century liberals understood the market as a space where nominally rational economic subjects came together in pursuit of their own self-interest. Liberals argued that, given the complexity of such encounters, market spaces were "naturally opaque and non-totalizable." It was therefore imperative that the state refrain itself from superintending the "totality of the economic process, 'for the proper performance of which no human knowledge could ever be sufficient.'"[7] In Foucault's analysis, liberals posited *Homo oeconomicus* as an ungovernable figure whose existence stripped the state of its power to manage the market. Although liberals initially called on the state to respect the market as a space structured by the principle of laissez-faire, they also accepted government intervention as an evil necessary to curb the excesses of economic activity. This uneasy compromise was overturned in the wake of World War II, when so-called neoliberals blamed socialist and Keynesian models of governmental practice for the political ascendancy of fascism. Fueled by an obvious disdain for welfare-statism, neoliberals embarked on a crusade to restore and maintain some form of market rule. While neoliberals shared their predecessors' commitments to free trade, labor market flexibility, and social state retrenchment, they nonetheless "sought to transcend the 'naïve ideology' of laissez-faire in favour of a 'positive' conception of the state as the guarantor of a competitive order."[8] They recognized that in a context such as war-torn Europe, the state would have to play a substantive role in reestablishing market infrastructures. The challenge facing neoliberals, therefore, was not to "cut out" a "free space of the market within an already given political society."[9] Rather, it was to "determine a set of tightly constrained, yet positive, functions for the state as the foundation for a designed market order."[10] Neoliberals, in other words, decided that government would have to be defined in relation to the market economy. Instead of passively responding to the excesses of the market, government must be made to actively serve its interests.

In order to achieve these political goals, neoliberals sought to "extend the rationality of the market to domains hitherto considered to be non-economic."[11] Market relations were increasingly seen as the key to deciphering and predicting a wide array of ostensibly extraeconomic behaviors. It was precisely this belief that distinguished neoliberals from both their intellectual forbears, as well as their avowed enemies. Neoliberals rendered this new logic of government "actionable through 'environmental technologies' orientated to the actions of a specific 'object-target'—*Homo oeconomicus*."[12] Under such new frameworks,

Homo oeconomicus went from being an "intangible element" to an "eminently governable" subject whose conduct responded "systematically to modifications in the variables of the environment": or, what Foucault calls "environmental-type interventions."[13] While Foucault never explicitly explains what he means by the term, Ben Anderson uses it as a shorthand for "attempts to manage and manipulate the contingent 'environments' in which action occurs in order to indirectly act on the investments that the subject of interest makes."[14] Through such interventions, action is brought to bear on the "rules of the game," rather than the bodies of the players.[15]

Foucault's comments on neoliberal governance remain partial and provisional. And yet, if Jamie Peck is correct to locate the origins of neoliberalism in a European crucible totally decimated by the global war on fascism, then it is all the more curious that the movement's connections to militarism and imperialism remain undertheorized in Foucault's lectures. In some sense, this is not surprising, given Foucault's well-established blind spots on the thorny questions of colonialism, race, and empire.[16] But from another perspective, Foucault notably launched his investigations into biopolitics through the prisms of (race) war and conflict.[17] It therefore seems generative to extrapolate from Foucault's work by asking what does neoliberal governmentality—or environmentality—look like when it becomes explicitly yoked to an imperial project of pacification and rule.

My starting point is Michelle Murphy's reflections on how Cold War encounters between imperialism and neoliberalism across the decolonizing world resulted in what she names as an "economization of life."[18] Murphy reads various development experiments at quantifying, aggregating, and intervening on rural life in 1970s Bangladesh—often in the forms of family planning or global health initiatives—to track the emergence of new infrastructures for combining population with economy. She emphasizes that while these infrastructures undoubtedly sustained and invested in certain forms of life, they also diminished or abandoned others in highly racialized and economized ways. Under conditions of neoliberal capitalism, such "noninnocent" entanglements of population and economy do not "just distribute life and death possibilities between bodies." Rather, they "bundle antagonistic arrangements of life potential and exposure to death as the very terms of living."[19]

Here, Murphy's theorization of the economization of life brings her into direct conversation with Ruth Wilson Gilmore's definition of racism as the "state-sanctioned or extralegal production and exploitation of group-differentiated vulnerability to premature death."[20] Murphy draws explicitly on Gilmore to argue that the economization of life has historically innovated new practices and techniques of racial violence that seek to govern racialized and gendered bodies on the basis of economic capacities, rather than innate bodily or biological differences.[21] This is to say, economizing life necessarily involves racializing life, or, in the case of DAI, using the heuristic of "economic futures" to parse populations into those who are capable of participating in global markets—and hence, worthy of living and reproducing under the current conditions of racial capitalism—and those who are destined to become surplus, or grist for the mill of accumulation, exploitation, and dispossession. As Murphy notes, when it comes to the economization of life, "race [does] not have to be named in order to enact racist practices."[22]

Murphy begins her analysis of the economization of life with imperial development projects that deal with reproduction in postcolonial contexts as a familiar problem of fertility, birth, and contraception. In so doing, she shows how "race is the grammar and ghost" of such interventions, especially given their commitment to using "population" as a seemingly technical term for naming a mass or multitude of beneficiary subjects. This, in turn, obscures how population "offers an epistemological framing of life that [is] profoundly dehumanizing," one that "facilitate[s] a distanced and managerial gaze toward optimizing the life and death of brown and black bodies at rates over time in need of adjustment."[23] But her ultimate goal is to theoretically stretch the concept of reproduction beyond individual bodies to encompass the "uneven relations and infrastructures" that shape how living being is nurtured, altered, sustained, destroyed, and contained under conditions of late racial capitalism and imperialism.[24] Murphy's new and expanded sense of "distributed reproduction" is therefore useful for reckoning with how market-based alternative development interventions were decomposing and recomposing rural life and household relations in eastern Afghanistan. DAI grounded ADP/E and IDEA-NEW in longer-standing Orientalist racializations of rural Afghans as fiercely independent and entrepreneurial subjects whose innate suspicion of governmental rule makes them intractable, yet not entirely ungovernable.[25] DAI championed market relations as a mechanism for bridging this gap, transforming both alternative development projects into important field sites for experimenting with and refining imperial environmentalities.[26]

And yet, following Murphy, both projects also doubled as multiscalar lynchpins that chained the intimate geographies of everyday rule in eastern Afghanistan to broader infrastructures of imperial violence. The projects themselves directly enmeshed beneficiary households in highly uneven regimes of accumulation and abandonment that disproportionately benefited propertied male farmers living in the central and well-irrigated areas of Nangarhar at the expense of women and other differentially marginalized subjects. But the slow violence of U.S. empire was also felt in more intimate and intersectional ways. DAI envisioned its alternative development projects helping rural women participate in emerging market infrastructures. In practice, however, DAI mobilized the language of gender integration to make domestic or interior spaces the preferred locus of women's economic activity. The net effect of these alternative development interventions was to legitimize and entrench a supposedly traditional and heteropatriarchal model of rural household management.

None of this should come as a surprise. As Patricia Owens and Oliver Belcher have shown, liberal counterinsurgents have long coveted the household as a key site for indirect rule and management.[27] Given these longer-standing connections to counterinsurgency, race war, and military occupation, it therefore follows that the violence of imperial household management is not always slow. Sometimes, it is explosive and lethal. Belcher documents how counterinsurgent forces in southern Afghanistan relied heavily on village razing as a technique for securing the most intimate spaces of rural—and hence, potentially insurgent—households and communities. Belcher situates these military operations within a longer transimperial tradition of counterinsurgency urbicide that includes the infamous Strategic Hamlet program in war-torn Vietnam, as well as the New Village concept in insurgent Malaya.[28] Following Katherine McKittrick, however, we might further connect these distinct yet related forms of counterinsurgency urbicide to the "practices of place annihilation" that have historically played a central role in targeting and destroying a "black sense of place in the Americas." While each of these case studies of place annihilation "certainly differ according to time and place," what they all bring into sharp focus are the diverse ways in which the everyday work of counterinsurgency, whether it is carried out in the domestic or foreign spheres, "functions to render specific human lives, and thus their communities, as waste."[29] Village razing did not feature as prominently—if at all—in the U.S. military's playbook for transforming "*hearths* and minds" in eastern Afghanistan.[30] Liberal counterinsurgents nonetheless repurposed other tried-and-tested techniques for targeting, crippling, and dismantling nonimperial infrastructures of household management. As in southern Afghanistan, crop eradication remained a centerpiece of the imperial war against poppy cultivation. Over time, however, higher-ranking agents of the regional narcotics–insurgency nexus also found themselves in the crosshairs of the same transnational military infrastructure of nexus targeting and extrajudicial assassination that was rapidly becoming infamous for waging drone warfare on insurgent leaders in the Af-Pak borderlands.[31] As the (indirect) beneficiary of such an imperial necropolitics, DAI's alternative development programming in eastern Afghanistan recalls nothing so much as the USAID complex's direct and enthusiastic involvement in the controversial Phung Hoang effort to eliminate insurgent infrastructures—which was a euphemism for extrajudicially murdering suspected members of the National Liberation Front—during the later phases of the Vietnam War.[32] Reading ADP/E and IDEA-NEW in relation to these Cold War genealogies of U.S. imperial household management, I argue, offers a way of clarifying DAI's role in bundling "antagonistic arrangements" of counternarcotics "anger" and alternative development "mercy" into the very infrastructural foundations for making, remaking, and unmaking rural life in eastern Afghanistan.

DAI's first post-9/11 opportunity to experiment with more commercial approaches to transforming rural household relations was ADP/E. Drawing on prior experiences of carrying out cross-border rural development programs across Soviet-occupied Afghanistan, DAI assembled an infrastructure of agricultural training centers and demonstration farms for schooling local farmers in the basics of commercial agricultural production. In these spaces, DAI laid the groundwork for transitioning farmers away from a traditional survival mindset toward more future-oriented perspectives. DAI expected that farmers would follow the example of Mohammad Muslim in producing agricultural commodities for the market, provisioning their households from the market, soliciting services from the market, and supplying white collar and professional labor to the market. In this sense, ADP/E was the first phase in DAI's long-term project of reorganizing everyday household relations in eastern Afghanistan around emerging market infrastructures.

"The Pride of the Eastern Region"

USAID awarded the four-year contract to DAI on February 15, 2005. Valued at $108.386 million, ADP/E's objective was to provide poppy cultivators in Nangarhar, Laghman, Kunar, and Nuristan provinces with alternative income sources.[33] It was conceived in part as a way of softening the regional blow of Nangarhar's 2004 decision to ban poppy cultivation. Initially, the ban was successful at forcing rural households to replace poppy with wheat. From 2004 to 2005, poppy cultivation in Nangarhar fell by approximately 96 percent.[34] But as the ban extended into a second year, its negative impacts were becoming increasingly difficult to ignore. The majority of affected households did not own enough land to achieve self-sufficiency in wheat: a problem that was exacerbated by rising food prices. Better-resourced households were able to close this subsistence gap by cultivating other high-value crops, seeking out off-farm wage labor opportunities, and cutting back on household consumption.[35] Households in the more remote regions of the provinces, however, experienced an economic shock so intense that many had no choice but to relapse into poppy cultivation.[36] The unsurprising corollary here was that households across the province became increasingly alienated from both provincial and national authorities.[37]

DAI launched ADP/E in a bid to reverse these worrying trends. The poppy problem in eastern Afghanistan, DAI argued, called for a lighter and more indirect touch. Bruce Brown, a USAID official linked with ADP/E, described DAI's alternative development approach as one of "resurrecting, or supporting, or enhancing what had been going on already." To this end, ADP/E introduced "some new concepts and approaches and . . . skills, as a way . . . of . . . enticing people into making choices that would support them and their families in a way that would ensure that they didn't have to rely on poppy cultivation."[38]

Brown's description of ADP/E as a form of "enticement" makes "setting conditions"—and not "manipulating outcomes"—the crux of the rural development model of alternative livelihoods.[39] As Brown recognized, DAI could not coerce poppy cultivators into doing "as they ought."[40] Instead, they had to be free to make their own individual choices. By anchoring alternative development in the everyday work of stimulating individual choices—and by extension, economizing life—Brown firmly positioned ADP/E as a key nodal point within a broader infrastructure of neoliberal governmentality.[41] The trick for DAI was to present rural households with the right constellation of dis/incentives so that poppy cultivation would become unthinkable for rational, self-interested, and utility-maximizing subjects.

How, then, did DAI go about nudging rural households away from poppies toward licit yet equally high-value alternatives? "Growing Hope" hypothesizes that rural farmers have historically turned to poppy cultivation because they lack the knowledge and training to do otherwise. When the Karzai regime banned poppy cultivation in eastern Afghanistan, farmers in the east returned to "ancient agricultural techniques" because "thirty years of war had destroyed all basic infrastructure."[42] This is, of course, a hyperbolic claim that traffics in Orientalist imaginative geographies of Afghanistan as a premodern land wracked by perpetual failure, disconnection, and underdevelopment.[43] DAI had previously played a key role in USAID's cross-border effort to rebuild and rehabilitate the everyday infrastructures of rural life in war-torn Afghanistan. And from the late 1980s onward, the opium economy also served as an alternative conduit of infrastructural power across the countryside. This was especially true in the post–Cold War period, when the USAID complex began to focus its attention elsewhere. But this simplistic framework was nonetheless useful for DAI, who was keen to explain the persistence of a "survival mindset" in eastern Afghanistan as stemming from an individualized lack of modern agricultural techniques, services, and inputs. DAI was convinced that farmers who cultivated high-value alternative crops in accordance with the "old ways" would never generate enough income to push beyond basic subsistence thresholds.[44] The implication here is that ADP/E would have to lay down the infrastructural "conditions" necessary to facilitate the proliferation of a more commercial mindset.[45]

Part of this effort was focused on either constructing or rehabilitating physical infrastructures, such as farm-to-market roads and community irrigation systems. DAI was most likely to wield this particular kind of infrastructural power in areas oscillating between insurgent and coalition control. While the neo-Taliban resurgence in eastern Afghanistan was never as marked as in the south, the central government's "extremely weak" presence in Kunar, Nuristan, and northern Laghman made it possible for insurgent forces to operate with ease. In comparison, Nangarhar's relatively coherent government and stronger nationalist ties meant that it was initially better positioned to resist insurgent incursions.[46] By the time that DAI launched ADP/E, however, insurgents were beginning to establish substantive footholds in some of the province's outlying districts. In these "transitional" areas, DAI relied on infrastructure-building activities as the "entry point" for more sophisticated rural development interventions.[47] Labor-intensive infrastructure projects generated a multitude of cash-for-work opportunities for young, underemployed men, ostensibly offering them a safer and hence more attractive source of income than the insurgency.[48] Wherever possible, DAI leveraged these quick-impact activities into more trusting relationships with marginalized communities, thereby setting the stage for carrying out longer-term forms of extension and demonstration work.

Over time, DAI built these foundations into a hierarchical infrastructure of sixteen large commercial demonstration farms, which reached out and touched rural households through a proliferation of smaller community-based plots.[49] "Growing Hope" features one of ADP/E's field technicians, Noor Mohammad, who details some of the techniques, inputs, and technologies that were demonstrated in these spaces. At the time of Noor's interview, he was training a group of farmers in how to properly plant, fertilize, and care for cauliflower seeds. Farmers who planted cauliflower seeds in traditional ways always ran the risk of burying them too far underground. This, in turn, often led to overirrigation and crop failure. Under such conditions, farmers netted on average 3,000 to 4,000 heads of cauliflower per *jerib* (2,000 square meters). Farmers armed with improved seeds and modern agricultural techniques, Mohammad enthused, could harvest around 9,000.[50] Mohammad also emphasized the importance of arranging fields, spacing crops, and staggering planting times. The last innovation was particularly effective in streamlining vegetable farming. DAI's training encouraged farmers who typically planted their vegetable seeds all at once to instead do so in phases. Every two weeks, farmers planted vegetables on a further two *jeribs* of land, repeating this process until they ran out of room. The net effect was to redistribute the intensive work of harvesting over a longer and more manageable time frame. Farmers were then able to sell their produce at local wet markets at intervals, which minimized the risk of creating commodity gluts and price shocks, while also stabilizing their cash flows and maximizing their profitability.[51]

Before farmers could experiment with these lessons and insights in the real world, they first required a mechanism for procuring modern inputs and technologies from regional markets. DAI took the first steps in addressing these emerging needs in the spring of 2007, when it refashioned earlier experiments in cross-border trade facilitation and market development into a number of input distribution initiatives that were tailored to serve different classes of beneficiaries. Technology Innovation and Market-Led Economic Rehabilitation (TIMER) for example, channeled subsidized packages of improved seeds and fertilizers to smaller-scale farmers, while the Regional Vegetable Marketing Program offered similar services to medium sized horticulturalists.[52] TIMER, in particular, was notable for breaking the "traditional input program model."[53] Unhappy with the tendency of local authorities— community development councils, *shuras,* and so on—to claim a central role in the distribution of inputs, DAI instead offered beneficiaries a way of bypassing these traditional infrastructures. The specific content of input packages would no longer be determined by political middlemen but rather by the needs and decisions of individual farmers. Farmers, of course, paid a premium for this right to choose, customize, and tailor. DAI justified these additional costs on the grounds of transparency and flexibility. But I would also read TIMER as another example of how ADP/E was ultimately about disconnecting rural households from traditional governance structures and reconnecting them in terms that better served the geopolitical economic interests of empire and neoliberal racial capitalism.[54]

Indeed, when considered in relation to ADP/E's overall trajectory, DAI clearly envisioned TIMER as a stepping stone for reinserting Afghan farmers into globalized circulations of agricultural commodities and capital. In ADP/E reports, rural households appear as generally unfamiliar with the "concept" of the "private sector."[55] While DAI acknowledges that eastern Afghanistan has long been home to a thriving merchant class, it had nonetheless been conditioned by a "long legacy of Communist-era policies" to focus on trade rather than agribusiness.[56] If the private sector was to become an engine of long-term economic growth, DAI would have to establish an "enabling environment" for agribusiness investment.[57] In this sense, ADP/E replicated its southern counterpart's obsession with entrepreneurializing local farmers. Much like Chemonics, DAI established a Private Sector Development Technical Unit that helped local farmers create business plans, secure investment capital, connect with global buyers, and establish regional business associations.[58] As in southern Afghanistan, one of the major achievements of this unit was the yearly organization of a Regional Agricultural Trade Fair in Jalalabad. Each fair was centered around a distinct yet related theme. In 2006, participants became experts at "Navigating the Value Chain."[59] The fair that followed argued for the necessity of "Linking Eastern Afghanistan with the World." The concluding 2008 iteration encouraged delegates to "Discover the Possibilities" of local agribusiness.[60] What linked these three fairs together was a general commitment to helping rural households forge transnational connections with emerging or already-established market infrastructures.

This commitment also manifested in other ways. DAI helped individual farmers exhibit their wares at similar trade events across Afghanistan. One farmer based in Nangarhar's Chaparhar district returned from an AgFair in Kabul with a contract to supply the famous Serena Hotel with 100 kilograms of strawberries per day.[61] The Private Sector Development Technical Unit also brought markets to rural households by collecting, analyzing, and disseminating crucial price data for common agricultural commodities.[62] Every morning, DAI disseminated this information among farming communities through communication technologies such as the radio or mobile phones. In "Growing Hope," one farmer sends a text message to this "market information system" asking for an update on loquat prices in nearby markets. He then uses this information to determine where he can sell his loquat crates for maximum profit.[63]

DAI's in-house metrics extol the virtues of this market-based approach to alternative development. Of the 145,994 farmers who availed themselves of ADP/E's demonstration and extension services, 99 percent reported increased productivity, 94 percent adopted higher-value crops, and 93 percent received better market prices.[64] DAI complemented these statistics with glowing farmer testimonials that praised demonstration training as a guaranteed pathway to higher income. In addition to improving the yield, quality, variety, and value of agricultural commodities, demonstration training also reorganized the temporal rhythms of rural life. Whereas vegetable production was once highly seasonal, "now," one farmer gushed, "we can grow [them] year-round."[65]

Taken together, all of these different alternative development interventions speak to the ways in which DAI understood poppy cultivation in eastern Afghanistan as an environmental problem. As Brown clarified, the "underlying motivation" of ADP/E was "more than just to grow . . . more food" or "begin to . . . weave carpets." In order to "strengthen" or "incite" or "improve" alternative value chains, ADP/E had to "look at" and "target" all of the different "elements"—"the related stakeholders, policies, private sector dynamics, motivations, impediments"—of its "ecosystem." I asked Brown if DAI's ecosystem approach was geared toward inducing desired behavioral changes in Afghan farmers. Brown agreed, suggesting that a project like ADP/E demonstrates to beneficiaries that there is a better "alternative," changing the ways in which they behave, prioritize, and make choices.[66]

But to what extent did ADP/E actually change the behavior of poppy cultivators? One evaluation produced by Checchi and Company Consulting suggests that ADP/E was plagued by many of the same problems as its southern counterpart. DAI, too, eschewed "complete development packages" in favor of shorter-term "demonstration events."[67] DAI compounded matters by having "exceedingly optimistic expectations" regarding the "potential behavioral change of the rural population."[68] Instead of benefiting all segments of rural society in eastern Afghanistan, ADP/E's various components strongly favored the "best endowed farmers and entrepreneurs," thereby exacerbating already existing geographies of uneven development. All of ADP/E's demonstration plots were managed by "progressive" or "lead" farmers.[69] These were the "early adopters" who were "just far enough ahead" of their neighbors to be recognized as positive examples for the broader community.[70] This, in turn, concentrated assistance and inputs in the hands of the most entrepreneurial members of farming communities. Even a component like TIMER, which specifically targeted smaller-scale farmers who were "less open to bet on change," imposed stringent preconditions—access to irrigation and markets—that disqualified many from participating.[71]

ADP/E's agribusiness interventions were similarly plagued by the problem of "thinking 'too big.'"[72] This more ambitious approach may have worked for some of the region's "larger and more commercial oriented farms."[73] But as DAI acknowledges, eastern Afghanistan still lacked a critical mass of "sincere investors" who were not merely looking for a "free lunch."[74] For this reason, DAI's agribusiness outreach failed to gain traction among the class of rural households who stood to gain the most from it. To solve this problem, DAI vowed to channel future market development dollars exclusively to small- and medium-scale enterprises that had proven themselves to be not only cheaper than agribusiness megaprojects but also more successful at actually getting off the ground. In the meantime, DAI's dream of "introducing" rural households in eastern Afghanistan to the private sector would remain somewhat elusive.

It is also important to stress that DAI's preliminary attempts at market integration largely conformed with Orientalist conceptions of rural household relations as carcerally heteropatriarchal.[75] DAI "exclusively" reserved agricultural programs for male farmers, while ostensibly empowering household women—described by "Growing Hope" as the most vulnerable and impoverished class of Afghan subjects—through more appropriate home-based activities, examples of which included establishing seedling greenhouses or poultry farms.[76] From DAI's perspective, Afghan women were vulnerable and marginalized because they lacked a means of substantively contributing to overall household incomes.[77] DAI's simplistic strategy of framing gender integration as a corollary of income potential unfortunately diverted critical attention away from the sociocultural norms that effectively constrained Afghan women from engaging in work outside of domestic spaces, or from accessing and participating in markets. By designing alternative development programming to account for one particular heteropatriarchal model of rural household management, DAI revealed its failures to understand how gender roles and relations in rural Afghanistan were less a timeless and innate element of tribal culture and more a flexible and geographical bundle of challenges and opportunities.[78] DAI's attempt at empowering Afghan women counterintuitively contracted their spatial horizons, rather than expanding them.

By the time that DAI terminated ADP/E on June 30, 2009, eastern Afghanistan—and in particular, Nangarhar—was being celebrated as the new national blueprint for counternarcotics efforts.[79] The extent to which DAI contributed to Nangarhar's ostensible counternarcotics successes nonetheless remains unclear. DAI's early attempts at helping rural households cope with the economic aftereffects of the 2004 ban clearly did little to prevent poppy cultivation from resurging from 4,872 hectares in 2006 to 18,739 hectares in 2007.[80] While Nangarhar did achieve poppy-free status in 2008, mainstream commentators were quick to credit this achievement to the province's governor, Gul Aga Sherzai. Having shouldered most of the blame for the 2007 spike in poppy cultivation, Sherzai was under heavy pressure to show a "significant" improvement in counternarcotics metrics.[81] He responded by pushing an even-more-aggressive strategy that ramped up eradication operations on the ground and from the air, while also imposing harsh punishments on poppy cultivators. Sherzai's renewed commitment to coercive law enforcement was clearly on display in his meeting with the Jalalabad Provincial Reconstruction Team on April 18, 2007, when he reportedly promised to fire uncooperative government officials and openly accused local authority figures of planting poppies on the side.[82] When negotiating with rural communities, Sherzai often secured consent for intensified eradication by promising to support alternative livelihoods. But his inevitable failure to deliver on these promises unsurprisingly plunged expectant rural households into economic distress.[83] The hardest hit households, in turn, became increasingly hostile to the government, and in some cases, assaulted eradication teams. On April 1, 2007, for instance, a number of Afghans protested poppy eradication efforts at the Bati Kot District Center. In the ensuing scuffle, 15 protestors were arrested, while 5 locals and 2 police officers were wounded.[84] A similar incident occurred in the Koghyani district, where a suicide bomber targeted and killed 20 policemen and a UNODC surveyor collecting counternarcotics data for a report.[85]

It was against this backdrop of mounting violence that DAI began the difficult work of transitioning ADP/E into its successor project, IDEA-NEW. IDEA-NEW built on and extended ADP/E's more market-based approach to the problem of poppy cultivation in eastern Afghanistan. Having familiarized rural households with the concept of the private sector, DAI planned to drag them even further up the value chain. With IDEA-NEW, the focus of alternative development went from improving agricultural production to further marketizing rural life-worlds. Over time, DAI came to believe that IDEA-NEW represented a new model for alternative development, one that had fully shed its negative counternarcotics baggage. But a closer reading of IDEA-NEW reveals that alternative development in eastern Afghanistan remained a conduit for imperial violence, in all of its diverse forms.

"We're Here to Help, Not for the Money"

Armed with a five-year $150 million contract from USAID, DAI officially launched IDEA-NEW on March 3, 2009. It did so as part of an alternative development consortium rounded out by two other implementing partners, the NGO Mercy Corps and the contractor ACDI/VOCA. As Figure 13 shows, each implementer was assigned its own area of operations. DAI was based in eastern and western Afghanistan, while ACDI/VOCA and Mercy Corps operated in the north and northeast, respectively.

Although DAI was highly critical of stabilization programs such as Afghanistan Vouchers for Increased Production in Agriculture, it nonetheless recognized the strategic importance of emphasizing how IDEA-NEW could support counterinsurgency objectives.[86] To this end, DAI promised that IDEA-NEW would reduce poppy cultivation in key insurgency hotspots and buffer zones. These included the unstable districts of southern Nangarhar, as well as Kunar's Korengal Valley, which, by 2008 had acquired the dubious distinction of being one of the most dangerous battle spaces in all of Afghanistan.[87] Fighting in these areas further intensified following the 2009 surge of U.S. soldiers in the south. In what senior U.S. commanders described as a "counter-surge," neo-Taliban forces opened a second front in the N2KL—Nangarhar, Nuristan, Kunar, and Laghman—region, where they distributed night letters, established shadow government structures, and harassed counterinsurgent forces.[88] These neo-Taliban incursions were tolerated—and in some cases, even welcomed—by a local population who saw the Karzai administration as corrupt, ineffective, and morally

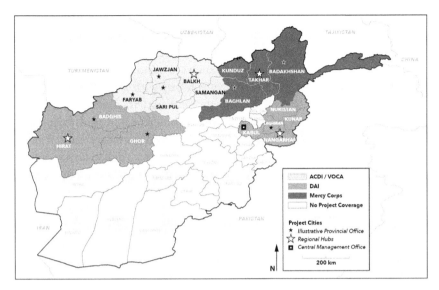

FIGURE 13. *IDEA-NEW's area of operations. Map by Richard Nisa, adapted from Office of Inspector General U.S. Agency for International Development, Audit of USAID/Afghanistan's Incentives Driving Economic Alternatives for the North, East, and West Program, 2012, https://oig.usaid.gov/ sites/default/files/2018–06/f-306-12-004-p.pdf.*

weak.[89] On June 27, 2010, U.S. and coalition forces responded to this neo-Taliban resurgence with a major offensive that targeted insurgent infrastructures across the region.[90]

These geographies of violence shaped how DAI carried out alternative development in the field. While everyday security precautions—traveling with Afghans in older-model cars or camouflaging gendered bodies in chadors—helped DAI employees navigate the spaces of battle, their safety was never guaranteed.[91] My interviewees confirmed that it was not uncommon for IDEA-NEW staff to be threatened, shot at, bombed, and kidnapped. But they also agreed that women were more likely to experience violence than men. This was especially the case with women who were working, in the words of one employee, "in a region where women shouldn't be working."[92] One particularly notorious incident unfolded in the fall of 2010, when a woman staff member was abducted by neo-Taliban forces and subsequently killed in the course of the rescue attempt.[93]

Despite these risks, DAI still believed that market-driven alternative development could support overall counterinsurgency efforts by intervening on and modulating the environment of poppy cultivation. From the outset, however, DAI employees such as Anthony Hoffman found it challenging to "motivate" farmers to "come up with what [IDEA-NEW] was doing."[94] As with ADP/E, cash-for-work activities went some way toward building rapport between DAI technicians and rural farming communities. Ultimately, however, such quick-impact interventions on their own were insufficient to the task of helping Afghans overcome their biggest constraint to development and marketization: themselves. According to Hoffman, most of IDEA-NEW's beneficiaries were subsistence farmers who only cared about growing just enough crops on their plots of land to get their family by. Helping these farmers develop a new "mind-set" was no easy task. As Hoffman lamented: "When you are saying, 'You know what, you're doing this and that's fine, it gets you by and your family's OK, but if you do this, in five years, your family is going to be awesome,' they . . . don't care. . . . The neo-Taliban could be back in five years and they might not have a farm, like it's just day by day, get through the day. . . . We're trying to bring people from . . . the 1300s up to 2012, and that takes a really long time."[95] There is nothing exceptional about how Hoffman locates Afghan farmers in a "space beyond the pale of the modern."[96] As we have seen, this is one of the key Orientalist imaginative geographies that has always undergirded alternative development work in Afghanistan. But what is important about Hoffman's reflections is how he explicitly draws attention to the *longue durée* of alternative development work. This highlights the extent to which the problem of sustainability was weighing heavily on the minds of alternative development professionals such as Hoffman.

Indeed, sustainability was one of the guiding leitmotifs of IDEA-NEW. As a way of motivating beneficiaries to adopt new materials or techniques, DAI experimented with "one-time" interventions that would not cover any subsequent costs. Further support would only be provided on a "diminishing basis, calculated to engender responsibility on the part of project participants."[97] Carrying on USAID's long history of doing development work in Afghanistan—and elsewhere—IDEA-NEW would help rural households help themselves. DAI's objective here was not, as Mark Duffield might argue, to push Afghan farmers toward a "homeostatic" state of resilient self-reliance.[98] Rather, it was to convince farmers to assume primary responsibility for their own self-improvement. From DAI's perspective, farmers who embraced this challenge were ready to be governed as economic subjects who "respond systematically to modifications in the variables of the environment."[99]

DAI kick-started these experiments in neoliberal governmentality by taking a "wide view" of each potential value chain under consideration.[100] At first blush, IDEA-NEW's "wide view" seemingly carries forward ADP/E's "ecosystem" approach to poppy cultivation. But whereas ADP/E ambitiously tried to account for all of the different elements and nodes in rural value chains, IDEA-NEW was interested in stress-testing more surgical methods for intervening on alternative development ecosystems. During our conversation, Hoffman emphasized how the seemingly simple task of helping farmers "produce more produce" actually required DAI to consider the complex infrastructure of relations linking them to other economic actors, including suppliers, companies, middlemen, and transporters. Confronted by such an unknowable totality, DAI had no choice but to identify the specific "areas" and "people" that could be targeted to generate the biggest impacts along each agricultural value chain. As Hoffman put it to me, if one value chain has six nodes in it, "we'll work at two of those nodes, but we're not just trying to improve those two, but rather to have an improvement for everyone."[101]

In keeping with ADP/E, one of these nodes was always the space of the farm itself. Amira Garner, one of DAI's senior livelihood specialists, stressed that Afghan farmers had not "changed any way of doing things for thirty to forty years." Most farmers were still reliant on "antiquated methods," which was ultimately holding them back.[102] DAI attempted to solve this problem by once again stringing together a multiscalar infrastructure of extension and demonstration spaces across eastern Afghanistan. The majority of IDEA-NEW's beneficiaries accessed these training services at larger 1.5-acre commercial production farms, where they learned how modern agricultural techniques—raised beds, staggered planting, compost usage, and so on—could be put to work in cultivating a diversity of horticultural crops. Over time, DAI gradually extended this infrastructure by establishing smaller-scale plots in more remote villages.[103]

In both of these spaces, DAI built and managed everyday lived relationships with individual farmers. In Garner's words: "We say, 'Look, apply this fertilizer this way and you are going to get a 30 percent yield in your crop at harvest time,' and you show them slowly, and it builds trust: 'OK, wow, alright, it's worth that investment in the fertilizer and seeds and so forth.'"[104] Such alternative development encounters were always asymmetrical.[105] This is to say, they were framed by broader imperial relations of power and violence.[106] DAI agents were the agricultural development experts, and rural farmers remained the beneficiaries of that expertise. And yet, DAI also believed that this multiplicity of individualized training relationships could be managed in such a way as to optimize the aggregate life chances of rural communities.[107] Whenever possible, Garner recalls, IDEA-NEW used communal land for demonstration plots in order to prevent one person from reaping all of the rewards. DAI also identified capable community members to serve as the everyday face of alternative development work. These "lead farmers" committed themselves to thirty- or ninety-day training sessions, during which they also received in-kind support in the form of tools, seeds, and fertilizers. DAI's hope was that after completing the program, the participants would return home, where they would share their training with their peers.[108]

In general, demonstration plots outperformed those being farmed in traditional ways. In the northern region, for example, wheat demonstration plots produced yields that were approximately 60 percent higher than average.[109] IDEA-NEW's extension and demonstration activities were also characterized by a high "rate of adoption." This was a metric that DAI used to measure the extent to which "neighboring farmers [were] keen to learn from IDEA-NEW beneficiaries."[110] DAI compiled one survey which found that "88% of trainees had shared the skills they learned from the project with other farmers, with each participant teaching an average of 11 other people."[111] DAI's interpretation of this data was that farmers were buying in to alternative development programming, and adjusting their attitudes and behaviors accordingly. But Figure 14 cautions against such an overly optimistic reading, revealing that IDEA-NEW's demonstration farms were unevenly distributed across the region. According to the statistics provided on the left-hand side of the map, approximately 53 percent (72 out of 136) of all satellite plots and 59 percent (10 out of 17) of all commercial production farms were located in Nangarhar. DAI, in contrast, only established seven demonstration farms in Nuristan, all of which were concentrated in the province's southern districts. The impacts of IDEA-NEW's demonstration farms, both positive or negative, were therefore felt unevenly across the broader region.

As IDEA-NEW ran its course, it gradually moved away from the initial production-centric focus that it inherited from ADP/E. As Hoffman tells the story, DAI spent much of IDEA-NEW's first few years working with farmers in their fields. In 2012, however, DAI "stopped

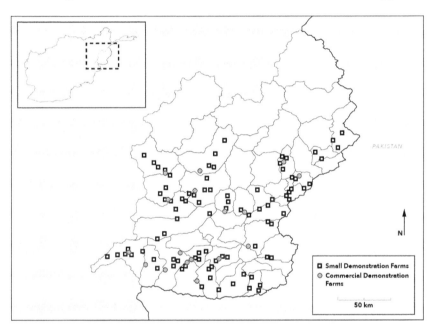

Small Demonstration Farms	
Province	Number of Farms
Kunar	33
Laghman	25
Nangarhar	72
Nuristan	6
Total	136

Commercial Demonstration Farms	
Province	Number of Farms
Kunar	3
Laghman	3
Nangarhar	10
Nuristan	1
Total	17

FIGURE 14. *Demonstration farm locations in the eastern region. Map by Richard Nisa. The map and tables are adapted from DAI, Summary Report: Year One, March 2, 2009—September 30, 2009, USAID DEC, 2009, https://pdf.usaid.gov/ pdf_docs/PDACU243.pdf, 6.*

doing seed subsidies and stuff like that." To quote Hoffman's defense of this decision: "We feel like we've shown [farmers] for the last x amount of years . . . 'Here's how to grow crops.'" "Now," he continued, "we're trying to help them move their crops down the value chain." DAI's turn toward "agricultural value chain enhancement" occurred at the expense of its investment in more conventional counternarcotics frameworks. This discursive reorientation is clearly evident in Hoffman's revisionist insistence that IDEA-NEW had "never really specifically been anti-poppy." Rather, it had "been an agricultural project that works in areas where there are also poppy growers."[112]

DAI confirmed this new alternative development direction in May 2012, when it refocused IDEA-NEW on helping beneficiary farmers participate in the "higher stages" of eight different value chains: vegetables, grapes, honey, livestock, orchard crops, poultry, silk, and wheat.[113] Convinced that rural Afghans were well positioned and motivated to "add value to their efforts," DAI ramped up IDEA-NEW's enterprise development efforts. As Garner informed me, Afghans are "entrepreneurial people by nature." If they were provided with the right skills and tools, "they could do a lot." In order to meet these presumed needs, DAI assembled a team tasked with helping small agro-entrepreneurs "get . . . the private sector going in Jalalabad." In theory, Garner argued, the proximity of Pakistan meant that IDEA-NEW's beneficiaries had all of these "great opportunities for trade." In practice, however, foreign merchants were "just crushing the local markets" with cheaper and better-quality produce.[114] IDEA-NEW's private sector development team provided beneficiary farmers with everything they needed to compete in this cutthroat environment: easier access to financing, enterprise registration programs, better business plans, SMS-based price fetching services, and a supportive network of community business associations, to name only a few examples.[115] Through these various activities, DAI wielded infrastructural power to establish and sustain a nurturing environment for everyday forms of entrepreneurialism.

Despite DAI's decision to move IDEA-NEW "beyond improved production," Garner's comments on the quality gap between foreign and local produce imply that beneficiaries, on average, continued to require some level of extension and demonstration assistance. Worried that government workers would not be able to "support" farmers after the termination of IDEA-NEW's contract, DAI gradually downloaded many of its key training and logistics responsibilities onto private sector partners.[116] In a neoliberal twist on established alternative development formulas, DAI pushed beneficiaries to "develop links" with these local subcontractors, who replaced IDEA-NEW field technicians as a source of inputs, agricultural techniques, and market development assistance.[117] DAI implemented one extension and demonstration program in 2012 where private sector partners not only prepared land and provided inputs, but also trained beneficiaries in transplanting seedlings, installing irrigation, controlling pests, weeding, and processing harvested crops.[118]

Thus far, the story of IDEA-NEW has been one of experimenting with various ways of nudging farmers toward "making good choices."[119] In DAI's hands, commercial production farms, smaller demonstration plots, business development centers, local markets, and even mobile phones became spaces where individual farmers entered into frictional relations with broader infrastructures of choice making. Michelle Murphy understands such deployments of infrastructural power as essential to the economization of life, and its attendant modes of neoliberal governmentality. But as she also reminds us, infrastructures concerned above all else with stimulating individual choices are always accompanied by pernicious investments in selectively undermining or abandoning key supports for life at an aggregate scale.[120] Following Murphy's invocation of Talal Asad, imperial and postcolonial development projects "do not reflect a simple expansion of the range of individual choice, but the creation of conditions in which only new (i.e., modern) choices can be made."[121] With IDEA-NEW, neoliberal infrastructures of choice making were shaped and supported by a more necropolitical combination of abandonment and outright violence. DAI's turn toward agricultural value chain enhancement was meant to bring about "improvement for everyone."[122] The concrete effect of IDEA-NEW, however, was to leave some of the more marginalized members of rural communities by the wayside. They were, in more Foucauldian terms, "let die."

Letting Die in Eastern Afghanistan

In her engagement with Foucault's lectures on neoliberalism, Li writes that all governmental assemblages are "guided by rationalities with distinct understandings of society, human nature, and the proper way of intervening in them."[123] Part of her project is to show that these distinctions matter. The same amalgamation of rural people can be governed as vulnerable children in need of protection, or as potential entrepreneurs who can be motivated by incentives and microcredit. It is for this reason that Li distinguishes the neoliberal art of government from its liberal equivalent. Liberals, Li argues, aspire to govern rural populations "in accordance with the grain of things."[124] They acquired detailed knowledge of the diverse capacities and characteristics of rural populations, which they then used to parse individuals who can be governed as autonomous and self-regulating subjects from those—women, the poor, colonial subjects—who were in need of more authoritarian and paternalistic forms of trusteeship, wardship, and protection.

As Patricia Owens subsequently makes clear, it is the latter approach, rooted in the older Greek tradition of *oikonomia*—a form of domestic governance where household members submit to the disciplinary authority of a benevolent and enlightened patriarch—that comes to predominate in liberal societies. Traditional histories of *oikonomia* emphasize that it was made obsolete by the ascendancy of liberalism in the eighteenth and nineteenth centuries, which had the effect of replacing the household with the contract as the dominant mode of social regulation. Owens counters that liberalism did not destroy household governance but merely transformed and upscaled it. The new liberal state governed, managed, and domesticated the life processes of the population as if it were simply the most modern, expansive, and bureaucratic iteration of the heteropatriarchal household. For Owens, the concept of *oikonomia* is better suited to capturing the various forms of violence that are both constitutive and unleashed by the liberal art of government.[125]

The neoliberal rationality of government, in contrast, advances a view of human nature that is explicitly universal. All humans have the capacity to act—and be governed—as *Homo oeconomicus.* Unlike *oikonomia,* neoliberal governing involves "setting conditions and devising incentives so that prudent, calculating individuals and communities choosing 'freely' and pursuing their own interests will contribute to the general interest as well."[126] In the interviews that I conducted, as well as the project documents that I consulted, DAI's turn toward agricultural value chain enhancement appears as an organic strategy for accommodating the increasing percentage of IDEA-NEW beneficiaries who were clearly demonstrating their ability to navigate risky environments as rational economic actors. A more careful and critical analysis, however, reveals the extent to which IDEA-NEW continued to be animated by a certain degree of *oikonomia*.

This is hardly surprising, considering how DAI was implementing IDEA-NEW under conditions of counterinsurgency, which, as Jairus Grove emphasizes in his reading of Owens's work, is what liberal *oikonomia* looks like when it "goes on the road."[127] Owens tracks how counterinsurgency has historically played a central role in disseminating the liberal model of household governance to colonial contexts. In particular, she identifies post-9/11 Afghanistan as the latest in a series of case studies that highlight this strategy of pacifying insurgent populations through infrastructures of indirect household rule. It was common for special forces brigades operating out of Village Stability Platforms to co-opt so-called tribal warlords with strategic disbursements of military and financial assistance.[128] This working relationship often culminated in the formation of an *arbakai*, or community militia. Although the U.S. military pitched *arbakai* as tools of counterinsurgency, all available evidence suggests that tribal warlords actually used them to consolidate or expand their personal bases of power. Elsewhere, counterinsurgents engaged in *oikonomia* to rearrange and reorganize some of the most intimate spaces of Afghan life. Owens argues that this was a fundamentally gendered and sexualized process. Counterinsurgents working in rural communities deliberately respected the authority of local elders, leaving them in charge of surveilling, controlling, and disciplining their households.[129] On those occasions when counterinsurgents felt compelled to intervene directly on household relations, they did so in ways that reproduced and entrenched their own Orientalist conceptions of Afghan gender hierarchies. Such attempts at "securing the intimate" reached their brutal climax in southern Afghanistan, where counterinsurgents infamously razed and rebuilt entire villages, deviating from the "local style" in ways that effectively carceralized community women inside household spaces.[130]

Much of the work on counterinsurgency *oikonomia* focuses on its military practitioners. But DAI's alternative development programming also implicates civilian counterinsurgents in the everyday work of imperial household management. With projects like IDEA-NEW, DAI was effectively carrying forward longer U.S. traditions of leveraging "home work" as a means of managing racialized populations. Mona Domosh's writings on the entanglements of race, gender, and development in the American South emphasize how government agents came to value home work as a method for repositioning women in historically racialized and marginalized communities as potential wellsprings of agricultural modernization and uplift. Much like the extension projects discussed in chapters 1 and 2, the home demonstration practices and techniques first honed in the Jim Crow South also went on to serve as the blueprint for subsequent U.S. gender development interventions across the decolonizing world. As Domosh writes, "Confronting the problem of how to establish some sort of control over 'foreign' peoples of different 'races' who were potential threats to American geopolitical rule, and hoping to shape these populations into 'better' producers and consumers, the U.S. government drew on its experiences with [home demonstration work] in the American South to conduct 'home work' overseas."[131] The forms of home work that circulated transnationally during the Cold War were undoubtedly shaped by the shifts from vulgar racism to liberal inclusion to multicultural neoliberalism that have been documented by scholars of U.S. empire building, such as Jodi Melamed, Takashi Fujitani, and Simeon Man. What began in the Jim Crow South as a suite of interventions that had the effect of upholding the racialized geographies of segregation and the color line morphed, over time, into a more technical or managerial project of optimizing the economic futures and potentials of beneficiary populations. And yet, throughout this transition, home development work remained a thoroughly racialized practice, making and manipulating the unequal distribution of life chances across new and intersecting axes of social differentiation.

This was especially true of IDEA-NEW, which struggled to reorganize rural household behaviors and relations in accordance with market logics. Over the course of IDEA-NEW, DAI tried to ascribe differing levels of economic fitness among beneficiary populations on the basis of certain entrenched cultural traits. This is to say, DAI broke with "an older racism's reliance on phenotype to innovate new ways of fixing human capacities to naturalize inequality."[132] But as DAI rapidly discovered, the average household in eastern Afghanistan was never a simple aggregation of market subjects. Some racialized and gendered forms of Afghan life were deliberately barred from acting—and being governed—as *Homo oeconomicus.* Others were interpellated in highly ineffective ways. Li observes that the complexities of different environments make it "all too easy to get the incentives wrong, creating outcomes quite different from the ones desired."[133] An ostensibly "environmental-type intervention" like IDEA-NEW therefore had to account for the diversity of contextual factors that influenced the decision-making processes of rural households.

To this end, DAI combined a diversity of quantitative and qualitative data collection techniques into an "epistemic infrastructure" that rendered rural households legible as a matrix of endlessly adjustable metrics.[134] DAI dispatched data collection teams to local communities, where they gathered up-to-date information on various aspects of the life of the population, including the number of families, yearly incomes, and the size of local economies.[135] Successive alternative development experiments were in turn powered and fueled by this thick data. By conjuring eastern Afghanistan as a biopolitical world amenable to experimentation, recomposition, and speculation, DAI's data collection drive promised the possibility of "making something different happen."[136] For DAI, "different" meant a technocratic dream of new market-based futures. But in order to modify the variables of the environment, DAI first had to know what they might be.

These epistemic infrastructures highlighted the geographical, agricultural, and economic diversity of eastern Afghanistan. DAI ostensibly fine-tuned its performance benchmarks to account for these regional differences.[137] But DAI nonetheless remained convinced that these differences would not serve as a source of friction to the extension of market infrastructures across the countryside. This is in line with the post-9/11 trend among both Afghan and international policy makers of championing market infrastructures as a replacement for the opium sector as the major driver of pro-poor economic growth.[138] Scholars who research Afghan livelihood strategies, however, were skeptical of this market exuberance. As early as June 2004, Sarah Lister and Adam Pain were calling on policy makers and development professionals to recognize that markets in rural Afghanistan were neither free nor equal.[139] They complicated such neoliberal discourses by foregrounding the intersection of extraeconomic factors—including class, race, ethnicity, gender, and geography—that conspire to prevent the majority of Afghans from participating in or benefiting from market activities.

As they clarify, it is always the elite who thrive under conditions of rural marketization, often at the expense of average farmers, who bear the brunt of any adverse consequences.[140]

DAI's turn toward agricultural value chain enhancement also produced "differentiated subjects of colonial rule."[141] David Mansfield's analysis of IDEA-NEW's impact on poppy cultivation in Nangarhar suggests that geography was one key axis of social sedimentation. He finds that IDEA-NEW had been "particularly active" in the fertile and well-irrigated districts straddling the Kabul River, including Surkhud, Kama, and Behsud.[142] Local farmers clearly took advantage of DAI's presence, as they were more likely to diversify their crops, engage in commercial horticulture, and seek out employment opportunities in urban economies. By contrast, the more remote communities located in key southern districts, such as Shinwar and Khogiani, were less well serviced. DAI initially made an explicit commitment to work with these marginalized households, which, at the time of IDEA-NEW's launch, were starting to relapse back into poppy cultivation. Mounting violence—which culminated in the killing of IDEA-NEW staff—curtailed these plans. DAI's decision to strategically minimize alternative development support in the south made it more difficult for farmers to generate the income levels necessary to subsist without poppy cultivation. Facing conditions of mounting economic distress, southern farmers became even less inclined to diversify their household subsistence strategies into higher value horticulture crops and off-farm income.[143] IDEA-NEW's success at adjusting behaviors and attitudes along the Kabul River Valley was therefore not replicated in the south.

In addition to entrenching Nangarhar's existing geographical fault lines, DAI also found it difficult to overcome long-standing gender inequalities. Mindful of ADP/E's strong gender bias, DAI tried to ensure that "women's economic activities" were integrated into—rather than marginalized from—emerging value chains.[144] To this end, DAI complemented existing microenterprise efforts with a new focus on nurturing "domestic" or "courtyard" economies. Following Lina Abirafeh, however, DAI reproduced many of the same problems that have long plagued "gender mainstreaming" activities in post-9/11 Afghanistan. Unsure of how best to define and operationalize the concept of gender, the USAID complex instead imported a narrow heteronormative framework that offered "technical solutions" to "women's problems."[145] This dearth of nuanced analysis and programming denied agency to rural women and men. This was particularly true in the economic sphere, where Afghan women continued to experience significant discrimination.[146] Most of the work done by Afghan women both inside and outside of the home has historically been "invisible, undervalued, and unpaid, providing few benefits."[147] Women who succeed at finding work are invariably burdened by what Lena Ganesh and her collaborators name as the "triple shift" of paid, reproductive, and emotional labor.[148] There are exceptions to this rule. Afghan women have historically played an outsized role in caring for and managing livestock herds.[149] But by and large, traditionally gendered divisions of labor have proved remarkably durable, such that rural women continued to find it difficult—if not impossible—to access the diverse spaces of economic activity. Overburdened by domestic responsibilities, rural women have little contact with market infrastructures on a day-to-day basis, as the purchasing or selling of items in public is narrowly scripted as a "man's task."[150] These problems are compounded by the fact that hegemonic sociocultural norms restrict women from accessing public spaces without a *mahram*—a male relative to act as a chaperone—making it difficult for them to participate in markets as self-regulating and autonomous subjects.[151]

All of this has serious implications for the growing percentage of economically active women who are making integral, if unrecognized, contributions to agricultural value chains. Although their "involvement is equal to that of men," Afghan women in agriculture face numerous access constraints—to land, credit, markets, and inputs—to moving beyond the "micro-scale of production."[152] Unfortunately, the USAID complex has a poor track record when it comes to helping Afghan women address these concerns. As Ganesh and her collaborators point out, extension training is often provided on the basis of land ownership, which automatically excludes most women farmers.[153] Trade facilitation activities have also done little to create an "enabling environment" or "level playing field" for women farmers who have otherwise found it difficult to break into highly gendered value chain infrastructures. IDEA-NEW's attempts at solving this problem have, in some ways, exacerbated the gendered geographies of rural labor. As Garner tells it, IDEA-NEW's "gender and micro-enterprise" unit promoted "mainly home-based activities" that were "actually kosher"— that "men would allow to happen"—such as cheese making, enterprise weaving, tailoring, and egg production, to name only a few examples. Garner claims that DAI confined its gender mainstreaming activities to domestic spaces because it was not an "easy process" to "identify different opportunities to engage women," just "given how strict the culture is in the east."[154] Some of Garner's colleagues were even more pessimistic, arguing that women in rural Afghanistan could not do a lot.[155] This was reflected in IDEA-NEW's own metrics, which show that alternative development activities once again overwhelmingly targeted men.[156] While DAI prepared Afghan men for a future of market participation, it simultaneously confined Afghan women to a present of household reproduction.

Patricia Owens argues that counterinsurgency claims to empower women yet actually bolsters heteropatriarchal family units. Helen Kinsella concurs, suggesting that one of the primary aims of counterinsurgency is to reinscribe women's position within household spaces. IDEA-NEW was no different. Instead of encouraging Afghan women to access markets and work, it steered them toward "courtyard" or "domestic" industries in which their "labour [was] (made) cheap." Women fixed within the space of the *domus* went from being autonomous political subjects with their own ideas of what justice and freedom might entail in the context of rural Afghanistan to an "object of social administration."[157] Following Laleh Khalili, they were massified into an "undifferentiated 'womenandchildren'" that was managed simultaneously as a "malleable mass, a docile subject, and a yielding terrain of domination."[158]

Despite all of this, mainstream commentators continued to celebrate IDEA-NEW as a "successful model for foreign aid" that actually "offers Afghans the help they need to improve their lives."[159] Guided by DAI's more humane hand, farmers went from being victims to beneficiaries. As Eyal Weizman cautions, however, we must always be aware of the stick that hides behind any carrot.[160] In order to create conditions "in which only new (i.e., modern) choices can be made," DAI minimized—and even abandoned—alternative development supports for various forms of marginalized Afghan life. But IDEA-NEW was also undergirded by— and provided a legitimating armature for—more destructive counternarcotics techniques, such as eradication and nexus targeting. In this way, the USAID complex became actively complicit in targeting and eliminating alternative infrastructures of rural life making.

Neutralizing the Nexus

For many commentators, Holbrooke's June 2009 promise to phase out American support for eradication operations signaled a turn toward kinder, gentler, and more therapeutic counternarcotics techniques and technologies. As in Helmand and Kandahar, however, counternarcotics in postsurge Nangarhar was very much business as usual.

Concerned by the latest resurgence of poppy cultivation in southern Nangarhar, Governor Sherzai inaugurated the 2010 fighting season by redispatching eradication units to remote districts such as Sherzad. It is now widely acknowledged that the Sherzai regime botched these efforts. Conducted on the cusp of the poppy harvest, they became bogged down in a protracted and difficult process of negotiation. Sherzai himself is reported to have insulted and threatened local elders and authority figures. Sherzad residents responded to these provocations by inviting antigovernment elements into the district to "protect" poppy fields: an act of insurgency that sparked deadly clashes with Afghan National Police forces.[161]

Sherzai's failure to reimpose a total ban on poppy cultivation in these districts proved to be the first of many decisive moments in a longer struggle for control over the countryside. Over the course of the 2010–2011 growing season, the collapse of Sherzai's 2007 ban accelerated. Poppy cultivation expanded further down the valleys of Sherzad, as well as into the southern districts of Khogiani, Achin, Pachir Wa Agam, and Hesarak.[162] Mansfield explains these dramatic increases in poppy cultivation as a function of Sherzai's shifting political fortunes. While Sherzai's endorsement of the botched 2010 eradication campaign damaged his reputation as a "bulldozer" who "gets things done," it was his subsequent involvement in the infamous Achin conflict that made it nigh impossible for him to project political power in these relapsing districts.[163]

The origins of the Achin conflict can be traced back to a dispute between two Shinwari subtribes—the Sepai and the Alisherkhel—over the ownership of a tract of desert land, approximately ten to fifteen square kilometers in size. In early 2010, a group of Sepai erected a building on the border of the contested plot of land, which was then demolished by the Alisherkhel. Undaunted, the Sepai retaliated by reestablishing a small settlement. Again, they were chased off by armed Alisherkhel in March 2010.[164] At this juncture, foreign interference escalated this localized land dispute into a full-blown conflict. As the Sepai were being evicted from their squatter settlement, they were also attacked by a local neo-Taliban offshoot. Although the Sepai were able to fend off the insurgents, they realized that the situation was beginning to spiral out of control and approached U.S. Special Forces for support. U.S. Special Forces signed a pact with the Sepai, offering them weapons, munitions, and cash in exchange for the establishment of an *arbakai* that would be tasked with keeping neo-Taliban forces out of the area. While this Shinwari Pact was "highly publicized as a significant development for the country's security," it backfired spectacularly, as the Sepai turned their newly acquired weapons on the Alisherkhel.[165] In response, the Alisherkhel requested and received support from Pakistani insurgents. After a number of false starts, Governor Sherzai finally brokered an agreement to disarm both subtribes on October 26, 2010. Although the Alisherkhel complied with the terms of the agreement, the Sepai did not. Two days later, a Sepai *lashkar* not only attacked a meeting of provincial authorities—which included Sherzai—but also shot at a U.S. helicopter, an act that triggered a number of retaliatory strikes.[166]

Sherzai's failure to peacefully resolve this dispute had a number of far-reaching consequences. According to Mansfield, the reputations of both the Sherzai regime and local authorities were "irrevocably damaged" among local farmers.[167] District elites who had previously managed the relationships linking locals and Jalalabad became increasingly superfluous. As antigovernment elements stepped into this vacuum of authority, farming communities became increasingly convinced that the provincial government no longer possessed the coercive power necessary to mount an effective eradication campaign.[168] Emboldened, local farmers decided that they were not only going to cultivate increasing amounts of poppy, but that they were going to resist eradication operations by any means necessary. Throughout the 2010 growing season, eradication resulted in the death of forty-eight people, yet only succeeded in destroying 748 hectares of poppy.[169] In an effort to stem the violence, provincial authorities and the Afghan security apparatus all but abandoned eradication, opting instead for a more consultative approach. Negotiations, however, quickly broke down, and by 2013, Nangarhar had once again become a "poppy paradise."[170]

Alongside these eradication efforts, the U.S. military also intensified its interdiction campaign in Regional Command–East (RC-East). In 2009, the Pentagon authorized U.S. forces to "remove" drug traffickers from the battlefield through "kill/capture" operations. According to two U.S. generals stationed in Afghanistan, Operation Enduring Freedom's "Rules of Engagement," as well as the internationally recognized "Laws of War," permitted the addition of "drug traffickers with proven links to the insurgency"—or "nexus targets"—on a Joint Integrated Prioritized Target List.[171] Derek Gregory explains the Joint Integrated Prioritized Target List as a heuristic used by the U.S. military to facilitate the interdiction of high-value targets. In the Afghan theatre, the U.S. military "maintains a subsidiary Joint Prioritized Effects List [JPEL] that identifies 'insurgent leaders' and 'nexus targets' . . . who may be killed or captured."[172] Once a week, the U.S. military's Joint Targeting Working Group met with military lawyers and other civilian representatives to vet "target nomination packs." By October 2009, reports were speculating that this working group had added hundreds—if not thousands—of names to the JPEL, at least fifty of which were nexus targets. Once identified, these nexus targets were scheduled for neutralization via "fix-and-finish missions" that were generally carried out by either Joint Special Operations Command or the U.S. Air Force.[173] Like the infamous Phung Hoang program of extrajudicial assassination that was the focus of so much consternation during the Vietnam War, these shadowy "kill/capture operations" targeted the political, operational, and economic infrastructures of insurgent life for extinguishment.[174]

In 2009, U.S. Central Command (CENTCOM) established a Combined Joint Interagency Task Force (CJIATF) to support and further streamline the everyday work of nexus targeting.[175] CENTCOM claims that the purpose of this civil–military task force—code-named Nexus—was to break the linkages between narcotics and insurgency by targeting "network functions (e.g. safe havens, movement, communications, and finance)" rather than individual traffickers.[176] There is a dearth of publicly available information on the nexus targeting process, making it difficult to verify these claims empirically. A close reading of job ads and LinkedIn profiles, however, suggests that Task Force Nexus was more directly involved in the work of nexus targeting than CENTCOM lets on. Task Force Nexus intelligence analysts, for example, supported "lethal and nonlethal operations against insurgent, narco-traffickers, malign influencers within GIRoA and Afghan National Security Forces (ANSF) to include JPEL targeting, law enforcement, and key leader engagements."[177] In his capacity as a Task Force Nexus targeting officer, Eric Camehl supported the U.S. counternarcotics mission by conducting "network analysis and development, named area of interest, development, high value persons pattern of life analysis, and illicit ratline studies."[178] Taken together, these sources call into question the Pentagon's claim that Task Force Nexus does not target individuals for neutralization.

While nexus targeting operations were undoubtedly commonplace in Afghanistan's unstable south, WikiLeaks's ICWATCH website reveals that Task Force Nexus was also active in RC-East. Consider, for instance, the profile of senior intelligence analyst, Jerod Harness. According to WikiLeaks,

> Mr. Harness was assigned to CJIATF-Nexus as a Counter Corruption Analyst and Counter Narcotics Target Developer. He worked in the RC-East HQ at Bagram [Air Base], Afghanistan, supporting DEA and Task Force Counter Narcotics Teams with target packages for their daily operations.[179]

These findings are further corroborated by the profile of Earl Owens, a "HUMINT Intelligence Analyst" who worked for a U.S. military contractor, BAE systems. Owens reportedly "worked closely with CJIATF-Nexus/counter-corruption-counter-narcotics cells for RC-East to coordinate action against drug labs and key leaders located in Nangarhar and Helmand Province." Over the course of his deployment, he produced "170 Story Boards" for killing or capturing fifty-four high-value targets, which included "two of the largest drug kingpins in Afghanistan."[180]

Counternarcotics analysts like Harness and Owens were assisted in their jobs by an Interagency Operations and Coordination Center.

A joint collaboration between the U.S. Drug Enforcement Administration and the United Kingdom's Serious Organized Crime Agency, the coordination center collated various forms of raw counternarcotics intelligence into "target packs," which were then vetted by Task Force Nexus officials to determine potential additions to the JPEL.[181] To a certain degree, it is striking how closely these coordination centers resembled the similarly named District Intelligence and Operations Coordinating Centers, which played a central role in supporting Phung Hoang operations in the Vietnam War.[182] But from another perspective, the coordination centers are an unsurprising testament to the enduring and highly citationary nature of U.S. imperial and infrastructural power. Techniques and technologies that prove their effectiveness in one theatre of U.S. imperialism are always repurposed for redeployment in another.

Unsurprisingly, nexus targeting proved highly controversial. Afghan officials such as General Mohammad Daud worried that foreign troops would neutralize nexus targets on the basis of secret evidence, rather than handing them over to Afghan forces for trial. Others such as Nur al-Haq Ulumi, a Kandahar-based politician, argued that the situation in the countryside would deteriorate rapidly if international forces started to neutralize drug dealers. According to Ulumi, Afghans already "feel that foreigners didn't really come here to reconstruct our country," but rather, "just came here to kill us." Similarly, the UNODC's Jean Luc Lemahieu cautioned international forces against escalating interdiction operations "a step too far."[183]

Although I am sympathetic with Ulumi's concerns, I argue that extrajudicial killing and reconstruction are not mutually exclusive processes but rather often occur in tandem in the Afghan countryside. Like the "other" war for Vietnamese "heart[h]s and minds" before it, the Afghan counternarcotics campaign was marked by an interplay between "catastrophic techniques that damage and destroy life" and "providential techniques that repair and improve life."[184] While alternative development programs like IDEA-NEW are not directly implicated in either eradication or nexus targeting, they are hardly innocent. As I have shown, they build and sustain certain forms of rural life, while simultaneously minimizing, abandoning, and eliminating others.[185] It is precisely this dialectical tension between life/death, violence/care, creation/destruction, and anger/mercy that IDEA-NEW inherited from its forbears; that, by extension, is constitutive of the U.S. imperial project more broadly.

Zombie Development?

In many ways, IDEA-NEW is the culmination of seventy years of rural development experimentation in the Afghan countryside. But U.S. imperial infrastructures are also restless and forward looking, always dreaming new ways of governing marginalized, insurgent, and decolonizing populations toward economy. The key political question then becomes, What kind of new blueprint of infrastructural power does IDEA-NEW offer moving forward?

While DAI's alternative development programming may have failed to reduce both poppy cultivation and violence in northeastern Afghanistan, it nonetheless had the effect, to paraphrase James Ferguson, of "expanding the exercise of a particular sort of [infrastructural] power," one that sought to establish the market economy as the general, defining index of government.[186] As alternative development programs like ADP/E and IDEA-NEW ran their course, DAI's "commercial" approach to the problem of poppy cultivation gradually acquired the force of common sense among practitioners and beneficiaries alike, who increasingly saw market participation as the only viable pathway to a brighter future and a better life. This is exemplified by how eastern Afghanistan, along with the southern region, became the site for a Regional Agricultural Development Program. Hoffman speculated that these "hard-core value chain ag-production projects" would be "very challenging." As he clarified:

> Even five years is impossible to get a lot of results in ag stuff. . . .
> It says you've got to have 60 million dollars in created revenues
> through sales of ag products . . . and I honestly don't know . . .
> how anyone's going to do that.[187]

DAI, of course, felt that it was up to the challenge and eventually secured the right to implement the Regional Agricultural Development Program for northern Afghanistan.

Hoffman's very real anxieties about the feasibility of generating at least $60 million in agricultural sales speaks to the increasingly precarious terrain of development-security work in contemporary Afghanistan. He exposes a clear incongruity between the expectations that the U.S. empire-state sets for itself, and its everyday, in-house capacity to actually meet these benchmarks in any substantive or meaningful way. From the outset, empire has been a fundamentally experimental and utopian project, one that unfolds and travels through models, plans, blueprints, calculations, speculations, and laboratories.[188] For this reason, U.S. empire building has always been defined by its seemingly limitless capacity to transmute failure into reinvention and renewal. Reading Jodi Byrd alongside Jamie Peck suggests that in this current conjuncture defined by everywhere warfare, racial and carceral capitalist crisis, ecological collapse, and resurgent white nationalism, this process has now entered its zombie phase: jaded and discredited, yet lurching haphazardly onward, its lethal defensive mechanisms still intact.[189]

Hoffman's ambivalent and frictional encounter with the broader USAID complex's stubborn commitment to rural marketization can be read, I think, as a simultaneous indictment and acceptance of how development theory and practice is also gradually taking on the increasingly zombie-like qualities that Peck diagnoses as typical of contemporary neoliberalism. But even if the USAID complex has contributed to the minimization, marginalization, and elimination of rural Afghans, to what extent has it followed other infrastructures of U.S. settler imperial power—such as the global war prison, the Middle Passage, or frontier countersovereignty—in reproducing the targets of development assistance as "living dead"?[190] Much like the tortured, the interned, the enslaved, and the colonized, marginalized and impoverished Afghans have demonstrated their capacity and willingness to resist the rollout of U.S. imperial power. Under such enduring conditions of zombie imperialism, then, what alternative, unaligned, or anti-imperial futures become possible?

Conclusion

Development in a Time of Abolition

> The colonized, underdeveloped man is today a political
> creature in the most global sense of the term.
>
> *Frantz Fanon,* The Wretched of the Earth

> Afghanistan was the "great experiment." There was a great
> DoD presence, it kind of worked. It's expensive to be engaged
> in a constant effort—it's like leaning into the fire. The surge
> politicized—nation building is a taboo term. Need for
> rebranding, kick the past aside for the sake of the future.
>
> *Anonymous, U.S. Army civil affairs officer,*
> *January 20, 2016, "U.S. Army Civil Affairs Officer,*
> *Lessons Learned Interview,"* The Afghanistan Papers

IN JULY 2012, John Sopko was sworn in as the special inspector general
for Afghanistan reconstruction (SIGAR). As the "chief watchdog of US
reconstruction spending in Afghanistan," his job was to "call strikes."[1]
This brought Sopko into direct conflict with USAID. In Sopko's eyes,
USAID had grossly mismanaged the Afghan reconstruction effort. It
had "constructed" buildings that subsequently disappeared into thin
air, channeled foreign assistance to Afghan subcontractors later revealed to be affiliated with insurgent groups, and actively conspired to
hide vital information from both auditors and lawmakers.[2]

At the time, the U.S. counterinsurgency campaign was already
sputtering. But in the intervening years since the U.S. empire-state's
ostensible "drawdown" from Afghanistan, things have only worsened.
Each subsequent fighting season has generally been more deadly than
the last. The violence peaked in 2018, when (para)military actors killed
3,804 civilians—an 11 percent increase from 2017 levels—and wounded
another 7,189. What made the 2018 fighting season the deadliest on

record was the fact that neo-Taliban insurgents were increasingly sharing rural battlespaces with Islamic State of Iraq and the Levant fighters.[3] According to the United Nations, both groups ramped up their use
of suicide attacks that disproportionately target civilian populations.
Their combined operations accounted for 63 percent of all civilian casualties in 2018. U.S. and Afghan air raids were the direct cause of the
other 37 percent, reportedly killing over 500 civilians.[4]

The USAID complex's impacts on the life chances of rural Afghans
have also remained fleeting and ephemeral. There is no better example of USAID's inability to "conduct the conduct" of rural populations
than the continued and explosive growth of poppy cultivation across
Afghanistan. In September 2014, Sopko was already offering a particularly grim assessment of counternarcotics progress in the countryside:

> The US has already spent nearly $7.6 billion to combat the
> opium industry. Yet by every conceivable metric, we've failed.
> Production and cultivation are up, interdiction and eradication
> are down, financial support to the insurgency is up, and ad-
> diction and abuse are at unprecedented levels in Afghanistan.
> During my trips to Afghanistan, I've met with US, Afghan, and
> international officials involved in implementing and evaluating
> counternarcotics programs. In the opinion of almost everyone
> I've met, the counternarcotics situation in Afghanistan is dire,
> with little prospect for improvement.[5]

Sopko was particularly astonished to find that counternarcotics programming, despite its overall importance to the Afghan reconstruction
effort, had not been prioritized by the Department of Justice, the State
Department, or the Pentagon during—as well as after—the transition
period. "Without an effective counternarcotics strategy and Afghan political will to tackle this problem," Sopko prophesied, "Afghanistan could
well become a narco-criminal state in the near future."[6]

It is now widely believed that Sopko's warnings have come to pass.
In 2017, Afghan farmers cultivated poppies on a record 328,000 hectares of land, harvesting a staggering 9,000 tons of raw opium. The total
area under poppy cultivation did subsequently decline back down to
263,000 hectares.[7] But Afghanistan, as Craig Whitlock recently wrote
for the *Washington Post,* remains "overwhelmed by opium."[8] Alfred

McCoy goes even further in *The Guardian*, arguing that "Afghanistan's unique ecology [has] converged with American military technology to transform this remote, landlocked nation into the world's *first true narco state*—a country where illicit drugs dominate the economy, define political choices, and determine the fate of foreign interventions." (In)famous for exposing the Central Intelligence Agency as one of the central drivers of Cold War drug production and trafficking, McCoy concludes his essay by observing that the U.S. empire-state is once again confronted by the same choice that it had to make in the run up to the Surge: continue to invest in a failed military drug war, or channel some of this "misspent" funding toward sustained rural development interventions that might offer "more economic options for the millions of farmers who depend upon the opium crop for employment."[9]

McCoy's article is striking for a number of reasons. He pushes an alternative development model rooted in the reestablishment of orchards, the repopulation of livestock herds, the replenishment of seed stocks, and the reconstruction of ruined irrigation infrastructures as a way of ending the U.S. drug war in Afghanistan. But as we saw in chapters 3 and 4, alternative development and the War on Drugs are not so easily disentangled. Across southern and eastern Afghanistan, rural communities experienced alternative development as simply another phase of the War on Drugs, one that took root in landscapes ruined by poppy eradication and police intervention, producing new geographies of slow violence, organized abandonment, and premature death. One might argue, then, that McCoy's call to replace counternarcotics ecologies with development ones is reformist in the sense that it simply entails shifting funding from one action arm of the U.S. empire-state to another.

More generally, however, McCoy's article contributes to an emerging genre of public commentary that, since 2014, has offered various postmortems of the U.S. empire-state's military occupation of Afghanistan. What, McCoy and so many others ask, went so terribly wrong in Afghanistan? And what lessons can we learn moving forward? SIGAR has been one of the main contributors to such debates, publishing massive reports that identify the most valuable lessons learned from the good war in Afghanistan. One such report focuses on the Afghan counternarcotics campaign. It recommends, "in flat, bureaucratic jargon," two ways of improving counternarcotics programming moving forward.

The first is to develop a "whole-of-government US counternarcotics strategy" for "[coordinating] various agencies around shared, long-term goals." The second is to align and integrate counternarcotics goals into the "larger security, development, and government objectives of the United States and the host nation."[10] SIGAR supposedly distilled these somewhat anemic lessons from the thousands of exit interviews that it conducted with military officers, development professionals, private contractors, Afghan government officials, and career diplomats between 2014 and 2018. Concerned that these "Lesson Learned" reports were deliberately downplaying some of the toughest criticisms contained in the source materials, the *Washington Post* successfully filed a Freedom of Information Act claim against SIGAR, forcing it to release the transcripts and interview notes. The resulting *Afghanistan Papers* exposé promised to reveal the "secret history" of the war in Afghanistan. In actuality, it largely confirmed what many already suspected: the U.S. counterinsurgency was defined—and ultimately derailed—by friction, confusion, and incoherence.

"Thanks USAID"

It is beyond the scope of this conclusion to inventory all of the different grievances aired in these 611 exit interviews. Of the 215 that dealt with questions of nation building from both civilian and military perspectives, most cover familiar and well-trodden ground. Many civilian interviewees trafficked in longer-standing skepticisms of the military turn toward stabilization. Back in 2013, Elaine Kingsley asserted to me in our interview that "AID does not do counterinsurgency." "We are assistance providers," she continued, working to build a "more developed, free-market economy with democratic principles." The military's "end-state," in contrast, is merely "end of hostilities," nothing more.[11] Six years later in the *Afghanistan Papers,* civilian nation builders reproduce such distinctions in their critiques of how military cash distribution initiatives like the infamous Commander's Emergency Response Program (CERP) were "out of control" because they made it possible for inexperienced junior officers to distribute destabilizing sums of "funny money" with little to no oversight.[12] Provincial reconstruction teams (PRTs) were similarly "inefficient and ineffective."[13] The soldiers who commanded PRTs "did not know what to do," nor did they engage the "overall development effort."[14] They "thought development [w]as just giving people money" and consequently prioritized "instant fixes" over "long-term plans."[15] All of this speaks to the ways in which military objectives, according to one USAID official, became the *only* driver of counterinsurgency. "Assumptions," they argued, "were made by people who had no understanding of the basic conditions in the country." Because civilians wanted to "play the game and be supportive," they went along with things, even when such assumptions were wildly "off-base."[16] But the truth for many civilians was that the "military had no business doing anything resembling dev."[17]

While some soldiers agreed that there were military development projects that "should not have been done"—one brigadier general acknowledged that PRT commanders were not prepared to lead stability operations in "complex environment[s]"—many still reserved their choicest criticisms for USAID.[18] The same brigadier general accused USAID of inappropriately trying to justify its own existence with projects that supposedly perpetuated an Afghan reliance on development expertise and capital.[19] Another U.S. Army Civil Affairs officer complained:

> USAID showed up in their Italian suits and shoes and would tell us, "We procured 40 million." That is twice what we spent on CERP. The Afghans didn't even need it. We just sat there and said, "Thanks USAID, you're totally ruining what we did." There was no shared vision—USAID was just going to pour money and that's what they were going to do. It was a total waste. There was no central plan, just running around, doing what they wanted.[20]

What is striking about this excerpt is how the interviewee inverts the civilian critique of CERP and stability operations, projecting it back on to USAID. Other soldiers do something similar in their own exit interviews when they express how they felt like "borrowed military power for USAID." USAID, from this perspective, "used" the U.S. military to achieve its own objectives, which was ultimately to the detriment of a "whole of government approach."[21]

Having diagnosed the key problems that plagued the U.S. nation-building effort in Afghanistan, civilian and military interviewees then distilled their diverse experiences into a series of "lessons learned" for future generations of counterinsurgents. Some of these lessons included "Occupation is a bad idea," "Operate much more like a business taking risks," "Aim small and make it personal," "Don't write things in your documents that you cannot do," and last but not least, base spending on "determined need, not arbitrary amounts passed down from Congress."[22] For the most part, these lessons were reformist, largely intended to improve the everyday workings of nation building and counterinsurgency across the decolonizing world. But some interviewees offered a more "structural" critique of their involvement in the war.[23] One former senior U.S. official noted that a lot of their colleagues were asking a vexing question: "Why are we doing the same things over and over?"[24] The U.S. empire-state went into the war cognizant of the need to confront the "lessons from previous eras."[25] But as the official observed, "We kept doing [development]" even though "We all recognized that it wasn't working."[26] To figure out why, they traced the USAID complex's structural issues all the way back to the Beltway. What they eventually singled out as a key issue of concern was the (sub)contracting infrastructures that organize the everyday work of development, enriching American contractors at the expense of ordinary Afghans. Big USAID contracts generally go to one of the major Beltway players, such as Chemonics or DAI. The winning bidder then subcontracts to smaller companies, who themselves outsource the actual job to Afghan implementers. Each subcontractor takes their cut, ensuring that less than 10 percent of the total contract actually gets to the village.

USAID adopted these practices in the post–Cold War era to appease deficit hawks such as Jessie Helms, who were questioning the value of international aid programming. After an intense period of negotiations, a compromise was reached. USAID could continue implementing aid programs as long as it spent the majority of its money domestically on American products and expertise. Under these new conditions, the USAID complex became a conduit for channeling public funds into the coffers of private contractors and NGOs. Many of the USAID employees who sat down for interviews with SIGAR often described their work in Afghanistan in terms of "re-establishing and expanding private sector development."[27] One might argue, however, that the USAID complex was ultimately more successful at spurring capitalist accumulation back home in the Beltway. As one USAID official succinctly put it: "We abandoned [the Afghans]. Chemonics made billions."[28]

But what might a structural fix to these problems look like? It is here that the political limitations of SIGAR's "Lessons Learned" project become most obvious. The former senior U.S. official who was most explicit in their call for "structural" fixes reportedly sat down with a friend "who knew the Afghan business side" to identify potential solutions. Changing the system, they determined, meant recruiting and retaining the "right people" who could think outside the box and solve problems through their good interpersonal skills. These new hires, in turn, would form the core of a new expeditionary force, capable of "[turning] on a dime" in a counterinsurgency environment.[29] The idea here is for USAID to build the "capacity for a surge beyond contracting."[30] Structural problems would be addressed at the scale of the individual.

This obsession with transforming USAID "to be more expeditionary" undoubtedly emerges out of a nostalgia for the immediate post-1945 moment: a time when the U.S. empire-state did "some of the best state and nation-building the world has ever seen."[31] Indeed, the Marshall Plan, the occupation of Japan, the Korean "police action," and the Vietnam War were all important historical touchstones for a number of interviewees. Both Marin Strmecki, Donald Rumsfeld's former civilian advisor, and Wais Barmak, Afghanistan's former minister of rural rehabilitation and development, hold up South Korea as a model of how a long-term, systematic approach to nation building can transform an "absolutely devastated place" into an "Asia Tiger."[32] Village stability platforms and PRTs also carried within them echoes of the integrated Civil Operations and Revolutionary Development Support (CORDS) model in Vietnam, which some interviewees pitched as a blueprint for how the USAID complex might move beyond its wasteful reliance on expensive subcontractors. The irony here is that the U.S. counterinsurgency track record in Vietnam was less than stellar. Richard Holbrooke reportedly "knew" that stability operations would not work in Afghanistan largely because of his formative experiences waging counterinsurgency in Vietnam.[33] But what this imperial rediscovery of the post-1945 moment as a golden age of nation building also conceals is the incredible violence of expeditionary development, both in Korea and Vietnam. Under the enabling umbrella of CORDS, USAID used development in a very "inhumane way," training police forces, managing prisons, covering up torture, and supporting kill/capture missions.[34] Reorienting USAID toward a more expeditionary future leaves the door open for its employees to once again take on the "dirty work of Empire."[35]

SIGAR's "Lessons Learned" project does float one other potential "structural fix" to the problem of rampant subcontracting, which is to simply channel development capital directly to the Afghan government. While many interviewees recognized the "value" of this approach, they nonetheless believed it would have been irresponsible to apply it in corrupt Afghanistan. But as Richard Boucher told his interviewer, "Sometimes you just have to spend money and hope that it is useful or assume that some of it will disappear." In Boucher's eyes, it is ultimately preferable that development capital "disappear in Afghanistan rather than in the Beltway" because "in the end, it is going to make sure that more of the money gets to some village."[36] And as Boucher and Jeffrey Eggers point out, if the U.S. empire-state was actually serious about cutting down on waste, then it would subject Pentagon budgets to equally sustained levels of scrutiny.[37] And yet the problem always seems to be the $2.5 billion earmarked for civilian development work, and not the $2.26 trillion tab that the Pentagon has racked up over the course of its two-decade occupation of Afghanistan.[38]

For obvious reasons, SIGAR's "Lessons Learned" project falls well short of articulating a structural critique of the USAID complex for public audiences. Boucher's and Eggers's exit interviews resonate with the critiques articulated by high-ranking Afghan technocrats, who consistently took the USAID complex to task for failing to "match the needs of the people."[39] From these interviewees, we learn that while ordinary Afghans embraced development, their everyday interactions with the USAID complex taught them that their wants have never been in alignment with the objectives of the broader mission.[40] What SIGAR's "Lessons Learned" project assumes is that this is a mismatch that can be smoothed over by enacting what abolitionists like Ruth Wilson Gilmore call "reformist reforms."[41] Boucher and Eggers cannot envision a world in which the USAID complex does not intervene on and mediate the basic needs of beneficiary populations. Even if the USAID complex is, by design, extractive, predatory, and asset stripping, the "structural fix" is not to slam on the brakes and reverse course, but rather, to find ways of helping it fail forward.

I conclude this book by arguing that the USAID complex needs to be the target of an explicitly internationalist or multiscalar politics of abolitionist organizing and struggle that encompasses both the domestic carceral state and the imperial national security state. Here, I am explicitly following the lead of scholars and activists such as Angela Davis, Ruth Wilson Gilmore, Mariame Kaba, Stuart Schrader, and Anun Kundnani, who have historically drawn upon the political and intellectual legacies of the Black radical tradition to foreground the "generative possibilities of applying an abolitionist approach not only domestically within the US, but also to its agencies of global security."[42] In the late 1960s and early 1970s, Black radicals and their Latinx, Puerto Rican, Asian American, and Indigenous allies were acutely aware of the "overlap between the structures of police violence at home and the structures of military violence abroad." Over time, they came to recognize that freedom struggles in the United States were but "one element in an international movement for liberation, from Vietnam to Puerto Rico and Palestine."[43] This explicitly internationalist framework has been carried forward by contemporary abolitionists such as Angela Davis, Mariame Kaba, and Ruth Wilson Gilmore, who have always called for antiprison organizing work to take on global infrastructures of migrant detention, as well as the carceral geographies of rendition and capture that have long defined the U.S. outer race war on terror.

In recent years, Stuart Schrader has been especially vocal in his calls for abolitionists to hold the foreign and the domestic "in a single frame, as indissolubly linked, as co-constituted."[44] For Schrader, dismantling the carceral state requires dismantling the national security state. As he explains in a recent *Intercepted* podcast:

When we talk about the carceral state, what we're talking about is, in part, the gross inflation of the amount of resources dedicated to punishment, policing, and disciplining populations. We can see an analog in the national security state, which of course itself also has a massive budget that far outstrips the budget for almost anything else in the United States. The logic behind both of these, I think, is very similar. The idea is security first, above all else. So in order to dismantle some of the institutions, we have to think about dismantling the logic. And when we see that they have a shared logic or a shared set of rationales, I think

it becomes imperative to start talking about them in the same
conversation.[45]

When Schrader invokes the national security state here and elsewhere,
he is particularly concerned with the transnational infrastructures of
police training, modernization, and violence that have long served as
one of the major pillars of U.S. global power. But as I have shown in
this book, the USAID complex's fundamental purpose has always been,
as David Bell put it so succinctly back in 1962, "national security." Abolishing the national security state, by implication, also means abolishing
the USAID complex.

 Mindful of how U.S. Republicans—including, most recently, former
President Trump—have historically threatened to defund USAID and
transfer its responsibilities to an already overburdened State Department, I want to clarify that this is not a call to move beyond small-d
development.[46] What threads through the everyday work of radical collectives such as No New Jails NYC, Critical Resistance, Californians
United for a Responsible Budget, or the Share-a-Ton organizers, I argue,
is a recognition that abolitionist struggles necessarily require a theory
and practice of development that is grounded in an internationalist
politics of collective solidarity, mutual aid, and community or grassroots organizing.[47] If abolition, following Dylan Rodriguez, is about
building liberatory futures of social transformation, then development,
it seems to me, has a role to play in such a project, both at home and
abroad.[48] There is, of course, a vibrant tradition of scholarly and political work that has struggled to imagine how development might be
mobilized for decolonial ends, one that is most famously associated
with the inaugural Afro-Asian Conference that took place from April
18 to 24, 1955, in Bandung, Indonesia (and to which the Kingdom of
Afghanistan sent a delegation).[49] In what remains of this conclusion, I
want to carry forward the internationalist spirit of Bandung and take
seriously the contradictory dialectic of critique and investment that has
shaped how ordinary Afghans relate to development. Vinay Gidwani
powerfully reminds us that development is "always anchored to a moral
geography of place-making" and "that its evaluation is, therefore, in-
separable from the freedoms it either enables or curtails."[50] How, then,
might development be reclaimed from militaries, empires, and markets
for abolitionist and decolonial ends?

Development, Refusal, Abolition

In the concluding section of *Golden Gulag*'s fourth chapter, which dissects the prison-building schemes that became popular across rural California from the late 1970s onward as engines of municipal economic development, Ruth Wilson Gilmore draws some tentative but generative connections between such highly localized carceral geographies and other more globalized projects of empire building and order making. More specifically, she wants to lead her readers "away from thinking of prison location as a siting problem for development ends and toward thinking of the prison as fully a development problem—or perhaps, more accurately, as an *antidevelopment problem*." Part of her aim here is to emphasize how the "particular forms and relations of developmentalism" that "further the underdevelopment of regions" in the global South find their corollaries in the geographies of capital flight and state restructuring that have historically "unfixed" rural and urban landscapes in the global North, exposing marginalized communities to evolving forms of slow violence, organized abandonment, and premature death. As Gilmore reminds us, however, while "unfixing" leaves behind "industrial residue—devalued labor, land made toxic, shuttered retail businesses, the neighborhood, or small city urban forms"—it does not inevitably lead to "absolute erasure." As it turns out, communities and households that have been unfixed or rendered surplus "do not abandon themselves." Instead, they learn how to live in and among the ruins, renovating already-existing activities to survive and make do under ongoing conditions of racial capitalism.[51]

By using liberal nation building abroad to better understand carceral state making at home, Gilmore helps us better understand the intellectual and political possibilities opened up by holding the foreign and the domestic spheres within a single frame of analysis. Building on Gilmore's generative claim that prison building might be best thought of as an *antidevelopment* problem, I ask: What role might *development* play in bringing about abolitionist futures? While abolition is simplistically understood by mainstream publics as a project of *absence* that aims to defund and dismantle all of the various interlocking elements of the carceral state, its advocates have always insisted that this is only half the struggle. At its core, abolition is a productive project of *presence*, concerned with building and supporting life-affirming infrastructures of social transformation.[52] Gilmore articulates this most poetically when she says that "abolition is life in rehearsal, not a recitation of rules, much less a relentless lament."[53] Or as Anun Kundnani clarifies in his recent call to "abolish national security":

> An abolitionist framework entails understanding that genuine security does not result from the eliminating of threats, but from the presence of collective well-being. It advocates building institutions that foster the social and ecological relationships needed to live dignified lives, rather than relatively identifying groups of people who are seen as threatening. It holds that true security rests not on dominance, but on solidarity, at both the personal and the international levels.

From this perspective, while abolishing national security would involve defunding the transnational infrastructures that comprise the U.S. military-detention-industrial complex, it would also entail the "construction of alternative institutions that can provide collective security in the face of environmental and social dangers."[54] What does this look like in concrete organizational practice? For collectives such as No New Jails, Red Canary Song, and Critical Resistance—to name only a few examples—abolition involves freeing the money and resources fixed in prisons, border walls, police forces, and detention camps and reinvesting it in historically marginalized communities. Closing Rikers Island in New York City, for example, also means ending the school-to-prison pipeline, or building up youth programs, or creating new jobs and positive neighborhoods. The everyday work of abolition, in other words, involves building collective infrastructures of community uplift and life making that are disconnected from the "logic[s] of racial security" that have historically animated the activities of the U.S. empire-state, both at home and across the decolonizing world.[55]

Abolitionist visions of "collective security" are, of course, not unique to the present moment. Instead, they emerge out of and draw strength from longer genealogies of Black radicalism and Third World internationalism. The pathbreaking work of Frantz Fanon has undoubtedly served as an important touchstone for abolitionists who are currently struggling to build more internationalist infrastructures of solidarity and struggle. In *The Wretched of the Earth*, Fanon offers a powerful, prescient theory of decolonization as both a "violent event" and an "agenda for total disorder" whose ultimate objective is nothing less than the "substitution of one species of man for another."[56] Fanon's description of the colonial world as one that is compartmentalized through the "language of pure violence" has long been fundamental to the work of Black, postcolonial, and settler colonial studies.[57] But *The Wretched of the Earth* has also resonated beyond the academy for what it has to say about dislocating and dismantling the colonial order of things. Decolonization, for Fanon, means building the material conditions of possibility for a new conception of humanity where the "last shall be first." Placing his own concrete experiences waging decolonial insurgency in Algeria with the struggles of the colonized—"the black, brown, and yellow hordes"—elsewhere across the globe, Fanon argued that "the great victory of the Vietnamese people [over French Union forces] at Điện Biên Phủ is no longer strictly a Vietnamese victory." The key political question for Fanon—and for all colonized subjects from July 1954 onward—was therefore, What must we do to achieve a Điện Biên Phủ? Given that a "Điện Biên Phủ was now within reach of every colonized subject," the "problem was mustering forces, organizing them, and setting a date for action."[58] What Fanon offers in *The Wretched of the Earth,* then, is a theory of decolonial revolution, one that begins with the fomenting of insurgency, carries forward into the moment of liberation, and culminates in a postcolonial project of development and nation building. What begins as a fight against colonial oppression, Fanon observes, gradually transitions into a fight against poverty, illiteracy, and underdevelopment. Life for (post)colonial subjects becomes an "unending struggle."[59]

How does Fanon narrate this struggle? On a very broad level, the ultimate aim of decolonization is the creation of new subjects. Initially, Fanon argues, (post)colonial nation builders are convinced European nations achieved development through self-help and hard work. They are therefore gripped by the desire to prove their capacity to do the same. Such was the case with Afghanistan in the early Cold War period, when it turned to the United States—and not, significantly, to Europe—for development assistance. Trained in the West, many members of Afghanistan's royal family not only adopted Western ideas as their own but also specifically expressed a deep sense of kinship with their "American friends." King Mohammad Zahir Shah, in particular, felt that "America and Afghanistan, with their pride of independence and their belief in the dignity of the individual, have always been close spiritual cousins."[60]

As Fanon reminds us, however, capitalist development is scandalous, for it is literally built on the "sweat and corpses" of the enslaved and the indentured.[61] From this perspective, former colonial regimes have a vested interest in maintaining the infrastructures of economic dependency that they had established to extract the resources that were fueling industrial development back home. In laying bare these colonial inheritances and sedimentations, Fanon's critique unsparingly highlights the ruse that would eventually become known as modernization: that European and American conceptions of development were, in fact, vehicles for maintaining and reproducing racial capitalist relations across the rapidly decolonizing world.[62] It is therefore unsurprising that Fanon would turn to socialism as a framework for political struggle that would allow decolonizing nations to "progress faster in greater harmony." Yet Fanon also recognized that the mere investment of human labor power was insufficient to the urgent task at hand. In order to truly divest from the economic infrastructures inherited from colonial regimes, Fanon argues, "everything needs to be started again."[63] This was an enormous undertaking that required considerable infusions of capital and expertise: precisely the critical resources that indigenous nation builders lacked, owing to decades—if not centuries—of colonial plunder, depredation, and dispossession.

Such inheritances, in Fanon's eyes, can and must be refused. For the formerly colonized, refusal means asserting a claim on the wealth of the imperialist nations, to demand development as a form of "just reparations." Development, in this context, becomes the "final stage of a dual consciousness—the consciousness of the colonized that it is their due and the consciousness of the capitalist powers that effectively they must pay up."[64] At the time that Fanon was writing *The Wretched of the Earth,* the highly developed worlds were encouraging the formerly colonized to articulate their political and economic aspirations within the narrow horizons of Cold War geopolitics. Framing the struggle for decolonization as a binary choice between capitalism or socialism effectively obscured an alternative and potentially more radical orientation grounded in a demand for an end to the Cold War—which was "[getting] us nowhere"—a wholesale divestment from the nuclear arms race, and a reinvestment of capital and technical expertise in what Fanon called the "underdeveloped regions."[65] What lay at the core of Fanon's theory of development, in other words, was a call for noncooperation with an emerging U.S. military-industrial-development complex bent on reshaping the decolonizing world in terms that feed capital.

This was, as Fanon acknowledged, easier said than done. He warns that grassroots struggles for decolonization are always at risk of being hijacked by an emerging class of colonized intellectuals, political functionaries, and petty-bourgeois actors for explicitly reformist or even counterrevolutionary ends. Fanon's worry here is that coopted movements might end up reproducing a "grotesque" reflection of the European nation-state form, thereby legitimizing entrenched hierarchical orderings of the world. It is for this reason that Fanon distinguishes between *nationalism,* which is reactionary and inward looking, and *national consciousness,* which produces a new kind of internationalist subject, eager to "walk in the company" of their comrades across the decolonizing world, "night and day, for all time."[66] Decolonization has to be internationalist because the capitalist powers would never willingly submit to any arrangement that allowed the formerly colonized to dictate the terms of international development to their own mutual benefit. Fanon was therefore hopeful that an internationalist coalition of solidarity between the colonized masses and an awakened European proletariat might pose a sufficient threat to the established order of things that capitalist regimes would "realize that their true interests lie in aiding, and massively aiding without too many conditions, the underdeveloped countries."[67]

This vision of revolutionary internationalism—or what one of the founders of the Black Panther Party, Huey Newton, would eventually call "revolutionary intercommunalism"—never came to pass.[68] Indeed, what became clear from the early 1960s onward is the extent to which the U.S. empire-state would seek to manage Cold War insurgencies in places like Vietnam and Afghanistan precisely through the racial liberal technology of development. As Simeon Man observes, "People who had spent their lives fighting the oppression of a single colonizer found themselves confronting a new and more complex imperial power." This new power ostensibly disavowed outright racism, domination, and dispossession in favor of "less coercive" methods for spreading democracy, freedom, and capitalism across the decolonizing world. In the hands of this "murkier," supposedly postracial U.S. empire, an increasingly militarized form of development became a tool for keeping decolonizing nations within the broader "capitalist orbit."[69] All of this speaks to the ways in which Fanon's concept of development-as-reparations could be coopted and leveraged to produce new entangled geographies of empire, militarism, and racial capitalism.

Fanon's writings on race and decolonization were invariably shaped by his own complex engagements with questions of class, gender, and sexuality. Fanon's relegation of colonized women to the role of revolutionary cheerleaders speaks, perhaps, to what Cedric Robinson once described as an "unflinchingly male arrogance."[70] And yet, his theory of revolutionary development undoubtedly went on to influence subsequent generations of radical thinkers. There are echoes of Fanon in Huey Newton's writings on U.S. imperialism and revolutionary intercommunalism, which called on the "people of the world" to "seize power from the small ruling circle and expropriate the expropriators, pull them down from their pinnacle and make them equals, and distribute the fruits of our labor that have been denied to us in some equitable way." Newton, like Fanon before him, emphasized the need for a largely Black revolutionary vanguard to work with and lead a diverse and growing *lumpenproletariat* into such a future of revolutionary intercommunalism, where the "last shall be first."[71]

For Newton and the rest of the Black Panther Party, revolutionary intercommunalism was merely an upscaled version of the organizing work and solidarity building that they had already been conducting, both in their home base of Oakland, California, and also in other cities across the rest of the United States. Newton himself had long recognized that

> in order to bring the people to the level of consciousness where they would seize the time, it would be necessary to serve their interests in survival by developing programs which would help them to meet their daily needs. . . . These programs satisfy the deep needs of the community, but they are not solutions to our problem. That is why we call them survival programs, meaning survival pending revolution.[72]

What the Black Panther Party built over the course of its lifespan was an extensive infrastructure for ensuring "survival pending revolution." The basic contours of this infrastructure were sketched out in the Panthers' "Ten-Point Party Platform and Program." In addition to calling for an immediate end to police brutality, forced military conscription, and mass incarceration, the Ten-Point Party Platform and Program also demanded full employment, decent housing, education, and an "end to the robbery by the capitalist of the Black community." What did this mean in concrete policy terms? According to Robin D. G. Kelley, "Panthers around the country patrolled the streets, held know-your-rights workshops, exposed the names of brutal cops, and in various places provided free medical care, free clothing and groceries, ran free breakfast and lunch programs for children, food banks, community gardens, drug rehab centers, ambulance services, and housing cooperatives."[73] In so doing, the Panthers showcased how community-based infrastructures of collective security and mutual aid could provide for the basic needs of racialized and marginalized communities that have historically been abandoned by the racial capitalist state.

In the intervening years, the infrastructural foundations laid down by the Black Panthers have continued to serve as practical building blocks for contemporary abolitionists. As I revise this conclusion, protests against the ongoing devaluation of Black lives by violence workers across the globe continue to rage across major urban centers, including Minneapolis, New York, London, Toronto, and Los Angeles. Reignited by the police murders of George Floyd, Breonna Taylor, and Tory McDade, this movement has followed scholar-activists like Ruth Wilson Gilmore, Angela Davis, and Mariame Kaba in making the abolition of the domestic carceral state its primary political objective. It has already won major victories on this front. It has secured concrete commitments to defunding—and in some cases, even abolishing—police departments in key battleground cities.[74] It has established autonomous zones—such as the Share-a-Ton takeover in Minneapolis—where abolitionist modes of life making and relation making have flourished, even if only temporarily.[75] And it has made great progress in mainstreaming abolitionist frameworks among wider and perhaps previously unreceptive audiences.[76]

Even now, much remains to be done. Much of the mutual aid work that has come to define leftist organizing in recent years—and especially during the ongoing COVID-19 pandemic—has been unfolding at the scale of the intimate and the everyday. According to Ruth Wilson Gilmore and Dean Spade, however, one of the key challenges moving forward is to find ways of mobilizing these highly localized struggles into a transnational movement of collective resistance and solidarity, geared toward tackling the "underlying causes" of broader social and economic crises.[77] Spade, in particular, shows how mutual aid can help bridge the gap between these two distinct yet complementary scales of abolition work. Bringing Spade into conversation with abolitionist scholars of the national security state like Schrader and Kundnani can help clarify how transnational infrastructures of mutual aid and collective security might serve as the basis for a theory and praxis of revolutionary development committed to ensuring that the "last shall be first." The resulting forms of "mutual development," in turn, can help us take the first steps toward internationalizing Newton's vision of surviving—and perhaps even thriving—pending revolutionary intercommunalism.

One of the main contributions of *The Quiet Violence of Empire* has been to expose USAID's commitment to bringing about precisely the inverse of Newton's vision, what he names *reactionary intercommunalism*. USAID emerged in the early 1960s as a handmaiden of U.S. empire and racial capitalism. Very little has changed in the intervening sixty years. One anonymous stabilization contractor captures this so perfectly in their exit interview with SIGAR:

> We didn't want stability. . . . We really wanted our side to win, but not necessarily stable. . . . We wanted to create conflict and disrupt things. . . . We're not neutral. We wanted to win. . . . We sought out conflict in [Taliban-] held territory because we wanted [the] Afghanistan [government] to be in charge. . . . That didn't mean *ending the violence; it meant instigating it to instill a very particular kind of stability.*[78]

What this stunning excerpt clarifies is the USAID complex's deep implication in the everyday violence work of U.S. empire. When considered as a whole, SIGAR's exit interviews contain little reason to believe that meaningful change is on the horizon. Both military and civilian counterinsurgents remain fundamentally convinced that the "right people" can transform U.S. empire building into a force for good across the decolonizing world. Under such circumstances, Fanon argues, "everything has to be started from scratch, everything has to be rethought."[79] To paraphrase one interviewee, the broader military-industrial-development complex remains a "bad idea." It must be abolished and something new must take its place. This is, I think, one of the key political tasks confronting anti-imperial scholars and activists moving forward.

Coda

In late February 2020, the United States and the Taliban signed an agreement to end the eighteen-year war. Under the terms of the agreement, the United States and its NATO allies agreed to withdraw all of their troops within fourteen months. The United States would also lift its economic sanctions against the Taliban and coordinate a prisoner swap between the insurgents and the Afghan security forces. In exchange, the Taliban "agreed not to allow al Qaeda or any other extremist group to operate in areas they control."[80] In the months immediately following the signing of the agreement, what any of this meant in concrete material terms remained largely unclear. Unfortunately, as I revise this concluding chapter in the dying days of August 2021, it seems that the peace agreement only emboldened the Taliban. Since August 6, 2021, Taliban forces have surprised both the United States and its Afghan allies, moving at "breakneck speed" and capturing over twenty provincial capitals, the most recent and significant being Afghanistan's capital city, Kabul. Writing for the Afghan Analysts Network in the short window of time between the Taliban's seizure of Mazr-e Sharif and Kabul, Martine van Biljert argues that while the "rapid fall of so many provincial capitals came as a surprise" and "looks like a complete reversal of fortune, which in many ways it is," it is "also an acceleration of the existing state of affairs in large parts of the country: an ongoing war with deaths, revenge killings, and aerial bombardments."[81] The almost total military and political collapse of the current Afghan government was confirmed on August 15, when the soon-to-be ex-president Ashraf Ghani fled Kabul for Oman. Ghani defended his decision to flee Afghanistan on the grounds that it would prevent a replay of April 1992, when the mujahideen battle for Kabul transformed the city into what Amnesty International describes as a "human rights catastrophe."[82] Rumors, however, are swirling that Ghani and his entourage fled the city with cars and helicopters stuffed full with cash, which, if true, would be just another example of the "galactic scale" corruption that has come to define successive Afghan governments over the last twenty years of war and occupation.[83]

News of Ghani's swift exit off stage seems all the more galling when one considers that Kabul—and Afghanistan more generally—is already in the grip of a mounting "human rights catastrophe." As van Biljert notes in her front-line report, the recent intensification of the conflict has meant that "parts of the country are . . . facing a possible grave humanitarian crisis due to mass displacement and destruction of shops, houses, and harvests, coupled with the existing hardships of poverty, drought, and unemployment." Of the 300,000 Afghans who have been uprooted and set in motion by the latest round of fighting, 13,500 have converged on Kabul, a figure that surely undercounts all of the "hidden" internally displaced persons who are currently living with and hiding among family in the capital. Van Biljert worries that "the influx of conflict-displaced Afghans into a city already facing the potential crumbling of services threatens to overburden a public health system already taxed by the COVID-19 pandemic and raises concerns about food security."[84] Meanwhile, the United States is also scrambling to arrange for the evacuation of nationals and local collaborators out of Kabul, offering a stark reminder to the rest of the city's population that they will ultimately bear the brunt of the coming regime change. The mainstream media has been quick to draw obvious comparisons between the current situation in Afghanistan and the fall of Saigon to National Liberation Front insurgents in 1975. The infamous photograph of an unnamed CIA employee helping Vietnamese collaborators onto the last Air America helicopter out of Saigon has been making the rounds in the news and on social media, serving as visual evidence of how history is now in the process of repeating itself in Kabul.[85] There are also reports emerging out of Hamid Karzai International Airport confirming that civilian flights are being cancelled to ensure the smooth logistical management of the U.S. evacuation.[86] These uneven geographies of circulation and mobility, of course, highlight the extent to which imperial lives have always been protected and nurtured at the expense of Afghan ones. But what it also reveals, I think, is the extent to which Vietnam and Afghanistan have always been conjoined in the U.S. imperial imagination by a "racial security logic" that conflates communism with terrorism, and that continues to undergird the everyday work of counterinsurgency across the decolonizing world.[87]

With regime change looming on the horizon, it seems as though ordinary Afghans, for the first time in approximately forty years, will be entering the fraught and uncertain time-space of "afterwar." Borrowing from Zoë Wool, Emma Shaw Crane recently defined afterwar as the "time after war formally ends, yet remains in embodied experience and spatial relationships."[88] For Shaw Crane, afterwar can be found in Homestead, a southern suburb of Miami where tract homes, strip malls, plant nurseries, and migrant communities coexist uneasily not only with U.S. Southern Command and the active duty soldiers that run the base, but also with the "excombatants from American proxy wars in Iraq, Lebanon, Colombia, and Panama."[89] This suburban space of afterwar is a ruined landscape of ongoing militarization, characterized not by spectacular, highly visible violence but by dispersed and everyday forms of harm. And yet, it is also a verdant, lush landscape that blooms through exploited labor provided by a largely undocumented migrant workforce. As a "spatial arrangement that absorbs people displaced and debilitated by war and enables ongoing militarization," the suburban afterwar embodies the many contradictions of the United States' entangled long wars on drugs, gangs, and terror.[90]

Similarly, Leah Zani has recently coined the term "bomb ecologies" to name the "zones in which war profoundly shapes the ecological relations, political systems, and material conditions of living and dying."[91] The term emerges out of her extensive fieldwork with unexploded ordinance clearance operators and development organizations in Laos, where she spent seventeen months exploring and reflecting on how everyday life can persist in the bombed out and bomb-riddled landscapes of afterwar.[92] Laotian bomb technicians, Zani argues, often treat unexploded ordinance both as military and toxic waste. Their preference for technical terminology such as "contamination," "hazardous area," and "residual risk" "invites analysis of 'postconflict landscapes' as distinct ecological zones" yet also "elides geopolitical conflict to the extent that it naturalizes war and obscures the politics that cut up battlefields, bracket conflicts, and count corpses."[93] Zani critically expands on this approach by theorizing processes of military wasting and ruination in afterwar Laos as constitutive of everyday ecologies in a time of ongoing development, liberalization, and global integration. "Engaging with ordinance as ecological waste," Zani writes, "opens the possibility of treating bombs as something other than weapons"; and, by extension, of moving "away from war" toward "the possibilities of everyday life."[94]

Placing Shaw Crane in conversation with Zani, I can't help but wonder: What might the ecologies of afterwar look like in Afghanistan? In some ways, this is, to return to Monica Kim, a "vast, impossible question" that lacks easy answers.[95] This, of course, has not stopped the rampant speculation over what the Taliban takeover means for everyday Afghan life making moving forward. In addition to widespread fears that uncontrolled Taliban fighters will be free to settle scores, enact punishments, and carry out revenge attacks, mainstream commentators are already sounding the death knell of gender rights across the country.[96] This is not to suggest that things were substantively better in the months and years leading up to this moment. As Juan Cole reminds us, the U.S. empire-state has, over the past twenty years, worked very closely with regional warlords who "were not easier on women or minorities than the Taliban had been, and were fundamentalists of a different stripe."[97] The Taliban's stated political commitment to imposing sharia law on subject populations, however, means that the future of gender and sexuality rights in Afghanistan moving forward looks undeniably grim. As van Biljert notes, "All signs are that although some local Taleban leaders are trying to convey a softened image ('the *burqa* is not compulsory, we prefer to convince people rather than force them'), the core of their rules has stayed very much the same."[98] The extent to which these rules are felt or enforced at the scale of the everyday, however, also seems to vary from district to district. In July 2021, the Afghan Analysts Network team published a report entitled *Between Hope and Fear,* featuring the testimony of rural women across Afghanistan. The Afghan Analysts Network team invited the interviewees to share their "fears about war and hopes for peace." While some of the interviewees living in contested or Taliban-controlled districts reported that they had stopped venturing outside without a *mahram* (male chaperone) or were no longer sending their children to school, others (such as an "older [Pashtun] woman from Panjwayi in Kandahar") reported that their mobility had actually increased, as improvements in security meant that they could start visiting family again.[99] These contradictory experiences, I think, are powerfully captured by the testimony provided by one "42-year-old mother of six from Tala wa Barfak, Baghlan," who told her interviewer:

> Since the Taleban came, I hate going out, to be honest. But the *whole family relies on me.* My elder sons are helping now—they started working, which is a huge relief. Otherwise, how can a woman provide for her family in a Taleban-controlled situation? We can't go out on our own. We have to take a mahram wherever we go. . . . I never thought that if the Taleban came, I would lose my job. I was a cleaner, not some officer who did something [important]. But I lost my job when they gained more power in the area. [Now] I need a mahram to go anywhere.[100]

Currently, the above interviewee is skirting Taliban decrees by pretending that her neighbor is her brother, so that she can "go to the doctor or run essential errands." This deception, she recognizes, is potentially dangerous, as the Taliban "have no mercy when it comes to punishing women." But what her testimony reveals is the sheer amount of labor that goes into making life livable in the ruins of war, counterinsurgency, and slow violence work. Such an everyday politics of what Thuy Linh Nguyen Tu describes elsewhere as "making do" will continue to grate against—and in some cases, exceed—the infrastructures of Taliban governmentality, clarifying how struggles over gender issues in rural Afghanistan are not well served by intensifying liberal handwringing over the need to once again save Afghan women from Afghan men.[101]

But a rural politics of "making do" also conjures up another image as well: a rural landscape lush with poppies. In the past, the Taliban tolerated—and even nurtured—poppy cultivation until it was politically expedient for them to turn around and declare the popular livelihood strategy to be haram, or forbidden. It is, at this stage, way too early to even speculate over how the incoming Taliban regime might go about tackling Afghanistan's raging poppy problem. From an imperial perspective, of course, poppies—and all of their illegal by-products— have come to symbolize the moral and ecological contamination of Afghanistan. As the surplus waste produced by decades of development, counterinsurgency, and war, poppies have long been a fixture of Afghanistan's ecological landscapes. But like the unexploded ordinance that continues to haunt the bomb villages of Laos, poppies might also be "better understood as a kind of surreal substrate" to everyday Afghan life; as something more than fuel for an ever-expanding illicit war economy. "We grow poppies out of poverty," one farmer tells Radio Free Europe. "We grow them because there are no factories, the drought has hurt us, the coronavirus has hit the economy," another confirms. Afghan farmers often stress that poppy cultivation is a last resort: "If we didn't have to, we wouldn't."[102] But the undisputable fact remains that poppy ecologies continue to provide communities of ordinary Afghan households with survival pending revolutionary intercommunalism. During this time of afterwar at Asia's edge, then, poppy ecologies are also development ecologies. They are the infrastructures that currently build and sustain ordinary Afghan life. What fraught, speculative futures might they enable?

From these and other conversations, it is abundantly clear that rural households do not see poppy development as the route to a true Afghan national consciousness, at least in the sense envisioned by Fanon. They long for a future where illicit economic activities are not the only viable pathway to subsistence and social reproduction. Prior to August 6, 2021, and the Taliban resurgence that followed, the USAID complex would have likely continued to intervene in afterwar Afghanistan with microfinance, value chain, and other alternative development initiatives designed to remediate, repair, and build up rural economies. It is fundamentally unclear, at this juncture, as to whether the USAID complex will even be permitted to maintain a mission in Afghanistan now that the Taliban has succeeded in ousting the Ghani regime. The immediate decriminalization of poppy cultivation—perhaps the more likely option, given the Taliban's policy history on this front—offers another potential pathway to forms of living and social reproduction that go beyond mere survival. But both of these models of alternative development ultimately leave rural Afghans at the mercy of broader racial capitalist infrastructures that buttress the agribusiness and pharmaceutical industries, respectively, and the planet-spanning geographies of uneven development that they leave in their wake. Decolonization, to be sure, has never been a sure-fire stepping stone to anticapitalism.

Fanon identifies the Việt Minh victory at Điện Biên Phủ as a model for decolonization in action. The National Liberation Front's successful insurgency against U.S. forces in occupied South Vietnam undoubtedly represents both a continuation and culmination of this fundamentally anticapitalist struggle. And yet, it was the victorious communist regime that decided in 1986 to launch the Đổi Mới—or "renovation"—reforms that eventually connected Vietnam to global markets in terms that fed and further entrenched racial capitalist formations across southeast Asia. Đổi Mới offers one vision of what national development might look like in a time of afterwar. But is "renovation" the only option available to Afghans?

Perhaps one way of moving forward into a fraught and uncertain future is by tentatively offering abolition as an alternative to renovation or, to put it differently, as a working blueprint for a genuinely decolonial form of alternative development. Drawing from Fanon, Newton, Gilmore, Kundnani, Spade, and Schrader, development in afterwar Afghanistan—like development elsewhere across the decolonizing world—must be oriented to the urgent task of building a decolonized national consciousness that is at once anticapitalist, antiracist, and abolitionist. Such a project is undoubtedly set back by the current situation in Afghanistan, which only seems to confirm Fanon's prescient suspicions of reactionary postcolonial nationalisms. And yet, tearing down the various interlocking complexes—military, development, prison, detention, and more—that make up the U.S. empire-state is "plodding" work that will not happen overnight.[103] Nor is this a burden that can—or should—be placed on the shoulders of ordinary Afghans alone. Given the extent of our complicity in the everyday work of U.S. empire building in places like Afghanistan, metropolitan abolitionists have a central role to play in the collective political project of rescaling our ongoing struggles to encompass the "speculative practices of immanent futurity" enacted by colonized peoples who are trying to build a life for themselves in spaces that have been so thoroughly transformed by the transnational infrastructures of poverty and violence work.[104] But if empire is sustained by infrastructures, this book shows that it can also be undone by them. As Deborah Cowen reminds us, it is infrastructure that makes it possible to connect the struggles of Afghan farmers "making do" in a time of afterwar with the struggles of Black Lives Matter activists, abolitionists, and racialized communities working to dismantle carceral and white supremacist geographies in the streets of cities the world over.[105] Thinking relationally across these "low freedom song[s]," to borrow Jackie Wang's evocative turn of phrase, exposes the importance of reclaiming infrastructures from militaries, markets, and empires and repurposing them toward the goal of building and sustaining new, speculative futures of revolutionary intercommunalism.[106] Such are, I think, the urgent political stakes of our current moment of crisis, emergency, and opportunity.

Acknowledgments

THIS BOOK IS THE PRODUCT of over a decade of thinking, researching, and writing in various spaces and places across Turtle Island. As academics, we are always encouraged to claim individual ownership over our scholarship. And yet I cannot imagine how this book would have taken shape without the intimate work of everyday relation making that has always been the very stuff of academic life. These geographies of what my sister Nadine and I name elsewhere as *relation work*—the work of being in relations with others—in turn have served as the basis for all sorts of generative conversations and collaborations, both inside and outside the spaces of academia. All of them, in their own way, have left their mark on this book.

This book began its life as a PhD dissertation in the University of British Columbia's Department of Geography. I am enormously grateful to my PhD supervisor, Derek Gregory, as well as the other members of my dissertation committee, Trevor Barnes and Jim Glassman, for patiently guiding the first version of this book from its inception to its eventual defense. I first articulated many of the book's key claims and arguments in their respective graduate seminars. The feedback they offered—first as seminar leaders, and then subsequently as committee members and mentors—was challenging yet generative, always pushing me to refine my ideas and put them to work in the world. Their contributions to this book are immense.

I also continue to learn so much from my fellow graduate students, with whom I shared both the joys and the struggles of PhD life. I wanted to give special thanks, in no particular order, to May Farrales, James Pangilinan, Vanessa Banta, Kyle Loewen, Andrew Shmuely, Tom Howard, Craig Jones, Jeffrey Whyte, Dawn Hoogeveen, Emily Rosenman, Nina Ebner, and Michael Fabris, who all helped make the PhD experience a little more bearable, both as generous interlocutors and as generous friends. If there is one thing that I have carried with me from graduate school, it is a recognition of how building and maintaining a close support network of comrades is required for surviving academia, both during and after the PhD program. These are relations that I hope will thrive for years to come.

I took the first steps in transforming my dissertation into a book project as a postdoctoral fellow in the Department of Geography and Planning at the University of Toronto. I could not have written this book without the strong mentorship and gentle encouragement of Matthew Farish, Deborah Cowen, and Emily Gilbert, who not only helped me craft the initial prospectus but also expertly guided me through the initial stages of editorial process. I also benefited enormously from the time that I spent with Martin Danyluk, David Roberts, Sam Walker, Dan Cohen, Cynthia Morinville, Connie Yang, Ben Butler, Adam Zendel, and Killian McCormack, who all made me feel so welcome in a new city. Finally, I am grateful for the words of advice and encouragement that were generously offered to me by other Toronto-based faculty, especially Michelle Murphy, Thy Phu, Vinh Nguyen, Lisa Yoneyama, and Tak Fujitani. They all modeled what a welcoming academic community can look like, even under academia's current conditions of austerity, underfunding, and retrenchment.

My time at New York University as a visiting assistant professor of Asian/Pacific/American studies in the Department of Social and Cultural Analysis was brief, but it shaped this book project—and my scholarship more generally—in profound ways. Thuy Linh Tu, Nikhil Pal Singh, and Heijin Lee opened up an opportunity for me to find a new intellectual and professional home in the field of Asian American and critical ethnic studies. Alongside Dean Saranillio, Crystal Parikh, Monica Kim, and Sophie Gonick, they encouraged me to understand Afghanistan through its connections to Asia and its diasporas, emphasizing the importance of thinking relationally across the multiple spaces and times of U.S. empire and its unmaking. My experience of academic life in New York City was undoubtedly enriched by the warmth and kindness of Emma Shaw Crane, Linda Luu, Ben Rubin, Stuart Schrader, Elliott Jun, Tenn Joe Lim, Maya Wind, Lydia Pelot-Hobbs, Tareq Radi, and Tyson Patros. And last, but not least, the students in my four courses in social and cultural analysis were a joy and an inspiration to teach. They pushed me to read beyond my comfort zone, and taught me so much about the everyday work of decolonization and abolition. Their investments in and commitments to building liberatory futures of social transformation shaped this book project more than they know.

When I returned back home to Vancouver in the middle of the global COVID-19 pandemic, I leaned heavily on an extensive support network to navigate a devastated job market. Phanuel Antwi, Danielle Wong, and J. P. Catungal kept me tethered to academic spaces in Vancouver, eagerly serving as both collaborators and co-conspirators, while Laura Chen-Schultz and Amita Manghani at NYU's A/P/A Institute provided me with an institutional base from which to apply for jobs and continue publishing. I am also eternally grateful to the transnational community of friends and colleagues that made time for me and kept me going even when the job market landscape looked increasingly bleak, especially Iyko Day, Laleh Khalili, Adrian De Leon, Christine Peralta, Rich Nisa, Emily Mitchell Eaton, Charmaine Chua, Naomi Paik, Hun Kim, Sylvia Nam, and Long Bui. It is these life-giving relationships that lead me to believe that academia can still play a role in struggles for decolonization, demilitarization, anti-imperialism, and abolition.

The research for this book would not have been completed without the generosity of Barbara Harslem, who opened her house in Alexandria to me as I conducted archival research at the National Archives and Records Administration campus in College Park and the National Security Archives at George Washington University. Jenn Fluri was also a similarly gracious host at Dartmouth, where she spent two weeks preparing me to navigate the fraught (sub)urban landscapes of the Beltway. I am also grateful for the patience of the archivists working for both NARA and the NSA, who entertained my endless questions in the early stages of the research, as well as the generosity of my anonymous key informants, who took time out of their busy schedules to sit down for interviews with a scholar doing field research for the very first time.

As a junior postdoctoral scholar who had yet to secure a tenure-track position, publishing a book with a major university press seemed like such a daunting—even insurmountable—task. My editor at the University of Minnesota Press, Jason Weidemann, played such a huge role in helping me achieve this goal. From our very first email conversations in the spring of 2018 to our more recent back-and-forth negotiations over the minutiae of the production process, Jason has been warm, supportive, flexible, and patient, showcasing a careful understanding of how editorial work is as much about building and maintaining relations as it is about the technical aspects of bringing a book into the world. Zenyse Miller and the rest of the team at the Press have also been exemplary, patiently entertaining my various questions, requests, and revisions. Many of the maps contained in this book were produced by my good friend Richard Nisa, who painstakingly re-created the fuzzy and low-resolution images that accompanied earlier versions of the manuscript, making them crisp and legible. I owe him many drinks at future conferences. I am also grateful for the support of my new chair at the University of Hong Kong, George Lin, who demonstrated his commitment to this book project by working with the Department of Geography to free up funds that helped me defray some of its publication costs. HKU's support on this front is essential, as it will help the University of Minnesota Press further its commitment to publishing the work of more precarious and less well-resourced scholars.

And finally, I owe an incalculable debt to family and the emotional and support labor they have performed on a day-to-day basis, especially these past few years. My sister Nadine has been the one mentoring constant who has followed me as I moved from Vancouver to Toronto to New York and to Hong Kong. She has read draft chapters, entertained my half-baked ideas, edited my job applications, and prepared me for interviews. She has been one of my biggest supporters, toughest critics, and most generative collaborators. My parents have been equally supportive and patient, helping me push through my biggest challenges and to find fulfillment in the everyday work of academia. My partner Lisa has also been extraordinarily generous with her time and labor. While she is one of the main reasons I am still working as an academic today, she also reminds me that there is a life beyond the walls of the university, one that should always be cherished, nurtured, and protected. This book would not exist without her continued love and commitment, always pushing me to be the best version of myself. Finally, there has been a very recent addition to the family that has turned our lives upside down for the best. Baby Juno, you have been the cause of many sleepless nights, but also the source of endless wonder and countless joys. The intellectual and political work of academia has never felt so urgent than since your arrival in the world.

Notes

Introduction

1. Julie Davis and Mark Landler, "Trump Outlines New Afghanistan War Strategy with Few Details," *New York Times,* August 21, 2017, https://www.nytimes.com/2017/08/21/world/asia/afghanistantroops-trump.html.

2. Mark Landler, "The Afghan War and the Evolution of Obama," *New York Times,* January 1, 2017, https://www.nytimes.com/2017/01/01/world/asia/obama-afghanistan-war.html.

3. See Rajiv Chandrasekaran, *Little America: The War within the War for Afghanistan* (New York: Vintage, 2012).

4. Andrew Rafferty, "The War in Afghanistan: By the Numbers," *NBC News,* August 21, 2017, https://www.nbcnews.com/politics/politics-news/war-afghanistan-numbers-n794626.

5. Inderpal Grewal, *Saving the Security State: Exceptional Citizens in Twenty-First-Century America* (Durham, N.C.: Duke University Press, 2017).

6. Henry L. Stimson, "The Challenge to Americans," *Foreign Affairs* 26 (1947): 5–14.

7. Monica Kim, *The Interrogation Rooms of the Korean War: The Untold History* (Princeton, N.J.: Princeton University Press, 2019); Stimson, "The Challenge."

8. Andrew Friedman, "US Empire, World War 2, and the Racializing of Labor," *Race & Class* 58, no. 4 (2017): 23–38; Laleh Khalili, "The Infrastructural Power of the Military: The Geoeconomic Role of the US Army Corps of Engineers in the Arabian Peninsula," *European Journal of International Relations* 24, no. 4 (2018): 911–33.

9. For a discussion of military Keynesianism, see Ruth Wilson Gilmore, "Globalisation and US Prison Growth: From Military Keynesianism to Post-Keynesian Militarism," *Race & Class* 4, no. 2–3 (1999): 171–88; Nikhil Pal Singh, *Race and America's Long War* (Berkeley: University of California Press, 2017), 3.

10. Singh, *Race and America's Long War,* 15.

11. Susan Roberts, "Development Capital: USAID and the Rise of Development Contractors," *Annals of the Association of American Geographers* 104, no. 5, (2014): 1030–51.

12. Jodi Melamed, "The Spirit of Neoliberalism: From Racial Liberalism to Neoliberal Multiculturalism," *Social Text* 24, no. 4 (2006): 2.

13. See, for example, Gunnar Myrdal, *An American Dilemma* (New York: Carnegie Corporation, 1944).

14. Zygmunt Bauman, "Wars of the Globalization Era," *European Journal of Social Theory* 4, no. 1 (2001): 11–28; Mark Duffield, *Development, Security, and Unending War: Governing the World of Peoples* (Malden, Mass.: Polity, 2007); Mark Duffield, *Global Governance and the New Wars: The Merging of Development and Security* (New York: Zed, 2001); Mary Kaldor, *New & Old Wars* (Stanford, Calif.: Stanford University Press, 2007); Herfried Munkler, *The New Wars* (Malden, Mass.: Polity, 2005); Marcus Power, *Geopolitics and Development* (London: Routledge, 2019).

15. David Del Testa, "'Imperial Corridor': Association, Transportation, and Power in French Colonial Indochina," *Science, Technology, and Society* 4, no. 2 (1999): 319–54; Manu Karuka, *Empire's Tracks: Indigenous Nations, Chinese Workers, and the Transcontinental Railroad* (Berkeley: University of California Press, 2019); Alfred McCoy, *Policing America's Empire: The United States, the Philippines, and the Rise of the Surveillance State* (Madison: University of Wisconsin Press, 2009); Gyan Prakash, *Another Reason: Science and the Imagination of Modern India* (Princeton, N.J.: Princeton University Press, 1999); James Scott, *Seeing Like a State: How Certain Schemes to Improve the Human Condition Have Failed* (New Haven, Conn.: Yale University Press, 1999); Stuart Schrader, *Badges without Borders: How Global Counterinsurgency Transformed American Policing* (Berkeley: University of California Press, 2019).

16. Keith Camacho, *Sacred Men: Law, Torture, and Retribution in Guam* (Durham, N.C.: Duke University Press, 2019); Adrian De Leon, "Sugarcane *Sakadas*: The Corporate Production of the Filipino on a Hawai'i Plantation," *Amerasia* 45, no. 1 (2019): 50–67; Juliet Nebolon, "'Life Given Straight From the Heart': Settler Militarism, Biopolitics, and Public Health in Hawai'i During World War II," *American Quarterly* 69, no. 1 (2017): 23–45; Dean Saranillio, *Unsustainable Empire: Alternative Histories of Hawai'i Statehood* (Durham, N.C.: Duke University Press, 2018).

17. Jim Glassman, *Drums of War, Drums of Development: The Formation of a Pacific Ruling Class and Industrial Transformation in East and Southeast Asia, 1945–1980* (Leiden: Brill, 2018); Simeon Man, *Soldiering through Empire: Race and the Making of the Decolonizing Pacific* (Berkeley: University of California Press, 2018); Lisa Yoneyama, *Cold War Ruins: Transpacific Critique of American Justice and Japanese War Crimes* (Durham, N.C.: Duke University Press, 2016).

18. Takashi Fujitani, *Race for Empire: Koreans as Japanese and Japanese as Americans during World War II* (Berkeley: University of California Press, 2011); Jodi Melamed, *Represent and Destroy: Rationalizing Violence in the*

New Racial Capitalism (Minneapolis: University of Minnesota Press, 2011); Michael Omi and Howard Winant, *Racial Formation in the United States: From the 1960s to the 1980s* (New York: Routledge, 1991); Singh, *Race and America's Long War.*

19. Fujitani, *Race for Empire*, 7.

20. Fujitani, 21.

21. Fujitani, 26.

22. Singh, *Race and America's Long War*, 125.

23. Melamed, *Represent and Destroy*, 10.

24. Mona Domosh, "Race, Biopolitics, and Liberal Development from the Jim Crow South to Postwar Africa," *Transactions of the Institute for British Geographers* 43, no. 2 (2018): 318; see also Mona Domosh, "International Harvester, the US South, and the Makings of International Development in the Early 20th Century," *Political Geography* 49 (2015): 17–29; Mona Domosh, "Practising Development at Home: Race, Gender, and the 'Development' of the American South," *Antipode* 47, no. 4 (2015): 915–41.

25. Harry Truman, "Inaugural Address of Harry S. Truman," January 20, 1949, Avalon Project, https://avalon.law.yale.edu/20th_century/truman.asp.

26. USAID, "A History of Foreign Assistance," April 3, 2002, https://pdf.usaid.gov/pdf_docs/PNACP064.pdf.

27. Truman, "Address."

28. Domosh, "Practising Development," 937.

29. Mark Berger and Douglas Borer, "The Long War: Insurgency, Counterinsurgency, and Collapsing States," *Third World Quarterly* 28, no. 2 (2007): 197–215.

30. Department of State, *United States Treaties and Other International Agreements: Volume 2 in Two Parts, Part 1, 1951* (Washington, D.C.: Government Printing Office, 1951), 592.

31. Harry Truman, "Special Message to the Congress on the Mutual Security Program," *American Presidency Project*, May 24, 1951, https://www.presidency.ucsb.edu/documents/special-message-the-congress-the-mutual-security-program-6.

32. Kim, *The Interrogation Rooms*; Richard Nisa, "Capturing the Forgotten War: Carceral Spaces and Colonial Legacies in Cold War Korea," *Journal of Historical Geography* 64 (2019): 13–24.

33. Berger and Borer, "The Long War"; Truman, "Special Message."

34. Jamey Essex, *Development, Security, and Aid: Geopolitics and Geoeconomics at the US Agency for International Development* (Athens: University of Georgia Press, 2013), 31; USAID, "A History."

35. William Lowenthal, "Oral History Interview," *Foreign Affairs Oral History Collection*, 1986, https://www.adst.org/OH%20TOCs/Lowenthal,%20William.toc.pdf.

36. William Lederer and Eugene Burdick, *The Ugly American* (New York: Norton, 1958).

37. Essex, *Development*, 31.

38. Sean Duffy, "The Origins of the Agency for International Development: Foreign Assistance Reorganization in 1961," USAID DEC, 1991, https://pdf.usaid.gov/pdf_docs/PNABL500.pdf.

39. Essex, *Development*, 32.

40. Melamed, *Represent and Destroy*, 10.

41. Melamed, 13.

42. John Norris, "Kennedy, Johnson, and the Early Years," *Devex*, July 23, 2014, https://www.devex.com/news/kennedy-johnson-and-the-early-years-83339.

43. Jodi Melamed, "Racial Capitalism," *Critical Ethnic Studies* 1, no. 1 (2015): 78.

44. Ruth Wilson Gilmore, *Golden Gulag: Prisons, Surplus, Crisis, and Opposition in Globalizing California* (Berkeley: University of California Press, 2007), 28.

45. Melamed, "The Spirit of Neoliberalism," 6.

46. Kim, *The Interrogation Rooms*, 5.

47. Kim. On counterinsurgency and race war in other Cold War hotspots of decolonization and insurgency, see Wesley Attewell, " 'From Factory to Field': USAID and the Logistics of Foreign Aid in Soviet-Occupied Afghanistan," *Environment and Planning D* 36, no. 4 (2018): 719–38; Wesley Attewell, "Ghosts in the Delta: USAID and the Historical Geographies of Vietnam's 'Other' War," *Environment and Planning A* 47, no. 11 (2015): 2257–75; Vincent Bevins, *The Jakarta Method: Washington's Anticommunist Crusade and the Mass Murder Program that Shaped Our World* (New York: Public Affairs, 2020); Kevin Gould, "The Old Militarized Humanitarianism: Contradictions of Counterinsurgent Infrastructure in Cold War Guatemala," *Critical Military Studies* 4, no. 2 (2018): 140–60; Bradley Simpson, *Economists with Guns: Authoritarian Development and US–Indonesia Relations, 1960–1968* (Stanford, Calif.: Stanford University Press, 2008); Quinn Slobodian and Stuart Schrader, "The White Man, Unburdened," *The Baffler* 40 (2018): np.

48. Kim, *The Interrogation Rooms*, 3.

49. For a more recent take on "transcalar" approaches to historical analysis, see Beth Lew Williams, *The Chinese Must Go: Violence, Exclusion, and the Making of the Alien in America* (Cambridge, Mass.: Harvard University Press, 2021). Williams's work was undoubtedly inspired by Neil Smith's classic work on "scale jumping." See, for example, Neil Smith, "Contours of a Spatialized Politics: Homeless Vehicles and the Production of Geographical Scale," *Social Text* 33 (1992): 54–81.

50. Michel Foucault, *Society Must Be Defended: Lectures at the Collège de France, 1975–76* (New York: Picador, 2003), 242.

51. Duffield, *Development*; Arturo Escobar, *Encountering Development: The Making and Unmaking of the Third World* (Princeton, N.J.: Princeton University Press, 1995).

52. Jim Glassman, "Critical Development Geography III: Critical Development Geography," *Progress in Human Geography* 35, no. 5 (2010): 706; Joel Wainwright, *Decolonizing Development: Colonial Power and the Maya* (Malden, Mass.: Blackwell, 2008), 9. See also Vinay Gidwani, *Capital, Interrupted: Agrarian Development and the Politics of Work in India* (Minneapolis: University of Minnesota Press, 2008); Vinay Gidwani, "The Unbearable Modernity of 'Development'? Canal Irrigation and Development Planning in Western India," *Progress in Planning* 58 (2002): 1–80.

53. Gillian Hart, "Geography and Development: Critical Ethnographies," *Progress in Human Geography* 28, no. 1 (2004): 92.

54. Gidwani, *Capital, Interrupted*, 129.

55. See Nick Cullather, "Damming Afghanistan: Modernization in a Buffer State," *Journal of American History* 89, no. 2 (2002): 530.

56. "Atlantic Report: Afghanistan," *The Atlantic*, October 1962, 26.

57. "Atlantic Report," 74.

58. Melamed, "Racial Capitalism," 78.

59. Singh, *Race and America's Long War*, 15.

60. Deborah Cowen, "Infrastructures of Empire and Resistance," *Verso*, January 25, 2017, https://www.versobooks.com/blogs/3067-infrastructures-of-empire-and-resistance; Michelle Murphy, "Distributed Reproduction, Chemical Violence, and Latency," *S&F Online* 11, no. 3 (2013): np.

61. Ara Wilson, "The Infrastructure of Intimacy," *Signs* 41, no. 2 (2016): 261.

62. Majed Akhter, "Adjudicating Infrastructure: Treaties, Territories, Hydropolitics," *Environment and Planning E* 2, no. 4 (2019): 831–49; Majed Akhter, "Infrastructure Nation: State Space, Hegemony, and Hydraulic Regionalism in Pakistan," *Antipode* 47, no. 4 (2015): 849–70; Prakash, *Another Reason*; Scott, *Seeing Like a State*; Christopher Sneddon, *Concrete Revolution: Large Dams, Cold War Geopolitics, and the US Bureau of Reclamation* (Chicago: University of Chicago Press, 2015).

63. Khalili, "The Infrastructural Power of the Military," 914.

64. Khalili, 927.

65. Kristen Byrne, "Reflections on Service," *Medium*, May 19, 2017, https://medium.com/usaid2030/reflections-on-service-46ee117f8268.

66. Emma Mawsdley, "The Millennium Challenge Account: Neo-Liberalism, Poverty, and Security," *Review of International Political Economy* 14, no. 3 (2007): 487–509.

67. Derek Gregory, "War and Peace," *Transactions of the Institute of British Geographers* 35, no. 2 (2010): 154–86.

68. Melamed, *Represent and Destroy*, 39.

69. U.S. Department of Defense, "Directive 3000.05: Military Support for Stability, Security, Transition, and Reconstruction (SSTR) Operations," November 28, 2005, https://policy.defense.gov/portals/11/Documents/solic/DoDD%203000.05%20SSTR%20(SIGNED)%2028NOV05.pdf, 2.

70. Jennifer Morrison Taw, *Mission Revolution: The US Military and Stability Operations* (New York: Columbia University Press, 2012).

71. U.S. Department of Defense, "Directive 3000.05," 2.

72. U.S. Department of the Army, *Stability Operations (FM 30-07)*, Federation of American Scientists, October 2008, https://irp.fas.org/doddir/army/fm3-07.pdf.

73. Taw, *Mission Revolution*. See also McCoy, *Policing America's Empire*.

74. Colleen Bell, "Hybrid Warfare and Its Metaphors," *Humanity* 3, no. 2 (2012): 226; see also Singh, *Race and America's Long War*.

75. John Morrissey, "Securitizing Instability: The US Military and Full Spectrum Operations," *Environment and Planning D* 33, no. 4 (2015): 615.

76. See Nomi Stone, "Imperial Mimesis: Enacting and Policing Empathy in US Military Training," *American Ethnologist* 45, no. 4 (2018): 533–45.

77. Melamed, "The Spirit of Neoliberalism," 16.

78. Michelle Murphy, *The Economization of Life* (Durham, N.C.: Duke University Press, 2017), 39.

79. Mark Duffield, "Challenging Environments: Danger, Resilience, and the Aid Industry," *Security Dialogue* 43, no. 5 (2012): 475–92; Jennifer Fluri, "Armored Peacocks and Proxy Bodies: Gender Geopolitics in Aid/Development Spaces of Afghanistan," *Gender, Place, & Culture* 18, no. 4 (2011): 519–36; Jennifer Fluri, "Bodies, Bombs, and Barricades: Geographies of Conflict and Civilian (In)Security," *Transactions of the Institute of British Geographers* 36, no. 2 (2011): 280–96; Lisa Smirl, *Spaces of Aid: How Cars, Compounds, and Hotels Shape Humanitarianism* (London: Zed, 2015).

80. Gidwani, *Capital Interrupted*; James Ferguson and Akhil Gupta, "Spatializing States: Toward an Ethnography of Neoliberal Governmentality," *American Ethnologist* 29, no. 4 (2002): 981–1002; Tania Li, *The Will to Improve: Governmentality, Development, and the Practice of Politics* (Durham, N.C.: Duke University Press, 2007).

81. Andrew Friedman, *Covert Capital: Landscapes of Denial and the Making of US Empire in the Suburbs of Northern Virginia* (Berkeley: University of California Press, 2013), 13.

82. For a discussion of the imperial war-finance nexus, see Karuka, *Empire's Tracks*.

83. Shareen Brysac and Karl Meyer, *Tournament of Shadows: The Great*

Game and the Race for Empire in Central Asia (New York: Basic Books, 2006).

84. Nivi Manchanda, *Imagining Afghanistan: The History and Politics of Imperial Knowledge* (Cambridge: Cambridge University Press, 2019), 30.

85. Manchanda, 39.

86. For an analysis of Conolly's supposed humanitarianism, see Malcolm Yapp, "The Legend of the Great Game," *Proceedings of the British Academy* 111 (2001): 182.

87. Derek Gregory, *The Colonial Present: Afghanistan, Palestine, Iraq* (Malden, Mass.: Blackwell, 2004).

88. Manchanda, *Imagining Afghanistan*.

89. Barnett Rubin, *The Search for Peace in Afghanistan: From Buffer State to Failed State* (New Haven, Conn.: Yale University Press, 1995). See also Martin Bayly, "Imperial Ontological (In)Security: 'Buffer States', International Relations, and the Case of Anglo-Afghan Relations, 1808–1878," *European Journal of International Relations* 21, no. 4 (2014): 816–40.

90. Manchanda, *Imagining Afghanistan*.

91. Manchanda.

92. For a more detailed discussion of imperial succession, see Jason Oliver Chang, "Four Centuries of Imperial Succession in the Comprador Pacific," *Pacific Historical Review* 86, no. 2 (2017): 193–227.

93. Barnett Rubin, "Political Elites in Afghanistan: Rentier State Building, Rentier State Wrecking," *International Journal of Middle East Studies* 24, no. 1 (1992): 78.

94. Rubin, *The Search for Peace*.

95. Duffield, *Development*, 155.

96. Barnett Rubin and Ahmed Rashid, "From Great Game to Grand Bargain," *Foreign Affairs*, November 1, 2008, https://www.foreignaffairs.com/articles/2008-11-01/great-game-grand-bargain.

97. Manchanda, *Imagining Afghanistan*, 43.

98. Ann Stoler and David Bond, "Refractions Off Empire: Untimely Comparisons in Harsh Times," *Radical History Review* 95 (2006): 95.

99. Stoler and Bond, 93.

100. Stoler and Bond, 95.

101. Sara Ahmed, *Strange Encounters: Embodied Others in Post-Coloniality* (New York: Routledge, 2000), 8.

102. Richard Cohen, "The Soviet's Vietnam," *Washington Post*, April 22, 1988, A23.

103. Attewell, "Ghosts in the Delta."

104. George Orwell, *Shooting an Elephant, and Other Essays* (London: Secker and Warburg, 1950).

105. Voice of America, "Afghan War Draws Comparisons to Vietnam War,"

November 2, 2009, https://www.voanews.com/archive/afghan-war-draws
-comparisons-vietnam-war.

106. Micol Seigel, *Violence Work: State Power and the Limits of Police* (Durham, N.C.: Duke University Press, 2018); Schrader, *Badges without Borders*; Singh, *Race and America's Long War*.

107. Schrader, *Badges without Borders*.

108. Alfred McCoy, *The Politics of Heroin: CIA Complicity in the Global Drug Trade* (Chicago: Lawrence Hill Books, 2003).

109. Teo Ballvé, "Everyday State Formation: Territory, Decentralization, and the Narco Landgrab in Colombia," *Environment and Planning D* 30, no. 4 (2012): 603–22; Teo Ballvé, "Grassroots Masquerades: Development, Paramilitaries, and Land Laundering in Colombia," *Geoforum* 50 (2013): 62–75; Emma Shaw-Crane, "Small Victories: Urban Politics, After War," *PoLAR*, November 24, 2020, https://polarjournal.org/2020/11/24/small-victories
-urban-politics-after-war/; Kevin Woods, "Ceasefire Capitalism: Military-Private Partnerships, Resource Concessions, and Military-State Building in the Burma-China Borderlands," *Journal of Peasant Studies* 38, no. 4 (2011): 747–70.

110. Emma Shaw Crane, "Afterwar at City's Edge," paper presented at the annual meeting of the Association of American Geographers, Washington, D.C., April 5, 2019.

111. Gregory, *The Colonial Present*, 12.

112. Singh, *Race and America's Long War*, 15.

113. Chen Kuan-Hsing, *Asia as Method: Toward Deimperialization* (Durham, N.C.: Duke University Press, 2010).

114. Roberts, "Development Capital."

115. Roberts, 15.

116. Ananya Roy, "Ethnographic Circulations: Space-Time Relations in the Worlds of Poverty Management," *Environment and Planning A* 44, no. 1 (2012): 31–41.

117. Roy, 33.

118. Roy, 37.

119. For an extended discussion of rumor as both a technique of continental imperialism and a mode of decolonial resistance, see Karuka, *Empire's Tracks* as well as Man, *Soldiering through Empire*.

120. Kim, *The Interrogation Rooms*, 20.

121. Friedman, *Covert Capital*, 14.

122. Ann Stoler, *Along the Archival Grain: Epistemic Anxieties and Colonial Common Sense* (Princeton, N.J.: Princeton University Press, 2009), 28.

123. Jim was a member of my dissertation committee at the University of British Columbia.

124. Stoler, *Along the Archival Grain*, 26.

125. USAID, "USAID History," last updated November 12, 2021, https://www.usaid.gov/who-we-are/usaid-history.

126. Stoler, *Along the Archival Grain,* 47.

127. Stoler, 50.

128. Stoler, 53.

129. Stoler, 20.

130. Jennifer Earl, Andrew Martin, John D. McCarthy, and Sarah A. Soule, "The Use of Newspapers in the Study of Collective Action," *Annual Review of Sociology* 30 (2004): 65–80; David Ortiz, Daniel Myers, Eugene Walls, and Maria-Elena Diaz, "Where Do We Stand with Newspaper Data?" *Mobilization: An International Quarterly* 10, no. 3 (2005): 397–419.

131. Stoler, *Along the Archival Grain,* 53.

132. John Kelly, Beatrice Jauregui, Sean Mitchell, and Jeremy Walton, eds., *Anthropology and Global Counterinsurgency* (Chicago: University of Chicago Press, 2010).

133. Stoler, *Along the Archival Grain,* 53.

134. On "afterwars," making do, and abolition, see Ruth Wilson Gilmore, "Race at Boiling Point: Movement We Make," July 17, 2020, https://www.youtube.com/watch?time_continue=3432&v=7UCvcL2nPbA&feature=emb_logo; Thuy Linh Nguyen Tu, *Experiments in Skin: Race and Beauty in the Shadows of Vietnam* (Durham, N.C.: Duke University Press, 2021); Shaw Crane, "Afterwar."

1. The Unfinished Symphony

1. Marvin Green, "Fourth of July Celebration—Kandahar," June 11, 1962, P 58, Box 1, Record Group 286: Records of the United States Agency for International Development (hereafter cited as RG 286), National Archives and Records Administration, College Park, Md. (hereafter cited as NARA).

2. Monica Whitlock, "Helmand's Golden Age," *BBC News,* August 7, 2014, http://www.bbc.co.uk/news/special/2014/newsspec_8529/index.html.

3. Whitlock.

4. Whitlock.

5. Rajiv Chandrasekaran. *Little America: The War within the War for Afghanistan* (New York: Vintage, 2013).

6. Whitlock, "Helmand's Golden Age."

7. Whitlock.

8. Derek Gregory, *The Colonial Present: Afghanistan, Palestine, Iraq* (Malden, Mass.: Blackwell, 2004), 9.

9. Andrew Friedman, *Covert Capital: Landscapes of Denial and the Making of US Empire in the Suburbs of Northern Virginia* (Berkeley: University of California Press, 2013), 11.

10. Munira Khayyat, Yasmine Khayyat, and Rola Khayyat, "Pieces of Us: The Intimate as Imperial Archive," *Journal of Middle East Women's Studies* 14, no. 3 (2018): 268–91.

11. Khayyat, Khayyat, and Khayyat, 283.

12. Maurice Williams, John Kean, Charles Jenkins, Joann Feldman, and Patricia Fisher-Harris, "Retrospective Review of US Assistance to Afghanistan, 1950–1979," Digital National Security Archive, October 31, 1988, http://www.afghandata.org:8080/xmlui/handle/azu/14011?show=full.

13. Jodi Melamed, *Represent and Destroy: Rationalizing Violence in the New Racial Capitalism* (Minneapolis: University of Minnesota Press, 2011), 10.

14. Nikhil Pal Singh, *Race and America's Long War* (Berkeley: University of California Press, 2017), 5.

15. Singh, 138.

16. Mona Domosh, "Race, Biopolitics, and Liberal Development from the Jim Crow South to Postwar Africa," *Transactions of the Institute for British Geographers* 43, no. 2 (2018): 312–24; Friedman, *Covert Capital*; Stuart Schrader, "To Secure the Great Global Society: Participation in Pacification," *Millennium* 7, no. 2 (2016): 225–53. On topological lines of connection, see Cindi Katz, "On the Grounds of Globalization: A Topography for Feminist Political Engagement," *Signs* 26, no. 4 (2001): 1213–34.

17. See Emma Shaw Crane, "Afterwar at City's Edge," paper presented at the annual meeting of the Association of American Geographers, Washington, D.C., April 5, 2019.

18. Galloway Report, "Rural Development Activities in Afghanistan," 1959, P 58, Box 5. RG 286, NARA, 14.

19. Charles Husick and Cecil Uyehara, "Organization of Political Effort to Gain People's Support of the Shamalan Project," August 3, 1970, Helmand Valley Archive, http://scottshelmandvalleyarchives.org/docs/sld-70-08.pdf.

20. Jamey Essex, *Development, Security, and Aid: Geopolitics and Geoeconomics at the US Agency for International Development* (Athens: University of Georgia Press, 2013).

21. Timothy Mitchell, *Rule of Experts: Egypt, Techno-Politics, Modernity* (Berkeley: University of California Press, 2002), 15.

22. Gyan Prakash, *Another Reason: Science and the Imagination of Modern India* (Princeton, N.J.: Princeton University Press, 1999), 4.

23. Deborah Cowen, "Following the Infrastructures of Empire: Notes on Cities, Settler Colonialism, and Method," *Urban Geography* 41, no. 4 (2020): 469–86; Iyko Day, *Alien Capital: Asian Racialization and the Logic of Settler Colonial Capitalism* (Durham, N.C.: Duke University Press, 2016); Manu Karuka, *Empire's Tracks: Indigenous Nations, Chinese Workers, and the Transcontinental Railroad* (Berkeley: University of California Press, 2019).

24. Prakash, *Another Reason,* 163.

25. Christopher Sneddon and Coleen Fox, "The Cold War, the US Bureau of Reclamation, and the Technopolitics of River Basin Development, 1950–1970," *Political Geography* 30 (2011): 450–60.

26. Sneddon and Fox, 452.

27. Majed Akhter, "The Hydropolitical Cold War: The Indus Waters Treaty and State Formation in Pakistan," *Political Geography* 46 (2015): 65.

28. Majed Akhter, "Infrastructure Nation: State Space, Hegemony, and Hydraulic Regionalism in Pakistan," *Antipode* 47, no. 4 (2015): 861.

29. Akhter.

30. Nick Cullather, "Damming Afghanistan: Modernization in a Buffer State," *Journal of American History* 89, no. 2 (2002): 536.

31. Cullather, 524.

32. Timothy Nunan, *Humanitarian Invasion: Global Development in Cold War Afghanistan* (Cambridge: Cambridge University Press, 2015), 92.

33. Deborah Cowen, "Infrastructures of Empire and Resistance," *Verso,* January 25, 2017, https://www.versobooks.com/blogs/3067-infrastructures-of-empire-and-resistance.

34. Malini Ranganathan, "Rule by Difference: Empire, Liberalism, and the Legacies of Urban 'Improvement,'" *Environment and Planning A* 50, no. 7 (2018): 1392.

35. Cullather, "Damming Afghanistan," 532.

36. Wesley Attewell, "Ghosts in the Delta: USAID and the Historical Geographies of Vietnam's 'Other' War," *Environment and Planning A* 47, no. 11 (2015): 2257–75; Wesley Attewell, "'The Planet that Rules Our Destiny': Alternative Development and Environmental Power in Occupied Afghanistan," *Environment and Planning D* 35, no. 2 (2017): 339–59; Domosh, "Race, Biopolitics, and Liberal Development"; Jennifer Greenburg, "The 'Strong Arm' and the 'Friendly Hand': Military Humanitarianism in Post-Earthquake Haiti," *Journal of Haitian Studies* 19, no. 1 (2013): 95–122; David Nally and Stephen Taylor, "The Politics of Self-Help: The Rockefeller Foundation, Philanthropy, and the 'Long' Green Revolution," *Political Geography* 49 (2015): 51–63.

37. Nally and Taylor, "The Politics of Self-Help," 60.

38. Tania Li, "Fixing Non-market Subjects: Governing Land and Population in the Global South," *Foucault Studies* 18 (2014): 34–48.

39. Daniel Immerwahr, *Thinking Small: The United States and the Lure of Community Development* (Cambridge, Mass.: Harvard University Press), 4.

40. Immerwahr, 8, 12.

41. Schrader, "To Secure the Great Global Society," 226.

42. Schrader.

43. Immerwahr, *Thinking Small,* 92.

44. Immerwahr.

45. Laleh Khalili, "The Infrastructural Power of the Military: The Geoeconomic Role of the US Army Corps of Engineers in the Arabian Peninsula," *European Journal of International Relations* 24, no. 4 (2018): 911–33.

46. Domosh, "Race, Biopolitics, and Liberal Development," 314.

47. Schrader, "To Secure the Great Global Society," 234.

48. Schrader, 228.

49. Quoted in Schrader, 244.

50. Nick Cullather, "'The Target Is the People': Representations of the Village in Modernization and US National Security Doctrine," *Cultural Politics* 2, no. 1 (2006): 29–48.

51. Brett Story, *The Prison in 12 Landscapes* (New York: Grasshopper Films, 2016).

52. Elizabeth Hinton, "'A War within Our Own Boundaries': Lyndon Johnson's Great Society and the Rise of the Carceral State," *Journal of American History* 102, no. 1 (2015): 100–112.

53. Schrader, "To Secure the Great Global Society."

54. On the idea of infrastructural friction and resistance, see Charmaine Chua, "Containing the Ship of State: Managing Mobility in an Age of Logistics," PhD diss., University of Minnesota, July 2017, https://conservancy.umn.edu/handle/11299/200214.

55. Lloyd Baron, "Sector Analysis Helmand-Arghandab Valley Region," February 1973, Helmand Valley Archive, http://scottshelmandvalleyarchives.org/docs/sld-73-02.pdf.

56. Williams et al., "Retrospective Review," 78.

57. Baron, "Sector Analysis."

58. Cullather, "Damming Afghanistan."

59. Louis Dupree, "An Informal Talk with Prime Minister Daud," *American Universities Field Staff Reports Service: South Asia Series* 3, no. 3 (1959): 1–4.

60. Morrison-Knudsen's partners in this endeavor included Utah Construction, Henry J. Kaiser Co., Bechtel Corporation, McDonald & Kahn, J. F. Shea Co., and Pacific Bridge. All of these firms would go on to be movers and shakers in the American military-industrial complex.

61. James Carter, *Inventing Vietnam: The United States and State Building, 1954–1968* (Cambridge: Cambridge University Press, 2008); Christopher Sneddon, *Concrete Revolution: Large Dams, Cold War Geopolitics, and the US Bureau of Reclamation* (Chicago: University of Chicago Press, 2015).

62. Lloyd Baron, "The Water Supply Constraint: An Evaluation of Irrigation Projects and Their Role in the Development of Afghanistan," March 15, 1975, Helmand Valley Archive, http://scottshelmandvalleyarchives.org/docs/tdh-75-01-1.pdf, 2.

63. Baron, 2; Ministry of Planning, "Survey of Progress 1961–62," 1963, P 168, Box 1, RG 286, NARA.

64. Williams et al., "Retrospective Review," 16. Emphasis added.

65. Baron, "The Water Supply Constraint," 9–10.

66. Louis Dupree, *Afghanistan* (Princeton, N.J.: Princeton University Press, 1973).

67. Tudor Engineering Company, "Report on Development of Helmand Valley—Afghanistan," November 1956, Helmand Valley Archive, http://scottshelmandvalleyarchives.org/docs/evl-56-09.pdf.

68. Cullather, "Damming Afghanistan," 523.

69. Ministry of Planning, "Survey of Progress 1961–62."

70. Aloys Michel, *The Kabul, Kunduz, and Helmand Valleys and the National Economy of Afghanistan: A Study of Regional Resources and the Comparative Advantages of Development* (Washington, D.C.: National Academy of Sciences National Research Council, 1959).

71. Peter Franck, *Obtaining Financial Aid for a Development Plan: The Export-Import Bank of Washington Loan to Afghanistan* (Washington, D.C.: U.S. Senate Committee on Banking and Currency, 1953).

72. Franck; Williams et al., "Retrospective Review."

73. Williams et al., "Retrospective Review," 80.

74. Franck, *Obtaining Financial Aid.*

75. Franklin Roosevelt, "Executive Order 6581 Creating the Import-Export Bank of Washington," *American Presidency Project,* February 2, 1934, https://www.presidency.ucsb.edu/documents/executive-order-6581-creating-the-export-import-bank-washington.

76. Gardner Pattison, "The Export-Import Bank," *Quarterly Journal of Economics* 29, no. 3 (1943): 487–502.

77. Pattison, 79, 81.

78. Franck, *Obtaining Financial Aid.*

79. Franck, 6.

80. Franck, 18.

81. Franck, 18.

82. Franck, 34.

83. Emily Baldwin and Cynthia Clapp-Wincek, *The Helmand Valley Project in Afghanistan,* A.I.D. Evaluation Special Study No. 18 (Washington, D.C.: USAID, 1983), https://pdf.usaid.gov/pdf_docs/Pnaalo28.pdf.

84. Franck, *Obtaining Financial Aid.*

85. U.S. Department of State, *Point Four General Agreement for Technical Cooperation Between the Royal Afghan Government and the Government of the United States of America,* 1951, http://www.cawater-info.net/afghanistan/pdf/afghanistan_usa_cooperation_1951_en.pdf.

86. Michel, *The Kabul, Kunduz, and Helmand Valleys.*

87. Franck, *Obtaining Financial Aid.*

88. Anonymous, "Afghanistan—Helmand Valley Development Project," April 18, 1955, P 157, Box 4, Record Group 469: Records of U.S. Foreign Assistance Agencies, 1948–1961 (hereafter cited as RF 469), NARA; Duval Stoaks, "A Critique of Approaches and Activities in the Helmand Valley Development Projects," September 8, 1955, P 157, Box 4. RG 469, NARA.

89. Tudor Engineering Company, "Report."

90. Saville Davis, "Hope Rises for New Survey Team to Rescue Afghan Irrigation Project," *Christian Science Monitor,* July 16, 1956, ProQuest.

91. Williams et al., "Retrospective Review," 82.

92. Michel, *The Kabul, Kunduz, and Helmand Valleys,* 165.

93. Susan Roberts, "Development Capital: USAID and the Rise of Development Contractors," *Annals of the Association of American Geographers* 104, no. 5 (2014): 1030–51.

94. Williams et al., "Retrospective Review," 10.

95. Cullather, "Damming Afghanistan."

96. Cullather, 530.

97. Baldwin and Clapp-Wincek, *The Helmand Valley Project,* viii.

98. Here, Director Snyder is referring to the breach of the Seraj Canal that occurred on December 14, 1955, flooding hundreds of acres and stopping flow below the town of Yakchal. See Robert Snyder, "Cablegram ICATO 282," January 10, 1956, RG 469, NARA.

99. Tudor Engineering Company, "Report."

100. Tudor Engineering Company, 41.

101. Tudor Engineering Company, 18.

102. J. Evans, "Memorandum of Conversation on Helmand Valley Project Agreement," May 6, 1954, P 157, Box 4, RG 469, NARA.

103. Paul von der Lippe, "Year-End Report Helmand Valley Advisory Services," 1954, P 157, Box 5, RG 469, NARA.

104. Anonymous, "Afghanistan—Helmand Valley Development Project."

105. Evans, "Memorandum"; Helmand Valley Advisory Service, "Organization Bulletin," March 31, 1954, P 157, Box 5, RG 469, NARA.

106. Chief of the HVAS, "HVAS Monthly Activities Report for August, 1954," September 23, 1954, P 157, Box 4, RG 469, NARA; Stoaks, "A Critique."

107. Nally and Taylor, "The Politics of Self-Help," 60. Emphasis in original.

108. J. Evans and Weston Drake, "Program Discussions with the Helmand Valley Authority," April 7, 1955, P 157, Box 4, RG 469, NARA.

109. Evans and Drake.

110. Cullather, "Damming Afghanistan," 530; L. Poullada, "United States Foreign Aid Program in Afghanistan," February 7, 1956, P 157, Box 5, RG 469, NARA.

111. Quoted in Poullada, "United States Foreign Aid."

112. Poullada.

113. Galloway Report, "Rural Development Activities."

114. Abdullah Malikyar, "Letter to Stellan C. Wollmar, Director, United States Mission to Afghanistan," July 21, 1959, P 58, Box 14, RG 286, NARA.

115. E. White, "The ICA Program and Foreign Relations," USAID Document Experience Clearinghouse, 1959, http://pdf.usaid.gov/pdf_docs/pnadq613.pdf.

116. Ara Wilson, "The Infrastructure of Intimacy," *Signs* 41, no. 2 (2016): 248, 261.

117. Truman, "Inaugural Address."

118. Domosh, "Race, Biopolitics, and Liberal Development."

119. Ayazi Hossein, "Race, Containment and the Settler Imperial Politics of the Green Revolution," PhD diss., University of California, Berkeley, 2018, https://digitalassets.lib.berkeley.edu/etd/ucb/text/Ayazi_berkeley_0028E_18098.pdf; Singh, *Race and America's Long War.*

120. Melamed, *Represent and Destroy*, 13.

121. Cowen, "Infrastructures of Empire and Resistance."

122. Galloway Report, "Rural Development Activities," 14.

123. Galloway Report, 15.

124. Galloway Report, 16.

125. Nurul Haw, "Five Year Plan for the Development of Villages," January 26, 1965, P 58, Box 1, RG 286, NARA.

126. Haw.

127. Nally and Taylor, "The Politics of Self-Help"; Schrader, "To Secure the Great Global Society," 228, 244.

128. Immerwahr, *Thinking Small.*

129. Weston Drake, "Helmand Valley," May 15, 1958, P 793, Box 16, RG 286, NARA, 2.

130. Anonymous, "Helmand Valley Review (Kabul)," July 27, 1963, P 58, Box 14, RG 286, NARA; James Cudney. "Memorandum of Conversation—Ministry of Planning Meeting," March 24, 1964, P 168, Box 3, RG 286, NARA.

131. P. Nalder. "Memorandum of Conversation—Helmand Valley Authority/USAID meeting," 1964, P 168, Box 3, RG 286, NARA.

132. Anonymous, "Ministry of Planning Meeting," November 12, 1963, P 168, Box 1, RG 286, NARA.

133. P. Nalder and G. Plymale, "Memorandum of Conversation—Proposed Application for Development Loan," July 1967, P 168, Box 3, RG 286, NARA.

134. Williams et al., "Retrospective Review."

135. Dana D. Reynolds, "What the Judges and Mullahs Can Do," July 4, 1962, P 168, Box 3, RG 286, NARA, 1.

136. Reynolds, 3.

137. Tania Li, *The Will to Improve: Governmentality, Development, and the Practice of Politics* (Durham, N.C.: Duke University Press, 2007).

138. Chandrasekaran, *Little America*.

139. Stewart L. Udall, Floyd Dominy, and F. G. Whitaker. "Shamalan Unit Draft Feasibility Report," September 1967, Helmand Valley Archive, http://scottshelmandvalleyarchives.org/docs/sld-67-04-1.pdf.

140. Mildred Caudill, "The Helmand-Arghandab Valley: Yesterday, Today, Tomorrow," 1969, Helmand Valley Archive, http://scottshelmandvalley archives.org/docs/evl-69-08.pdf, 3.

141. Adam Curtis, "Kabul: City Number One—Part 3," *The Medium and the Message* (blog), October 13, 2009, http://www.bbc.co.uk/blogs/adamcurtis/posts/kabul_city_number_one_part_3; E. Long. "The Performance of the Agricultural Sector of AID-Assisted Countries," December 3, 1964, P 168, Box 1, RG 286, NARA.

142. Curtis, "Kabul."

143. Richard Scott and Cecil Uyehara, "The Shamalan, Its People, and USAID Responsibilities," May 9, 1972, Helmand Valley Archive, http://scottshelmandvalleyarchives.org/docs/sld-72-34.pdf.

144. Udall, Dominy, and Whitaker, "Shamalan Unit."

145. Richard Scott, "Another Visit to the North Shamalan," May 29, 1972, Helmand Valley Archive, http://scottshelmandvalleyarchives.org/docs/sld-72-33.pdf.

146. Richard Scott, "The Shamalan Land Development Project: An Introduction," 2011, Helmand Valley Archive, http://scottshelmandvalleyarchives.org/docs/sld-11-23.pdf.

147. Udall, Dominy, and Whitaker, "Shamalan Unit."

148. Michelle Murphy, *The Economization of Life* (Durham, N.C.: Duke University Press, 2017).

149. Husick and Uyehara, "Organization of Political Effort," 2–5.

150. Immerwahr, *Thinking Small*, 92.

151. Husick and Uyehara, "Organization of Political Effort," 5.

152. Bartlett Harvey, "Shamalan Project," March 22, 1971, Helmand Valley Archive, http://scottshelmandvalleyarchives.org/docs/sld-71-13.pdf.

153. Richard Scott, "Comments on Programs," April 3, 1971, Helmand Valley Archive, http://scottshelmandvalleyarchives.org/docs/sld-71-27.pdf.

154. Richard Scott, "Further Studies in the Shamalan Valley," May 6, 1971, Helmand Valley Archive, http://scottshelmandvalleyarchives.org/docs/sld-71-15.pdf.

155. Scott, "Comments on Programs."

156. Richard Scott, "The North Shamalan: A Survey of Land and People,"

November 24, 1971, Helmand Valley Archive, http://scottshelmandvalley archives.org/docs/sld-71-16.pdf.

157. Richard Scott, "Attitudes in the North Shamalan," March 9, 1972, Helmand Valley Archive, http://scottshelmandvalleyarchives.org/docs/ sld-72-12.pdf.

158. Richard Scott, "The Long Wait in the North Shamalan," October 17, 1972, Helmand Valley Archive, http://scottshelmandvalleyarchives.org/docs/ sld-72-19.pdf.

159. Richard Scott, "A Discussion with Mohammad Ibrahim Khan of Khalaj," October 16, 1972, Helmand Valley Archive, http://scottshelmand valleyarchives.org/docs/sld-72-22.pdf.

160. Scott, "Further Studies."

161. J. Shankland, "End of Tour Report—Afghanistan, Project No. 4," May 14, 1973, Helmand Valley Archive, http://scottshelmandvalleyarchives .org/docs/sld-73-28.pdf, 3.

162. Shankland; USAID/Afghanistan, "USAID-Assisted Development in the Helmand Arghandab Valley: Notes on Program Successes and Problems," 1973, Helmand Valley Archive, http://scottshelmandvalleyarchives. org/docs/evl-73-01.pdf.

163. Chandrasekaran, *Little America*; Cullather, "Damming Afghanistan."

164. Chandrasekaran, *Little America*.

165. Essex, *Development, Security, and Aid,* 53–54.

166. USAID/Afghanistan, "Central Helmand Drainage," April 8, 1975, Helmand Valley Archive, http://scottshelmandvalleyarchives.org/docs/ hdp-75-05.pdf, 2.

167. Ernest Barbour, "Central Helmand Drainage and Irrigation Improvement, No. 306-11-120-146," March 5, 1975, Helmand Valley Archive, http:// scottshelmandvalleyarchives.org/docs/hdp-75-14.pdf.

168. Richard Scott, "Need for Systematic Information Program in Central Helmand Drainage Project," June 2, 1975, Helmand Valley Archive, http:// scottshelmandvalleyarchives.org/docs/hdp-7528.pdf.

169. Richard Scott, "Comments on 'Central Helmand Drainage and Irrigation Improvement Helmand-Arghandab Valley' Project Paper and the Social Context within Which the Projects Must Function," March 3, 1975, Helmand Valley Archive, http://scottshelmandvalleyarchives.org/docs/hdp-75-18.pdf.

170. Scott, "Need for Systematic Information Program."

171. Cowen, "Infrastructures of Empire and Resistance"; Cullather, "Damming Afghanistan," 536.

172. Frantz Fanon, *The Wretched of the Earth* (New York: Grove, 2007).

173. P. R. Nadler, "Progress Report—Number 3," December 29, 1959, RG 286, P 58, Box 14, 1.

174. Nadler.

175. Chandrasekaran, *Little America*, 33.

176. Ghulam Farouq, Richard Scott, and Frydoon Shirzai, "Farm Economic Survey of the Helmand Valley," 1975, Helmand Valley Archive, http://scottshelmandvalleyarchives.org/docs/fes-78-03.pdf.

2. From Factory to Field

1. David Edwards, *Before Taliban: Genealogies of the Afghan Jihad* (Berkeley: University of California Press, 2002), 25.

2. Barnett R. Rubin, *The Fragmentation of Afghanistan: State Formation and Collapse in the International System* (New Haven, Conn: Yale University Press, 2002), 118.

3. Edwards, *Before Taliban*.

4. Rubin, *The Fragmentation of Afghanistan*.

5. Rubin.

6. Steve Coll, *Ghost Wars: The Secret History of the CIA, Afghanistan, and Bin Laden* (New York: Penguin Press, 2004).

7. Laleh Khalili, "The Infrastructural Power of the Military: The Geoeconomic Role of the US Army Corps of Engineers in the Arabian Peninsula," *European Journal of International Relations* 24, no. 4 (2018): 11.

8. Charmaine Chua, Martin Danyluk, Deborah Cowen, and Laleh Khalili, "Introduction: Turbulent Circulations: Building a Critical Engagement with Logistics," *Environment and Planning D* 36, no. 4 (2018): 618.

9. Martin Danyluk, "Capital's Logistical Fix: Accumulation, Globalization, and the Survival of Capitalism," *Environment and Planning D* 36, no. 4 (2018): 631.

10. Wesley Attewell, "Just-in-Time Imperialism: The Logistics Revolution and the Vietnam War," *Annals of the American Association of Geographers* 111, no. 5 (2021): 1329–45.

11. Kenneth Hobson, "Logistics Is the Lifeline," *Air University Review* 18, no. 5 (1967): 4.

12. Hobson, 4. Emphasis added.

13. J. Heiser, "Debrief Report," 1969, A1 887, Box 281, Record Group 472: Records of the US Forces in Southeast Asia, 1950–1972 (hereafter cited as RG 472), National Archives and Records Administration (hereafter cited as NARA), 25–26.

14. D. Eisenhower, *Public Papers of the Presidents of the United States: Dwight D. Eisenhower* (Washington, D.C.: US Government Printing Office, 1953), 541.

15. Anonymous, "Aid Trips," 1967, P 999, Box 2, Record Group 286: Records of the Agency for International Development (hereafter cited as

RG 286), NARA; E. Staats, "Survey of the Agency for International Development's Management and Operation of the Commercial Import Program for Viet Nam," 1967, A1 302, Box 2, RG 472, NARA.

16. J. Clancy, "GAO Report B-159451," 1967, A1 302, Box 2, RG 472, NARA.

17. J. Fuson, *Transportation and Logistics: One Man's Story* (Washington, D.C.: Center of Military History, 1994).

18. Anonymous, "Opening Remarks," 1965, P 999, Box 1, RG 286, NARA, 1. Emphasis added.

19. Ara Wilson, "The Infrastructure of Intimacy," *Signs* 41, no. 2 (2016): 261.

20. Jodi Melamed, "Racial Capitalism," *Critical Ethnic Studies* 1, no. 1 (2015): 78.

21. Deborah Cowen, *The Deadly Life of Logistics: Mapping Violence in Global Trade* (Minneapolis: University of Minnesota Press, 2014), 30.

22. Charmaine Chua, "Containing the Ship of State: Managing Mobility in an Age of Logistics," PhD diss., University of Minnesota, July 2017, https://conservancy.umn.edu/handle/11299/200214; Derek Gregory, "Supplying War in Afghanistan: The Frictions of Distance," openDemocracy, June 11, 2012, https://www.opendemocracy.net/en/supplying-war-in-afghanistan-frictions -of-distance/.

23. Vanessa Agard-Jones, "Body Burdens: Toxic Endurance and Decolonial Desire in Martinique," Lecture, Society of Fellows in the Humanities, Columbia University, New York, March 6, 2015; Vanessa Agard-Jones, "Bodies in the System," *Small Axe* 42 (2013): 182–92.

24. Derek Gregory, "The Everywhere War," *Geographical Journal* 177, no. 3 (2011): 239–40.

25. Gloria Anzaldúa, *Borderlands/La Frontera: The New Mestiza* (San Francisco: Aunt Lute Books, 1987), 3–4.

26. Mark Duffield, "Governing the Borderlands: Decoding the Power of Aid," *Disasters* 25, no. 4 (2001): 309.

27. Gregory, "The Everywhere War," 240.

28. Priya Satia, "To Understand Afghanistan's Future, Reckon with the Region's Colonial Past," *Foreign Policy,* August 19, 2021, https://foreignpolicy .com/2021/08/19/afghanistan-pakistan-india-south-asia-british-colonial -past-partition-durand-line/.

29. Lester Grau and Ali Ahmad Jalali, "Forbidden Cross-Border Vendetta: Spetsnatz Strike into Pakistan During the Soviet-Afghan War," *Journal of Slavic Military Studies* 18, no. 4 (2005): 661–72.

30. Timothy Nunan, *Humanitarian Invasion: Global Development in Cold War Afghanistan* (Cambridge: Cambridge University Press, 2015), 210.

31. Magnus Marsden, "Being a Diplomat on the Frontier of South and Central Asia: Trade and Traders in Afghanistan," In *Beyond Swat: History,*

Society, and Economy along the Afghanistan-Pakistan Frontier, ed. Magnus Marsden and Benjamin Hopkins (London: Hurst, 2012), 97; Magnus Marsden, *Trading Worlds: Afghan Merchants across Modern Frontiers* (Oxford: Oxford University Press, 2016).

32. Helga Baitenmann, "NGOs and the Afghan War: The Politicization of Humanitarian Aid," *Third World Quarterly* 12, no. 1 (1990): 62.

33. Nunan, *Humanitarian Invasion*, 221.

34. Baitenmann, "NGOs and the Afghan War."

35. C. W. Greenleaf, "Establishing an Office of the Aid Representative for Afghanistan Affairs in Pakistan," 1985, AF01644, Records of "Afghanistan: The Making of US Policy, 1973–1990," the Digital National Security Archive, George Washington University, Washington, D.C. (hereafter cited as DNSA); Gordon Humphrey, "Humphrey Calls for Humanitarian Aid for Afghans," 1988, AF02224, RA, DNSA.

36. Baitenmann, "NGOs and the Afghan War"; Rubin, *The Fragmentation of Afghanistan.*

37. Raphael Arnold, "Afghanistan—FY 89 Congressional Presentation," 1987, AF02059, RA, DNSA; Steve Galster, "Volume II: Afghanistan: Lessons from the Last War," National Security Archive, October 9, 2001, https://nsarchive2.gwu.edu//NSAEBB/NSAEBB57/essay.html.

38. Elaine Kingsley, Skype interview, November 25, 2012.

39. Baitenmann, "NGOs and the Afghan War," 76.

40. George D'Angelo et al., "Assessment of the Afghanistan Humanitarian Relief Project (Project 306–0206)," 1989, AF02295, RA, DNSA, 15.

41. Kingsley, Skype interview.

42. Tish Butler et al., "Management Assessment of the Cross-Border Humanitarian Assistance Program," 1988, AF02119, RA, DNSA, 1.

43. Butler et al., 14.

44. Baitenmann, "NGOs and the Afghan War."

45. Richard English, "Transitional Resettlement and Reconstruction Strategy," 1988, AF02233, RA, DNSA, 4.

46. Baitenmann, "NGOs and the Afghan War"; USAID, "Cross-Border Humanitarian Assistance Program for Afghanistan," 1988, AF02237, RA, DNSA.

47. Mike Martin, *An Intimate War: An Oral History of the Helmand Conflict, 1978–2012* (Oxford: Oxford University Press, 2014).

48. Barnett R. Rubin, "The Fragmentation of Afghanistan," *Foreign Affairs*, Winter 1989/1990: 153.

49. Rubin, 153.

50. English, "Transitional Resettlement."

51. USAID, "Cross-Border Humanitarian Assistance."

52. USAID, "Project Assistance Completion Report: Commodity Export

Program (306–0205)," USAID DEC, 1994, http://pdf.usaid.gov/pdf_docs/
PDABJ204.pdf.

53. USAID, "Project Assistance Completion Report: Commodity Export
Program (306–0205)"; Wesley Attewell, "The Lifelines of Empire: Logistics as
Infrastructural Power in Occupied South Vietnam," *American Quarterly* 72,
no. 4 (2020): 909–35; Khalili, "The Infrastructural Power of the Military."

54. Development Associates, "An Assessment of the Commodity Export
Program (Afghanistan): Final Report," USAID DEC, 1988, http://pdf.usaid
.gov/pdf_docs/XDABA102A.pdf.

55. English, "Transitional Resettlement."

56. Development Associates, "An Assessment."

57. D'Angelo et al., "Assessment," 52.

58. Butler et al. "Management Assessment."

59. Development Associates, "An Assessment," 4.

60. Development Associates, 4.

61. Rubin, *The Fragmentation of Afghanistan.*

62. Alan Kuperman. "The Stinger Missile and US Intervention in Afghanistan," *Political Science Quarterly* 114, no. 2 (1999): 219–63.

63. Rubin, *The Fragmentation of Afghanistan.*

64. Anonymous, "Afghanistan Private Sector Agribusiness Project"
(#902–0204), 1989, P 638, Box 51, RG 286, NA, 45.

65. Curt Wolters, "Agriculture Sector Support Project: VITA ARS Cooperative Agreement (Subproject)," USAID DEC, 1992, http://pdf.usaid.gov/
pdf_docs/PDABD925.pdf.

66. Thomas C. Frederic, Helen A. Cruz, and Radun S. Laban, "Final
Report, Afghanistan: Agriculture Rural Rehabilitation Evaluation," USAID
DEC, 1991, http://web.archive.org/web/20170224054656if_/http://pdf.usaid
.gov/pdf_docs/Pdabd526.pdf.

67. VITA, "Project Review—ARR VITA," USAID DEC, 1994, http://pdf
.usaid.gov/pdf_docs/PDABJ329.pdf.

68. USAID, "Agriculture Sector Support Project/Private Sector Agribusiness Subproject (ASSP/PSA)," USAID DEC, 1992, http://pdf.usaid.gov/
pdf_docs/PDABE157.pdf.

69. VITA, "Rural Works Component: Agriculture Sector Support Project," USAID DEC, 1987, http://pdf.usaid.gov/pdf_docs/pdaba219.pdf, 2.

70. VITA, "Rural Works Component," 3.

71. USAID, "Agriculture Sector Support Project," 5.

72. VITA, "Rural Works Component," 5.

73. Oakley, "Afghanistan Agriculture Sector Support Project (AAM)
Amendment," 1988, P 638, Box 52, RG 286, NA, 2.

74. Andrew Friedman, "US Empire, World War 2, and the Racializing of
Labor," *Race & Class* 58, no. 4 (2017): 23–38.

75. RONCO Consulting Corporation, "Assessment of the Agriculture Sector Support Project," USAID DEC, 1989, http://pdf.usaid.gov/pdf_docs/PDABB828.pdf, 41.

76. Frederic, Cruz, and Laban, "Final Report."

77. VITA, "Rural Works Component," 6–7.

78. VITA, "Rural Works Component," 7.

79. VITA, "Rural Works Component," 7.

80. Stuart Schrader, "To Secure the Great Global Society: Participation in Pacification," *Millennium* 7, no. 2 (2016): 225–53.

81. RONCO, "Assessment," 4, 32.

82. Thomas Frederic et al., "Notes Regarding Contractor Operations," 1991, P 638, Box 51, RG 286, NA, 147.

83. DAI, "Afghanistan Agricultural Sector Support Project: Technical Proposal, Volume One," USAID DEC, 1989, http://pdf.usaid.gov/pdf_docs/PDABJ431.pdf, 33.

84. Rubin, *The Fragmentation of Afghanistan.*

85. Aldelmo Ruiz, "Consolidated Annual Implementation Plan, Third Year—1992/93," USAID DEC, 1992, http://pdf.usaid.gov/pdf_docs/PDABJ333.pdf.

86. DAI, "Afghanistan Agricultural Sector Support Project," 21.

87. Frederic, Cruz, and Laban, "Final Report."

88. Frederic et al., "Notes Regarding Contractor Operations," 152.

89. DAI, "Agricultural Developments in Afghanistan, 1.2," Afghanistan Centre at Kabul University, 1992, Afghan Data Archives, http://afghandata.org:8080/xmlui/handle/azu/7330; Robert McCorkle and Clyde Hostetter, "A Farmer-to-Farmer Training Program for Afghanistan," Afghanistan Centre at Kabul University, 1990, Afghan Data Archives, http://afghandata.org:8080/xmlui/handle/azu/4628, ii, 7–8.

90. DAI, "Agricultural Developments in Afghanistan, 1.8," Afghanistan Centre at Kabul University, 1992, Afghan Data Archives, http://afghandata.org:8080/xmlui/handle/azu/7336, 23.

91. McCorkle and Hostetter, "A Farmer-to-Farmer Training Program," ii.

92. DAI, "Agricultural Developments in Afghanistan, 1.8," 26.

93. RONCO, "Assessment," 11.

94. DAI, "Strategy," 11.

95. Frederic et al., "Notes Regarding Contractor Operations."

96. DAI, "Strategy," 11.

97. Frederic et al., "Notes Regarding Contractor Operations," 144.

98. DAI, "Agricultural Developments in Afghanistan, 1.2," 8.

99. DAI, "Agricultural Developments in Afghanistan, 1.7," Afghanistan Centre at Kabul University, 1992, Afghan Data Archives, http://afghandata.org:8080/xmlui/handle/azu/7335, 1.

100. Eugene Saari, "Assessment of Wheat Production," Afghanistan Centre at Kabul University, 1992, Afghan Data Archives, http://afghandata.org:8080/xmlui/handle/azu/4741; Mir Mohammad Sediq, "Quarterly Report, July–September," Afghanistan Centre at Kabul University, 1989, Afghan Data Archives, http://afghandata.org:8080/xmlui/handle/azu/14181.

101. Anonymous, "Afghanistan Private Sector Agribusiness Project," 11.

102. DAI, "Afghanistan Agricultural Sector Support Project," 27.

103. DAI, "Afghanistan Agricultural Sector Support Project," 35.

104. DAI, "Afghanistan Agricultural Sector Support Project," 22.

105. DAI, "Afghanistan Agricultural Sector Support Project," 22.

106. USAID, "Agriculture Sector Assistance, 306–0204: Activity Approval Memorandum," USAID DEC, 1987, https://pdf.usaid.gov/pdf_docs/PDABE157.pdf.

107. John Conje, "Agricultural Extension System for Afghanistan: Approach, Strategy, and Features of a Reformed Extension Service," Afghanistan Centre at Kabul University, 1991, Afghan Data Archives, http://afghandata.org:8080/xmlui/handle/azu/3046; Tariq Husain, "Loosely Connected Notes with a Useful Attachment," USAID DEC, 1990, https://pdf.usaid.gov/pdf_docs/PNABS664.pdf.

108. Conje, "Agricultural Extension," 16.

109. DAI, "Agricultural Developments in Afghanistan, 1.8," 3.

110. John De Boer, Carl N. Hittle, and Michael E. Evnin, "Assessment of the Afghanistan Private Sector Agribusiness Component of the Agriculture Sector Support Project," USAID DEC, 1992, https://pdf.usaid.gov/pdf_docs/XDABE157A.pdf, 11.

111. Tania Li, "Fixing Non-Market Subjects: Governing Land and Population in the Global South," *Foucault Studies* 18 (2014): 44.

112. Husain, "Loosely Connected Notes," 4.

113. Anonymous, "Afghanistan Private Sector Agribusiness Project," 2.

114. Anonymous, "Afghanistan Private Sector Agribusiness Project," 2; Roger Poulin, "Private Sector Agribusiness Report," Afghanistan Centre at Kabul University, 1990, Afghan Data Archives, http://afghandata.org:8080/xmlui/handle/azu/13498.

115. USAID, "Project Assistance Completion Report: Agriculture Sector Support Project (306–0204)," USAID DEC, 1994, https://pdf.usaid.gov/pdf_docs/PDABJ203.pdf, 10.

116. Denny Freed, "Restraints and Possible Interventions to Increase Agricultural Inputs to and Outputs from Afghanistan," Afghanistan Centre at Kabul University, 1990, Afghan Data Archives, http://afghandata.org:8080/xmlui/handle/azu/4638.

117. Poulin, "Private Sector Agribusiness Project," 9.

118. Freed, "Restraints," 1–2.

119. Cary Raditz, "Financing Cross-Border Trade: Reconstructing Agriculture and Agribusiness in Afghanistan," Afghanistan Centre at Kabul University, 1990, Afghan Data Archives, http://afghandata.org:8080/xmlui/handle/azu/3568.

120. Poulin, "Private Sector Agribusiness Project."

121. Poulin, 10.

122. DAI, "Strategy for the Afghanistan Agriculture Sector Support Project," 9.

123. Freed, "Restraints."

124. James Ferguson, *The Anti-Politics Machine: "Development," Depoliticization, and Bureaucratic Power in Lesotho* (Minneapolis: University of Minnesota Press, 2017).

125. Alfred McCoy, *The Politics of Heroin: CIA Complicity in the Global Drug Trade* (Chicago: Lawrence Hill Books, 2003), 526–28.

126. See, for example, Ruth Wilson Gilmore, *Golden Gulag: Prisons, Surplus, Crisis, and Opposition in Globalizing California* (Berkeley: University of California Press, 2007); Elizabeth Hinton, *From the War on Poverty to the War on Crime: The Making of Mass Incarceration in America* (Cambridge, Mass.: Harvard University Press, 2016); Stuart Schrader, *Badges without Borders: How Global Counterinsurgency Transformed American Policing* (Berkeley: University of California Press, 2019).

127. Kingsley, Skype interview.

128. Gretchen Peters, *Seeds of Terror: How Drugs, Thugs, and Crime Are Reshaping the Afghan War* (New York: St. Martins, 2009), 49.

129. Peters, 51.

130. A. Samin, "Poppy Planting and Opium Production in Afghanistan," USAID DEC, 1992, https://pdf.usaid.gov/pdf_docs/PDABK074.pdf; USAID, "Narcotics Awareness and Control Project History," USAID DEC, 1992, https://pdf.usaid.gov/pdf_docs/PDABK049.pdf.

131. USAID, "Activity Approval Memorandum: Afghanistan—Narcotics Awareness and Control Project," USAID DEC, 1989, https://pdf.usaid.gov/pdf_docs/PDABK069.pdf; USAID, "Activity Information Memorandum: Anti-Narcotics Project," USAID DEC, 1992, https://pdf.usaid.gov/pdf_docs/PDABU395.pdf.

132. USAID, "Activity Information Memorandum: Anti-Narcotics Project," 34.

133. USAID, "AID Grant No. 306-0201-C-00-0820-00 to Development Alternatives Inc. in Support of the Narcotics Awareness Control Project in Afghanistan," USAID DEC, 1990, https://pdf.usaid.gov/pdf_docs/PDFCG165.pdf.

134. Curt Wolters, "Rural Development and Opium Production: Lessons

Learned in Pakistan and Afghanistan," USAID DEC, 1992, https://pdf.usaid
.gov/pdf_docs/PDABK050.pdf.

135. USAID, "Activity Approval Memorandum," 68.

136. USAID, 68.

137. USAID, "Activity Information Memorandum," 2.

138. Anonymous, "NACP Research Idea," P 638, Box 72, RG 286, NA, 1; G. Martin, "Inter-Agency Coordination in Support of the Afghanistan Narcotics Awareness and Control Project," 1990, P 638, Box 72, RG 286, NA, 2.

139. USAID, "Activity Approval Memorandum."

140. G. Martin, "Inter-Agency Coordination," 2.

141. USAID, "Interim Narcotics Strategy Related to Assistance Provided to Afghanistan," USAID DEC, 1988, https://pdf.usaid.gov/pdf_docs/PDABU396 .pdf.

142. DAI, "Afghanistan Narcotics Research and Awareness Project: Plan for Project Reconfiguration," USAID DEC, 1991, https://pdf.usaid.gov/pdf_ docs/PDABK071.pdf, 29.

143. DAI, "Afghanistan Narcotics Research and Awareness Project," 26; John Dixon, "End of Tour Report," USAID DEC, 1991, https://pdf.usaid.gov/ pdf_docs/PDABU385.pdf, 3.

144. Dixon, "End of Tour Report," 3; Gary Lewis, "Narcotics Awareness and Control Project Refocused Implementation Plan," 1991, P 638, Box 72, RG 286, NA, 11.

145. Gerald Owens, "Final Report," USAID DEC, 1991, https://pdf.usaid. gov/pdf_docs/PDABU386.pdf, 5–6.

146. Anonymous, "Working Level Meeting on Narcotics," P 638, Box 72, RG 286, NA, 3; USAID, "Activity Information Memorandum," 17.

147. Richard English, "Letter to Bev Eighmy," 1991, P 638, Box 72, RG 286, NA, 1–2.

148. USAID, "Activity Approval Memorandum."

149. USAID, "Activity Approval Memorandum," 51.

150. USAID, "Activity Approval Memorandum," 23.

151. USAID, "Activity Approval Memorandum," 23.

152. Steven Weerts, "End of Contract Report," USAID DEC, 1992, https:// pdf.usaid.gov/pdf_docs/PDABU382.pdf.

153. American Consul Peshawar, "Poppy Eradication in Malakand Division," 1991, P 638, Box 72, RG 286, NA.

154. Lawrence Smith and Stephen Solarz, "Letter to Ronald Roskens," 1990, P 638, Box 72, RG 286, NA, 3.

155. USAID, "Activity Information Memorandum."

156. Steven Weerts, "End of Tour Report," USAID DEC, 1992, https://pdf .usaid.gov/pdf_docs/PDABU383.pdf, 5.

157. Weerts, 5.

158. Bradford Miller, "End of Tour Report," USAID DEC, 1991, https://pdf
.usaid.gov/pdf_docs/PDABU387.pdf.

159. USAID, "Activity Approval Memorandum."

160. USAID, "Advice of Program Change," 1991, P 638, Box 72, RG 286, NA.

161. C. Rose, "Assistance Ban Study," USAID DEC, 1992, https://pdf.usaid
.gov/pdf_docs/PDABJ486.pdf.

162. Rose, 8.

163. Agard-Jones, "Bodies in the System"; Lauren Berlant, "Slow Death
(Sovereignty, Obesity, Lateral Agency)," *Critical Inquiry* 33, no. 4 (2007):
754–80; Rob Nixon, *Slow Violence and the Environmentalism of the Poor*
(Cambridge, Mass.: Harvard University Press, 2011).

164. VITA, "Project Review—ARR VITA," USAID DEC, 1994, https://pdf
.usaid.gov/pdf_docs/PDABJ329.pdf.

165. USAID, "Project Assistance Completion Report: Agriculture Sector
Support Program (306–0204)."

166. Gerry Owens, "End of Contract and Final Report from the Chief of
Party: Afghanistan Agriculture Sector Support Project/Private Sector Agribusiness," USAID DEC, 1993, https://pdf.usaid.gov/pdf_docs/PDABJ349.pdf, 3.

167. Owens, 3.

168. Jamey Essex, *Development, Security, and Aid: Geopolitics and Geoeconomics at the US Agency for International Development* (Athens: University
of Georgia Press, 2013), 51.

169. De Boer, Hittle, and Evnin, "Assessment," xii.

170. De Boer, Hittle, and Evnin, 5, 54.

171. De Boer, Hittle, and Evnin, 81, 59.

3. Fast Development, Slow Violence

1. Stuart Schrader, "Defining Key Policing Terms," *Stuart Schrader*
(blog), June 15, 2016, https://www.stuartschrader.com/blog/defining-key
-policing-terms.

2. Bench Ansfield, "The Broken Windows of the Bronx: Putting the Theory in Its Place," *American Quarterly* 72, no. 1 (2020): 103.

3. Ansfield, 104.

4. Stuart Schrader, *Badges without Borders: How Global Counterinsurgency Transformed American Policing* (Berkeley: University of California Press, 2019); Micol Seigel, *Violence Work: State Power and the Limits of
Police* (Durham, N.C.: Duke University Press, 2018).

5. Andy Bell, "Fixing Afghanistan's Broken Windows: A Low Tech Tool
in the Fight against Terror," *Small Wars Journal*, August 13, 2013, https://

smallwarsjournal.com/jrnl/art/fixing-afghanistan%E2%80%99s-broken
-windows-a-low-tech-tool-in-the-fight-against-terror.

6. Personal conversation, Elliott Jun.

7. *The Economist,* "Broken Windows in Afghanistan," January 19, 2010, https://www.economist.com/democracy-in-america/2010/01/19/broken-windows-in-afghanistan.

8. Sandeep Gopalan, "Pulling the Afghan Bus from the Ditch: 'Broken Windows' Strategy to Fix Government Can Inspire Hope," *Washington Times,* May 6, 2010, B04.

9. Ansfield, "The Broken Windows of the Bronx," 104.

10. Elizabeth Hinton, *From the War on Poverty to the War on Crime: The Making of Mass Incarceration in America* (Cambridge, Mass.: Harvard University Press, 2016). See also Ruth Wilson Gilmore, *Golden Gulag: Prisons, Surplus, Crisis, and Opposition in Globalizing California* (Berkeley: University of California Press, 2007).

11. Ansfield, "The Broken Windows of the Bronx," 104.

12. Bret Stephens, "Our Broken Windows World," *New York Times,* August 24, 2021, https://www.nytimes.com/2021/08/24/opinion/united-states-worlds-policeman.html.

13. Daniel Drezner, "Let's Shatter the 'Broken Windows' Theory of American Foreign Policy," *Washington Post,* January 2, 2015, https://www.washingtonpost.com/posteverything/wp/2015/01/02/lets-shatter-the-broken-windows-theory-of-american-foreign-policy-right-now/. See also Peter Munson, "Through a Broken Window Darkly: A False Vision of Foreign Policy," *War on the Rocks,* April 2, 2015, https://warontherocks.com/2015/04/through-a-broken-window-darkly-a-false-vision-of-foreign-policy/.

14. W. E. B. Du Bois, *Black Reconstruction: An Essay toward a History of the Part Which Black Folk Played in the Attempt to Reconstruct Democracy in America, 1860–1880* (New York: Harcourt, Brace and Company, 1935), 16.

15. Katherine McKittrick, "On Plantations, Prisons, and a Black Sense of Place," *Social & Cultural Geography* 12, no. 8 (2011): 947–63.

16. James Baldwin, "A Report from Occupied Territory," *The Nation,* July 11, 1966, https://www.thenation.com/article/archive/report-occupied-territory/; Hinton, *From the War on Poverty to the War on Crime*; Keeanga Yahmatta-Taylor, *Race for Profit: How Banks and the Real Estate Industry Undermined Black Homeownership* (Chapel Hill: University of North Carolina Press, 2019).

17. Pierre-Arnaud Chouvy, *Opium: Uncovering the Politics of the Poppy* (Cambridge, Mass.: Harvard University Press, 2009); United Nations Office on Drugs and Crime, *Global Illicit Drug Trends 2002* (New York: United Nations, 2002).

18. USAID, "The United States Agency for International Development and Counternarcotics: An Overview," USAID DEC, 1991, https://pdf.usaid.gov/pdf_docs/pnabh921.pdf.

19. Elaine Kingsley, Skype interview.

20. Barnett R. Rubin, *The Fragmentation of Afghanistan: State Formation and Collapse in the International System* (New Haven, Conn: Yale University Press, 2002).

21. Derek Gregory, *The Colonial Present: Afghanistan, Palestine, Iraq* (Malden, Mass.: Blackwell, 2004).

22. Rubin, *The Fragmentation of Afghanistan*, 271.

23. Gregory, *The Colonial Present*.

24. Amnesty International, *Women in Afghanistan: A Human Rights Catastrophe* (London: Amnesty International, 1995).

25. Andrew Hartman, " 'The Red Template': US Policy in Soviet-Occupied Afghanistan," *Third World Quarterly* 23, no. 3 (2002): 467–89; Kingsley, Skype interview.

26. Kingsley, Skype interview.

27. Jonathan Goodhand, "Frontiers and Wars: The Opium Economy in Afghanistan," *Journal of Agrarian Change* 5, no. 2 (2005): 191–216; Human Rights Watch, "Afghanistan's Civil Wars," https://www.hrw.org/reports/2001/afghan2/Afghan0701-01.htm; Alfred McCoy, "Can Anyone Pacify the World's Number One Narco-State?" *TomDispatch* (blog), March 30, 2010, http://www.tomdispatch.com/blog/175225/alfred_mccoy_afghanistan_as_a_drug_war.

28. Gregory, *The Colonial Present*, 40.

29. McCoy, "Can Anyone Pacify?"

30. Barbara Crosette, "Taliban's Ban on Poppy a Success, US Aides Say," *New York Times*, May 20, 2001, https://www.nytimes.com/2001/05/20/world/taliban-s-ban-on-poppy-a-success-us-aides-say.html; Jonathan Goodhand, "From War Economy to Peace Economy? Reconstruction and State-Building in Afghanistan," *Journal of International Affairs* 58, no. 1 (2004): 155–74.

31. Crosette, "Taliban's Ban."

32. Tim Golden, "A War on Terror Meets a War on Drugs," *New York Times*, November 25, 2001, https://www.nytimes.com/2001/11/25/weekinreview/the-world-a-war-on-terror-meets-a-war-on-drugs.html; Tim Weiner, "With Taliban Gone, Opium Farmers Return to Their Only Cash Crop," *New York Times*, https://www.nytimes.com/2001/11/26/world/nation-challenged-drug-trade-with-taliban-gone-opium-farmers-return-their-only.html.

33. Gopalan, "Pulling the Afghan Bus."

34. Seigel, *Violence Work*.

35. Eric Tang, *Unsettled: Cambodian Refugees in the New York City*

Hyperghetto (Philadelphia: Temple University Press, 2015); Thuy Linh Nguyen Tu, *Experiments in Skin: Race and Beauty in the Shadows of Vietnam* (Durham, N.C.: Duke University Press, 2021).

36. Jim Glassman, *Drums of War, Drums of Development: The Formation of a Pacific Ruling Class and Industrial Transformation in East and Southeast Asia, 1945–1980* (Leiden: Brill, 2018); Jim Glassman, "The Geopolitical Economy of Global Production Networks," *Geography Compass* 5, no. 4 (2011): 154–64; Jim Glassman and Young-Jin Choi, "The Chaebol and the US Military-Industrial Complex: Cold War Geopolitical Economy and South Korean Industrialization," *Environment and Planning A* 46, no. 5 (2014): 1160–80; David Keen, "The Political Economy of War," in *The Social and Economic Costs of Conflict in Developing Countries*, ed. Frances Stewart (London: ESCOR, DFID, 1997); Erica Schoenberger, "The Origins of the Market Economy: State Power, Territorial Control, and Modes of War Fighting," *Comparative Studies in Society and History* 50, no. 3 (2008): 663–91.

37. Jonathan Goodhand, "From Holy War to Opium War? A Case Study of the Opium Economy in North-Eastern Afghanistan," *Disasters* 24, no. 2 (2000): 155.

38. Goodhand, "From Holy War to Opium War?" 157.

39. Goodhand, "From War Economy to Peace Economy."

40. Dietrich Jung, *Shadow Globalization, Ethnic Conflicts, and New Wars: A Political Economy of Intra-State War* (London: Routledge, 2003).

41. Barnett Rubin, "The Political Economy of War and Peace in Afghanistan," *World Development* 28, no. 10 (2000): 1799.

42. Nikhil Pal Singh, *Race and America's Long War* (Berkeley: University of California Press, 2017).

43. Sven Beckert, *Empire of Cotton: A Global History* (New York: Alfred Knopf, 2014), xv–xvi.

44. Singh, *Race and America's Long War*, 30.

45. Ruth Wilson Gilmore, "Globalisation and US Prison Growth: From Military Keynesianism to Post-Keynesian Militarism," *Race & Class*, 40, no. 2/3 (1998/99): 176.

46. Schrader, *Badges without Borders*, 39.

47. Ara Wilson, "The Infrastructures of Intimacy," *Signs* 41, no. 2 (2016): 270.

48. Schrader, *Badges without Borders*.

49. Schrader, 131–32.

50. George Orwell, *Shooting an Elephant, and Other Essays* (London: Secker and Warburg, 1950).

51. Schrader, *Badges without Borders*, 261–62.

52. Schrader, 39.

53. Seigel, *Violence Work*, 9, 187.

54. Fred Moten, "Do Black Lives Matter? Robin D. G. Kelley and Fred Moten in Conversation," Vimeo video, January 6, 2015, https://vimeo.com/ 116111740.

55. Deborah Cowen, "Infrastructures of Empire and Resistance," *Verso,* January 25, 2017, https://www.versobooks.com/blogs/3067-infrastructures -of-empire-and-resistance; Michelle Murphy, "Distributed Reproduction, Chemical Violence, and Latency," *S&F Online* 11, no. 3 (2013): np.

56. David Mansfield, "Turning Deserts into Flowers: Settlement and Poppy Cultivation in Southwest Afghanistan," *Third World Quarterly* 39, no. 2 (2018): 331–49.

57. Moten, "Do Black Lives Matter?"

58. Lauren Berlant, "Slow Death (Sovereignty, Obesity, Lateral Agency)," *Critical Inquiry* 33, no. 4 (2007): 761.

59. Neferti Tadiar, "Life Times in Fate Playing," *South Atlantic Quarterly* 111, no. 4 (2012): 793.

60. Chemonics, *Afghanistan Alternative Livelihoods Program South (ALP/S): Revised Life of Project Work Plan, February 15, 2005 through February 15, 2009,* USAID DEC, 2006, https://pdf.usaid.gov/pdf_docs/Pdacks591.pdf.

61. Serge Schmemann, "Afghanistan Issues Order Taking Hard Line on Opium Production," *New York Times,* January 17, 2002, https://www.nytimes .com/2002/01/17/world/nation-challenged-drugs-afghanistan-issues-order -taking-hard-line-opium.html.

62. Craig Smith, "Poppy Ban Pleases Dealers in Opium," *New York Times,* January 19, 2002, https://www.nytimes.com/2002/01/19/world/a-nation -challenged-drug-trade-poppy-ban-pleases-dealers-in-opium.html.

63. Cyrus Hodes and Mark Sedra, "The Opium Trade," *Adelphi Papers* 47, no. 391 (2007): 35–42.

64. Carlotta Gall, "UN Aide Says Afghan Drug Trade Pays for Terrorist Attacks," *New York Times,* September 5, 2003, https://www.nytimes.com/ 2003/09/05/world/un-aide-says-afghan-drug-trade-pays-for-terrorist-attacks .html.

65. Gall, "UN Aide"; United Nations Office on Drugs and Crime, *The Opium Economy in Afghanistan: An International Problem* (New York: United Nations, 2003).

66. "Urban Cancer," *New York Times,* January 17, 1973, https://www .nytimes.com/1973/01/18/archives/urban-cancer.html.

67. John Lancaster, "Karzai Urges War on Opium Trade," *Washington Post,* December 10, 2004, https://www.washingtonpost.com/wp-dyn/articles/ A52402-2004Dec9.html.

68. Antonio Giustozzi, *Koran, Kalashnikov, Laptop: The Neo-Taliban Insurgency in Afghanistan* (New York: Columbia University Press, 2008). Giustozzi distinguishes the neo-Taliban (2002–present) from the "old Movement"

(1996–2001). He argues that the Taliban who survived the invasion traded their previous top-down approach to establishing and maintaining political hegemony for one that was better suited to waging an insurgent among a population. The neo-Taliban demonstrated their new flexibility by actively cultivating the popular support of rural communities and by recruiting foreign jihadists.

69. Gretchen Peters, *Seeds of Terror: How Drugs, Thugs, and Crime Are Reshaping the Afghan War* (New York: St. Martins, 2009).

70. Ashraf Ghani, "Where Democracy's Greatest Economy Is a Flower," *New York Times*, December 11, 2004, https://www.nytimes.com/2004/12/11/opinion/where-democracys-greatest-enemy-is-a-flower.html.

71. U.S. Senate Caucus on International Narcotics Control, *U.S. Counternarcotics Strategy in Afghanistan*, July 2010, https://fas.org/irp/congress/2010_rpt/counternarc.pdf.

72. Victoria Allen, Luke K. Handley, Ryan R. Stranahan, and Jacob Wells, *Sustainable Opium Poppy Elimination & Replacement in Afghanistan*, WikiLeaks, November 7, 2007, https://wikileaks.org/gifiles/attach/136/136481_Opium%20Poppy%20in%20Afghanistan%20ono%20slides.pdf.

73. D. Norland, *Trip Report PDAS Schweich to Afghanistan*, WikiLeaks, January 24, 2006, https://wikileaks.org/plusd/cables/06KABUL317_a.html; U.S. Office of Inspector General, Middle East Regional Office, *Status of the Bureau of International Narcotics and Law Enforcement Affairs Counternarcotics Program in Afghanistan: Performance Audit*, December 2009, https://www.stateoig.gov/system/files/134183.pdf.

74. U.S. Government Accountability Office, *Afghanistan Drug Control*, March 2010, https://www.gao.gov/new.items/d10291.pdf.

75. Inspectors General, US Department of State and US Department of Defense, *Interagency Assessment of the Counternarcotics Program in Afghanistan*, July 2007, https://media.defense.gov/2007/Jul/01/2001712995/-1/1/1/Counternarcotics_Pgr_Afghan%20_Final%20Rpt.pdf.

76. U.S. Government Accountability Office, *Afghanistan Drug Control*.

77. Barnett Rubin and Jake Sherman, "Counter-Narcotics to Stabilize Afghanistan: The False Promise of Crop Eradication," Centre on International Cooperation, February 2008, https://cic.es.its.nyu.edu/sites/default/files/counternarcoticsfinal.pdf.

78. United Nations Office on Drugs and Crime, *Afghanistan Opium Survey 2005* (New York: United Nations, 2005).

79. David Cloud and Carlotta Gall, "US Memo Faults Afghan Leader on Heroin Fight," *New York Times*, May 22, 2005, https://www.nytimes.com/2005/05/22/world/asia/us-memo-faults-afghan-leader-on-heroin-fight.html.

80. David Mansfield, *Resurgence and Reductions: Explanation for Changing Levels of Opium Poppy Cultivation in Nangarhar and Ghor in 2006–07,*

AREU, May 2008, https://areu.org.af/wp-content/uploads/2008/05/810E
-Resurgence-and-Reduction-CS-print.pdf.

81. United Nations Office on Drugs and Crime, "Alternative
Development—Overview," http://www.unodc.org/unodc/en/alternative
-development/overview.html.

82. David Mansfield, *Development in a Drugs Environment: A Strategic
Approach to "Alternative Development,"* Development-Oriented Drug
Control Programme, February 2006, http://www.mamacoca.org/docs_de_
base/Cifras_cuadro_mamacoca/strategic_approach.pdf; David Mansfield,
"Alternative Development in Afghanistan: The Failure of Quid Pro Quo,"
Helmand Valley Archives, August 2001, http://www.scottshelmandvalley
archives.org/docs/nar-01-03.pdf; David Mansfield and Adam Pain, *Alternative Livelihoods: Substance or Slogan,* AREU, October 1, 2005, https://areu
.org.af/publication/524/.

83. Chemonics, *Afghanistan Alternative Livelihoods Program South
(ALP/S): Implementation Strategy,* USAID DEC, 2005, https://pdf.usaid.gov/
pdf_docs/pdack676.pdf.

84. Joel Havfenstein, *Opium Season: A Year on the Afghan Frontier* (Guilford, Conn.: Lyon, 2008).

85. Theo Farrell and Antonio Giustozzi, "The Taliban at War: Inside the
Helmand Insurgency, 2004–2012," *International Affairs* 4 (2013): 845–71;
Giustozzi, *Koran, Kalashnikov, Laptop;* Carter Malkasian, *War Comes to
Garmser: Thirty Years of Conflict on the Afghan Frontier* (London: Hurst
and Company, 2013); Mike Martin, *An Intimate War: An Oral History of the
Helmand Conflict, 1978–2012* (London: Hurst and Company, 2014).

86. Chemonics, *Implementation Strategy,* 2.

87. Terence Hopkins and Immanuel Wallerstein, "Commodity Chains
in the World-Economy Prior to 1800," *Review (Fernand Braudel Center)* 10,
no. 1 (1986): 159.

88. Gary Gereffi, "A Commodity Chains Framework for Analyzing Global
Industries," *Institute of Development Studies* 8, no. 12 (1999): 1–9; Gary
Gereffi, "Global Chains in a Post-Washington Consensus World," *Review of
International Political Economy* 21, no. 1 (2014): 9–37; Gary Gereffi, "Global
Value Chains and International Competition," *Antitrust Bulletin* 56, no. 1
(2011): 37–56; Gary Gereffi and Stacey Frederick, "Value Chain Governance,"
USAID DEC, https://pdf.usaid.gov/pdf_docs/Pnadqo30.pdf.

89. Marion Werner, Jennifer Bair, and Victor Ramiro Fernández, "Linking Up to Development? Global Value Chains and the Making of a Post-
Washington Consensus," *Development and Change* 45, no. 6 (2014): 1242.

90. Chemonics, *Revised Life of Project Work Plan.*

91. Werner, Bair, and Ramiro Fernández, "Linking Up to Development?"

92. Neil Smith, "Contours of a Spatialized Politics: Homeless Vehicles and the Production of Geographical Scale," *Social Text* 33 (1992): 54–81.

93. Werner, Bair, and Ramiro Fernández, "Linking Up to Development?" 1228.

94. Chemonics, *Implementation Strategy*, 5.

95. Chemonics, *Revised Life of Project Work Plan*, 10.

96. Chemonics, *Afghanistan Alternative Livelihoods Program South (ALP/S): Year Two Work Plan, July 1, 2006 Through June 30, 2007*, USAID DEC, 2006, https://pdf.usaid.gov/pdf_docs/PDACK592.pdf.

97. Chemonics, 16–17.

98. Chemonics, 17–18.

99. Chemonics, 14.

100. Chemonics, 10; Chemonics, *Afghanistan Alternative Livelihoods Program South (ALP/S): Quarterly Report: October–December 2006*, USAID DEC, 2007, https://pdf.usaid.gov/pdf_docs/PDACK590.pdf; Chemonics, *Afghanistan Alternative Livelihoods Program South (ALP/S): Year Three Work Plan, July 1, 2007 through June 30, 2008*, USAID DEC, 2007, https://pdf.usaid.gov/pdf_docs/pdack593.pdf.

101. Mark Mazetti and David Rhode, "Amid US Policy Disputes, Al Qaeda Grows in Pakistan," *New York Times*, June 30, 2008, https://www.nytimes.com/2008/06/30/washington/30tribal.html.

102. Farrell and Giustozzi, "The Taliban at War," 850–51.

103. U.S. Office of Inspector General, "Audit of USAID/Afghanistan's Alternative Development Program—Southern Region," USAID DEC, 2008, https://pdf.usaid.gov/pdf_docs/PDACS006.pdf.

104. Chemonics, *Quarterly Report: October—December 2006*, 3.

105. Chemonics, *Year Three Work Plan*, 6.

106. Chemonics, 12–13.

107. "The Magnificent Seven Agricultural Fairs in Afghanistan in 2007," WikiLeaks, December 29, 2007, https://www.wikileaks.org/plusd/cables/07KABUL4211_a.html.

108. Checchi and Company Consulting, *Evaluation Report for Alternative Development Program (ADP) Southern Region by USAID in the Islamic Republic of Afghanistan*, USAID DEC, 2010, https://pdf.usaid.gov/pdf_docs/PDACS236.pdf; Checchi and Company Consulting, *Midterm Evaluation Alternative Livelihoods Program USAID/Afghanistan*, USAID DEC, 2007, https://pdf.usaid.gov/pdf_docs/pdacm813.pdf; U.S. Office of Inspector General, "Audit"; Special Inspector General for Afghanistan Reconstruction, *Audit of Costs Incurred by Chemonics International, Inc., in Support of USAID's Alternative Livelihoods Program—Southern Region*, 2013, https://www.sigar.mil/pdf/audits/Financial_Audits/Financial%20Audit%2013-1.pdf.

109. Checchi and Company Consulting, *Evaluation Report.*

110. Checchi and Company Consulting, 75.

111. Checchi and Company Consulting, 66.

112. Chemonics, *Afghanistan Alternative Livelihoods Program South (ALP/S): Economic Safety Net and Gender Analysis,* USAID DEC, 2005, https://pdf.usaid.gov/pdf_docs/Pnadk466.pdf.

113. Checchi and Company Consulting, *Evaluation Report,* 69.

114. Diana Davis, "A Space of Her Own: Women, Work, and Desire in an Afghan Nomad Community," in *Geographies of Muslim Women: Gender, Religion, and Space,* ed. Ghazi-Walid Falah and Caroline Nagel (New York: Guilford, 2005); Joanne Sharp, John Briggs, Hoda Yacoub, and Nabila Hamed, "Doing Gender and Development: Understanding Empowerment and Local Gender Relations," *Transactions of the Institute of British Geographers* 28 (2003): 281–95.

115. Checchi and Company Consulting, *Evaluation Report.*

116. Checchi and Company Consulting, 30.

117. Lorene Flaming and Alan Roe, *Opportunities for Pro-Poor Agricultural Growth,* AREU, 2009, https://areu.org.af/wp-content/uploads/2017/04/929E-Opportunities-for-Pro-Poor-Agricultural-Growth-SP-2009.pdf, 10.

118. David Mansfield and Adam Pain, *Evidence from the Field: Understanding Changing Levels of Opium Poppy Cultivation in Afghanistan,* AREU, November 1, 2007, https://areu.org.af/publication/722/, 16.

119. Flaming and Roe, *Opportunities*; Government of Afghanistan, *National Agriculture Development Framework: Economic Regeneration Programme* (Kabul: Government of Afghanistan, 2008).

120. Liz Wily, *Land, People, and the State in Afghanistan: 2002–2012,* AREU, February 28, 2013, https://areu.org.af/publication/1303; Liz Wily, *Looking for Peace on the Pastures: Rural Land Relations in Afghanistan,* AREU, 2004, https://econpapers.repec.org/paper/agsareusr/14626.htm.

121. Gilmore, *Golden Gulag,* 28.

122. Lisa Lowe, *The Intimacies of Four Continents* (Durham, N.C.: Duke University Press, 2015); Jodi Melamed, *Represent and Destroy: Rationalizing Violence in the New Racial Capitalism* (Minneapolis: University of Minnesota Press, 2011), 2.

123. Pamela Constable, "Success of Afghan Drug War Is Waning," *Washington Post,* January 14 2011, http://www.washingtonpost.com/wp-dyn/content/article/2011/01/13/AR2011011306701.html.

124. Victoria A. Greenfield, Keith Crane, Craig A. Bond, Nathan Chandler, Jill E. Luoto, and Olga Oliker, Reducing the Cultivation of Poppies in Southern Afghanistan, RAND, 2015, https://www.rand.org/content/dam/rand/pubs/research_reports/RR1000/RR1075/RAND_RR1075.pdf; U.S. Government Accountability Office, *Afghanistan Drug Control.*

125. United Nations Office on Drugs and Crime, *Afghanistan Opium Survey 2007* (New York: United Nations, 2007), iv.

126. Mansfield and Pain, *Evidence from the Field*, 14.

127. United Nations, "We Can End Poverty: Millennium Development Goals and Beyond," 2015, https://www.un.org/millenniumgoals/poverty.shtml.

128. Committee on Foreign Relations, *Afghanistan's Narco War: Breaking the Link between Drug Traffickers and Insurgents* (Washington, D.C.: U.S. Government Printing Office, 2009); Peters, *Seeds of Terror*.

129. Michael Watts, "Petro-Insurgency or Criminal Syndicate? Conflict and Violence in the Niger Delta," *Review of African Political Economy* 34, no. 114 (2007): 637–60.

130. United Nations Office on Drugs and Crime, "Afghan Opium Production in Significant Decline," September 2, 2009, http://www.unodc.org/unodc/en/frontpage/2009/September/afghan-opium-production-in-significant--decline.html.

131. Thomas Schweich, "Is Afghanistan a Narco-State?" *New York Times*, July 27, 2008, https://www.nytimes.com/2008/07/27/magazine/27AFGHAN-t.html?pagewanted=all&_r=0.

132. Tom Shanker and Eric Schmitt, "NATO Aims at Afghans Whose Drugs Aid Militants," *New York Times*, October 1, 2008, https://www.nytimes.com/2008/10/02/world/asia/02military.html.

133. Thomas Schweich, "The Pentagon Is Muscling in Everywhere. It's Time to Stop the Mission Creep," *Washington Post*, December 21, 2008, https://www.washingtonpost.com/wp-dyn/content/article/2008/12/19/AR2008121902748.html; Senate Caucus of International Narcotics Control, *US Counternarcotics Strategy*; Tom Shanker, "Obstacles in Bid to Curb Afghan Trade in Narcotics," *New York Times*, December 22, 2008, https://www.nytimes.com/2008/12/23/world/asia/23poppy.html.

134. U.S. Department of the Army, *Stability Operations (FM 30-07)*, Federation of American Scientists, October 2008, https://irp.fas.org/doddir/army/fm3-07.pdf, 14–15.

135. U.S. Department of the Army, 17–18.

136. Barack Obama, "Remarks by the President on a New Strategy for Afghanistan and Pakistan," *New York Times*, March 27, 2009, https://www.nytimes.com/2009/03/27/us/politics/27obama-text.html.

137. Richard Holbrooke, "Still Wrong in Afghanistan," *Washington Post*, January 23, 2008, http://www.washingtonpost.com/wp-dyn/content/article/2008/01/22/AR2008012202617.html.

138. Obama, "Remarks"; Associated Press, "US to Shift Approach to Afghanistan Drug Trade," *Los Angeles Times*, June 28, 2009, https://www.latimes.com/archives/la-xpm-2009-jun-28-fg-afghan-drugs28-story.html.

139. Reuters, "Highlights of Interview with US Envoy Holbrooke," June 27, 2009, https://www.reuters.com/article/usg8-holbrooke-sb/highlights-of -interview-with-u-s-envoy-holbrooke-idUSTRE55Q1GJ20090627.

140. Holbrooke, "Still Wrong."

141. Bruce Brown, interview, October 18, 2012.

142. Office of Inspector General—US Agency for International Development, *Audit of USAID/Afghanistan's Incentives Driving Economic Alternatives for the North, East, and West Program,* June 29, 2012, https://oig.usaid .gov/sites/default/files/2018-06/f-306-12-004-p.pdf.

143. Special Inspector General for Afghan Reconstruction, *Quarterly Report to the United States Congress,* January 30, 2010, https://www.sigar.mil/ pdf/quarterlyreports/2010-01-30qr.pdf.

144. Special Inspector General for Afghan Reconstruction.

145. Nathan Hodge, *Armed Humanitarians: The Rise of the Nation Builders* (New York: Bloomsbury, 2011), 84; USAID Office of Military Affairs, *Civil-Military Operations Guide,* April 27, 2010, https://mirror.explodie.org/ Civilian-Military%20Operations%20Guide.pdf.

146. Thomas Briggs, "New Bahar Districts 2010–11: A Case Study of Counterinsurgency Conducted by Naval Special Warfare in Afghanistan," *Small Wars & Insurgencies* 25, no. 1 (2014): 122–36; E. M. Burlingame, "Irregular Warfare: Village Stability Operations and the Venture Capital Green Beret," *Small Wars Journal,* May 14, 2012, https://smallwarsjournal .com/jrnl/art/irregular-warfare-village-stability-operations-and-the-venture -capital-green-beret; Daniel Green, "Retaking a District Center: A Case Study in the Application of Village Stability Operations," *Military Review* 95, no. 2 (2015): 118–24; Seth Shreckengast, "The Only Game in Town: Assessing the Effectiveness of Village Stability Operations and the Afghan Local Police," *Small Wars Journal,* March 27, 2012, https://smallwarsjournal.com/jrnl/art/ the-only-game-in-town-assessing-the-effectiveness-of-village-stability -operations-and-the-a; Jennifer Morrison Taw, *Mission Revolution: The US Military and Stability Operations* (New York: Columbia University Press, 2012).

147. Emily Gilbert, "Money as a 'Weapons Systems' and the Entrepreneurial Way of War," *Critical Military Studies* 1, no. 3 (2015): 202–19; Sloan Mann, "Taking Interagency Stability Operations to a New Level: The Integration of Special Operations Forces and USAID in Afghanistan," *Small Wars Journal,* 2008, https://smallwarsjournal.com/documents/79-mann.pdf.

148. Judy Patton, interview, July 18, 2013.

149. Mann, "Taking Interagency Stability Operations," 1.

150. Kingsley, Skype interview.

151. Sippi Azarbaijani-Moghaddam, Mirwais Wardak, Idrees Zaman, and Annabel Taylor, *Afghan Hearts, Afghan Minds: Exploring Afghan Perceptions of Civil-Military Relations,* British & Irish Agencies Afghanistan Group

Refugee Council, 2008, https://www.diplomatie.gouv.fr/IMG/pdf/Afghan_H_and_M_Exec_Summ_and_C_and_R.pdf.

152. Gilmore, *Golden Gulag*; Schrader, *Badges without Borders*, 268–69.

153. Mansfield and Pain, *Evidence from the Field*, 18.

154. Teo Ballvé, "Everyday State Formation: Territory, Decentralization, and the Narco Landgrab in Colombia," *Environment and Planning D* 30, no. 4 (2012): 603–22; Teo Ballvé, "Grassroots Masquerades: Development, Paramilitaries, and Land Laundering in Colombia," *Geoforum* 50 (2013): 62–75; Kevin Woods, "Ceasefire Capitalism: Military-Private Partnerships, Resource Concessions, and Military-State Building in the Burma-China Borderlands," *Journal of Peasant Studies* 38, no. 4 (2011): 747–70.

155. Dell, "What's Required to Make Alternative Livelihood Programs Succeed," WikiLeaks, December 9, 2008, https://wikileaks.org/plusd/cables/08KABUL3183_a.html.

156. Dell.

157. "Food Zone Initiative and High Wheat Prices Will Reduce Poppy Crop in 2009," WikiLeaks, January 9, 2009, https://wikileaks.org/plusd/cables/09KABUL45_a.html.

158. United Nations Office on Drugs and Crime, *Afghanistan Opium Survey 2009: Summary Findings* (New York: United Nations, 2009).

159. Eliza Villarino, "USAID Blocks IRD from Receiving New Contracts," *Devex*, January 27, 2015, https://www.devex.com/news/usaid-blocks-ird-from-receiving-new-contracts-85354.

160. USAID, "Afghanistan Vouchers for Increased Productive Agriculture—Plus (AVIPA Plus)," USAID, December 2010, http://web.archive.org/web/20190210010435/https://www.usaid.gov/sites/default/files/documents/1871/Fact_Sheet_AVIPA_Plus_FINAL_Dec_2010.pdf.

161. Office of Inspector General—US Agency for International Development, *Audit of USAID/Afghanistan's Afghanistan Vouchers for Increased Productive Agriculture Program*, April 20, 2010, https://oig.usaid.gov/sites/default/files/2018-06/5-306-10-008-p.pdf.

162. Rajiv Chandrasekaran, *Little America: The War Within the War for Afghanistan* (New York: Vintage, 2012), 109.

163. Greenfield et al., "Reducing the Cultivation," 117–18.

164. Dell, "Governance Improves Despite Security and Political Challenges," WikiLeaks, February 25, 2009, https://wikileaks.org/plusd/cables/09KABUL409_a.html.

165. "Food Zone Initiative."

166. "UNODC Report Anticipates Significant Decline in Opium Cultivation," WikiLeaks, February 9, 2009, https://wikileaks.org/plusd/cables/09KABUL280_a.html.

167. Karl Eikenberry, "AVIPA Plus Progress in RC-SOUTH," WikiLeaks,

February 3, 2010, https://wikileaks.org/plusd/cables/10KABUL433_a.html; Yaroslav Trofimov, "US Hires Afghan Farmers to Hold Off Taliban," *Wall Street Journal,* May 18, 2010, https://www.wsj.com/articles/SB1000142405274 8704250104575238442531337592.

168. Chandrasekaran, *Little America,* 192.

169. Andrew Metcalf, Skype interview, October 26, 2012.

170. Chandrasekaran, *Little America.*

171. Joel Havfenstein, "The Helmand Food Zone Fiasco," Registan, August 26, 2010, http://registan.net/2010/08/26/helmandfood-zone-fiasco.

172. Prisca Benelli, Antonio Donini, and Norah Niland, *Afghanistan: Humanitarianism in Uncertain Times,* Feinstein International Centre, November 2012, https://fic.tufts.edu/publication-item/afghanistan -humanitarianism-in-uncertain-times.

173. David Mansfield, *Managing Concurrent and Repeated Risks: Explaining the Reductions in Opium Production in Central Helmand Between 2008 and 2011,* AREU, August 25, 2011, https://areu.org.af/publication/1122; see also David Mansfield, *A State Built on Sand: How Opium Undermined Afghanistan* (Oxford: Oxford University Press, 2016).

174. Mansfield and Pain, *Evidence from the Field,* 13.

175. Paul Fishstein, *Despair or Hope: Rural Livelihoods and Opium Poppy Dynamics in Afghanistan,* AREU, August 2014, https://areu.org.af/wp -content/uploads/2016/02/1421E-Despair-or-Hope-Web-Version.pdf, 46.

176. Fishstein, *Despair or Hope*; David Mansfield, *"From Bad They Made It Worse": The Concentration of Opium Poppy in Areas of Conflict in the Provinces of Helmand and Nangarhar,* AREU, May 22, 2014, https://areu.org.af/ publication/1411.

177. David Mansfield, "Where Have All the Flowers Gone? The Real Reasons for the Drop in Poppy Crop in Afghanistan in 2015," *ALCIS,* October 20, 2015, https://stories.alcis.org/where-have-all-the-flowers-gone-7de7b34e8478.

178. Fishstein, *Despair or Hope*; David Mansfield, *All Bets Are Off! Prospects for (B)reaching Agreements and Drug Control in Helmand and Nangarhar in the Run Up to Transition,* AREU, January 23, 2013, https://areu.org.af/ publication/1302.

179. Mansfield, "Turning Deserts into Flowers."

180. Mansfield, "Where Have All the Flowers Gone?"

181. David Mansfield, *Helmand on the Move: Migration as a Response to Crop Failure,* AREU, October 15, 2015, https://areu.org.af/publication/1521.

182. Mansfield, 12.

183. Amira Garner, Skype interview, October 19, 2012.

184. David Axe, "US Kicks Drug-War Habit, Makes Peace with Afghan Poppies," *Wired,* May 9, 2013, https://www.wired.com/2013/05/afghan-poppies.

185. Anthony Hoffman, interview, October 23, 2012.

186. Tania Li, "Fixing Non-Market Subjects: Governing Land and Population in the Global South," *Foucault Studies* 18 (2014): 38.

4. Alternative Developments?

1. USAIDAfghanistan, "Growing Hope in Afghanistan Part 1," YouTube video, 2011, http://web.archive.org/web/20120219040944/ https://www.youtube.com/watch?v=a4W-ABaijIk; USAIDAfghanistan, "Growing Hope in Afghanistan Part 2," YouTube video, 2011, http://web.archive.org/web/20120219040933/https://www.youtube.com/watch?v=v4FeLc7jFfM.

2. USAIDAfghanistan, "Growing Hope in Afghanistan Part 1"; USAIDAfghanistan, "Growing Hope in Afghanistan Part 2."

3. Ahmidullah Archiwal and Casey Johnson, "Afghanistan's Better History, with Lessons for Today," USIP, August 13, 2015, https://www.usip.org/blog/2015/08/afghanistans-better-history-lessons-today; DAI, *Agricultural Developments in Afghanistan, 1.1,* Afghanistan Centre at Kabul University, http://afghandata.org:8080/xmlui/handle/azu/7329.

4. Michel Foucault, *The Birth of Biopolitics: Lectures at the Collège de France, 1978–1979* (New York: Palgrave Macmillan, 2008).

5. Special Inspector General for Afghan Reconstruction, *Quarterly Report to the United States Congress,* January 30, 2010, https://www.sigar.mil/pdf/quarterlyreports/2010-01-30qr.pdf; Special Inspector General for Afghan Reconstruction, *Quarterly Report to the United States Congress,* January 30, 2014, https://www.sigar.mil/pdf/quarterlyreports/2014Jan30QR.pdf, 14.

6. Jonathan Goodhand, "Corrupting or Consolidating the Peace? The Drugs Economy and Post-conflict Peacebuilding in Afghanistan," *International Peacekeeping* 15, no. 3 (2008): 414.

7. Foucault, *The Birth of Biopolitics,* 282.

8. Jamie Peck, "Remaking Laissez-Faire," *Progress in Human Geography* 32, no. 3 (2008): 14–15.

9. Foucault, *The Birth of Biopolitics,* 131.

10. Peck, "Remaking Laissez-Faire," 14–15.

11. Foucault, *The Birth of Biopolitics,* 329.

12. Ben Anderson, "Affect and Biopower: Towards a Politics of Life," *Transactions of the Institute of British Geographers* 37 (2012): 14.

13. Foucault, *The Birth of Biopolitics,* 240.

14. Anderson, "Affect and Biopower," 39.

15. Foucault, *The Birth of Biopolitics,* 260.

16. See Ann Stoler, *Race and the Education of Desire: Foucault's History of Sexuality and the Colonial Order of Things* (Durham, N.C.: Duke University Press, 1995).

17. Michel Foucault, *Society Must Be Defended: Lectures at the Collège de France, 1975–76* (New York: Picador, 2003).

18. Michelle Murphy, *The Economization of Life* (Durham, N.C.: Duke University Press, 2017).

19. Murphy, 140.

20. Ruth Wilson Gilmore, *Golden Gulag: Prisons, Surplus, Crisis, and Opposition in Globalizing California* (Berkeley: University of California Press, 2007), 28.

21. Murphy, *The Economization of Life*.

22. Murphy, 12.

23. Murphy, 135.

24. Murphy, 141.

25. Nivi Manchanda, "The Imperial Sociology of the 'Tribe' in Afghanistan," *Millennium* 46, no. 2 (2018): 165–89.

26. See also Vinh Kim Nguyen, "Government-by-Exception: Enrolment and Experimentality in Mass HIV Treatment Programmes in Africa." *Social Theory and Health* 7, no. 3 (2009): 196–217.

27. Oliver Belcher, "Anatomy of a Village Razing: Counterinsurgency, Violence, and Securing the Intimate in Afghanistan," *Political Geography* 62 (2018): 94–105; Patricia Owens, *Economy of Force: Counterinsurgency and the Historical Rise of the Social* (Cambridge: Cambridge University Press, 2015).

28. Wesley Attewell, "Ghosts in the Delta: USAID and the Historical Geographies of Vietnam's 'Other' War," *Environment and Planning A* 47, no. 11 (2015): 2257–75; Maureen Sioh, "Anxious Enactments: Postcolonial Anxieties and the Performance of Territorialization," *Environment and Planning D* 28, no. 3 (2010): 476–86; Maureen Sioh, "An Ecology of Postcoloniality: Disciplining Nature and Society in Malaya, 1948–1957," *Journal of Historical Geography* 30, no. 4 (2004): 729–46.

29. Katherine McKittrick, "On Plantations, Prisons, and a Black Sense of Place," *Social & Cultural Geography* 12, no. 8 (2011): 952.

30. Belcher, "Anatomy of a Village Razing," 98.

31. Derek Gregory, "From a View to a Kill: Drones and Late Modern War," *Theory, Culture, and Society* 27, no. 7–8 (2011): 188–215.

32. Attewell, "Ghosts in the Delta."

33. USAIDAfghanistan, "Growing Hope in Afghanistan Part 1"; USAIDAfghanistan, "Growing Hope in Afghanistan Part 2."

34. David Mansfield, *Development in a Drugs Environment: A Strategic Approach to "Alternative Development,"* Development-Oriented Drug Control Programme, February 2006, http://www.mamacoca.org/docs_de_base/Cifras_cuadro_mamacoca/strategic_approach.pdf.

35. David Mansfield and Adam Pain, *Evidence from the Field:*

Understanding Changing Levels of Opium Poppy Cultivation in Afghanistan, AREU, November 1, 2007, https://areu.org.af/publication/722/.

36. David Mansfield, *Resurgence and Reductions: Explanation for Changing Levels of Opium Poppy Cultivation in Nangarhar and Ghor in 2006–07,* AREU, May 2008, https://areu.org.af/wp-content/uploads/2008/05/810E -Resurgence-and-Reduction-CS-print.pdf.

37. Barnett Rubin and Jake Sherman, "Counter-Narcotics to Stabilize Afghanistan: The False Promise of Crop Eradication," Centre on International Cooperation, February 2008, https://cic.es.its.nyu.edu/sites/default/files/ counternarcoticsfinal.pdf.

38. Bruce Brown, personal interview, October 15, 2012.

39. Tania Li, "Fixing Non-market Subjects: Governing Land and Population in the Global South," *Foucault Studies* 18 (2014): 44.

40. David Scott, "Colonial Governmentality," *Social Text* 43 (1995): 202–3.

41. Murphy, *The Economization of Life.*

42. USAIDAfghanistan, "Growing Hope in Afghanistan Part 1."

43. Nivi Manchanda, "Rendering Afghanistan Legible: Borders, Frontiers, and the 'State' of Afghanistan," *Politics* 37, no. 4 (2017): 386–401.

44. USAIDAfghanistan, "Growing Hope in Afghanistan Part 1."

45. Checchi and Company Consulting, *Evaluation Report for Alternative Development Program (ADP) Eastern Region by USAID in the Islamic Republic of Afghanistan,* USAID DEC, 2010, https://pdf.usaid.gov/pdf_docs/ pdacs234.pdf, 10.

46. Antonio Giustozzi, *Koran, Kalashnikov, Laptop: The Neo-Taliban Insurgency in Afghanistan* (New York: Columbia University Press, 2008), 64.

47. DAI, *Alternative Development Program—Eastern Region Final Report, 2005–2009,* 2009, http://web.archive.org/web/20140719143312/https://www .dai.com/sites/default/files/pdfs/adpe_final_report.pdf, 69.

48. Although in practice, nothing prevented young men from working for both DAI and the neo-Taliban.

49. USAIDAfghanistan, "Growing Hope in Afghanistan Part 1"; USAIDAfghanistan, "Growing Hope in Afghanistan Part 2."

50. USAIDAfghanistan, "Growing Hope in Afghanistan Part 1"; USAIDAfghanistan, "Growing Hope in Afghanistan Part 2."

51. USAIDAfghanistan, "Growing Hope in Afghanistan Part 1"; USAIDAfghanistan, "Growing Hope in Afghanistan Part 2."

52. DAI, *Alternative Development Program—Eastern Region Final Report*; DAI, *Alternative Livelihoods Program—East: Quarterly Report, January–March 2007,* USAID DEC, 2007, https://pdf.usaid.gov/pdf_docs/pdacn321.pdf.

53. DAI, *Alternative Development Program—Eastern Region Final Report,* 74.

54. See also Jodi Melamed, "Racial Capitalism," *Critical Ethnic Studies* 1, no. 1 (2015): 76–85.

55. DAI, *Alternative Development Program—Eastern Region Final Report, 2005–2009,* 70–71.

56. DAI, 48; Magnus Marsden, "Being a Diplomat on the Frontier of South and Central Asia: Trade and Traders in Afghanistan," In *Beyond Swat: History, Society, and Economy along the Afghanistan-Pakistan Frontier,* ed. Magnus Marsden and Benjamin Hopkins (London: Hurst, 2012); Magnus Marsden, *Trading Worlds: Afghan Merchants across Modern Frontiers* (Oxford: Oxford University Press, 2016).

57. DAI, *Alternative Livelihoods Program East (ALP/E): Quarterly Report, January–March 2006,* USAID DEC, 2006, https://pdf.usaid.gov/pdf_docs/pdacn317.pdf, 17.

58. DAI, *Alternative Development Program—Eastern Region Final Report, 2005–2009.*

59. DAI, *Alternative Livelihoods Program—East (ALP/E): Quarterly Report, April–June 2006,* USAID DEC, 2006, https://pdf.usaid.gov/pdf_docs/Pdacn319.pdf.

60. DAI, *Alternative Development Program—Eastern Region Final Report, 2005–2009,* 56–58.

61. USAIDAfghanistan, "Growing Hope in Afghanistan Part 1"; USAIDAfghanistan, "Growing Hope in Afghanistan Part 2."

62. DAI, *Alternative Livelihoods Program—East (ALP/E): January–March 2006*; DAI, *Alternative Livelihoods Program—East (ALP/E): Quarterly Report, April–June 2006*; DAI, *Alternative Livelihoods Program—East (ALP/E): Quarterly Report, October–December 2006,* USAID DEC, https://pdf.usaid.gov/pdf_docs/pdacn320.pdf; DAI, *Alternative Development Program—Eastern Region Final Report, 2005–2009.*

63. USAIDAfghanistan, "Growing Hope in Afghanistan Part 1"; USAIDAfghanistan, "Growing Hope in Afghanistan Part 2."

64. DAI, *Alternative Development Program—Eastern Region Final Report, 2005–2009.*

65. USAIDAfghanistan, "Growing Hope in Afghanistan Part 1"; USAIDAfghanistan, "Growing Hope in Afghanistan Part 2."

66. Bruce Brown, personal interview, October 15, 2012.

67. Checchi and Company Consulting, *Evaluation Report for Alternative Development Program (ADP) Eastern Region,* 23, 29.

68. Checchi and Company Consulting, 31.

69. Checchi and Company Consulting; DAI, *Alternative Livelihoods Program—East (ALP/E): January–March 2006*; DAI, *Alternative Livelihoods Program—East (ALP/E): Quarterly Report, April–June 2006.*

70. John Woods, *Rebuilding Afghanistan's Agricultural Markets Program*

(RAMP): *RAMP Guidelines for Establishing Farmer Demonstration Plots,* USAID DEC, 2003, https://pdf.usaid.gov/pdf_docs/PNACY292.pdf.

71. Checchi and Company Consulting, *Evaluation Report for Alternative Development Program (ADP) Eastern Region,* 36; DAI, *Alternative Development Program—Eastern Region Final Report, 2005–2009.*

72. DAI, *Alternative Development Program—Eastern Region Final Report, 2005–2009,* 71.

73. Checchi and Company Consulting, *Evaluation Report for Alternative Development Program (ADP) Eastern Region,* 36.

74. DAI, *Alternative Development Program—Eastern Region Final Report, 2005–2009,* 71.

75. Owens, *Economy of Force.*

76. Checchi and Company Consulting, *Evaluation Report for Alternative Development Program (ADP) Eastern Region,* 17–18.

77. USAIDAfghanistan, "Growing Hope in Afghanistan Part 1."

78. Jennifer Fluri, "Armored Peacocks and Proxy Bodies: Gender Geopolitics in Aid/Development Spaces of Afghanistan," *Gender, Place, & Culture* 18, no. 4 (2011): 519–36; Jennifer Fluri, "The Beautiful 'Other': A Critical Examination of 'Western' Representations of Afghan Feminine Corporeal Modernity," *Gender, Place, and Culture,* 16, no. 3 (2009): 241–57; Manchanda, "The Imperial Sociology"; Nivi Manchanda, "Queering the Pashtun: Afghan Sexuality in the Homo-Nationalist Imaginary," *Third World Quarterly* 36, no. 1 (2015): 130–46.

79. Nangarhar, Inc., "Nangarhar Regional Development Plan: Building a Rich Past with a Bright Future," *We Meant Well* (blog), 2008, https://wemeantwell.com/blog/wp-content/uploads/2012/09/NANGARHAR-INC-BUSINESS-PLAN-MAR-08.pdf.

80. United Nations Office on Drugs and Crime, *Afghanistan Opium Survey 2009: Summary Findings* (New York: United Nations, 2009).

81. Gordon Phillips, "150500Z, NANGARHAR PRT, PRT CDR, PRT S2; STB XO ATTENDED GOV SHERZAI'S COUNTERNARCOTICS PLANNING MEETING AT GOVERNOR'S PALACE," WikiLeaks, 2007, https://wardiaries.wikileaks.org/id/A1B10E28-9445-40BA-A99A-E9A557C0DFEE/; Mark Corcoran, "The Bulldozer," *Foreign Correspondent,* 2009, https://www.abc.net.au/foreign/the-bulldozer/1323302.

82. "PRT Jalalabad: What Next for Poppy Eradication," WikiLeaks, 2007, https://www.wikileaks.org/plusd/cables/07KABUL1356_a.html.

83. Vanda Felbab-Brown, "Afghanistan Trip Report VI: Counternarcotics Policy in Afghanistan: A Good Strategy Poorly Implemented," Brookings, May 10, 2012, https://www.brookings.edu/opinions/afghanistan-trip-report-vi-counternarcotics-policy-in-afghanistan-a-good-strategy-poorly-implemented/.

84. Task Force Spartan, "D1 020509Z TF Vanguard LN Demonstration at Bati Kot DC (mod)," WikiLeaks, 2007, https://wardiaries.wikileaks.org/id/AF028814-CFA3-42B7-884C-7A992F1B93DB/.

85. United Nations Office on Drugs and Crime, _Afghanistan Opium Survey 2008_, https://www.unodc.org/documents/data-and-analysis/ExSum25August-standard.pdf.

86. DAI, "Summary Report: Year One, March 2, 2009–September 30, 2009," USAID DEC, 2009, https://pdf.usaid.gov/pdf_docs/PDACU243.pdf, 6.

87. Tim Hetherington and Sebastien Junger, _Restrepo_ (Outpost Films, 2010).

88. Greg Jaffe, "US and Afghan Forces Launch Major Assault in Eastern Province of Kunar," _Washington Post,_ June 28, 2010, http://www.washingtonpost.com/wpdyn/content/article/2010/06/28/AR2010062804376.html?hpid=moreheadlines.

89. Spencer Ackerman, "East Afghanistan Sees Taliban as 'Morally Superior' to Karzai," _Wired: Danger Room,_ July 6, 2010, https://www.wired.com/2010/07/in-afghanistans-east-taliban-seen-as-morally-superior-to-karzai/.

90. Bill Roggio, "Afghan, US Forces Launch Offensive in Kunar," _FDD's Long War Journal,_ June 28, 2010, https://www.longwarjournal.org/archives/2010/06/afghan_us_forces_lau.php.

91. Jennifer Fluri, "Bodies, Bombs, and Barricades: Geographies of Conflict and Civilian (In)Security," _Transactions of the Institute of British Geographers_ 36, no. 2 (2011): 280–96.

92. Garner, personal interview.

93. Rob Nordland, "Killings of Afghan Relief Workers Stir Debate," _New York Times,_ December 13, 2010, https://www.nytimes.com/2010/12/14/world/asia/14afghan.html?_r=0.

94. Anthony Hoffman, personal interview, October 23, 2012.

95. Anthony Hoffman.

96. Derek Gregory, _The Colonial Present: Afghanistan, Palestine, Iraq_ (Malden, Mass.: Blackwell, 2004), 28.

97. DAI, _Incentives Driving Economic Alternatives—North, East, and West (IDEA-NEW): Annual Report No. 2, October 1, 2009–September 30, 2010,_ USAID DEC, 2010, https://pdf.usaid.gov/pdf_docs/PDACU248.pdf, 19.

98. Mark Duffield, _Development, Security, and Unending War: Governing the World of Peoples_ (Malden, Mass.: Polity, 2007).

99. Foucault, _The Birth of Biopolitics,_ 269.

100. DAI, _Incentives Driving Economic Alternatives—North, East, and West (IDEA-NEW): Annual Report No. 3, October 1, 2010–September 30, 2011,_ USAID DEC, 2011, https://pdf.usaid.gov/pdf_docs/PDACU251.pdf, 4.

101. Hoffman, personal interview.

102. Garner, personal interview.

103. DAI, *Incentives Driving Economic Alternatives—North, East, and West (IDEA-NEW): Annual Report No. 3*, 32.

104. Garner, personal interview.

105. Mary Louise Pratt, *Imperial Eyes: Travel Writing and Transculturation* (New York: Routledge, 1992).

106. Sara Ahmed, *Strange Encounters: Embodied Others in Post-Coloniality* (New York: Routledge, 2000).

107. Murphy, *The Economization of Life*.

108. Garner, personal interview.

109. DAI, *Incentives Driving Economic Alternatives—North, East, and West (IDEA-NEW): Annual Report No. 3*.

110. DAI, *Incentives Driving Economic Alternatives—North, East, and West (IDEA-NEW): Annual Report No. 4, October 1, 2011–September 30, 2012*, http://www.ideanew.af/getpdf.php?f=201209/reports122.pdf, 25.

111. DAI.

112. Hoffman, personal interview.

113. DAI, *Incentives Driving Economic Alternatives—North, East, and West (IDEA-NEW): Annual Report No. 4*.

114. Garner, personal interview.

115. DAI, *Incentives Driving Economic Alternatives—North, East, and West (IDEA-NEW): Annual Report No. 3*.

116. Office of Inspector General U.S. Agency for International Development, *Audit of USAID/Afghanistan's Incentives Driving Economic Alternatives for the North, East, and West Program*, 2012, https://oig.usaid.gov/sites/default/files/2018-06/f-306-12-004-p.pdf.

117. DAI, *Incentives Driving Economic Alternatives—North, East, and West (IDEA-NEW): Annual Report No. 4*, 12.

118. DAI.

119. Murphy, *The Economization of Life*, 129.

120. Murphy, 139.

121. Talal Asad, "Conscripts of Western Civilization," in *Dialectical Anthropology: Essays in Honour of Stanley Diamond, vol. 1*, ed. Christine Gailey (Gainesville: University of Florida Press, 1992), 337.

122. Hoffman, personal interview.

123. Li, "Fixing Non-market Subjects," 47.

124. Li, 35–36.

125. Owens, *Economy of Force*.

126. Li, "Fixing Non-market Subjects," 37.

127. Jairus Grove, "The Stories We Tell about Killing," *The Disorder of Things*, 2016, https://thedisorderofthings.com/2016/01/06/the-stories-we-tell-about-killing/.

128. Oliver Belcher, "Tribal Militias, Neo-Orientalism, and the US Military's Art of Coercion," In *War, Police, and Assemblages of Intervention,* ed. Jan Bachmann, Colleen Bell, and Caroline Holmqvist (New York: Routledge, 2014); Jonathan Goodhand and Aziz Hakimi, *Counterinsurgency, Local Militias, and Statebuilding in Afghanistan,* United States Institute of Peace, 2014, https://www.usip.org/sites/default/files/PW90-Counterinsurgency -Local-Militias-and-Statebuilding-in-Afghanistan.pdf; Markus Kienscherf, "Producing 'Responsible' Self-Governance: Counterinsurgency and the Violence of Neoliberal Rule," *Critical Military Studies* 2, no. 3 (2016): 173–92.

129. Owens, *Economy of Force.*

130. Belcher, "Anatomy of a Village Razing."

131. Mona Domosh, "Practicing Development at Home: Race, Gender, and the 'Development' of the American South," *Antipode* 47, no. 4 (2015): 937.

132. Melamed, *Represent and Destroy,* 14.

133. Li, "Fixing Non-market Subjects," 47.

134. Murphy, *The Economization of Life,* 6.

135. DAI, *Incentives Driving Economic Alternatives—North, East, and West (IDEA-NEW): Annual Report No. 2.*

136. Murphy, *The Economization of Life,* 80–81.

137. DAI, *Incentives Driving Economic Alternatives—North, East, and West (IDEA-NEW): Annual Report No. 2.*

138. Anna Paterson, *Going to Market: Trade and Traders in Six Afghan Sectors,* AREU, 2006, https://areu.org.af/publication/622/.

139. Sarah Lister and Adam Pain, *Trading in Power: The Politics of 'Free' Markets in Afghanistan,* AREU, 2004, https://areu.org.af/publication/423/.

140. Deniz Kandiyoti, "Between the Hammer and the Anvil: Post-Conflict Reconstruction, Islam, and Women's Rights," *Third World Quarterly* 28, no. 3 (2007): 503–17; Mohammad Abed Shirzai, "Farmers Without Markets: Afghanistan's Struggle toward an Agricultural Economy," *The Diplomat,* December 30, 2016, https://thediplomat.com/2016/12/farmers-without -markets-afghanistans-struggle-toward-an-agricultural-economy/.

141. Li, "Fixing Non-market Subjects," 38.

142. David Mansfield, *Examining the Impact of IDEA-NEW on Opium Production: Nangarhar, a Case Study,* USAID DEC, 2015, https://pdf.usaid .gov/pdf_docs/PA00KCPT.pdf, 66.

143. Mansfield, 65.

144. DAI, *Incentives Driving Economic Alternatives—North, East, and West (IDEA-NEW): Annual Report No. 2,* 9.

145. Lina Abirafeh, *Gender and International Aid in Afghanistan: The Politics and Effects of Intervention* (Jefferson, N.C.: McFarland, 2009), 68.

146. AREU, *Women's Rights, Gender Equality, and Transition: Securing*

Gains, Moving Forward, AREU, September 25, 2013, https://areu.org.af/
publication/1308/.

147. AREU, 23; see also Jo Grace, *Gender Roles in Agriculture: Case Studies of Five Villages in Northern Afghanistan,* AREU, March 1, 2004, https://
areu.org.af/publication/408/; Kandiyoti, "Between the Hammer and the
Anvil."

148. Lena Ganesh, Massouda Kohistani, Rahim Azami, and Rebecca L.
Miller, *Women's Economic Empowerment in Afghanistan, 2002–2012: Information Mapping and Situation Analysis,* AREU, July 3, 2013, https://areu.org
.af/publication/1311/, 4.

149. Diana Davis, "A Space of Her Own: Women, Work, and Desire in an
Afghan Nomad Community," in *Geographies of Muslim Women: Gender,
Religion, and Space,* ed. Ghazi-Walid Falah and Caroline Nagel (New York:
Guilford, 2005).

150. Chona Echavez, *Gender and Economic Choice: What's Old and What's
New for Women in Afghanistan,* AREU, March 19, 2012, https://areu.org.af/
publication/1206/, 24; Kandiyoti, "Between the Hammer and the Anvil."

151. Echavez, *Gender and Economic Choice.*

152. Ganesh et al., *Women's Economic Empowerment,* 24.

153. Ganesh et al., 26.

154. Garner, personal interview.

155. Hoffman, personal interview.

156. Office of Inspector General U.S. Agency for International Development, *Audit of USAID/Afghanistan's Incentives Driving Economic Alternatives for the North, East, and West Program.*

157. Owens, *Economy of Force,* 271.

158. Laleh Khalili, "Gendered Practices of Counterinsurgency," *Review of
International Studies,* 37, no. 4 (2014): 1479; Laleh Khalili, "A Habit of Destruction," *Society and Space,* August 25, 2014, https://www.societyandspace
.org/articles/a-habit-of-destruction.

159. Trudy Rubin, "Successful Model for Foreign Aid Is IDEA-NEW," *The
Inquirer,* 2010, https://www.inquirer.com/philly/columnists/trudy_rubin/
Trudy_Rubin_Successful_model_for_foreign_aid_is_IDEA-NEW_.html.

160. Eyal Weizman, *The Least of All Possible Evils: Humanitarian Violence
from Arendt to Gaza* (New York: Verso, 2011).

161. David Mansfield, *Managing Concurrent and Repeated Risks: Explaining the Reductions in Opium Production in Central Helmand Between 2008
and 2011,* AREU, August 25, 2011, https://areu.org.af/publication/1122.

162. Mansfield.

163. Corcoran, "The Bulldozer"; David Mansfield, *"From Bad They Made
It Worse": The Concentration of Opium Poppy in Areas of Conflict in the*

Provinces of Helmand and Nangarhar, AREU, May 22, 2014, https://areu.org
.af/publication/1411.

164. Fabrizio Foschini, "How Outside Interference Politicized the Achin
Land Conflict," Afghanistan Analysts Network, October 30, 2011, https://
www.afghanistan-analysts.org/how-outside-interference-politicised-the
-achin-land-conflict/.

165. Foschini.

166. Foschini.

167. Mansfield, *Managing Concurrent and Repeated Risks,* 15.

168. Mansfield, 15.

169. Mansfield, *Examining the Impact.*

170. Mansfield.

171. Committee on Foreign Relations, *Afghanistan's Narco War: Breaking
the Link between Drug Traffickers and Insurgents* (Washington, D.C.: U.S.
Government Printing Office, 2009), 15.

172. Derek Gregory, "Lines of Descent," openDemocracy, November 8,
2011, https://www.opendemocracy.net/en/lines-of-descent/.

173. Gregory.

174. Gregory; Attewell, "Ghosts in the Delta."

175. Robert Pope, "Interagency Task Forces: The Right Tools for the Job,"
Strategic Studies Quarterly, 2011, https://apps.dtic.mil/dtic/tr/fulltext/u2/
a545502.pdf.

176. Department of Defense, *Progress Toward Security and Stability in
Afghanistan,* July 2013, https://dod.defense.gov/Portals/1/Documents/pubs/
Section_1230_Report_July_2013.pdf, 25.

177. Steak, "CIATF ALL SOURCE ANALYST $13–17K/MONTH
(OCONUS)(TS/SCI REQUIRED)," Socnet, 2011, http://www.socnet.com/
showthread.php?t=101068.

178. WikiLeaks, "Eric Camehl," ICWATCH, 2015, https://icwatch.wikileaks.
org/search?action=index&controller=search&location_facet=Land+O%27+
Lakes%2C+FL&page=1&tools_mentioned_facet=IMINT.

179. Jerod Harness, "Jerod Harness," LinkedIn, https://www.linkedin.com/
in/jerod-harness-35b95666; Jerod Harness, "Jerod Harness," ICWATCH,
https://icwatch.wikileaks.org/search?action=index&area_facet=Arkansas+
Area&controller=search&page=1&tools_mentioned_facet=Military&type_
facet=Privately+Held.

180. WikiLeaks, "Earl Owens," ICWATCH, 2015, https://icwatch.wikileaks
.org/docs/rEarl-Owens21eda1e9e2260fdc%3Fsp=0HUMINTCollectionTeam
Leader2008-12-01icwatch_indeed.

181. Department of Defense, *Report on Progress Toward Security and
Stability in Afghanistan: United States Plan for Sustaining the Afghanistan*

National Security Forces, April 2012, https://dod.defense.gov/Portals/1/Documents/pubs/Report_Final_SecDef_04_27_12.pdf; Nic Jenzen-Jones, "Chasing the Dragon: Afghanistan's National Interdiction Unit," *Small Wars Journal,* September 5, 2011, https://smallwarsjournal.com/blog/chasing-the-dragon-afghanistan's-national-interdiction-unit.

182. Attewell, "Ghosts in the Delta."

183. Craig Whitlock, "Afghans Oppose US Hit List of Drug Traffickers," *Washington Post,* October 4, 2009, http://www.washingtonpost.com/wp-dyn/content/article/2009/10/23/AR2009102303709_pf.html.

184. Ben Anderson, "Population and Affective Perception: Biopolitics and Anticipatory Action in US Counterinsurgency Doctrine," *Antipode* 43: 1.

185. Michelle Murphy, "Distributed Reproduction, Chemical Violence, and Latency," *S&F Online* 11, no. 3 (2013): np.

186. James Ferguson, *The Anti-Politics Machine: "Development," Depoliticization, and Bureaucratic Power in Lesotho* (Minneapolis: University of Minnesota Press, 2017), 21; Paul Fishstein, *Despair or Hope: Rural Livelihoods and Opium Poppy Dynamics in Afghanistan,* AREU, August 2014, https://areu.org.af/wp-content/uploads/2016/02/1421E-Despair-or-Hope-Web-Version.pdf; on Daesh's arrival in eastern Afghanistan, see Haseeb Ahmadzai, "Nangarhar Residents Voice Concerns over Security Issues," *TOLO News,* May 21, 2015, https://www.tolonews.com/afghanistan/nangarhar-residents-voice-concerns-over-security-issues; "Daesh in Afghanistan," *Khaleej Times,* 2015, https://www.khaleejtimes.com/opinion/daesh-in-afghanistan.

187. Hoffman, personal interview.

188. Murphy, *The Economization of Life*; James Scott, *Seeing Like a State: How Certain Schemes to Improve the Human Condition Have Failed* (New Haven, Conn.: Yale University Press, 1999).

189. Jodi Byrd, *The Transit of Empire: Indigenous Critiques of Colonialism* (Minneapolis: University of Minnesota Press, 2011); Jamie Peck, "Zombie Neoliberalism and the Ambidextrous State," *Theoretical Criminology* 14, no. 1 (2010): 104–10.

190. Achille Mbembe, "Necropolitics," *Public Culture* 15, no. 1 (2003): 40.

Conclusion

1. Ernesto Londono, "John Sopko, Watchdog for US Reconstruction Spending in Afghanistan, Isn't Looking to Make Friends," *Washington Post,* August 8, 2013, https://www.washingtonpost.com/world/national-security/john-sopko-watchdog-for-us-reconstruction-spending-in-afghanistan-isnt-looking-to-make-friends/2013/08/08/3cfc9c10-0053-11e3-96a8-d3b921c0924a_story.html.

2. Charles Clark, "USAID Accused of Covering Up Failures in Afghanistan," *Defense One,* April 2014, https://www.defenseone.com/business/2014/04/usaid-accused-covering-failures-afghanistan/81922/; Jessica Donati and Mirwais Harooni, "Afghan Businessmen Accused of Channeling Aid Money to Insurgency," *Reuters,* October 22, 2013, https://www.reuters.com/article/us-afghanistan-funding-haqqanis/afghan-businessman-accused-of-channeling-aidmoney-to-insurgency-idUSBRE99L09F20131022; Michael Igoe, "USAID Refutes SIGAR Report on Funds Misuse in Afghanistan," *Devex,* September 6, 2013, https://www.devex.com/news/usaid-refutes-sigar-report-on-funds-misuse-inafghanistan-81752.

3. The Islamic State of Iraq and the Levant (ISIL) is the U.S. government's preferred name for an extremist paramilitary group that first emerged as a response to the American counterinsurgency in Iraq. Over time, ISIL fighters made their way to other hotspots of the U.S. long War on Terror, including Afghanistan, Syria, and the Philippines.

4. Al Jazeera, "Afghanistan Civilian Deaths Hit Record High in 2018: UN," *Al Jazeera,* February 24, 2019, https://www.aljazeera.com/news/2019/2/24/afghanistan-civilian-deaths-hit-record-high-in-2018-un.

5. John Sopko, "Remarks Prepared for Delivery," *SIGAR,* 2014, https://www.sigar.mil/newsroom/ReadFile.aspx?SSR=7&SubSSR=29&File=speeches/14/Georgetown_University_ Speech.html.

6. Sopko.

7. United Nations Office on Drugs and Crime, *Afghanistan Opium Survey 2018: Cultivation and Production,* 2018, https://www.unodc.org/documents/cropmonitoring/Afghanistan/Afghanistan_opium_survey_2018.pdf.

8. Craig Whitlock, "Overwhelmed by Opium," *Washington Post,* December 9, 2019, https://www.washingtonpost.com/graphics/2019/investigations/afghanistan-papers/afghanistan-war-opium-poppy-production/.

9. Alfred McCoy, "How the Heroin Trade Explains the US-UK Failure in Afghanistan," *The Guardian,* January 9, 2018, https://www.theguardian.com/news/2018/jan/09/how-the-heroin-trade-explains-the-us-uk-failure-in-afghanistan.

10. Quoted in Whitlock, "Overwhelmed."

11. Kingsley, Skype interview.

12. Anonymous, "Aid Coordinator in Kabul," *The Afghanistan Papers,* January 26, 2015, https://www.washingtonpost.com/graphics/2019/investigations/afghanistan-papers/documents-database/?document=background_ll_02_xx_kabul2_01262015; Douglas Lute, "Douglas Lute, Lessons Learned Interview," *The Afghanistan Papers,* February 20, 2015, https://www.washingtonpost.com/graphics/2019/investigations/afghanistan-papers/documents-database/?document=lute_doug_ll_01_d5_02202015. See also Emily Gilbert, "The Gift of War: Cash, Counterinsurgency, and

'Collateral Damage,'" *Security Dialogue* 46, no. 5 (2015): 403–21; Emily Gilbert, "Money as a 'Weapons Systems' and the Entrepreneurial Way of War," *Critical Military Studies* 1, no. 3 (2015): 202–19.

13. Anonymous, "Aid Coordinator in Kabul, Lessons Learned Interview," *The Afghanistan Papers*, January 31, 2015, https://www.washington post.com/graphics/2019/investigations/afghanistan-papers/documents-database/?document=background_ll_02_xx_kabul_01312015.

14. Anonymous, "Aid Coordinator in New York, Lessons Learned Interview," *The Afghanistan Papers*, January 23, 2015, https://www.washingtonpost.com/graphics/2019/investigations/afghanistan-papers/documents-database/?document=background_ll_02_xx_nyc_01232015.

15. Anonymous, "U.S. Special Forces Adviser, Lessons Learned Interview," *The Afghanistan Papers*, January 22, 2016, https://www.washington post.com/graphics/2019/investigations/afghanistan-papers/documents -database/?document=background_ll_05_xx_phone_01222016; Anonymous, "USAID Official, Lessons Learned Interview," *The Afghanistan Papers*, November 10, 2016, https://www.washingtonpost.com/graphics/2019/investigations/afghanistan-papers/documents-database/?document=background_ll_07_xx_dc_11102016.

16. Anonymous, "USAID Official, Lessons Learned Interview," *The Afghanistan Papers*, December 9, 2015, https://www.washingtonpost.com/graphics/2019/investigations/afghanistan-papers/documents-database/?document=background_ll_05_a6_12092015.

17. Anonymous, "USAID Official, Lessons Learned Interview," *The Afghanistan Papers*, August 15, 2016, https://www.washingtonpost.com/graphics/2019/investigations/afghanistan-papers/documents-database/?document=background_ll_07_xx_dc_08152016.

18. Brian Copes, "Brian Copes, Lessons Learned Interview," *The Afghanistan Papers*, February 25, 2016, https://www.washingtonpost.com/graphics/2019/investigations/afghanistan-papers/documents-database/?document=copes_brian_ll_05_c15_02252016.

19. Copes.

20. Eric Wahner, "Eric Wahner, Lessons Learned Interview," *The Afghanistan Papers*, January 5, 2015, https://www.washingtonpost.com/graphics/2019/investigations/afghanistan-papers/documents-database/?document=wahner_eric_ll_05_c2_01052015.

21. Anonymous, "U.S Army Civil Affairs Officer, Lessons Learned Interview," *The Afghanistan Papers*, January 20, 2016, https://www.washingtonpost.com/graphics/2019/investigations/afghanistan-papers/documents-database/?document=background_ll_05_xx_phone_01202016.

22. Anonymous; Anonymous, "Former Official in U.S. Embassy in Kabul, Lessons Learned Interview," *The Afghanistan Papers*, June 9, 2015, https://

www.washingtonpost.com/graphics/2019/investigations/afghanistanpapers/
documents-database/?document=background_ll_02_xx_dc_06092015;
Anonymous, "USAID Official, Lessons Learned Interview," *The Afghanistan
Papers*, October 7, 2016, https://www.washingtonpost.com/graphics/2019/
investigations/afghanistan-papers/documents-database/?document=
background_ll_07_xx_dc2_10072016; James Bullion, "James Bullion, Lessons
Learned Interview," *The Afghanistan Papers*, November 18, 2015, https://
www.washingtonpost.com/graphics/2019/investigations/afghanistan-papers/
documents-database/?document=bullion_james_ll_05_c1_11182015; Tariq
Esmati, "Tariq Esmati, Lessons Learned Interview," *The Afghanistan Papers*,
December 12, 2016, https://www.washingtonpost.com/graphics/2019/
investigations/afghanistan-papers/documents-database/?document=esmati_
tariq_ll_12122016.

23. Anonymous, "Former Senior USAID Official, Lessons Learned
Interview," *The Afghanistan Papers*, December 2, 2015, https://www
.washingtonpost.com/graphics/2019/investigations/afghanistan-papers/
documents-database/?document=background_ll_05_a1_12022015.

24. Anonymous, "Former Senior US Official, Lessons Learned Interview,"
The Afghanistan Papers, December 11, 2015, https://www.washingtonpost
.com/graphics/2019/investigations/afghanistan-papers/documents
-database/?document=background_ll_03_xx_dc_12112015.

25. Stephen Hadley, "Stephen Hadley, Lessons Learned Interview," *The
Afghanistan Papers*, September 16, 2015, https://www.washingtonpost.com/
graphics/2019/investigations/afghanistan-papers/documents-database/?
document=hadley_stephen_ll_01_d12_09162015.

26. Anonymous, "Former Senior US official."

27. Gordon Weynand, "Gordon Weynand, Lessons Learned Interview,"
The Afghanistan Papers, February 26, 2016, https://www.washingtonpost
.com/graphics/2019/investigations/afghanistan-papers/documents
-database/?document=weynand_gordon_ll_05_a8_02262016.

28. Donald Dwyer, "Donald Dwyer, Lessons Learned Interview," *The
Afghanistan Papers*, February 10, 2016, https://www.washingtonpost.com/
graphics/2019/investigations/afghanistan-papers/documents-database/?
document=dwyer_donald_ll_5_c18_02102016.

29. Anonymous, "Former Senior US Official."

30. Anonymous, "Former National Security Council Staffer, Lessons
Learned Interview," *The Afghanistan Papers*, September 14, 2015, https://
www.washingtonpost.com/graphics/2019/investigations/afghanistanpapers/
documents-database/?document=background_ll_01_xx_dc_09142015.

31. Marin Strmecki, "Marin Strmecki, Lessons Learned Interview," *The
Afghanistan Papers*, October 19, 2015, https://www.washingtonpost.com/

graphics/2019/investigations/afghanistan-papers/documents-database/?
document=background_ll_01_xx_xx_10192015.

32. Strmecki; Wais Barmak, "Wais Barmak, Lessons Learned Interview," *The Afghanistan Papers*, January 17, 2017, https://www.washingtonpost.com/graphics/2019/investigations/afghanistan-papers/documents-database/?document=barmak_wais_ll_01172017.

33. Barnett Rubin, "Barnett Rubin, Lessons Learned Interview," *The Afghanistan Papers*, February 17, 2017, https://www.washingtonpost.com/graphics/2019/investigations/afghanistan-papers/documents-database/?document=background_ll_07_xx_nyc_rubin_02172017/.

34. Kim Willenson, "Congress Kills Program of US Police Advisers," *Ludington Daily News*, January 16, 1974, https://news.google.com/newspapers?nid=110&dat=19740115&id=lY1aAAAAIBAJ&sjid=IEoDAAAAIBAJ&pg=6828,1148031.

35. George Orwell, *Shooting an Elephant, and Other Essays* (London: Secker and Warburg, 1950).

36. Richard Boucher, "Richard Boucher, Lessons Learned Interview," *The Afghanistan Papers*, October 15, 2015, https://www.washingtonpost.com/graphics/2019/investigations/afghanistan-papers/documents-database/?document=boucher_richard_ll_01_b9_10152015.

37. Jeffrey Eggers, "Jeffrey Eggers, Lessons Learned Interview," *The Afghanistan Papers*, August 25, 2015, https://www.washingtonpost.com/graphics/2019/investigations/afghanistan-papers/documents-database/?document=background_ll_01_xx_dc_08252015.

38. Andrew Cockburn, "How the US Military Got Rich from Afghanistan," *Spectator World*, July 19, 2021, https://spectatorworld.com/topic/pentagon-rich-afghanistan-military-budget/.

39. Esmati, "Lessons Learned Interview."

40. Hedayatullah Babakarkheil, "Hedayatullah Babakarkheil, Lessons Learned Interview," *The Afghanistan Papers*, December 29, 2016, https://www.washingtonpost.com/graphics/2019/investigations/afghanistanpapers/documents-database/?document=babakarkheil_hedayatullah_ll_12292016; Barmak, "Wais Barmak, Lessons Learned Interview."

41. See, for example, Ruth Wilson Gilmore, "In the Shadow of the Shadow State," in *The Revolution Will Not Be Funded*, ed. INCITE! Women of Color Against Violence (Boston: South End 2009).

42. Anun Kundnani, "Abolish National Security," *The Transnational Institute*, June 2021, https://www.tni.org/files/publication-downloads/abolish_national_security_online.pdf. See also Angela Y. Davis, Gina Dent, Erica R. Meiners, and Beth E. Richie, eds., *Abolition. Feminism. Now.* (Chicago: Haymarket, 2021); Mariame Kaba, *We Do This 'Til We Free Us*

(Chicago: Haymarket, 2021); Stuart Schrader, *Badges without Borders: How Global Counterinsurgency Transformed American Policing* (Berkeley: University of California Press, 2019).

43. Kundnani, "Abolish National Security."

44. Schrader, *Badges without Borders*, 272.

45. Keisha Blain and Stuart Schrader, "The Rebellion in Defense of Black Lives Is Rooted in US History. So, Too, Is Trump's Authoritarian Rule," *Intercepted,* June 3, 2020, https://theintercept.com/2020/06/03/the-rebellion -in-defense-of-black-lives-is-rooted-in-u-s-history-so-too-is-trumps -authoritarian-rule/.

46. Michael Igoe, "Disrupt and Compete: How Trump Changed US Foreign Aid," *Devex,* August 21, 2020, https://www.devex.com/news/ disrupt-and-compete-how-trump-changed-us-foreign-aid-97955.

47. See, for example, Charmaine Chua, "Abolition Is a Constant Struggle: Five Lessons from Minneapolis," *Theory & Event* 23, no. 4 (2020): S-127–S-147.

48. Dylan Rodriguez, "Abolition as a Praxis of Human Being: A Foreword," *Harvard Law Review* 132 (2018–2019): 1575–612.

49. See for example Vijay Prashad, *The Darker Nations: A People's History of the Third World* (New York: New Press, 2007).

50. Vinay Gidwani, "The Unbearable Modernity of 'Development'? Canal Irrigation and Development Planning in Western India," *Progress in Planning* 58 (2002): 5.

51. Ruth Wilson Gilmore, *Golden Gulag: Prisons, Surplus, Crisis, and Opposition in Globalizing California* (Berkeley: University of California Press, 2007), 179.

52. Ruth Wilson Gilmore, "Covid 19, Decarceration, and Abolition (Full)," YouTube video, April 28, 2020, https://www.youtube.com/watch?v= hf3f5i9vJNM.

53. Ruth Wilson Gilmore, "Abolition on Stolen Land," *UCLA Luskin* (video), October 9, 2020, https://vimeo.com/467484872?ref=fb-share&fbclid= IwAR3Oy9Ov9P5rXGPBEMshpULMy7iBVtLEyMTadH7trAOD3kSMsbcj PoDNo9A.

54. Kundnani, "Abolish National Security."

55. Kundnani.

56. Frantz Fanon, *The Wretched of the Earth* (New York: Grove, 2007), 1–2.

57. Glen Coulthard, *Red Skin, White Masks: Rejecting the Colonial Politics of Recognition* (Minneapolis: University of Minnesota Press, 2014); Glen Coulthard, "Subjects of Empire: Indigenous Peoples and the 'Politics of Recognition' in Canada," *Contemporary Political Theory* 6 (2007): 437–60; Paul Gilroy, "Fanon and the Value of the Human," *Reading Fanon* (blog), 2011, http://readingfanon.blogspot.com/2012/01/fanon-and-value-of-human.html;

Lewis Gordon, T. Denean Sharpley-Whiting, Renee White, eds., *Fanon: A Critical Reader* (London: Wiley, 1996); Sylvia Wynter, "Towards the Sociogenic Principle: Fanon, Identity, and the Puzzle of Conscious Experience and What It Is Like to Be 'Black,'" in *National Identities and Socio-Political Changes in Latin America,* ed. Antonio Gomez-Moriana and Mercedes Duran-Cogan (New York: Routledge, 2001).

58. Fanon, *The Wretched,* 30–31.

59. Fanon, 51.

60. Louis Dupree, "An Informal Talk with King Mohammad Zahir of Afghanistan," *American Universities Field Staff Reports Service: South Asia Series* 7, no. 9 (1963): 4.

61. Fanon, *The Wretched,* 53.

62. See Walt Rostow, "The Stages of Economic Growth," *Economic History Review* 12, no. 1 (1959): 1–16.

63. Fanon, *The Wretched,* 56.

64. Fanon, 59.

65. Fanon, 61.

66. Fanon, 180.

67. Fanon, 61.

68. Huey Newton, "Intercommunalism," *Viewpoint Magazine,* 1974, https://www.viewpointmag.com/2018/06/11/intercommunalism-1974/.

69. Simeon Man, *Soldiering through Empire: Race and the Making of the Decolonizing Pacific* (Berkeley: University of California Press, 2018), 6. See also Patrick Chung, "From Korea to Vietnam: Local Labor, Multinational Capital, and the Evolution of US Military Logistics, 1950–97," *Radical History Review* 133 (2019): 31–55; Jim Glassman, *Drums of War, Drums of Development: The Formation of a Pacific Ruling Class and Industrial Transformation in East and Southeast Asia, 1945–1980* (Leiden: Brill, 2018); Jim Glassman and Young-Jin Choi, "The Chaebol and the US Military-Industrial Complex: Cold War Geopolitical Economy and South Korean Industrialization," *Environment and Planning A* 46, no. 5 (2014): 1160–80.

70. Cedric Robinson, "The Appropriation of Frantz Fanon," *Race & Class* 35, no. 1 (1993): 80.

71. Newton, "Intercommunalism."

72. Huey Newton, *To Die for the People* (New York: Writers and Readers, 1995), 104.

73. Robin D. G. Kelley, "What Abolition Looks Like, from the Panthers to the People," *LEVEL,* October 25, 2020, https://level.medium.com/what-abolition-looks-like-from-the-panthers-to-the-people-6c2e537eac71.

74. Dionne Searcey and John Eligon, "Minneapolis Will Dismantle Its Police Force, Council Members Pledge," *New York Times,* June 7, 2020, https://www.nytimes.com/2020/06/07/us/minneapolis-police-abolish.html.

75. Arun Gupta, "Seattle's CHOP Went Out with Both a Bang and a Whimper," *The Intercept*, July 2, 2020, https://theintercept.com/2020/07/02/seattle-chop-zone-police/.

76. See Ruthie Gilmore, "Is Prison Necessary? Ruth Wilson Gilmore Might Change Your Mind," *New York Times*, April 17, 2019, https://www.nytimes.com/2019/04/17/magazine/prison-abolition-ruth-wilsongilmore.html.

77. Ruth Wilson Gilmore, "Covid-19"; Dean Spade, *Mutual Aid: Building Solidarity During This Crisis (and the Next)* (Verso: New York, 2020), 2.

78. Anonymous, "U.S. Stabilization Contractor, Lessons Learned Interview," *The Afghanistan Papers*, September 27, 2016, http://washingtonpost.com/graphics/2019/investigations/afghanistan-papers/documents-database/?document=background_ll_07_xx_dc_09272016. Emphasis added.

79. Fanon, *The Wretched*, 56.

80. "Afghan Conflict: US and Taliban Sign Deal to End 18-Year War," *BBC*, February 29, 2020, https://www.bbc.com/news/world-asia-51689443.

81. Martine van Biljert, "Is This How It Ends? With the Taleban Closing In on Kabul, President Ghani Faces Tough Decisions," *Afghan Analysts Network*, August 15, 2021, https://www.afghanistan-analysts.org/en/reports/war-and-peace/is-this-how-it-ends-with-the-taleban-closing-in-on-kabul-president-ghani-faces-tough-decisions/.

82. Hamza Mohamed and Ramy Allahoum, "Taliban Enters Afghan Presidential Palace After Ghani Flees," *Al Jazeera*, August 15, 2021, https://www.aljazeera.com/news/2021/8/15/taliban-continues-advances-captures-key-city-of-jalalabad.

83. Juan Cole, "The Great Washington Ponzi Scheme in Afghanistan Comes Crashing Down," *Informed Comment*, August 13, 2021, https://www.juancole.com/2021/08/washington-afghanistan-crashing.html?fbclid=IwAR0xNkhpwoBfJ6aPOqmjUC9sRwAzPZ_UsJMN41k6umDua2Fk35SyiaR21-Q; "Russia Says Afghan President Fled with Cars and Helicopter Full of Cash—RIA," *Reuters*, August 16, 2021, https://www.reuters.com/world/asia-pacific/russia-says-afghan-president-fled-with-cars-helicopter-full-cash-ria-2021-08-16/.

84. Van Biljert, "Is This How It Ends?"

85. Gillian Brockell, "The Fall of Saigon: As Taliban Seizes Kabul, the Vietnam War's Final Days Remembered," *Washington Post*, August 16, 2021, https://www.washingtonpost.com/history/2021/08/15/saigon-fall-kabul-taliban/.

86. Kaamil Ahmed, Kevin Rawlinson, Caroline Davies, and Helen Sullivan, "Chaos at Hamid Karzai International Airport in Kabul—As It Happened," *The Guardian*, August 16, 2021, https://www.theguardian.com/world/live/2021/aug/16/afghanistan-taliban-kabul-evacuation-live-news-updates.

87. Kundnani, "Abolish National Security."

88. Emma Shaw Crane, "Afterwar at City's Edge," paper presented at the annual meeting of the Association of American Geographers, Washington, D.C., April 5, 2019, 4; See also Zoë Wool, *After War: The Weight of Life at Walter Reed* (Durham, N.C.: Duke University Press, 2015).

89. Emma Shaw Crane, "Afterwar at City's Edge."

90. Emma Shaw Crane, "Afterwar at City's Edge," 1.

91. Leah Zani, "Bomb Ecologies," *Environmental Humanities* 1, no. 2 (2018): 528.

92. See also Davorn Sisavath, "The US Secret War in Laos: Constructing an Archive from Military Waste," *Radical History Review* 133 (2019): 103–16; Emma Shaw-Crane, "Afterwar."

93. Zani, "Bomb Ecologies," 530.

94. Zani.

95. Monica Kim, *The Interrogation Rooms of the Korean War: The Untold History* (Princeton, N.J.: Princeton University Press, 2019), 5.

96. Van Biljert, "Is This How It Ends?"

97. Cole, "The Great Washington Ponzi Scheme."

98. Van Biljert, "Is This How It Ends?"

99. Martine van Biljert, "Between Hope and Fear: Rural Afghan Women Talk About Peace and War," Afghanistan Analysts Network, July 2021, https://reliefweb.int/report/afghanistan/between-hope-and-fear-rural-afghan-women-talk-about-peace-and-war.

100. Van Biljert, 27. Emphasis added.

101. Thuy Linh Nguyen Tu, *Experiments in Skin: Race and Beauty in the Shadows of Vietnam* (Durham, N.C.: Duke University Press, 2021).

102. Radio Free Europe, "Afghan Farmers Supply Opium Trade as Money Dries Up," YouTube video, May 8, 2020, https://www.youtube.com/watch?v=wrPyEdYKrmY&t=21s.

103. Gilmore, "Is Prison Necessary?"

104. Dylan Rodríguez, "Abolition as Praxis of Human Being: A Foreword," *Harvard Law Review* 132 (2019): 1575–612.

105. Deborah Cowen, "Infrastructures of Empire and Resistance," *Verso*, January 25, 2017, https://www.versobooks.com/blogs/3067-infrastructures-of-empire-and-resistance; Tu, *Experiments in Skin*.

106. Newton, "Intercommunalism"; Jackie Wang, *Carceral Capitalism* (South Pasadena, Calif.: Semiotext(e), 2018), 298; on abolition as an "infrastructure of making," see Rodriguez, "Abolition."

Index

Abirafeh, Lina, 202
abolitionist approach, 221–31
ACDI/VOCA, 190
Achin conflict, 205–6
ADP/E (Alternative Development
Program East): as alternative
development, 175; demonstration farms, 184–85; as favoring
male landowners, 187–88; and
"Growing Hope in Afghanistan"
(documentary), 174, 183, 184, 186;
and market-based approaches,
186–87; obstacles, 188; replacing
poppy with wheat crops, 182. *See
also* DAI (Development Alternatives, Inc.)
ADS (area development schemes),
106–9
ADT (Agricultural Development
Training), 113–14
Afghani farmers: displacement of,
38, 139, 146, 165, 168–69, 171;
and IDEA-NEW, 193–94; and
women's inequality, 203. *See also*
agricultural projects
Afghani resistance: to development, 80; Kandahar riots, 78–79;
mapped to rural development,
106; to poppy eradication,
141–42, 146, 150–51, 160–61,
189, 206; to SLDF, 74–76. *See also*
insurgency
Afghanistan: broken windows approach in, 130–34; Central Asian

location, 29; civil war in, 25,
135–36; communist coup, 81, 87;
development in, during Cold War,
15; as field site for development,
13–14; government collapse,
231–32; as narco-criminal state,
214–15; overview of USAID in,
4–5; and Point Four program,
10; post-9/11 nation building in,
1–2; and returning refugees, 111;
shaped by development infrastructures, 3; as site of imperial struggle, 22–30; as site of
U.S.–Soviet proxy war, 24; Soviet
invasion of, 83–84, 87; USAID
abandonment of, 125–28; USAID
mismanagement in, 213–14; U.S.
withdrawal from, 231; wars with
Britain, 22–24
Afghanistan–Pakistan Transit Trade
Agreement (1965), 115–16
*Afghanistan Papers: A Secret History
of the War,* 216–20
Afghanistan Vouchers for Increased
Production in Agriculture
(AVIPA). *See* AVIPA (Afghanistan
Vouchers for Increased Production in Agriculture)
Af-Pak borderlands: and humanitarian relief operations, 95–96; logistics management on, 100–102;
mujahideen insurgents in, 94–95;
and Soviet–Afghan conflict,
93–103; violence in, 101. *See also*

29, 44; on "Great Game," 23–24,
26; on targeted killings, 207; on
war after 9/11, 93
Grove, Jairus, 199
"Growing Hope in Afghanistan"
(documentary), 173–74, 183, 184,
186

Harness, Jerod, 208
Helmand Food Zone (HFZ). *See* HFZ
(Helmand Food Zone)
Helmand Province, 41–43
Helmand Valley Advisory Service,
62
Helmand Valley Authority. *See* HVA
(Helmand Valley Authority)
Helmand Valley Project (HVP). *See*
HVP (Helmand Valley Project)
Helms, Jessie, 218
heroin manufacturing, 120
HFZ (Helmand Food Zone), 138–39,
165–70
Hobson, Kenneth B., 36–37
Hoffman, Anthony, 192, 193, 195–96,
210, 211
Holbrooke, Richard, 162–63, 166–67,
171, 219
Homestead, Fla., 233
Hopkins, Terence, 152
Hostetter, Clyde, 111
household management, 174–75,
198–200
Humanitarian Relief Program,
100–101
Huntington, Samuel, 53
Husain, Tariq, 115
Husick, Charles, 73
HVA (Helmand Valley Authority),
59, 68
HVP (Helmand Valley Project):
and agricultural training efforts,
62–63; anticommunism, 46;

and community development,
49–50; consequences of, 49–50;
failures of, as damaging to U.S.
prestige, 60; funding for, 57–61;
and infrastructural power, 51–52;
and Morrison-Knudsen, 55–57,
59–60; overview of, 35–36, 45–46;
pre–Cold War history, 54–55;
and salinization, 47; salinization
as effect of, 56–57, 59; "total" development approach, 66–70; and
water scarcity, 49

ICA (International Cooperation Administration): and "competitive
coexistence," 60; origins of, 11;
technical assistance programs,
64–65
IDEA-NEW (Incentives Driving
Economic Alternatives—North,
East, and West): and Afghani
farmers, 193–94; as alternative
development, 175; demonstration
farms, 194–95; effects of, on marginalized populations, 197–205;
market-based approaches,
190–97; and poppy cultivation,
190
IDEA-South (Ideas Driving Economic Alternatives), 162
Immerwahr, Daniel, 51
imperialism, of United States, 6–8
Incentives Driving Economic
Development—North, East,
and West (IDEA-NEW). *See*
IDEA-NEW (Incentives Driving
Economic Alternatives—North,
East, and West)
Indus River Basin, 48–49
infrastructural power: counternarcotics as, 149–50; defined, 17;
and HVP, 51–52; and stability

operations, 21; and technical assistance, 65–66; USAID's use of, 18
infrastructure: development as, 14–22; types of, 48; use of term, 16–17; VITA's rural works program, 104–11. *See also* development
insurgency: and counternarcotics operations, 152–53; and poppy cultivation, 141–42, 146, 160–61. *See also* Afghani resistance
International Cooperation Administration (ICA). *See* ICA (International Cooperation Administration)
International Medical Corps, 101

Jalali, Ali Ahmad, 94–95
Japan, 6–7
Jim Crow, 8, 52, 65, 200
Johnson, Lyndon, 52
Joint Prioritized Effects List (JPEL). *See* JPEL (Joint Prioritized Effects List)
JPEL (Joint Prioritized Effects List), 207
just-in-time imperialism, 36–37, 88–90

Karzai, Hamid, 147–48
Kelley, Robin D. G., 229
Kelling, George, 130, 145
Kennedy, John F., 11
Khalili, Laleh, 17, 51–52, 85, 88, 204
Khan, Fayaz, 111
Khan, Wazir Akbar, 23
Kim, Monica, 2, 13, 32
Kingsley, Elaine: on CBHAP, 96; on cross-border constraints, 97; on poppy cultivation, 119–20; on stability operations, 163–64; on

USAID and counterinsurgency, 216; on USAID inaction after Gorbachev resignation, 135–36
Kinsella, Helen, 204
Kissinger, Henry, 76
Kundnani, Anun, 224

Laos, 233–34
Lederer, William, 11
Lemahieu, Jean Luc, 209
Li, Tania, 15, 172, 197–98, 201
Lister, Sarah, 201
logistics management: American Manufacturer's Export Group, 100–102; and antirelationality, 91; as CBHAP focus, 85; defined, 88; development as, 87–93; just-in-time imperialism, 36–37, 88–90; supply chain disruptions, 92, 126; and U.S. intervention in Soviet–Afghan conflict, 85, 87–88, 91–92, 97–102. *See also* Af-Pak borderlands; CBHAP (Cross Border Humanitarian Assistance Program)

Mahmood, Saeeda, 43
Man, Simeon, 227
Manchanda, Nivi, 23, 24, 26
Mangal, Golub, 165, 167
Mansfield, David: on alternative development, 151, 158; on daily income in Afghanistan, 161; on IDEA-NEW, 202; on poppy cultivation, 165, 168–69, 205; on Sherzai's failure, 206
market-based approaches: and ADP/E, 186–87; and biopolitics, 176–82; IDEA-NEW, 190–97; O/AID/REP program, 111–19; post-9/11 USAID work, 128. *See also* capitalism
Marsden, Magnus, 94

special inspector general for
Afghanistan reconstruction
(SIGAR). *See* SIGAR (special
inspector general for Afghanistan
reconstruction)
stability operations: and AVIPA,
166–171; and counternarcotics,
159–65; Directive 3000.05, 19–20;
and infrastructural power, 21;
shift toward, 159
stabilization model, 138, 163
Stephens, Bret, 133
Stimson, Henry, 2
Stoler, Ann, 26, 33
Strmecki, Marin, 219
supply chains. *See* logistics
management

Tadiar, Neferti, 146
Taliban: and poppy cultivation, 136,
148–49, 161, 235–36; resurgence
of, 191–92, 213–14; rise of,
136; and U.S. withdrawal from
Afghanistan, 231; and women,
234–35
tanzeems (mujahideen parties), 99
Task Force Nexus, 207–9
Taw, Jennifer Morrison, 18–19
Taylor, Stephen, 62
TCA (Technical Cooperation
Agency), 10–11
technical assistance: Helmand Val-
ley programs, 64; and racialized
violence, 65; and racial liberalism,
64–65. *See also specific projects*
Technical Cooperation Administra-
tion (TCA). *See* TCA (Technical
Cooperation Agency)
Technology Innovation and Market-
Led Economic Rehabilitation
(TIMER). *See* TIMER (Technol-

ogy Innovation and Market-Led
Economic Rehabilitation)
TIMER (Technology Innovation and
Market-Led Economic Rehabilita-
tion), 185
"total" development approach: and
ADS (area development schemes),
109; in Helmand Valley, 66–70;
and VITA, 86
training centers and classes: ADT
(Agricultural Development
Training), 113–14; DAI, 181–82;
gender issues, 157; for Helmand
Valley farmers, 62–63
Truman, Harry S., 8–9, 10
Trump, Donald, 1
Tu, Thuy Linh, 235
Tudor Engineering Company, 61

Udall, Stewart L., 73
Ugly American, The (Burdick and
Lederer), 11
Ulumi, Nur al-Haq, 209
United Nations Office on Drugs and
Crime (UNODC). *See* UNODC
(United Nations Office on Drugs
and Crime)
United Nations Technical Assis-
tance Mission (UNTAM). *See*
UNTAM (United Nations Tech-
nical Assistance Mission)
United States: development aid as
tool of imperialism, 5–14; and
proxy war with Soviets, in Af-
ghanistan, 24; soft power wielded
by, 2; withdrawal from Afghani-
stan, 231. *See also* imperialism, of
United States
UNODC (United Nations Office on
Drugs and Crime), 147, 150
unrest. *See* Afghani resistance

Wesley Attewell is assistant professor of political geography and urban governance in the Department of Geography at the University of Hong Kong.

Ingram Content Group UK Ltd.
Milton Keynes UK
UKHW020921030423
419517UK00011B/1291